Cybercrime

Cybercrime

Vandalizing the Information Society

STEVEN FURNELL

ADDISON-WESLEY
An imprint of PEARSON EDUCATION

Boston • San Francisco • New York • Toronto • Montreal • London • Munich • Paris
Madrid • Cape Town • Sydney • Tokyo • Singapore • Mexico City

PEARSON EDUCATION LIMITED

Head Office:
Edinburgh Gate
Harlow CM20 2JE
Tel: +44 (0)1279 623623
Fax: +44 (0)1279 431059

London Office:
128 Long Acre
London WC2E 9AN
Tel: +44 (0)20 7447 2000
Fax: +44 (0)20 7240 5771

Website: www.it-minds.com
www.aw.com/cseng

First published in Great Britain in 2002

The right of Steven Furnell to be identified as the Author of this Work has been asserted by him in accordance with the Copyright, Designs and Patents Act 1988.

ISBN: 0 201 72159 7

British Library Cataloguing in Publication Data
A CIP catalogue record for this book can be obtained from the British Library.

Library of Congress Cataloging in Publication Data
Applied for.

Many of the designations used by manufacturers and sellers to distinguish their products are claimed as trademarks. Pearson Education Limited has made every attempt to supply trademark information about manufacturers and their products mentioned in this book.

10 9 8 7 6 5 4 3 2 1

Typeset by Land & Unwin, Bugbrooke, Northamptonshire
Printed and bound in Great Britain by Biddles Ltd of Guildford and King's Lynn

The Publishers' policy is to use paper manufactured from sustainable forests.

Contents

Preface vii
About the author x
Acknowledgments xi

1 "You are here" – welcome to the information society 1
The opportunity – the brave new world 1
The dependency – society's reliance upon information technology 11
The danger – why we need security 13
Some basic principles of IT security 17
Summary 20

2 Crime in the information society 21
What is cybercrime? 21
Assessing the scale of the problem 26
Some examples of notable incidents 29
Summary 39

3 Hackers – anti-heroes of the computer revolution? 41
Who or what is a hacker? 41
Phreaking out the phone company 45
Stereotype and self-image 47
What's the motivation? 52
Elements of the hacker culture 58
Hackers as celebrities 77
Summary 93

4 Delving deeper – what hackers do and how they do it 95
Getting in and staying there 95
Common forms of attack 102
Getting the tools to do it for you 116
Using less technological approaches 136
Summary 142

5 Manifestations of malware 143
What is malware? 143
Motivations of the malware writers 149
The evolution of viruses 151
Notable malware incidents 155
Causing problems without writing code 177
Future directions for malware 186
Summary 188

6 Societal impacts of cybercrime 189
Implications for society at large 189
Public attitudes and awareness 191
Electronic commerce – an example of society's need for protection 202
Policing the problem 207
Legislating against computer crime and abuse 210
The problems of enforcing the law 212
Understanding the issues involved 216
Global inconsistency 220
Did the crime, did the time – what next? 225
Summary 230

7 Commercial and political evolution 231
Hackers for hire 231
Hacktivism 239
Information warfare 245
Cyberterrorism 253
When the boot is on the other foot 261
Summary 267

8 Where do we go from here? 269
Preventative measures 269
Vandalizing the information society? 280

Glossary of terms 285
Online resources for cybercrime and security 288
Online news sites 288
Security sites 288
Hacker-related sites 290
Notes on sources 291
Index 309

Preface

THE TOPIC OF CYBERCRIME HAS RECEIVED AN IMMENSE AMOUNT OF coverage in recent years, with the media, law enforcers, and governments all doing their bit to bring the issue to our attention. For those unfamiliar with the term, the concept of cybercrime covers a wide range of crimes and abuses relating to information technology, with the most commonly reported incidents being those involving hackers and computer viruses. Although the last few years have witnessed an explosion of interest in the area, the problem of computer crime is not new, and there have been incidents that could be placed in this bracket since the early days of computing. The difference now is the increased scope available to would-be attackers – largely due to the popularity of the Internet. The numerous benefits offered by the Internet and, in its turn, the World Wide Web have now led to their widespread public adoption. At the same time, however, the increased usage has served to fuel interest in the accompanying problems and it seems that not a day goes by without a cybercrime incident of some sort being reported.

This book is intended as an introduction to the topic of cybercrime and considers the significance and impacts of the issue in the context of modern society. The chapters that follow examine the various forms in which cybercrime may be encountered and present numerous examples of incidents that have already occurred. Chapter 1 sets the scene for subsequent discussion by tracing the origins of the so-called "information society" and introducing the technologies that have put us where we are today. The discussion also establishes our increasingly widespread dependence upon information technologies, and the problems that can consequently be encountered when things go wrong. The chapter concludes by identifying the basic principles of IT security – principles that are basically disregarded and undermined by cybercriminals. Chapter 2 proceeds to define the problem of cybercrime, considering the ways in which it has previously been classified by other sources. The scale of the problem is then assessed, based upon a consideration of recent survey results in the area. The chapter concludes with some examples of how cybercrime can manifest itself in practice, considering some real incidents that have occurred in recent years. Chapter 3 is the first of two chapters focusing upon issues relating to computer hackers. It begins by considering potential definitions of hacking and then examines various aspects that can be considered to constitute the hacker "culture." The discussion also considers the emergence of celebrity figures from the hacker community and the effect that this may have upon public perception. Chapter 4 continues with the hacking theme, and proceeds to look at the methods that are often employed in the attack and compromise of systems. Common forms of attack, such as denial of service and web site defacement are considered, along with less technically-oriented methods that also form part of the hacker's repertoire. A significant theme of the discussion is the relative ease with which Internet systems can now be targeted, using automated tools that enable even comparative novices to get involved. Chapter 5 moves on from hackers to consider another significant aspect of cybercrime – namely the problems of viruses and other forms of malicious software, collectively known as "malware." The different manifestations of malware are examined, followed by consideration of a series of examples of specific malware incidents that have been encountered in practice. These combine to show the various negative effects that can be unleashed by suitably motivated individuals. Chapter 6 moves away from examining specific categories of cybercrime to consider how the issues discussed in previous chapters have impacted upon various aspects of society. Some specific perspectives considered here are the effects upon organizations, implications and responses from the legal system, and the attitudes and awareness of the general public in relation to cybercrime issues. Chapter 7 considers the commercial and political evolution of the computer hacker, looking at ways in which techniques such as system penetration are now being applied in a variety of contexts other than those that are purely criminal. These include the hiring of hacker expertise as a means of legitimately testing systems and the application of hacking skills in the context of warfare. Politically motivated applications of hacker techniques are also considered, with the examination of issues such as "hacktivism" and "cyberterrorism." Chapter 8 concludes the overall discussion, by briefly considering the ways in which cybercrime may evolve in the future. It also presents summary information in relation to preventative measures, which is geared towards those readers who, having read the earlier material, are interested in looking at potential means of securing their systems. A glossary of terms and list of supporting sources is provided at the end of the book.

It is hoped that the material presented here will be of interest to a broad audience, including business professionals, students and any other members of the general public who come into regular contact with information technology. Readers are not required to have any prior knowledge of computer security or any detailed understanding of information technology itself. A general familiarity with using PC systems and their applications will be of assistance in relating to some elements of the discussion, although this should not be regarded as essential, and computer novices should still be able to come away with a good level of understanding. Attempts have been made to ensure that the examples are presented in an appropriate level of detail, without over-simplifying the nature of the activities involved. At the same time, however, specific technical details are avoided in many cases to make the material as accessible as possible for non-experts.

The book does not aim to provide any sort of guide for would-be cybercriminals to learn from. It will not teach you how to hack or commit other forms of cybercrime and abuse. The omission of technical details in many of the examples again aims to reduce the risk of copycat activities here. Conversely, the discussion also says very little in relation to safeguarding systems against the various types of threat – although some sections, particularly in Chapter 8, do offer elements of general advice. The overall intention of this book is to draw attention to the cybercrime problem and the forms it may take, and to offer some thoughts regarding its implications for society as a whole.

Given the range of examples presented in the book, a great many of them are not drawn directly from personal experience. As a result, where examples are cited from elsewhere, references are provided to indicate the original sources from which information was obtained. Where the original sources are media reports, attempts have been made to check the accuracy of any claims, by cross-referencing the details with other articles or reports. As such, it is hoped that the details presented can be considered factual and reliable. It must also be observed that trying to write a book about cybercrime is very much like trying to hit a moving target. The daily occurrence of new incidents means that, within a relatively short period of time, new aspects of the problem are likely to have emerged that will not be reflected in these pages. Nonetheless, it is hoped that the discussion will help people to appreciate the breadth of the cybercrime issue, to understand that it is not necessarily as black and white as it may sometimes be presented and that, occasionally, even those people cast as cybercriminals may have valid perspectives to offer.

About the author

DR. STEVEN FURNELL is the head of the Network Research Group at the University of Plymouth in the United Kingdom. He specializes in computer security and has been actively researching in the area for nine years. During this time he has contributed to a number of U.K. and European projects, as well as presenting his work and findings at a variety of international events. Dr. Furnell is a member of the British Computer Society (BCS) and the Institute of Electrical and Electronics Engineers (IEEE), and is a U.K. representative in two International Federation for Information Processing (IFIP) working groups, relating to Network Security and Information Security Education. He is also a frequent reviewer for a variety of international journals covering Internet and security issues, and has recently acted as an advisor to the London Science Museum in relation to an exhibition exposing the cybercrime problem.

Acknowledgments

THE TOPIC OF CYBERCRIME IS ONE THAT I HAVE LONG FOUND FASCINATING and it is a problem that has underscored much of the computer security research that I have performed and supervised in recent years. Although this research has led me to write a number of papers about cybercrime and related issues, I never felt that these offered the scope to explore the topic in enough detail – particularly in relation to the societal implications. This book is, therefore, my attempt to provide a more comprehensive discussion of the issue.

It has been a fairly long process and there are several people that I wish to thank. I must begin by acknowledging the help and support that I received from staff at Pearson Education. In particular, thanks are owed to Alison Birtwell, who was my initial contact and provided advice and encouragement when I originally approached her with the idea for this book, and Michael Strang, who subsequently provided invaluable help and advice throughout the writing process.

A number of people provided input and opinions regarding the content of the book and helped to ensure that I did not stray too far away from my intended topics. Special thanks are owed to Bogdan Ghita, Paul Dowland, Maria Papadaki, Dr. Michael Evans and Professor Peter Sanders for their useful and insightful comments on the early drafts and for giving up their spare time to read them. I would also like to thank other members of the Network Research Group for their continual support during the writing period.

Finally, I would like to acknowledge the support of my parents, who always believed I would get the book finished, despite my frequent claims to the contrary.

"You are here" – welcome to the information society

AS YOU WILL HAVE GATHERED FROM THE TITLE, THIS BOOK CONCERNS the issue of cybercrime – a major and increasing problem that has arisen through our adoption and use of computer systems and networks. To understand the significance of the problem, it is necessary to appreciate the context in which it exists. The underlying theme of this book is that cybercrime is a major issue because it has the ability to impede, or even undermine, the information society of which it is a part. It is, therefore, appropriate to examine the foundations of this society and see how we come to be in our current position.

This chapter provides scene-setting material for the discussions that follow, explaining the importance of information technology in today's society. It illustrates the extent to which technology pervades the vast majority of the activities and services that we take for granted in modern society and, hence, the extent to which we are dependent upon it. In view of this, the importance of IT security will be identified and the basic principles defined in terms of the requirements for confidentiality, integrity and availability of systems and data – the aspects that cyber criminals would typically seek to undermine.

The opportunity – the brave new world

So, what is the information society? Whether you realize it or not, it is the world in which we are living today. Looking back through history, it is clear that the nature of society has fundamentally changed through the ages. The first phase of this evolution was the agrarian society, based upon farming and agriculture, and was the basic shape of society for many centuries. The years between 1750 and 1850 witnessed the Industrial Revolution, heralding the shift to an industrially based society, based on the manufacture of physical goods. This was accompanied by a huge increase in the use of fossil fuels and the construction of transport infrastructures such as railways and canals. During this time, the main wealth creation and employment opportunities shifted to these directions. Although agriculture clearly did not disappear, it ceased to represent the main focus of life for the majority of people.

Industry and manufacturing are still clearly a significant feature in the developed world of today. However, in the 1940s and 1950s, defining technologies emerged in the form of computers, which would gradually alter the fabric of society once again. In this post-industrial context, the possession, handling and exchange of information have become the central focus, leading to the new age being christened the Information Society. In his book *The Next World War*, James Adams, CEO of iDEFENSE, talks of information being a strategic resource, the same as oil, gas or diamonds.[1] Indeed, information is now seen as being a more valuable commodity than things that can be grown or manufactured.

The concept of the information society is closely linked to the use of information technology and the transition is being driven by the reduction in the costs of computing power and telecommunications. Such technology can now be seen to shape the way in which we work, learn, play, shop and communicate with each other. These factors, in combination with advances in the core technologies, are making information resources available to an increasing number of people. While it would be wrong to argue that technology and the information society are the same thing, the technology is basically the enabler of the new age and the changes would not have been possible without it. Global information networks are now an integral part of the way in which modern businesses and economies operate. A rudimentary comparison arising from this is that the population of the Internet now exceeds that of some industrialized nations. In the developed world, information technologies form an intrinsic part of all aspects of modern life. Commerce, banking, healthcare, education and government, to name but a few, are all areas that now have a significant dependence upon IT in their day-to-day operations. This is not to say that nothing at all could happen without IT, but its absence would at least cause disruption and difficulties. As a consequence, there is now a widespread reliance on computers and network technology, with the ability to communicate and receive information via these channels being recognized as an essential ingredient for competitiveness in the global market.

The fact that our lives are changing as a result of the spread of technology is widely accepted and numerous authors – for example, in Toffler's *Third Wave*[2] and Martin's *Information Society*[3] – have forecast the nature of the "society" that will result. Although differing in many respects, all share the common vision of the computer as the foundation upon which the society is built. Leading industrial figures are also excited by this revolution, with people such as Microsoft's Bill Gates having predicted that its effects will be as far reaching as the introduction of electricity.[4] The concept has also received significant publicity and backing from national governments in various countries with, for example, the United States having pushed the idea of an "information superhighway," an open network of information that will be as accessible as the conventional telephone system. In Europe, a whole range of research and development projects are currently receiving support from the European Commission under the auspices of the Information Society Technologies program. It is, therefore, clear that this route is perceived to be an important element in ensuring future national development and competitiveness.

How did it begin and how far have we come?

Today's information society is inextricably linked to the revolution in electronic communications, the origins of which can be traced back to the development and patenting of the telegraph by William Cooke and Charles Wheatstone in 1836. Within thirty years, this event had been followed by the laying of the first trans-atlantic cable, enabling instantaneous communications between the Old World and the New one (the first attempt, in 1858, had short-lived success and stopped working after less than a month. By 1866, however, a truly successful link had been established).[5] The telegraph was followed by the telephone, patented by Alexander Graham Bell in 1876. From this point, a means for remote voice communication was established and, in the decades that followed, advances in the technology witnessed the evolution of long-distance and international telephony services. More than a century has passed since Bell's original invention and the telephone now provides a global communications infrastructure, with domestic phones and international direct dialling capability being a standard feature in homes in many developed countries.* However, voice communication is, of course, only part of the story. In the last two decades, the role of the telephone network itself has evolved from carrying purely voice communications to also encompass data transmissions from devices such as fax machines and computers. In actual fact, the volume of data communications is now very close to exceeding that of voice traffic in worldwide networks. The main catalyst for this change in the nature of telecommunications traffic has, of course, been the networking of computer systems. And, of all the networking technologies that form part of the information society, none to date have had greater impact or significance than the Internet.

The origins of the Internet lie in the military domain and it is based upon a communications concept called "packet switching." The basic idea is that any messages to be sent are broken up into discrete elements (the packets), sent off over the network and then reassembled in the correct order at the destination end. Intuitively, this may not seem to be particularly advantageous – why bother breaking the message up in the first place? Why not send it in a continuous transmission and avoid the overhead of having to reassemble it? From a military or defence perspective, there are actually two reasons why packet switching is attractive – both

---

* Having said this, it is also worth noting that the penetration of telephones on a global basis still only reaches a very small percentage of the population.

relating to the fact that once the message has been split up into packets, the packets themselves may travel through the network via different routes. The first advantage of this is secrecy. If someone is tapping the network at an intermediate point, they are unlikely to see the whole message. Secondly, it is possible to route around points of failure. Therefore, if a network link is broken or a switch goes down at an intermediate point, packets may still have a chance of finding their way to the intended destination by trying another route. As such, the overall communications process has an increased level of resilience to failure. This is important from a defence perspective, and was a particular consideration during the 1960s when the shadow of potential nuclear war still loomed large. Using the normal telephony communications approach (known as circuit switching), a connection must be established and held between source and destination points (albeit via intermediate exchanges) for the duration of the call. With calls only able to take this fixed path through the network, any disruption to the intermediate infrastructure could result in contact being lost with certain destinations. So, if a nuclear strike was to take out major parts of the cabling infrastructure, it was desirable to ensure that communications could still continue. Hence, the concept of packet-based communications was born, being originally proposed by Paul Baran at Rand in 1964.

Within a few years, the packet communication concept had been adopted by the Advanced Research Projects Agency (ARPA), part of the U.S. Department of Defense, as the basis for its own network – the ARPANET. Today's Internet is a direct descendent of this early work and, following the establishment of the underlying concepts, 1967 saw the publication of plans proposing the architecture for a worldwide network based on the new approaches. By the end of 1968, hardware development was underway to support this network – the realization of the actual technology that would route the packet data over the ARPANET. By late 1969 the technology was ready and the first tests were made by four U.S. universities: UCLA, Stanford Research Institute, University of California Santa Barbara and University of Utah. In the years that followed, the use of the ARPANET was largely confined to universities and government agencies, linking members of the scientific and academic research communities, but further developments continued to occur. Applications such as electronic mail emerged in the early 1970s and further pioneering work resulted in the development of the communication protocols* that would later support the entire Internet. Over time, other networks arrived to accompany the ARPANET – some examples being the U.K.'s JANET (Joint Academic NETwork – for educational institutions), the U.S. MILNET (a military network, which resulted from splitting defense systems away from the ARPANET in 1983) and

---

* A protocol specifies the "rules" for communication, such that both sender and receiver ends can understand each other.

NSFNET (from the U.S. National Science Foundation). Being based upon the same underlying protocols for communication, all of these networks were able to inter-connect and talk to each other – with the resulting infrastructure being referred to as the Internet. So, in short, the Internet itself is the result of the interconnection of thousands of individual networks, now collectively containing hundreds of millions of computers around the world.

The original ARPANET was officially decommissioned by the U.S. Government in 1990. By this time, however, the wider Internet infrastructure was in place and, over time, more and more networks were becoming part of it. That said, it was not until the 1990s that the world at large really became aware of the Internet and its usage skyrocketed. Although it is difficult to determine the exact number of Internet users at any given time, the growth of the network itself can be more easily quantified. The preferred measure for assessing the growth of the Internet is the number of end systems (or hosts) that are connected to it. A general, if rather formal, definition of a host is "the ultimate consumer of communication services [which] executes application programs on behalf of user(s), employing network and/or Internet communication services in support of this function."[6] The number of Internet hosts has risen dramatically every year, as evident from studies carried out by Network Wizards[7] and illustrated in Figure 1.1, which depicts the eleven years from January 1991 to January 2001 (the "old," "adjusted," and "new" lines in the figure reflect different ways in which the hosts have been counted – the method having changed in January 1998. For the purposes of this discussion, the significance to note is simply the overall upward trend).

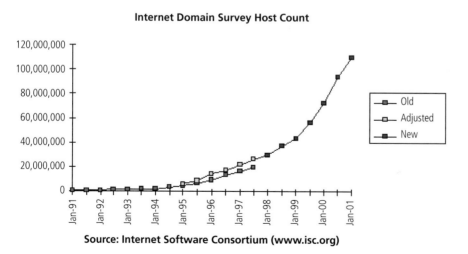

Internet Domain Survey Host Count

Source: Internet Software Consortium (www.isc.org)

FIGURE 1.1 Internet growth 1991 to 2000 (number of hosts)

The original uses of the Internet were very much related to the requirements of existing IT users, encompassing applications such as file transfer, remote login to other systems, network news and email services. There was little amongst this group of applications that would be exciting enough to attract a total newcomer to the Internet unless they had a particular fascination with the technology or a particular need to perform one of the tasks. A 1991 survey of three large networks (University of California, Berkeley, University of Southern California and Bellcore Laboratories) revealed that these applications accounted for about 90 percent of the Internet traffic at the time.[8] However, the landscape changed fundamentally over the next few years, with the widespread acceptance of the World Wide Web and associated browser technologies (starting with a program called Mosaic, which then evolved into today's familiar names such as Netscape's Navigator and Microsoft's Internet Explorer). Indeed, in contrast to the earlier applications, the web was a catalyst for Internet adoption in its own right. People wanted to get onto the web and see what it was all about. It created a buzz.

The effect of the web on the overall Internet landscape was dramatic. Whereas the 1991 survey had shown a predominance of text-based applications, a sub-sequent study in 1997 on a U.S. East Coast domestic link revealed that 75 percent of traffic was web-related (with the older applications now accounting for only 10 percent of the traffic between them).[9] This does not necessarily mean that the older applications had become less popular – the same people were still using them. However, the new users had arrived in their droves, and they had come to see the web.

So how many Internet users are there? As previously mentioned, it is more difficult to determine the number of users, as there is not an exact correlation to the number of hosts (because of factors such as several people sharing access through a single system). However, an estimate in 2000 put the figure at 369 million,[10] additionally predicting that it would increase to 640 million by 2003. If the number of users was considered in the same way as the population of a country, then the current population of cyberspace currently exceeds that of all but two countries on Earth, the exceptions being India and China.

It is, however, easier to assess the number of countries that are connected to the Net. Figure 1.2 shows the trend throughout the 1990s, based upon figures from the International Telecommunications Union (ITU). This shows that the Internet is a truly global phenomenon – although it can also be assumed that, as 95.5 percent of Internet hosts are located in either the U.S., Canada, Europe, Australia, or Japan,[11] there are still vast sections of the world's population whose lives have not been significantly affected.

History shows that the introduction of any significant new technology is followed by a period during which the public assesses it, adopts it and becomes used to its existence. After this, the technology can be considered to have been assimilated into everyday life and culture. This can be seen to have been the case with each of the major advances in communications technologies in the nineteenth and twentieth centuries: the telegraph, the telephone, the radio and the television. However, the period over which such assimilation of technology occurs is variable and it is by no means an overnight process. The television, for example, is now considered to have had a fundamental and revolutionary effect upon domestic life in the developed world. It would be no exaggeration to say that the typical evening activity for most households and families is now dominated by television. Yet, if we were to look back sixty years we would see a completely different picture of life. Although television as we now know it had been invented in the 1930s (the British Broadcasting Corporation was running the first public television service by 1936), it was not until the 1950s and 1960s that its real effects upon leisure time would be seen. So, the mainstream adoption of television took a good fifteen to twenty years (although admittedly the occurrence of World War II in the intervening period did serve to impede progress).

The Internet (and particularly the World Wide Web) represents a technology of a similarly landmark nature to those previously listed. However, a dramatic difference with the Internet is the speed with which it has been accepted into popular culture – particularly if you take the creation of the web to represent the real starting point (which is a reasonably valid assumption, given that the Internet had no real public visibility prior to this point). The web was originally conceived in the late 1980s by Tim Berners-Lee (then a researcher at CERN, the European Particle Physics Laboratory, located near Geneva) as a means for particle physicists to share information.[12] However, the concept was so revolutionary and so flexible that, within a few years,

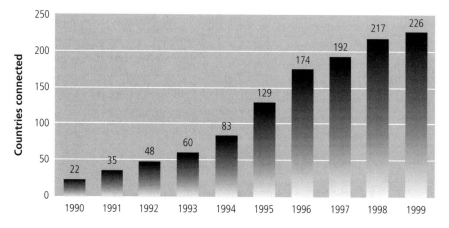

FIGURE 1.2 Number of countries connected to the Internet
Source: International Telecommunications Union

the web led to the mainstream visibility of the Internet. Certainly by 1996, the web browser was a standard application for desktop PCs and web addresses started to become an increasingly familiar occurrence – appearing in other media, such as television and printed advertisements.

The web opened the eyes of the populace at large and, through this, they have also discovered other aspects of the Internet, such as email, chat, gaming, and the wealth of materials that can be downloaded (e.g. MP3 music files). As a consequence, the word "Internet" is now part of everyday vocabulary. Even if people have not used it, they have certainly heard or read about it. It is virtually inescapable. Furthermore, the sheer range of applications in which the Internet has now found a role go far beyond its academic and military origins, as illustrated in Figure 1.3.

Most of the headings in Figure 1.3 are fairly self-explanatory, but a couple of them probably warrant some further clarification for the uninitiated. As the name may suggest, virtual communities are scenarios where people have formed social or professional groupings through the medium of cyberspace. In some cases, such communities may mirror real ones that also exist in the physical world – e.g. the virtual community provides an online adjunct to a real town. More typically, however, the members of a virtual community will be geographically dispersed and the Internet provides the means by which they can come together to share their common interests. A good example is The Well (Whole Earth 'Lectronic Link – see **www.well.com**), as described by Howard Rheingold in his book on the topic of virtual communities.[13]

Distributed processing relates to the fact that the Internet actually comprises millions of individual systems, each with their own computing capabilities. This

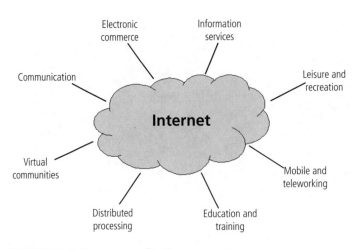

FIGURE 1.3 Internet application areas

represents a massive distributed resource – the power of which vastly exceeds that which any single organization alone could amass for itself. The ability to harness this combined power (or a subset of it) enables large and complex tasks to be shared out between many systems – an online analogy to the old adage that "many hands make light work." An example is the SETI@home (Search for Extraterrestrial Intelligence) project, in which individuals from around the globe can participate in a search for alien life that is being conducted by a wider project called SERENDIP. Volunteers can download a SETI@home program for their PC, which then contributes to the scanning and analysis of radio telescope data, searching for extraterrestrial signals. The program works during idle time on the participating PCs, in parallel with thousands of other volunteer systems elsewhere on the Internet – each downloading a chunk of data, analyzing it and returning the results to the SERENDIP team. As of March 2001, the effort had attracted over 2.8 million volunteers, from 226 countries and, since its commencement in May 1999, had contributed the equivalent of 582,978 years worth of computing time.[14] It is the largest computation ever performed – and the Internet made it possible.

In parallel with the emergence of these application areas, the means by which one can achieve Internet access are continually increasing. Although the options just a few years ago would have centered entirely around standard computers, the range of potential access devices now includes television set-top boxes, mobile phones, personal digital assistants and public kiosks. A few of the options available at the time of writing are depicted in Figure 1.4. Each individual device may not necessarily be able to support all applications, but all make some degree of Internet access possible.

This selection by no means represents the limit of Internet connectivity. Another frequent example is the Internet-enabled refrigerator, from which the owner may then access online shopping services to order fresh supplies from the supermarket when necessary. This would have sounded like nonsense a few years ago and, to many people, it will not sound very plausible today. However, it is actually a reality – at least in prototype form.[15] An Internet washing machine is also under development at the time of writing (enabling new wash programs to be downloaded), as well as the Internet microwave oven (which can download recipes).[16] In the future, it appears that kitchen appliances will be wired in more ways than one. It could, of course, be argued that such applications of the Internet are hardly the ones that will change the world. The point is, however, that such applications are becoming possible at all – which is testament to the capabilities of the technologies and the networking between them. When we are networked to that degree, the interdependency of systems will clearly have advanced one stage further.

Readers who do not use the Internet may take issue with the earlier statement that it has become part of our everyday lives. However, you do not have to actually *use* it for this assertion to still hold true. Use it or not, there are still myriad everyday situations in which it is likely to pop up. Consider, for example, the pervasion of World Wide Web addresses. They now routinely turn up in magazine and newspaper adverts (having become as ubiquitous as postal addresses and telephone numbers as means of further contact), in television adverts and at the end of television programs themselves (e.g. everything on the BBC, from soap operas to sports events, now encourages you to check out its web site). You may not use it, but you almost cannot help but see it.

As for business and commerce, the situation has changed in just a few years from being one where having an Internet presence set you apart from the crowd, to one in which *not* having it is now a more distinguishing characteristic. The following

FIGURE 1.4 Internet access devices

Clockwise from the top, these are a standard PC, an Internet kiosk, a games console, a set-top box, a laptop computer, a personal digital assistant (PDA), a WAP-enabled mobile phone and a landline phone with email capability.

quotation illustrates the extent to which Internet connectivity is now virtually a standard expectation:

> Anyone who stands up and says how much they're doing in the internet should imagine themselves proclaiming that their company uses electricity.[17]

The discussion so far has been of a uniformly positive nature, extolling the virtues of technology and the opportunities that it offers us. However, the title of this book, of course, betrays the fact that there is also a darker side to be considered. Within any sufficiently mature society there will always be a criminal or destructive element. The information society is no exception to this and the perceived undesirables have been collectively christened under various names – including "hackers," "crackers," and "cyberpunks" – and have received a high degree of publicity in the process. As a consequence, many people may know the information society as much for its problems as for its benefits.

The dependency – society's reliance upon information technology

Whether we like it or not, modern society has become very much dependent upon the use and correct operation of information technologies. Even where people choose to avoid contact with IT and cling rigidly to the practices of the past, they are often only succeeding in making themselves one step removed from it. For example, many people (particularly the older generation) dislike using ATM machines to withdraw money from their bank accounts. As a result of their dislike or mistrust of the technology, they prefer to go to their branch in person and withdraw money over the counter from a human teller. Similarly in shops, they may feel more comfortable with the idea of writing a cheque rather than making an electronic payment via debit cards and the like. However, while they may choose to avoid direct contact with the technology, they are still significantly dependent upon the underlying IT infrastructure, which will be handling things such as the maintenance of their account, the issuing of statements, the calculations of payments and withdrawals, and many more besides. If some undesirable fate were to befall the bank's customer accounts system, then they would be as affected as any other customers.

Technology, of course, continues to advance and opens further opportunities for those who are willing to embrace it. For example, in addition to the ATM machines that have now been with us for years, other options such as telephone banking, web-based online banking, WAP-based mobile services and interactive television banking have all emerged in recent years. These are new opportunities that are intended to offer increased flexibility to the bank's customers. However, they also serve to implicitly increase the IT dependence of both parties.

Banking is, of course, just one domain in which IT has a major role to play. Looking at the issue more generally, the developed world's IT dependence can be illustrated extremely well by the so-called Year 2000 (Y2K) problem, also known as the Millennium Bug. This was an issue that received massive attention in both the IT industry and the media in the years leading up to the beginning of 2000. It is not a story of computer crime and abuse, but it is indicative of a society in which cybercrime could have a great effect. For those readers who managed to escape the Y2K issue, a brief summary of the problem is provided below (for those who are thoroughly sick of hearing about it, the summary is kept relatively brief!).

The basic problem related to concern over how a large proportion of the world's computer systems maintained date information – specifically the way in which they represented the year element. In the early days of computing, back in the 1950s, and throughout the 1960s and 1970s, computer memory was a precious commodity, because most systems had very little of it. Therefore, in order to economize on their storage requirements, software developers used to make savings wherever possible. One common example of this was the way in which years were held. It was generally considered that storing the leading "19" in a year such as "1970" would be redundant in the context of most applications, as a date such as "3/8/70" would naturally be interpreted to mean "3/8/1970" anyway. Doing this meant that it only required half as much storage space to store each year (two bytes as opposed to four) – not a great saving in a one-off instance, but very significant if you are holding a database containing thousands of records. During most of the late twentieth century this caused no problem but, as the millennium approached, the realization increasingly dawned that the two-digit year format would be insufficient and could lead to significant ambiguity. For example, in a database of personal details, it would be impossible to distinguish between someone born in 1900 and someone else born in 2000, as the two-digit representation of these years would be the same.

At the time the affected programs were originally written, the problem was largely unforeseen, as the developers in the 1970s and 1980s had never expected that their programs would still be in use so many years later. However, in many cases (including both commercial software and systems developed in-house) programs were more often built upon and extended than replaced from scratch as new features were required. As a result, the two-digit year format remained inherent. It was only by the mid-1990s that the potential of the problem was recognized and it became the focus of ever-increasing attention throughout the remaining years of the decade, as people speculated about the possibility of disaster. Would millions of computer systems crash on 1st January 2000? Would finance and trading systems fall apart? Would planes fall out of the sky? Would timer-based video recording ever work again? The list of potential disasters was seemingly endless.

A major aspect of the problem was that nobody could be sure *where* it might manifest itself. Date information is held by all manner of computer-based systems and devices – many of which you might not instinctively suspect would hold a date at all, but which might nevertheless rely on it in order to maintain normal operation. Of particular concern were embedded systems, where microcontrollers and microprocessors are used to form part of a wider system that, on the surface at least, would not seem to be computer-related. Examples here would potentially include burglar alarm systems, lifts, temperature control units and a variety of other devices.[18]

Certainly, many problem scenarios were known about, but even in these cases the situation was not straightforward. For example, older PCs running pre-Windows 98 versions of Microsoft's operating systems would, upon reaching 23:59 on 31st December 1999, then proceed to announce that the next day was 1st April 1980.[19] Software-based tests and fixes were made available to enable people to determine whether their systems were vulnerable, but the real problem was not so much the technical solution as the major awareness campaign required to ensure that people could take advantage of it.

At the end of the day, the actual impact of the Millennium Bug was nowhere near the level that the prior hype suggested it could have been (of course, many would argue that this was because of the successful campaign of awareness that had preceded the arrival of the date itself). From a financial perspective, however, the impact had been huge. As a result of the scale of the problem, millions were spent by national governments in an effort to minimize the negative effects. In addition, many person hours were expended within companies and other organizations to assess and reduce their vulnerability. If IT were not so pervasive, and if society were not so dependent upon it, then these impacts could have been lessened.

Our dependence upon information technology is nicely summed up by the following quotation from Eric Chien, chief researcher from the European laboratory of the anti-virus company Symantec:

These computers may take you into cyberspace – but they are also running the world.[20]

As the next section will indicate, this dependency can result in dangers when things do not work quite as they should.

The danger – why we need security

The discussion has already examined the significance of the Internet and how it has changed the face of computing during recent years. Growth and access opportunities have both increased dramatically, which from many perspectives can be viewed as being positive trends. At the same time, however, as more people use the Internet, the number of potential targets can be considered to have increased. As more organizations rely upon the Internet and other networked systems to conduct their business activities, the greater the potential for related loss or damage to affect them.

Disregarding for a moment longer the cybercrime focus of this book, the following incidents illustrate examples of the sort of problems that can occur simply by accident, without any criminal or malicious intent involved. On 7th July 2000, U.K. utility company PowerGen was found to have a major security vulnerability when it was discovered that customer debit card details could be downloaded from its web server.[21] The problem was discovered by one of PowerGen's customers, John Chamberlain, who had connected to the company's web site in order to utilize the online bill payment facility. By modifying the target address of the site (e.g. removing the reference to the specific page that he was viewing and just leaving the directory path), he was able to see the content of the web server directory, containing various other files. In doing so, he was then able to access three files containing name, address and debit card details of over 7,000 PowerGen customers. The details about customers also included telephone numbers and email addresses, as well as the date and amount of their last payment. The debit card details included the card number and expiry date. The combination of this information would be sufficient to facilitate the misuse of the customer's debit card.

Upon being notified of the issue, PowerGen refused to notify the numerous other customers whose details had been at risk. As a consequence, Chamberlain decided to do something about it himself and took the story to the U.K. Data Protection Commissioner and online news service silicon.com. Silicon then began to contact other customers to make them aware of the issue. Upon being contacted by Silicon, PowerGen's attitude changed and they claimed that Chamberlain's actions constituted hacking of their system and chose to refer the matter to the police. Although it is true that modifying the URL is not something that all web surfers would be expected to engage in (e.g. they would typically be expected to navigate to pages by following hyperlinks), it is not that unusual and it is certainly not an action that can be claimed to qualify as attempted hacking (the same effect could even be caused by accidentally mistyping the URL). Chamberlain did, however, acknowledge that his action had been prompted by watching a documentary about hacking that had been shown by BBC Television a few days earlier. Even with this knowledge, his actions do not seem unreasonable or malicious – having seen examples of how systems may be left insecure, it is somewhat natural to want to reassure yourself that the companies you deal with are not leaving your data at risk in the same way.

In the end, the hacking allegations against Chamberlain were dropped and PowerGen admitted that the breach had been the result of a technical error. The company also acted to restore confidence by offering £50 to each customer affected by the breach.[22] Although the latter meant a direct financial impact to the company, it is likely that it paled by comparison to the bad publicity that the company received as a result of the incident. The Data Protection Commissioner ultimately decided not to issue an enforcement notice against the company, on the basis that it did not have evidence to suggest that there were ongoing security issues to be concerned about (stating that issues that occurred in the past are outside its remit).[23]

The security arrangement described in this incident breaks a couple of fundamental rules of web security. Firstly, sensitive information such as customer card details should ideally not be held on a public-facing server to which anyone can gain easy access (even if files are not referenced by hyperlinks from actual web pages, inquisitive users can still discover their existence – as the incident proves). Secondly, the server should be configured to prevent users from being able to gain access to unintended views of the site, such as a directory listing of the underlying files, by altering the URL. Both of these aspects represent an open invitation to computer criminals. The implications of the case extend beyond PowerGen and serve to raise questions about various other forms of online commerce.

PowerGen are by no means alone in falling victim to such accidental incidents and another example can actually be cited from the same month – this time in the banking community. 1999 and 2000 witnessed a number of U.K. banks beginning to offer online banking services for their customers via the World Wide Web. However, these were not without their teething problems from a security perspective. On 31st July 2000, Barclays Bank was forced to suspend its online banking services after four of its customers reported logging in and being presented with someone else's account details.[24] With over 1.2 million registered customers, Barclays claimed to be the U.K.'s largest Internet bank and, as such, a security failing of this nature could not be dismissed lightly. The incident consequently made headline news on the television that evening, as well as on the front page of newspapers the next day – ensuring a significant degree of bad publicity that would have done little to improve public confidence in the opportunities offered by emerging technologies (and, given that the whole business of banking relies upon customer trust, this was not good for Barclays or the various others offering online banking services). The bank, of course, was not the only party to be concerned. From the affected customers' perspective, not only were they being presented with somebody else's confidential information, but it also introduced the immediate fear that maybe their own account details were being similarly compromised.

The cause of the problem was found to be an upgraded version of the software that ran the bank's online services, which had been installed during the preceding weekend (31st July was a Monday, the first working day after the upgrade). Barclays responded by taking their service offline at 3.30pm in order to enable the previous version of the software to be reinstalled and the system was available to customers again later the same evening. Although this rapid response to the problem was reassuring in terms of the bank's ability to handle its security issues, it is unlikely whether this would have been as apparent to people as the fact that a security incident had occurred. It can also be argued that the new software was probably in need of greater testing before going live – especially as problems were apparent so quickly after it was deployed. This is not to say that Barclays had not undertaken a period of testing prior to deployment – they had in fact performed a six week trial including some 15,000 customers.[25] However, the fact that 85,000 customers used the system in practice between the point at which it went live and the time at which it was taken down again suggests that the level of testing was not a realistic approximation of normal system loading. Barclays subsequently argued that their security architecture remained unbreached. This is true in the sense that no one managed to penetrate it via an attack, but the system was still plainly insecure in its implementation and the resulting effect upon customer trust was probably much the same.

Barclays was by no means the only bank to encounter security-related problems with its Internet banking services. The Cahoot service, offered by the U.K.'s Abbey National bank, suffered problems during its first day of operation, when unexpectedly high levels of demand served to make it inaccessible for three to four hours.[26] Whereas Barclays' problem had related to the issue of confidentiality, the Cahoot incident was related to availability (both of these issues are defined and discussed in the next section). The demand on the web site was such that, at some points, there were over 1,000 people attempting to login at once – which apparently proved to be too much for the server. To quote Cahoot's managing director, the occurrence of such an incident was "an extremely large bummer" for the new service and he admitted that it left them with the task of having to restore confidence.

The incidents described here were, of course, accidental and (other than PowerGen's short-lived allegations of hacking against Mr. Chamberlain) there was no suggestion of any cybercrime implications. However, even before picking up this book, most readers were probably aware that not all that goes wrong in the information society happens by accident. Indeed, as later discussion will show, without having taken the proper precautions, the information society is not necessarily a safe place to be. It is, in fact, a place where:

- personal details that are held about you on a computer system may be disclosed or modified by unauthorized third parties.
- innocuous looking email messages may actually be attempts to compromise and damage your system.
- web sites established to provide information or services to the public or potential customers may be defaced and left containing defamatory materials.

- people with a minimum amount of information can effectively masquerade as you online.
- a program that you utilized in good faith, believing it to be relevant to your needs, may in fact have a concealed purpose such as the destruction of data or the extortion of money.
- any system that is visible on the Internet is a potential target – able to be automatically scanned for vulnerabilities and then subjected to an attack.
- tools that may be used to attack and potentially cripple a system can be freely downloaded and used by anyone who cares to do so.

As a result, the information society is a place where trust is beginning to run out and it is not surprising that we need to give consideration to appropriate protection and safeguards.

Some basic principles of IT security

The issues of IT security and computer crime are clearly interlinked, in that appropriate attention to the former will typically reduce opportunities for the occurrence of the latter. As such, before considering in any detail the nature of computer crime and abuse, it is useful to appreciate the aspects of security that should be preserved. At the highest level, IT security relates to maintaining the properties of confidentiality, integrity and availability – three issues that will be examined in the paragraphs that follow. In order to make the discussion less abstract, a series of examples, this time set in a healthcare context, will be considered as a basis for illustrating the practical implications in each case.

Confidentiality

The maintenance of confidentiality refers to the prevention of unauthorized information disclosure, and is normally the aspect that people most closely associate with the concept of security. In the majority of organizations it is desirable to restrict access and allow only authorized users (those possessing a legitimate "need to know") to see specific systems and data. The seriousness of an unauthorized disclosure may often be dictated by whether it occurs to a member of the same organization or a total outsider (with the consequences from the latter being potentially more severe).

Confidentiality may be viewed as more important in healthcare than in many other sectors as there are several aspects to the problem that must be considered. These result from the handling of potentially sensitive data relating to both patients and the institution. Firstly, the principle of confidentiality is fundamental to medical practice in that it provides an assurance to the patient that discussions with their doctor will not be divulged to others. This is central to maintaining a necessary relationship of trust between patient and practitioner. Secondly, the unauthorized disclosure of patient information has the potential to lead to a number of undesirable consequences for the affected individual. At the most basic level it will represent the infringement of their general rights to privacy. However, more serious or damaging effects may be:

- potential to cause embarrassment.
- potential to cause discrimination, prejudice or even social ostracision.
- potential to invite blackmail or bribery.

Particularly relevant in this context will be especially sensitive classes of data, examples of which include information about sexually transmitted diseases, mental health, drug addiction or alcoholism. All of these tend to have a certain stigma attached to them, which could affect the way that an individual is perceived. The maintenance of patient confidentiality is also in the interest of the healthcare establishment itself, in order to avoid the risks of litigation and adverse publicity.

There are also various types of information that an establishment may wish to remain confidential. For example, there may be organizational implications if data relating to issues such as financial constraints, resource shortages or poor performance indicators (e.g. relating to staff or the organization) were to become generally known (especially in the context of the more performance-related healthcare environments now emerging).

However, despite the fact that confidentiality may be the most easily identified view of security, it is not the only issue to be considered.

Integrity

Maintaining integrity relates to preventing the unauthorized modification of information. Users must be able to trust their systems and be confident that the same information can be retrieved as was originally entered. While the integrity of a system or its data may be compromised as a result of accidental error or malicious activity, it is the latter aspect that is relevant to the context of this book.

Considering our healthcare example, the loss of data integrity is potentially the worst problem scenario. Unauthorized modifications to data could lead to misinformed decisions which, in a clinical context, could result in serious harm to patients. There have been documented incidents of such unauthorized modifications in the healthcare community. For example, a 1994 survey of computer crime and abuse from the U.K. Audit Commission reported a case in which a nurse hacked into a computer system and prescribed potentially lethal drugs for a patient and made unauthorized changes to the treatment records of others.[27] Luckily the changes were spotted before drugs were administered to the patient and the perpetrator was prosecuted under the U.K. Computer Misuse Act. Another integrity-related example can also be cited from 1994, in which a hacker entered the computer system of a local health services authority in London. A routine letter about cervical cancer was modified and, instead of a polite request to attend for a smear test, the text invited the patients to come in and "have your fanny checked."[28] The letter was posted to 5,000 women before the mistake was highlighted, causing embarrassment for both the health authority and the recipients. Such incidents illustrate that even a caring profession such as healthcare is not immune from the effects of computer abuse.

From the perspective of healthcare establishments, there are again additional considerations in relation to integrity, in that they may risk legal action being taken against clinicians or the organization as a result of a failure to protect information. This would be particularly the case with information relating to individuals, as failure to provide appropriate safeguards would represent a breach of data protection legislation in many countries. This issue is by no means unique to healthcare and the same kind of legal obligations would also apply in other domains.

Availability

The property of availability relates to the need for data and systems to be accessible and usable (by authorized parties) when and wherever they are required. This necessitates both the prevention of unauthorized withholding of information or resources, as well as adequate safeguards against system failure. The seriousness of any denial of service will, in most cases, increase depending upon the period of unavailability.

In the healthcare context, the continual availability of systems and data may be significant at various levels. In general, the unavailability of even the most mundane healthcare systems (e.g. patient appointments) could result in inconvenience and delays. It is fair to say that most healthcare professionals now expect their IT systems to be available on demand, and a significant proportion (particularly those directly relating to care delivery) will be required to be operational 24 hours a day.

In terms of care delivery and decision-making, healthcare professionals are not only reliant upon their own skills, but also upon the information that is at their disposal. Although there is an expectation that competent and experienced clinicians would be able to cope in many situations even if patient records were unavailable, most would still prefer access if records were known to exist (in case additional beneficial information was available). The unavailability of data (e.g. patient medical histories or diagnoses) could significantly reduce the quality and effectiveness of treatment, given that decisions would be made on a less informed basis. Although, in most cases, unavailability would be unlikely to be life threatening, such scenarios are not inconceivable (e.g. a system controlling the automatic administration of drugs could be seriously affected if data was unavailable for even a short period).

SUMMARY

Information technology undoubtedly has a significant and positive role to play in the everyday lives of many people. However, while it can clearly offer a myriad of benefits, the same technology can also provide an environment for misuse and criminal exploitation. This chapter has set the scene for later discussion by establishing our increasing dependence upon IT and some of the difficulties that can occur when things go wrong. Any problems here, whether the result of accidental or deliberate activities, can be considered to fall within the domain of IT security, with impacts on the confidentiality, integrity and availability of systems and data. A variety of security measures can be employed to guard against such threats and reduce the associated vulnerabilities. However, such measures are not used in all cases and, in others, determined abusers may still find a way to bypass or overcome them. As a result, few (if any) systems can be considered completely secure and the risk of cybercrime consequently looms large for many organizations.

The remainder of the book focuses upon the problems that can occur when individuals or groups set out with the deliberate intent to compromise systems, as well as the wider implications that must be considered as a result. The next chapter begins this discussion by classifying the problem of cybercrime and presenting some initial examples of how it can manifest itself in practice.

Crime in the information society

THIS CHAPTER CONSIDERS THE GENERAL ISSUE OF CYBERCRIME AND provides introductory material about the different types that may be encountered. The capabilities and uses of IT have resulted in the emergence of various new classes of crime. Having examined the issue of technology dependence in the previous chapter, the discussion now moves on to highlight the potential threats to which individuals and organizations may be exposed. A number of the themes introduced here are expanded upon in later chapters.

What is cybercrime?

At the most basic level, what we are clearly considering are types of crime involving the use of computers. However, this is obviously a very broad classification and anyone who has read or heard media reports about hacking and viruses will be aware that there are sub-categories to be considered. Therefore, in order to answer the question more precisely, it is useful to consider previous interpretations of computer crime and abuse that have been offered by some authoritative sources.

Renowned computer crime expert Donn Parker, a security veteran with thirty years of related experience, distinguishes between the concepts of computer crime and cybercrime, and offers definitions of the terms as follows:[29]

Computer crime: A crime in which the perpetrator uses special knowledge about computer technology.

Cybercrime: A crime in which the perpetrator uses special knowledge of cyberspace.

Although perfectly acceptable as far as they go, these definitions are still rather too vague to enable the various dimensions of the problem to be appreciated. It is, therefore, appropriate to consider some other sources in an attempt to add some more specific definition.

One organization that has taken a specific interest in cybercrime is the U.K. Audit Commission, an independent body that is principally responsible for auditing the activities of local government and the health service in England and Wales. Since its formation in the early 1980s, the Commission has conducted a series of surveys to determine the extent of computer crime and abuse in both the public and private sectors. The respondent organizations in these studies have included representatives from a number of domains including, from the public sector, local and central government, healthcare and education and, from the private sector, manufacturing, financial and leisure companies, as well as various other commercial organizations. Looking at the issues encompassed by the surveys, it can be seen that, over the years, the recognized range of crimes has broadened. For example, in the 1981 survey the only categories were fraud and theft. However, by the time of the most recent survey in 1998, the range had more than quadrupled to encompass a variety of other problems. The full range of categories, along with the Audit Commission's own definitions of them, are presented in Table 2.1. Later sections will consider the level of incidents reported under some of these headings and the financial losses associated with them.

It should be noted that the categories are not mutually exclusive. For example, hacking may be used as a means by which someone might commit an invasion of privacy, whereas both hacking and viruses might be regarded as methods of sabotaging a system. It should also be noted that, strictly speaking, the term "virus" is rather too narrow for the Audit Commission's accompanying definition, which also serves to encompass other categories of malicious software such as worms and Trojan Horse programs (as will be considered in later chapters).

Looking at the Audit Commission categories more closely, it is possible to draw a distinction between those crimes that are computer-assisted and those that are computer-focused, as defined below.

- Computer-assisted crimes. Cases in which the computer is used in a supporting capacity, but the underlying crime or offence either predates the emergence of computers or could be committed without them. The headings of fraud, theft, unauthorized private work, misuse of personal data, sabotage, and pornography can all be considered to fit into this category.

- Computer-focused crimes. Cases in which the category of crime has emerged as a direct result of computer technology and there is no direct parallel in other sectors. From the Audit Commission's headings, the problems of hacking and viruses clearly fall within this category.

Categorizing the use of illicit software is a debatable point, as it clearly would not be feasible without a computer. However, the underlying nature of the offence is a breach of copyright – something that frequently occurs in other domains, such as music and publishing. As such, for the purposes of this discussion, it will be considered to fall into the computer-assisted class.

The categorization of offences as being computer-assisted rather than computer-focused is not intended to imply that they are in any way less serious – indeed, survey results presented later in this chapter reveal that the losses resulting from computer fraud alone dwarfs all of the others put together. However, it is likely that, if computers did not exist, the perpetrators of these crimes would generally find alternative means to achieve the same ends (although, admittedly, computers frequently serve to make the commission of the crime easier and, thus, may influence the likelihood of it taking place). By contrast, it can be argued that the computer-focused crimes are the ones perpetrated by true cybercriminals – directly attacking the technologies that the information society has ushered in. All of the

TABLE 2.1 Computer crime and abuse categories from U.K. Audit Commission[30]

Crime/abuse	Description
Fraud	■ for private gain or benefit: – altering input in an unauthorized way; – destroying/suppressing/misappropriating computer output; – altering computerized data; – alteration or misuse of programs (excluding virus infections).
Theft	■ of data; ■ of software.
Use of unlicensed software	■ using illicit copies of software.
Private work	■ unauthorized use of the organization's computing facilities for private gain or benefit.
Misuse of personal data	■ unofficial "browsing" through computer records and breaches of data protection legislation.
Hacking	■ deliberately gaining unauthorized access to a computer system, usually through the use of communication facilities.
Sabotage	■ interfering with the computer process by causing deliberate damage to the processing cycle or to equipment.
Introducing pornographic material	■ Introducing pornographic material, for example, by downloading from the Internet.
Virus	■ distributing a program with the intention of corrupting a computer process.

categories are undesirable, but few would seriously argue that the computer-assisted crimes actually undermine the attractiveness of the technologies to which they are related. Hacking and viruses are viewed somewhat differently, and appear to be the categories most heavily emphasized in the media and, hence, the ones with the most name-recognition with the public at large. For this reason, cybercrimes of this nature will represent particular areas of focus in the examples and discussions that follow in subsequent chapters.

It should, however, be noted that the Audit Commission categories discussed here are only one way of looking at the cybercrime issue. Another view on the matter can be obtained by considering a categorization used by the U.S.-based Computer Security Institute (CSI). Working in association with the FBI, the CSI has conducted a series of annual Computer Crime and Security Surveys and the following thirteen headings were used as the basis for classifying incidents reported in their 2001 results:[31]

- Theft of proprietary information
- Sabotage of data or networks
- Telecom eavesdropping
- System penetration by outsider
- Insider abuse of Net access
- Financial fraud
- Denial of service

- Spoofing
- Virus
- Unauthorized insider access
- Telecom fraud
- Active wiretapping
- Laptop theft

It can be seen that, in many cases, the headings refer to much more specific types of incident than the Audit Commission. For example, the issue of "denial of service," which is specifically denoted by the CSI, would fit under the more generic heading of "hacking" or "sabotage" in the Audit Commission breakdown. At the same time, other classes of crime that were identified by the previous classification (e.g. use of unlicensed or pirated software), do not appear to be encompassed by the CSI's headings.

The classifications presented here are by no means exhaustive, and various other sources can be found that present alternative versions. However, what should be apparent from this discussion is that the topic of cybercrime can be interpreted in many different ways. It is also worth noting that the extent to which the problems are regarded as criminal offences actually varies from country to country. For example, although all countries can be expected to have laws relating to issues like theft, the feasibility of legal recourse for problems such as viruses is more variable (this inconsistency is considered in more detail in later chapters).

So who are the computer criminals? Where do the threats come from? For many years the accepted view of the situation has been that the vast majority of abuse has actually come from within affected organizations, with their own staff being responsible. In fact, the widely quoted statistic is a ratio of 80:20 between internally and externally sourced abuse. This is supported by the results of previous surveys, such as that of the U.K. Audit Commission in 1994, which found that external perpetrators were only responsible for 15 percent of reported incidents, with the remaining 85 percent being split between different categories of insiders. However, with the increasing role of the Internet in recent years (which serves to make systems significantly more visible to outsiders), the apparent trend has changed dramatically. The U.K.'s Defence Evaluation and Research Agency (DERA) has estimated that the reality of the split is now probably closer to a 50:50 ratio.[32] This is supported to some degree by more recent survey evidence. For example, the Audit Commission's 1998 results reveal that the proportion of outside abusers has risen to 39 percent. The 2001 CSI/FBI Computer Crime and Security Survey also supports the view of the increasing outsider threat, albeit though a more focused set of statistics, which specifically consider attacks on web sites. Here, 47 percent of incidents came from outside, 4 percent came from insiders and 22 percent of respondents had experienced incidents from both directions (a further 26 percent were not sure of the source).[33] The number of outsider incidents was a significant increase from the 38 percent reported just two years earlier, in the 1999 version of the same survey.

In a sense, the predominance of outsider attacks in the CSI/FBI results is to be expected, given that the context is specifically related to web sites. These are, almost by definition, public facing systems and, therefore, represent a visible target to the outside world. At the same time, they would tend not to represent very attractive targets for internal abusers, as there are few benefits to be gained from attacking them (unless the employee has an axe to grind and simply wishes to cause embarrassment or adverse publicity for the organization by affecting the content or performance of its site). From the insider perspective, more desirable targets would be systems holding confidential information or those with a potential to yield a financial reward if successfully breached.

A more specific classification of the types of human abuser was provided by James Anderson in 1980.[34]

- *External penetrators*
  Outsiders gaining (or attempting to gain) unauthorized access to the system. This is the category that best equates to the traditional perception of a hacker – they have no legitimate purpose and should consequently play no part in the system.

- *Internal penetrators*
  Authorized users of the system who access data, resources or programs to which they are not entitled. These are sub-categorized into:

  - *Masqueraders* – users who operate under the identity of another user.
  - *Clandestine users* – users who evade access controls and auditing.

- *Misfeasors*

    Users who are authorized to use the system and resources accessed, but misuse their privileges. These will typically be the most difficult group to identify, as they have legitimate access to the systems and applications that they are utilizing.

Barring the first category, all of Anderson's groupings can be seen to relate to internal abusers of some description. This is not to suggest that external penetrators cannot be further subdivided and, indeed, Chapter 3 will consider potential classifications in its consideration of hackers. It should also be noted that Anderson's categorizations fail to take into account any of the categories of abuse that may result from software activity (e.g. viruses, Trojan Horses, etc.). The collective term for this is "malware" and its omission from Anderson's work is understandable when it is considered that the analysis was made in 1980, before such incidents became commonplace. In more recent years, however, saying that such incidents are commonplace almost seems like an understatement and the various problems are examined in Chapter 5.

Assessing the scale of the problem

As networked systems have grown and matured, so has the nature of abuse within the environment. In the earlier days of computing, abuse was largely restricted to fraud and theft related activities, which simply represented the extension of traditional crimes into the electronic environment. However, as time has moved on, new and more advanced forms of abuse have emerged (e.g. computer viruses), which often appear not so much a means to an end, but an objective in themselves. Whatever form they take, it is clear that cybercrimes will not disappear and computers have firmly become part of the criminal landscape. To quote detective sergeant Clive Blake, from the U.K. Metropolitan Police Computer Crime Unit, "Computers are the future of crime . . . They will become as crucial to the criminal as a gun or a getaway vehicle."[35]

A number of surveys can be cited that provide a good indication of the level of computer crime. A good example comes from the aforementioned U.K. Audit Commission, with studies dating back to 1984 and, hence, enabling the long-term trend to be tracked. The results from these surveys, categorized by some of the main incident types, are presented in Table 2.2.

It is clear that over the last decade there has been a significant increase in the reported cases and, in the 1998 survey, 46 percent of the 900 U.K. respondents reported some form of incident.[36] A clear factor influencing this increase is the explosion in virus incidents that can be observed in the 1990s. It is also worth noting that, in the latest results, "hacking" is the only category of abuse in which the reported incidents have risen (in both absolute terms and as a percentage of incidents reported) when compared to the previous 1994 survey. A possible reason for this, which will be discussed in more detail later, is that the technological barriers to entry have been reduced in recent years and there are now numerous tools that provide automated support for would-be hackers.

While the Audit Commission's U.K. surveys have been conducted every three to four years, the Computer Security Institute has been conducting annual surveys in the United States since 1996. Their statistics give a more specific picture of the problem in recent years and, as Figure 2.1 illustrates, there has been a general upward trend in the number of respondent organizations experiencing unauthorized use of their computer systems.

TABLE 2.2 Reported incidents of computer crime and abuse (U.K. Audit Commission)

	Fraud	Viruses	Theft	Hacking	Other	Total
1984	60	–	17	–	–	77
1987	61	–	22	35	–	118
1990	73	54	27	26	–	180
1994	108	261	121	47	–	537
1998	67	247	88	56	52	510

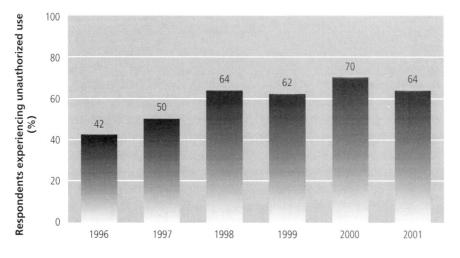

FIGURE 2.1 CSI/FBI Computer Crime and Security Survey results 1996–2001

Going back to the Audit Commission figures, Table 2.3 shows that the overall costs incurred by computer abuse have also increased over the last fifteen years. However, averaging the totals with those from Table 2.2 reveals that the loss per incident is now less. This can again be explained by the prevalence of viruses and the fact that their financial impact (upon an individual organization) is generally much less than other classes of abuse.

Even though the costs are running into the millions, it may be observed that the total figures are actually quite small when compared to the amount of attention and publicity that cybercrime seems to attract. However, when considering the figures from both of the previous tables, there are several points that should be kept in mind:

- the figures only relate to *reported* incidents from one particular set of surveys. It is often conjectured that the true level of computer crime remains much higher than reported,[37] as organizations do not wish to risk undesirable consequences such as bad publicity, legal liability, or loss of custom.

- from the most recent results, the average cost per incident is £6,448, which is a significant figure to contemplate for individual organizations.

- financial loss is merely one type of impact that may result from cybercrime. Other impacts, such as disruption to services, loss of data or damage to reputation, are more difficult to quantify and may actually be more significant in many contexts.

It can also be observed that the Audit Commission's U.K. figures are dwarfed by those from the CSI, whose 2001 survey results reported losses approaching $378 million from the 186 respondents who were willing and able to quantify the financial impacts of their incidents.[38] With an average loss per incident of over $2 million, this is not a problem that one should dismiss lightly.

Although computer crime is certainly on the increase, there are also indications that the public perception of malicious abuse is somewhat inflated. For example, a previous survey into computer security breaches by the U.K. National Computing Centre[39] indicated that some 53 percent of respondents perceived a threat from

TABLE 2.3 Costs of computer crime and abuse (U.K. Audit Commission)

	Fraud	Viruses	Theft	Hacking	Other	Total
1984	£1,131,186	–	£2,301	–	–	£1,133,487
1987	£2,526,751	–	£34,500	£100	–	£2,561,351
1990	£1,102,642	£5,000	£1,000	£31,500	–	£1,140,142
1994	£3,042,318	£254,925	£394,725	£130,245	–	£3,822,213
1998	£2,360,646	£403,921	£62,480	£360,860	£100,740	£3,288,647

hacking. However, within the same survey, hacking accounted for only 2.5 percent of the reported incidents. Nevertheless, the fact that hacking (and other types of malicious abuse) may account for only a small proportion of computer security problems is, in a sense, immaterial because it is normally these cases that are seized on by the mass media. The stories are often presented in a dramatic, even scare-mongering, fashion, which may in turn influence public opinion of the activity (an issue that will be examined in more detail in Chapter 6). In some cases, this will reduce confidence in IT in general and impede progress, while in others it may unduly glamorize the concept of computer abuse (i.e. promoting the anti-establishment, cyberpunk image) and thereby encourage others to enter the fray. It is in this sense that much damage may be caused.

Also of concern is the fact that people have widely differing perspectives over what is right and what is wrong in cyberspace. For example, a poll of 47,235 elementary level and middle school students in the United States revealed that 48 percent of them did not consider hacking into systems to be a crime.[40] Given that the U.S. is one of the leading countries in terms of domestic IT ownership, and that unauthorized system access is definitely regarded as being illegal, this statistic is worrying. The lack of awareness suggests both the need for stronger enforcement of cyber-ethics and that, in the meantime, there may be a large population of young IT users at risk of becoming cyber criminals.

Some examples of notable incidents

Having looked at some general definitions of the problem and its scale in recent years, it is now appropriate to consider some brief examples of cybercrime in practice, based upon incidents that have made media headlines in recent years. Later chapters will present examples of more specific types of incident – those presented here are intended to give a general flavor of the ways in which problems can manifest themselves. The scope of the incidents can be seen to vary – some affect individuals, some affect multiple organizations; some are restricted to a particular country, whereas others have a global significance. In this sense, they provide a good indication of the rich diversity of cybercrimes. The only common factor is that the incidents were all conducted via the Internet – and, indeed, none of them would have been possible, or as noteworthy, were it not for society's mass adoption of the Net.

Denial of service – simple but effective

February 2000 witnessed one of the most significant and widely reported examples of IT systems vulnerability, with the launch of a series of major denial of service attacks upon popular Internet sites, including Amazon.com (bookseller), eBay (online auctions) and CNN (news). A denial of service (DoS) attack results when legitimate user access to a computer or network resource is intentionally blocked or degraded as a result of malicious action taken by another user. These attacks do not necessarily cause direct or permanent damage to data, but they intentionally compromise the availability of the resources. This type of attack tends to affect the availability of computer systems for legitimate usage. At the very least, therefore, the result is disruption and inconvenience, but in an extreme case it could result in the total unavailability of a system.

The software required to carry out denial of service attacks is widely available on the Internet. The tools utilized in the February 2000 attacks had been available for several months prior to the incidents and included programs entitled Tribal Flood Net (TFN), Stacheldraht (German for "barbed wire") and Trinoo. This occasion did not represent the first time their use had been noted, but it was certainly the most concerted incident up to that point. Similarly, this was by no means the first widely reported Internet security incident (the honors there go to an incident from 1988, when a U.S. university student inadvertently brought a large proportion of the network to a standstill with a worm program). However, although other high-profile attacks had been reported, this incident differed in the sense that its effect was so widespread and the sites affected were specifically those that average Net users would be wishing to access.

The impact of the attacks was significant. For example, according to Keynote (**http://www.keynote.com**), a U.S. Internet monitoring company, the average performance of the Net was "degraded by as much as 26.8%."[41] This assertion was based upon their Business 40 Index which, to quote Keynote, is based upon "the average response time of accessing and downloading the home pages of 40 important business Web Sites as measured Monday through Friday every 15 minutes between 6am and noon." The Index included three of the sites attacked, namely Excite, Yahoo!, and ZDNet. Keynote's figures indicate that Yahoo! is normally one of the best performing sites on the web in terms of its accessibility, with a 99.3 percent availability rate. However, during the DoS attack it became virtually unavailable for three hours, with accessibility rates of between zero and 10 percent.

Another popular site, Amazon.com, was also badly affected. Amazon was targeted on 8th February and, within a few minutes, the site became 98.5 percent unavailable to legitimate users.[42] During this period (which lasted about thirty minutes), it took about 300 seconds for legitimate visitors to be able to get to the site's home page. Anyone wishing to make a purchase would probably have given up in this time, resulting in lost revenue for the company.

On 15th April 2000, almost two-and-a-half months after the attacks, the Royal Canadian Mounted Police arrested a suspect – a fifteen-year-old high-school student known online by the identity "Mafiaboy" (his real name could not be divulged due to a Canadian law designed to protect young offenders). The evidence that led to the arrest included the log files of a computer system at University of California, Santa Barbara, which was amongst those used to attack the CNN.com site. In addition, the FBI obtained logs from Internet chat rooms that showed Mafiaboy asking others which sites he should attack before they were targeted.[43] He was originally charged with two counts of "mischief to data" in relation to the attacks on CNN.com. However, on 3rd August 2000, a further sixty-four charges were added after additional evidence was found that linked him to attacks on five other sites – namely those of Yahoo!, Amazon, eBay, Dell and Outlawnet. Ten of the new charges related to mischief against the sites listed, whereas the other fifty-four were associated with illegal use of computer systems (mainly located in U.S. universities). In January 2001, Mafiaboy pleaded guilty to fifty-eight charges and, at the time of writing, the case had not concluded. However, it was reported that, if convicted, he could face up to two years in a juvenile detention centre (an adult faced with the same charges could face ten years in prison).[44] The recommendation made by a court-appointed social worker was that Mafiaboy should spend at least five months in custody because, despite pleading guilty, he had not acknowledged the serious-ness of his activities and could, therefore, still pose a moderate risk if released.[45]

By February 2000, denial of service attacks were certainly nothing new. They had been experienced in network and Internet-based systems many times previously. The difference in this instance was the sheer scale of the attack and the fact that so many well-known sites were targeted simultaneously.

Many of the media reports at the time of the attacks included quotes attributed to hackers, claiming that the incidents were probably the result of actions by "script kiddies" or "packet monkeys" (i.e. those without the technical skill or inclination to mount a more ingenious type of attack and relying upon the automated tools and scripts to do the work for them). Indeed, these views are echoed by Sgt. Jean-Pierre Roy of the Royal Canadian Mounted Police, who made the following comments at the time of Mafiaboy's arrest:

> It is in our estimation that Mafiaboy wasn't that good . . . He wasn't what we would call a genius . . . almost anyone with knowledge of a computer [could have launched the attacks].[46]

In a sense, such observations make the results of the attacks even more worrying. If this effect can be achieved by the average Joe, using a technique that is effectively a no-brainer, then it does not inspire much confidence in the security of the systems and raises a significant concern about what someone could therefore do if they were really trying. Later discussion will give more focus to the issue of the automated tools that are available for attacking systems and exploiting the vulnerabilities within them.

"President Clinton" supports online pornography!

February 2000 was certainly a fun month for CNN's online services. Not only were they amongst the victims of the denial of service assaults described in the previous section, but about a week later a further incident caught the headlines.[47] President Clinton was giving his first live online interview to CNN . . .

In the middle of the dialogue, the President began to offer contributions such as "Personally, I would like to see more porn on the Internet." Now, given the President's controversial reputation in office, some may not have been surprised to read such statements. In actual fact, however, the words did not belong to him at all – an impostor had managed to hijack the President's identity.

During the interview, the chat room system had become overloaded with users and then crashed – disconnecting users from the session and forcing them to connect again. At this point, the impostor was able to reselect a nickname under which to appear in the chat session – and chose the one that the President had been using up to that point (selecting it before the typist entering the President's responses was able to re-login). From this point, the impostor, rather than the President's typist, had control over what the President appeared to be saying.

The perpetrator of the impersonation was actually a New York-based computer security officer. He subsequently claimed that his activities had been unplanned and that the remark about pornography was the first thing that came into his head.[48] He described the activity as a "harmless prank," but also pointed out that it illustrated the insecurity of the system being used to host the interview. CNN rightly pointed out that the incident was not a result of its site having been hacked. Nonetheless, it is easy to see that what took place was not trivial from a security perspective. The average member of the public could rightly observe that, if it is possible to successfully target the U.S. President, then what chance do the rest of us have? One would instinctively assume that a Presidential webcast would be afforded a better than average level of protection.

What if the impersonator had used more subtle replies? How long could the deception have been maintained? If a live session can be so easily hijacked, to what extent may other online materials have been tampered with? Subtle changes to information content could go unnoticed, but could have significant consequences. Consider for a moment a hypothetical example. What if someone were to perform subtle modifications to the information presented on a public advisory web site, covering an issue such as medical and health matters? Such a site might contain advice on the medication that individuals could administer for themselves if feeling unwell. What if someone were to modify the information regarding the suggested dosage? Make too significant a change and someone will probably notice quite quickly. If the alteration were of a less obvious nature, such that the information presented did not intuitively seem unreliable, then people would continue to follow it. The consequences in such a scenario could conceivably be life threatening.

Hackers unite to expose email

In August 1999, a group calling themselves Hackers Unite publicized a security vulnerability that allowed any web user to gain open access to the private email accounts belonging to subscribers to the popular Hotmail service. For those readers who are unfamiliar with it, Hotmail is a web-based email service, which represented a revolution in electronic messaging when it was launched in 1996. It allows users to access, send and receive their email messages on any machine that has web access. This can be contrasted to traditional email access, which often require specific "client" software to be installed on the machine and, at the very least, requires some reconfiguration for each email account that is to be accessed (which would often mitigate against people being able to get temporary access from a machine in a location they are just visiting). Hotmail allows easy access from anywhere in the world, just by going to the Hotmail web site and entering a username and password at the prompt. What's more, the service is completely free. It is a boon to anyone working on the move or wanting to get themselves an email address in a quick and hassle-free manner. It has provided a successful model for web-based mail services, which are now offered by numerous other companies such as Yahoo, Excite and Netscape. The Hotmail service was originally offered by an independent company of the same name, but was bought by Microsoft in 1998 and incorporated into its Microsoft Network (MSN) offerings. By the time of the security breach in August 1999, the service was estimated to have attracted 50 million subscribers.

The vulnerability that was exploited allowed anyone to log into other people's email accounts by knowing just their user name – without the need to know the accompanying password. User names can, of course, be determined relatively easily (for Hotmail they are actually part of the email address) and it is meant to be the password that is protected and kept secret. As such, this blew a major hole in the privacy of the service. The hack involved the utilization of an alternative login process to the one that Hotmail normally uses when someone enters his or her user details. This alternative script would allow any account to be accessed using the constant password of "eh." Security experts conjectured that this was a backdoor route into the Hotmail system, originally created by the developers but then overlooked and left operational by mistake. Such backdoors are actually quite common and are often included for testing and maintenance purposes, with the developers assuming that they are safe to leave in because no one will find them or expect that they are there.

The breach presented problems at several levels. First, there were direct effects upon the individual Hotmail subscribers. Most obviously, opening their accounts to casual inspection was a threat to their personal privacy. Any sensitive or confidential correspondence was put at risk of exposure. More than this, however, was the threat of impersonation. Having gained access to the email account, an impostor would be perceived by both the Hotmail service and any subsequent message recipient to be the legitimate user. The ability to send out messages that appeared to be from somebody else could be used for a variety of mischievous or malicious purposes against an individual or a company. It is difficult to assess how many people suffered from such incidents, but many were certainly concerned and indignant that their privacy could have been violated in this way. In one rather memorable quotation, which appeared in a Wired News report at the time, a Hotmail user (who feared that messages containing his credit card number might have been exposed) offered the following opinion:

> I feel like I've been bent over the table by hackers, had my pants lowered to my ankles, and Vaseline smeared all over my [expletive] while the great staff of Hotmail tied my hands together with a sturdy piece of rope.[49]

Although this reaction was possibly a bit extreme, many people shared the underlying view that both the hackers and the Hotmail service had to take some level of responsibility for the breach. The typical reaction from existing users seemed to be that the incident would not prevent them from using Hotmail, but they would be more careful about what they sent with it.

At the level above the individual users, Hotmail's reputation for security (and, by association, that of Microsoft) took a bit of a knock. Overall, however, this did not dent the popularity of the service and the price of Microsoft stock was not noticeably affected. At the end of the day, Microsoft's market value is based upon its software sales and so a problem with a free email service was unlikely to worry its stockholders. The most lasting impact was probably at a more generic level, relating to the image of the Internet (and its security) in the eyes of the public at large. For those who did not use Hotmail or the Internet in general, the publicity surrounding the incident could have simply placed another psychological barrier in the way of them doing so.

Hackers Unite, the group responsible for the incident, comprised seven Americans and one Swede. Their claimed motivation for publicizing the hole was to draw attention to the weak security in a service that millions of people routinely used and, presumably, trusted. To quote one of the group members:

> We did not do this hack to destroy, we want to show the world how bad the security on Microsoft really is, and that company nearly have monopoly on [all] the computer software.[50]

From a certain perspective, it can be seen that a useful point is being made here – if a system or service is vulnerable to compromise, then people should ideally be told, so that they can make an informed decision about whether they wish to trust it. The problem in this case was that, in opening people's eyes to the vulnerability, Hackers Unite was also placing them directly into the scenario that they would most like to avoid, with their email accounts being exposed to all and sundry. As with many other hacking cases, it was the means rather than the message that was the problem, serving to make the hackers the ultimate villains of the piece in the eyes of the media and the public. However, it does not have to be this way, as a similar incident that occurred almost a year later can be used to illustrate. In August 2000, a hacker called "Blue Adept" discovered a security vulnerability at ZKey, an information storage portal that provides protected file space and personal information management facilities that can be accessed over the Internet.[51] The vulnerability allowed ZKey users to obtain the usernames and passwords of other users (and thereby access their information) by sending them an email message containing some embedded program code. Rather than shout about the issue to all and sundry, Blue Adept reported the problem to the web-based news service Wired News, but specifically asked them not to publicize it until ZKey had the chance to rectify the issue. In this sense, he can be considered to have acted in a more responsible manner than the Hackers Unite group – retrospectively alerting people to the possible risks of Internet-based services, without leaving ZKey's users open to abuse before a solution was found. As a consequence of the hole being fixed before it was reported, it can be observed that there was considerably less media coverage than with the Hotmail incident and it did not make headline news in the same way. In part, this can be put down to the fact that a big name such as Microsoft was not involved in the story, but there was also less potential for media commentary and speculation (making the story less attractive). As a result, the reports were only really likely to have reached the sort of strongly IT-literate audience who would potentially be affected by the incident (rather than raising unnecessary spectres in the minds of the public and Internet users at large).

In response to the Hotmail incident, Microsoft allowed an independent audit of the service and its security. It was judged that the subsequent repairs conducted to patch the holes in the service were effective and new quality controls were also introduced to guard against future incidents. Overall, however, Microsoft's view was that the blame for the breach ultimately lay with the hackers:

> Unfortunately, malicious hackers target all technology platforms, but we believe this effort will help ensure that we have the right security controls in place to protect customers of Hotmail.[52]

Being the most recognized name in the IT industry, Microsoft and its products continue to attract a significant degree of attention from the hacker community and later discussion will illustrate other relevant examples.

The Saint of e-commerce?

The ability to engage in electronic commerce is one of the much-vaunted advantages of the web. In the last few years, numerous sites have sprung up offering customer-facing web sites that enable all manner of goods and services to be purchased online. In addition to the advantages, however, a downside has also been apparent and there have been a rash of incidents in which associated web sites have been penetrated and customer credit card details stolen. A good example of the problem was demonstrated in early 2000, when a hacker calling himself Curador began hacking into small e-commerce sites and posting stolen card details elsewhere on the web. Curador's hacking spree began in late January and continued throughout February and into early March. During this period he penetrated some nine sites, variously located in Britain, the U.S., Canada, Japan and Thailand, stealing between 750 and 5,000 card numbers in each case. It was estimated that some 26,000 cards may have been compromised in total.[53]

Stealing the information was not the end of the story – Curador also took steps to share his findings and, during the course of his activities, he set up two web sites upon which he listed the stolen card details (**www.free-creditcard.com** and **e-crackerce.com** – with the site registrations being paid for using stolen cards!). An example of one of the sites is shown in Figure 2.2. In the original version, the information shown here was also followed by a list of 1,000 stolen card numbers and associated cardholder names.

On another of his sites, Curador also posted information that purported to be the credit card details of Microsoft's Bill Gates – a story that was picked up and reported by Reuters. The details were subsequently shown to be bogus, but the stunt probably had the effect that Curador desired by drawing more attention to his

FIGURE 2.2 One of Curador's stolen credit card sites

actions. It was, however, later reported that Curador had actually obtained Gates' credit card details, but kept them to himself, and used them to send the billionaire a consignment of Viagra tablets.

As can be seen from the figure, Curador was proclaiming himself to be "The Saint" of e-commerce (a reference to the character created by Leslie Charteris) and he subsequently attempted to justify his actions by claiming that he wanted to draw the web site providers' attention to their security vulnerabilities. Indeed, he had been able to gain access to the various sites by exploiting well-known vulnerabilities in the underlying software systems and, according to his logic, that meant that the web site owners were actually the ones at fault for not having addressed the weaknesses. However, by giving such a practical and public demonstration, he also served to put the compromised card details at risk – which would, of course, have punished the customers rather than the e-commerce sites concerned.

Having evaded capture for over a month, Curador began to get quite cocky and, in early March 2000, was quoted as saying:

> Law enforcement couldn't hack their way out of a wet paper bag. They're people who get paid to do nothing. They never actually catch anybody.[54]

It was probably with some satisfaction, then, that the FBI and Welsh police arrested him (and an unnamed accomplice) just a couple of weeks later, after having traced him to the Welsh village of Clynderwen (in Welsh, the word "curador" means "custodian"). Both Curador and his accomplice were eighteen years old and it was revealed that Curador had previously worked as an e-commerce consultant, actually helping to set up the type of sites that he later broke into.[55] The FBI estimated that the losses associated with the various intrusions were in excess of $3 million, taking into account the cost of closing down Curador's sites and issuing new cards. In March 2001, Curador pleaded guilty to two charges of obtaining services by deception (in relation to setting up the two Internet sites), as well as six charges of intentionally accessing sites containing the original card details. He was finally sentenced in early July, but contrary to what many would have expected, Curador managed to escape a custodial sentence. Tried under his real name, Raphael Gray, the court was told that he was suffering from a mental condition, and that medical treatment was more appropriate than imprisonment. Taking this into account, the judge consequently ordered that Gray should undergo psychiatric treatment under a three-year community rehabilitation order. After the trial, Gray maintained that his aim had been to expose the weaknesses of Internet-based e-commerce, and suggested that it was only his methods that had been questionable:

> I would do it all again but another time I would choose to ensure that I acted legally.[56]

Many in the security industry felt that Gray had got off lightly, and that the sentence gave the wrong impression to other hackers who might consider emulating his activities. In this respect, it can also be observed that the comments reported from the judge sent out a rather mixed message. Media reports after the trial included the following quotes:

> You demonstrated some sense of humour by sending Viagra to Bill Gates to mock him.
>
> Even the prosecution had difficulty identifying the criminality of what you did. You have computer skills which many, including myself, envy.[57]

Considered in conjunction with the perceived leniency of the sentence, such comments do not help to reinforce any impression that what Gray did was wrong. Indeed, the headline that accompanied these quotes was "Hacker praised by judge for Bill Gates prank." Consequently, anyone reading about the case might well have come away with the impression that Curador was indeed the hero that he always set out to be.

An unwanted lesson in customer relations

On 12 August 2000, U.K. supermarket chain Safeway experienced a hacking incident in which a customer database was compromised and customers were sent a hoax email message, purporting to come from Safeway themselves.[58] The message appeared to originate from **info@safeway.co.uk** (an account normally used to inform registered customers of current bargains), and the main text read as follows:

> We are pleased to announce that from Monday Safeway will be increasing prices on all our goods to by 25%. If this doesn't sound good to you then you can piss off to another supermarket chain such as Tesco or Sainsbury.

On the surface, and from the perspective of the individual responsible, this may seem like a wryly-amusing stab at a big organization, which most people would not take very seriously. However, it was estimated that the message was received by around 3,000 customers, 1,000 of whom then contacted Safeway to complain about it. The supermarket chain confirmed that the message did appear to have originated from within their system, but were unclear on whether external hackers or internal misuse were to blame. In either event, not only was the breach of security embarrassing for Safeway, it could also have had the effect of alienating customers and driving them in the direction of the competing stores, as the message suggested. In addition, while the affected system did not contain any financial information about customers, the incident would nonetheless have given them concern about the safety of their personal details. Indeed, from the customer perspective, it would not be immediately clear what information about them is maintained on which Safeway system. They would be aware, for example, that their debit and credit card details are taken at the store's point-of-sale terminals. As such, without being told differently, they might assume that these details would be maintained and handled centrally, on the same system as their email address – a system that must have been breached or misused to send them a fake and irresponsible message. In order to avoid such misunderstandings, Safeway had to act to contact and reassure its customers.

It is this sort of publicly visible incident that a well-known high street company can clearly do without and, at the same time, reflects badly upon the idea of using information technology. In offering such an email notification service, Safeway was clearly trying to innovate and take advantage of new opportunities to communicate with its customers. The occurrence of such an incident could potentially be off-putting for both sides, undermining customers' faith in the technology and stifling attempts by the store to make further inroads into the electronic marketplace. A possible upside to this argument is that, if the customers were IT literate enough to have an email address and to have provided it in order to receive online bargain notifications, then they would probably be more sympathetic toward the kind of problems that can occur. The media reporting of the incident would, however, have reached a wider audience than the existing users, and could well have tarnished the image of the online service in the minds of other customers before they had a chance to try it.

SUMMARY

It is clear from the discussion in the early part of this chapter that, whichever way you look at it, cybercrime is a multifaceted problem. Furthermore, the issue is an international one and impacts have been felt by organizations and individuals around the globe. Indeed, as some of the brief examples have already shown, the involvement of the Internet enables a single incident to affect thousands, or even millions, of people.

Most of the examples presented so far have highlighted activities that observers would class as hacking. The topic of hackers will now be considered in detail during the next two chapters. The first chapter examines the issue of hacking in general, and those responsible for it, whereas the one that follows considers some of the methods that may typically be employed.

Hackers – anti-heroes of the computer revolution?

THIS CHAPTER BEGINS TO FOCUS UPON THE WORLD OF THE COMPUTER hacker. Before later discussion examines some of the techniques that they employ, this section considers the factors that may motivate people to become hackers, how they justify their activities and how they are perceived as a result. It also considers elements of hacker culture, illustrating that hackers are frequently part of an organized community, with groups, publications, and events dedicated to their activities. Consideration will also be given to how the whole issue of hacking has captured public attention and to the celebrity figures that have emerged from the computer underground as a result. Before any of this, however, the discussion will begin by asking what may at first appear to be a fairly straightforward question . . .

Who or what is a hacker?

You may have picked up this book and read the first couple of chapters feeling certain that you had a fairly clear understanding about what a hacker is. However, as the following discussion will illustrate, the usage and intended meaning of the term can often be extremely variable. In fact, to say that opinion is divided on the issue could be considered something of an understatement.

The definition of the term "hacker" has changed considerably over the last thirty years. The title of this chapter is actually a play on the title of the 1984 book by Steven Levy, *Hackers: Heroes of the Computer Revolution*.[59] Levy's book was not about computer criminals, but the pioneers of 1950s and 1960s computing to whom the term "hacker" was originally applied as a mark of respect for their skills. In the 1960s, hackers were the dedicated software and hardware gurus, and the term largely referred to persons capable of implementing elegant, technically advanced solutions to technologically complex problems. Hackers then were basically very gifted programmers and, when Levy wrote his book, he was reflecting upon a different era. In the new millennium, the moniker implies something rather different and is commonly used to refer to persons who gain unauthorized access to systems and data. At the extreme are a subset (often distinguished by the term "crackers") that perform openly malicious actions upon the systems they enter, such as deleting files, modifying data and stealing information. Such activities would be frowned upon by the original hackers of the 1960s, who regarded technology as a means of liberation rather than a tool for causing damage and destruction.

The application of such labels is, however, the source of some controversy. Some texts, such as The Jargon File[60] (an online compendium of hacker slang), make the specific and strong point that hackers and crackers are fundamentally different groups, as illustrated by the following definitions:

Hacker: 1. A person who enjoys exploring the details of programmable systems and how to stretch their capabilities, as opposed to most users, who prefer to learn only the minimum necessary. 2. One who programs enthusiastically (even obsessively) or who enjoys programming rather than just theorizing about programming. 3. A person capable of appreciating hack value. 4. A person who is good at programming quickly. 5. An expert at a particular program, or one who frequently does work using it or on it; as in "a Unix hacker." (Definitions 1 through 5 are correlated, and people who fit them congregate.) 6. An expert or enthusiast of any kind. One might be an astronomy hacker, for example. 7. One who enjoys the intellectual challenge of creatively overcoming or circumventing limitations. 8. [deprecated] A malicious meddler who tries to discover sensitive information by poking around. Hence "password hacker," "network hacker." The correct term for this sense is cracker.

Cracker: One who breaks security on a system. Coined ca. 1985 by hackers in defense against journalistic misuse of hacker . . . though crackers often like to describe *themselves* as hackers, most true hackers consider them a separate and lower form of life.

The argument that often emerges from this is that the term "hacker" is still a mark of respect that should not be used to refer to those who abuse and misuse systems. The media is largely credited with misusing the term and an explicit distinction is maintained in certain writings. However, to argue that it is just the media that misuses the term is itself misleading – indeed, it is debatable whether this interpretation should be considered misuse at all. The nature of the computing industry has now changed and the commonly accepted meaning of the word "hacker" (in an IT context) can be illustrated by considering a series of dictionary definitions from recent years:

A computer fanatic, esp. one who through a personal computer breaks into the computer system of a company, government, etc.

COLLINS ENGLISH DICTIONARY (3RD EDITION), 1994

A (computer) hacker is a person who hacks into other people's computer systems.

CAMBRIDGE INTERNATIONAL DICTIONARY OF ENGLISH, 1995

A person who uses computers to gain unauthorized access to data.

THE NEW OXFORD DICTIONARY OF ENGLISH, 1998

A skilled and enthusiastic computer operator, *esp* an amateur; an operator who uses his or her skill to break into commercial or government computer or other electronic systems.

THE CHAMBERS DICTIONARY, 1998

A person who uses computer for a hobby, *esp.* to gain unauthorized access to data.

DK ILLUSTRATED OXFORD DICTIONARY, 1998

It can be seen that specific emphasis is placed upon the issues of unauthorized access and breaking into systems. As such, for the public at large, the act of hacking is generally synonymous with these factors. In fact, the nature of the wording in some cases serves to imply that if an individual uses a computer for a hobby, but does not engage in unauthorized access, then they do not meet the definition of a true hacker. Clearly, these definitions are not compatible with the viewpoint of first-generation hackers, but they nonetheless seem to represent the generally accepted interpretation in modern society. As such, the general term "hacker" will be used in much of the remaining discussion to refer to persons who gain or attempt unauthorized access to systems.

Whatever your preference, the use of a term such as "hacker" or "cracker" is sometimes rather too vague. It is analogous to the use of a simple label such as "criminal" to refer to a lawbreaker – the label alone is not very informative and there are a number of sub-categories that can be used to enable a more specific classification. As you can probably imagine, if there is a dispute over the correct top-level term, then the underlying groupings are likely to be far from standardized. Indeed, there is no overall set of hacker sub-groups that is regarded as definitive. There are, however, numerous terms that can be used to provide more specific focus and meaning.

A fairly high-level distinction can be made using the terms "Black Hat" and "White Hat" hackers. The former refers to the majority of hackers – those intruding into systems in an unauthorized, and frequently malicious, manner (to add yet another term, these may also be referred to as "dark-side" hackers). White Hats, by contrast, are "ethical" hackers, working for the good of system security. So, in a sense, these groupings can be considered to represent the same basic distinctions as the hacker and cracker labels defined earlier (except, of course, that in this case both types are being referred to as hackers!). It should also be noted that another term, "Grey Hat," is used to refer to individuals who fall somewhere between these two camps – those whose motives are unclear or may be prone to change.

In order to further illustrate the lack of a clear-cut black and white, good and bad distinction, here are some other names that are frequently ascribed to members of the hacker community (it should be noted that even this still does not provide an exhaustive list):

Cyberterrorists: Terrorists who employ hacker-type techniques to threaten or attack against systems, networks, and/or data. As with other forms of terrorism, cyberterrorist activities are conducted in the name of a particular political or social agenda. The underlying objective will typically be to intimidate or coerce another party (e.g. a government).

Cyber warriors: Persons employing hacking techniques in order to attack computer systems that support vital infrastructure, such as emergency services, financial transactions, transportation and communications. This essentially relates to the application of hacking in military and warfare contexts.

Hacktivists: Hackers who break into computer systems in order to promote or further an activist agenda. Incidents such as the defacement of web sites are very often linked to these individuals.

Malware writers: Not strictly a classification of hacker – but often considered alongside them – these individuals are responsible for creating malware programs such as viruses, worms and Trojan Horses.

Phreakers: Individuals who specifically focus upon hacking telephone networks and related technologies. Their objectives may range from simple exploration of the infrastructure to actually manipulating elements of it (e.g. to enable free phone calls to be made).

Samurai: Individuals who are hired to conduct legal cracking jobs, penetrating corporate computer systems for legitimate reasons. Such hackers may also be termed "Sneakers."

Script kiddies: Individuals with fairly limited hacking skills who rely upon scripts and programs written by other, more competent, hackers. Hackers of this type typically cause mischief and malicious damage and are generally viewed with scorn by more accomplished members of the hacking community. Such individuals may also be referred to as "Packet monkeys" or "Code kiddies."

Warez d00dz: A sub-class of crackers, who obtain and distribute illegal copies of copyrighted software (after first breaking any copy protection mechanisms if appropriate). The spelling used is representative of a common form of hacker slang – in this case the two words, when written properly, are "Wares Dudes." More commonly, these individuals are known as Software pirates.

Of these groups, the Samurais and Cyber warriors can be argued to represent forms of White Hat hacker, whereas the remaining activities will more typically be regarded as Black Hat behavior. There are also other names by which hackers refer to and describe those that they encounter, such as "lamers," "lusers" and "wannabees." However, these terms are generally used to pass comment on their opinions of the individuals concerned, rather than representing completely distinct categories of ability or proficiency (for example, a script kiddie could also be labeled a lamer due to the weak nature of their targets). At the other end of the scale, a proficient hacker could be referred to as being "elite" or being a "wizard." We will not dwell upon these additional terms, as there are already enough to be going on with.

So, what do hackers do? The title of this book refers to vandalizing the information society. However, this is not meant to imply that vandalism is the only activity in which hackers are involved (although it certainly plays its part in some cases). To consider the question properly, it is appropriate to look at the origins of hacking, the nature of hacker culture and the factors that motivate the individuals involved.

Phreaking out the phone company

The origins of hacking, in the sense of technological exploration and tampering, can be traced back to the phone phreakers of the 1960s and 1970s. Although a detailed exposition of phreaking is outside the scope of this book, a brief overview is appropriate to set the scene and provide a basis for comparison with the hackers that followed them. A more comprehensive account of the early phreaking scene can be found in Clough and Mungo's *Approaching Zero*.[61]

The passion of the phreaker was the telephone system, and learning how to explore, manipulate and control it. The fascination lay in the fact that it was a globally connected network, enabling you to communicate with virtually any other place on the planet (a similar attraction to that which many modern hackers find with the Internet and other computer networks). Entering the system, the phreakers could commandeer control of the telephone switches and route their own calls. In many cases, they did not have much of an interest in actually *talking* to anybody – the goal was just to understand how the system could be manipulated. Indeed, a favorite demonstration of phreaking skill would be to have two phones in the same room and then to use one of them to get into the network and route a call through a series of international switches until, ultimately, the other phone in the room would ring. For example, in *Approaching Zero*, Clough and Mungo describe an incident in which legendary phreaker John Draper (discussed later in this chapter) phreaked a call around the world, beginning in the U.S. and routing it via Tokyo, India, Greece, South Africa, South America, Great Britain, New York and Los Angeles, before terminating it in an adjacent phone booth. Of course, going to all this trouble in order to then literally talk to oneself was of no practical benefit. For the phreaker, however, the act of achieving it was its own reward.

Although playing with the phone system was fun, an obvious problem for such would-be explorers was the cost of the associated calls. Clearly, making sustained use of the phone and placing international calls was an expensive proposition (especially in the 1960s, when making international calls at all was extremely rare), and so the associated cost was something that phreakers did their best to avoid. A means to this end, as well as other aspects of controlling the system, was a device called a "Blue Box" – the essential companion of the early phone phreaker. A Blue Box is basically a tone generator, used to generate pairs of tones for telephone dialing, as well as a single 2600 Hz tone, used for in-band signaling to control the telephone network.* When using such a box, a phone number would first be dialed as normal but then, at the point where the number starts to ring, the Blue Box could be used to send the 2600 Hz tone. The receipt of this tone would signal to the telephone switch to clear the call. This then leaves the switch in a state where it is ready to receive tone dial information for another call (which can also be generated by the Blue Box) to substitute for the original dialed number. If the original dialed number was an 800 toll-free number, then at this point any further call placed through the switch would effectively also be free, as the 800 call would be the only one that was registered.

The telephone companies, of course, were less than enamored with the phreakers and their activities. The bottom line was that they were effectively depriving the telco of revenue. However, it should be noted that the roots of phreaking can actually be traced back to the Bell Telephone company itself, which essentially let the genie out of the bottle by publishing two articles in its technical journal that described the operation of its multi-frequency direct dial phone system. First, a 1954 article described the concept of in-band signaling, explaining the way in which signals were used to route and charge for calls. Then, in 1960, a second article presented details of the tone frequencies used to dial the telephone numbers. Armed with this combination of information, anyone with the required engineering knowledge could put together a Blue Box to produce the multi-frequency tones and then avoid the associated call charges by manipulating the signaling system.

* Clough and Mungo report how the name Blue Box originated from the first incident in which the Bell company encountered the use of an electronic device to enable the theft of long distance calls. Investigating a series of unusually long calls from Washington State College, engineers discovered that a "strange looking device on a blue metal chassis" had been attached to the phone line.

Although the articles had appeared in Bell's in-house journal, and thus made available to telco staff, the company had overlooked the fact that it was also sent out to various engineering colleges – thus placing the material in the hands of the very students in a position to exploit it.

The advent of all-digital telephone switches enabled the network operators to move the signaling information out of band and, as such, Blue Boxes are largely obsolete in the modern telecommunications arena. Correspondingly, phone phreakers requiring free calls have moved toward methods such as hacking telco computer systems, or exploiting PBXs (Private Branch Exchanges) owned by other organizations. As such, the required skills are closely related to other forms of hacking, because the underlying system is likely to be a computer of some description. Emerging technologies, such as Internet telephony, will further reinforce this convergence – with the result that any distinction between phreakers and other forms of hacker will be simply motivational, rather than technological.

Stereotype and self-image

So, how are hackers perceived by the world around them? For years, the standard image in the public mind has been that of the schoolboy or college student causing havoc from the computer in his bedroom. This image was reinforced, and often conjured up in the first place, by Hollywood films such as *WarGames* (discussed later). That is not to suggest, however, that it is without foundation, and practical evidence indicates that the typical hacker has a number of notable characteristics:

- almost always male.
- aged from mid-teens to mid-20s.
- lacking in social skills.
- fascination (possibly even an obsession) with technology.
- an underachiever in other areas (e.g. education) – who sees the computer as a means of being important or powerful.

In a way, this is not a surprising set of attributes, as they collectively describe someone of the right age and temperament to become hooked on IT. Fitting this stereotype does not, of course, automatically make you a hacker or indeed a cyber criminal. Many of the above characteristics could also be attributed to the pioneers of modern personal computing – individuals like Steve Wozniak (co-founder of Apple), Bill Gates and Paul Allen (the co-founders of Microsoft) were all what would commonly be described as nerds and possessed at least some of the characteristics above when they made their first landmark contributions to the fledgling PC industry in the 1970s.

Of course, the stereotype above did not evolve without justification and numerous cases can be found in which the perpetrators very much fit the bill. In more recent years, however, with the soaring popularity of the Internet and the web, the nerd image associated with computing has abated to some extent. The Net is cool and so, by association, are those who can claim to be in tune with it. This change is reflected in the way that hackers are presented to the general public by the media – a claim that can be illustrated, for example, by the way that they are portrayed in the movies. Contrasting 1983's *WarGames* with 1995's *Hackers* (two Hollywood films in which hacking is the central element), it can been seen that the portrayal of hackers in the later film attempts to endow them with personalities and behavior that the audience will hopefully regard as being "cool." So, whereas in *WarGames* the main hacker character is simply known as David and conforms quite closely to the stereotype presented above, in *Hackers* they all have handles (aliases) like Zero Cool, Acid Burn and The Plague, and the film attempts to show them as skilled masters of the technology. It is debatable whether this really succeeds, and the general audience may have found the hackers difficult to identify with. Indeed, it can be observed that the impact of the earlier film was by far the greater (as is discussed later in this chapter).

A couple of the examples above, and earlier elements of the discussion, have made reference to the use of handles instead of real names and, indeed, this is something that can also be considered to be part of the hacker stereotype (a trait which is also common to other cyber criminals like virus writers). The names that hackers choose for themselves can often be quite revealing – in terms of the hacker's self image if not the physical reality. In fact the names that are chosen are often the last thing that would come to mind if presented with the hacker in person. For example, as highlighted in Chapter 2, the individual behind the potentially sinister-sounding handle of "Mafiaboy" was a fifteen year-old high-school student with no connection to the Mafia whatsoever.

There are, of course, practical reasons for utilizing an alias, as it makes it more difficult to trace things to the real person – especially useful if you are intending to engage in illegal activities. However, rather than being simply an alias, many hackers regard their online name as being a whole new character that they have created, as a cyberspace alter ego. As a result, the names chosen are rarely neutral-sounding ones, of the "John Smith" variety, and they are more often selected in order to create an aura of mystique, power or importance – things that the hacker may feel that he lacks in the real world. Some examples of the grandiose titles that hackers and virus writers have given themselves include The Black Baron, The Dark Avenger, Knight Lightning, Dark Dante and Eric Bloodaxe. This is not to say that all hackers choose titles of this nature, or to suggest that, without exception, those choosing such names are doing so because they feel inadequate in the real world. What can be said is that the choice of handle generally reflects the way in which the individual would like to be perceived. In this respect, some hackers clearly have a sense of humor and, evidently, motivations other than conveying a sense of power or importance. Take for example, the choice of the name "Tweety Fish" – the moniker adopted by a member of the hacking group Cult of the Dead Cow (cDc). Explaining his choice, Tweety Fish says:

> I wanted a name so ridiculous that if I ever got arrested, a judge would laugh it out of court.[62]

In some cases, however, Joe Public may not appreciate the rationale by which hackers select their handles. Consider, for instance, the name Sir Dystic – the alias adopted by a colleague of Tweety Fish in the cDc. To the casual observer, this name may convey considerable menace and suggest an intention to cause harm. However, the background to the name is somewhat different. It is actually taken from a 1920s bondage comic book, in which the character Sir Dystic was one who tried to do evil things but ended up inadvertently doing good instead. Sir Dystic the hacker feels that the handle suits his self-image.[63]

The issue of self-image raises the wider questions of how hackers see themselves and how they justify activities that others would often regard as criminal. It may not be surprising to learn that, while the world at large may simply regard them as unauthorized intruders within the systems that they penetrate, hackers themselves do not necessarily subscribe to this worldview. A popular self-image is as a pioneer of the cyberspace frontierland, exploring systems and the network connections between them in a continual process of learning and discovery.

In terms of the threat to security, hackers often have a different (some may say convenient) interpretation of the issue. In some cases, the fact that they are not meant to be in the system seems to elude them, or at least is considered to be a secondary security consideration to the fact that they have been *able* to get in. For example, Emmanuel Goldstein, editor-in-chief of *2600: The Hacker's Quarterly*, offers the following opinion regarding unauthorized exploration of systems by hackers:

> If some kid somewhere can access your medical records or your phone records, he or she is not the one who put them there. The true violator of your privacy is the person who made the decision to make them easily accessible.[64]

This viewpoint overlooks the fact that the aforementioned "kid" does not have the right to look at the information. Unless the organization hosting the information had posted them in a publicly accessible part of their system, the implicit indication is that they are not meant to be generally available and, hence, such access represents an invasion of privacy.

To further examine the issue of self-image, a series of quotations are presented from a pair of genuine hackers. They were featured as the focus of a U.K. Channel Four documentary a few years ago[65] and the quotations are taken from things that they said during their commentary. However, the likely truth and ethics of their statements were not considered during the program, leaving viewers to weigh things up for themselves. The quotations are considered here, as the sentiments are by no means unique to the hackers in the program. For example, the first one typifies the viewpoint of many hackers in justifying their intrusion into other people's systems:

We're not doing any harm.

This might be more accurately expressed as "We do not intend to do any harm," or "We're not altering or destroying anything, so that must be okay," or "We know it isn't right, but we're not doing any harm." What the hackers are doing is invading someone else's privacy. Just because the victim might not realize that a breach has occurred, this does not mean that they have not been harmed.

The plain fact is that hackers cannot know for sure that they are not doing any harm. They represent an uncontrolled element within the system, which may fundamentally conflict with its planned operation. For example, they may unwittingly prevent someone else's legitimate access – the system may limit the overall number of logged in accounts, limit the number of active copies of applications that may be running or prevent concurrent access from the same user account. Furthermore, their mere presence in the system may steal CPU cycles, memory, disk storage and network capacity that may degrade or prevent other essential activities (any form of real-time control system would be an example of where this might be significant). A relevant example can be cited here from 1997, when U.S. space shuttle astronauts were put at risk when a hacker broke into a NASA computer system and overloaded it such that medical communications between the shuttle and the NASA center were impeded.[66] These systems continually monitor the astronaut's heartbeat, pulse and medical condition and, at the point when the hacker struck, the shuttle was in the process of attempting to dock with the Mir space station. The hacker, however, was unaware of this context and, from his perspective, the unauthorized presence in the system was exploratory and harmless. In reality, of course, it was anything but harmless and disrupted the system at a crucial time.

A final observation in relation to this point is that a so-called "harmless" hacker could still share his knowledge with colleagues and contacts (who may well have more destructive or malicious motives). They would then effectively lose control of the situation and would be unable to say with confidence that intentional harm would not be caused.

Here is another quotation from the same hacker (the text in brackets has been added for clarity):

> If they [the system administrators] are stupid enough to let me get in [to the system], and there's absolutely no reason why I should [be able to], then they have no right to keep that information to themselves.

This sort of logic does not stand up to anything but the most lazy-minded scrutiny. The competence (or otherwise) of the system administrator does not have any relationship to the nature of the information and the need to prevent unauthorized access to it. While it is possible that a hacker's presence in the system may have been assisted by inadequate system administration, it still does not give him any right to be there. Moreover, in most cases, system administrators (or more accurately their parent organizations) *do* have a right to keep their information to themselves. Furthermore, other people will often expect that right to be enforced by means of security. Data may have originally been collected on the understanding that it would not be further disseminated or used for anything other than the purpose stated at the time it was obtained. Therefore, the data subjects (e.g. you and me) may well have the implicit expectation that the organization will keep the information to itself. Indeed, in certain scenarios, it may even be a legal requirement for them to do so. For example, the provision of appropriate security is one of the requirements of the U.K. Data Protection Act 1998,[67] which is itself derived from the European Directive on the Protection of Personal Data.[68]

Sometimes, of course, the administrators may have taken what they consider to be reasonable precautions to safeguard their data (indeed, risk analysis may have suggested the level of protection to be commensurate with the value of the data assets – further protection could be provided, but the cost-benefit may not be justified). As such, it should be clear to any hacker that some attempt to incorporate protection had been made (even if it was no more than the use of a simple password at login) and, consequently, the system and its data are not intended for open, public access. Therefore, no *right* exists for them to do anything further with any information they gain access to. Equally, provided that reasonable protection measures have been employed, the target organization should not automatically be assumed to be at fault because a breach has occurred.

A final quotation, providing another potential defense and justification for the hacker's actions:

> If you didn't have hackers you'd have every corporation running rings round the public and they [the public] would never know about it.

The implicit message here is that corporations are generally up to no good. In a small percentage of cases, this might actually be true, but it would be a nonsense to suggest that most hackers chose their targets on the basis of this kind of suspicion. The fact is that hackers are not generally recognized as a major source of corporate exposés. For the most part, any misdeeds and wrongdoing are more likely to be brought to light as a result of inside leaks and/or journalistic endeavors. So, whereas many hackers may like to think of themselves as campaigners working in the public interest to free information, there is not a great deal of evidence to substantiate the claims. The closest thing is probably hacktivism (discussed in detail in Chapter 7), where hackers target and modify web sites in order to protest about an issue of interest. All this really involves is hacking the site and replacing the intended page with one that contains your own opinions. It does not mean that hacking methods have been used to uncover any hard evidence – they are just being used to get information published (whether it is credible or not). If the opinion being offered on the hacked pages was valid and worthy of public note then it would be possible for it to be more effectively promoted to a wide audience via legitimate news media. If a regulatory force is required, then is it really desirable that this should come in the form of hackers – unwanted guests within the system, who are knowingly breaking the law in order to gain access and are not answerable to anyone other than themselves? The answer from most people is probably no, and so this justification of hacker activity also fails to hold up in practice.

For a comprehensive assessment and analysis of the personality of a typical hacker, readers are referred to "A Portrait of J. Random Hacker," part of The Jargon File.[69] It should, however, be noted that this portrait relates to the classical hacker rather than the online vandals with whom the term has become more commonly associated. Some of the traits will be common to both, but this should not be assumed to be the case across the board.

What's the motivation?

There is no doubt that, for the individual, the formation of computer networks can represent an extension of conventional freedoms. They introduce the concept of an electronic presence, which offers the opportunity and ability to roam beyond the confines of one's physical environment, into the cyberspace world of the Net. This is a world that you can enter without even leaving your home and one in which factors that might cause restrictions or discrimination in the real world can be forgotten. Gender, sexual orientation, race, skin color, religion, disability, physical appearance – none of them need be known about you online unless you choose to reveal the information. This consequently makes the Net a place in which people may feel significant freedom when compared to their everyday environments. However, we must not allow an individual's cyberspace existence, and their activities within it, to become entirely divorced from the responsibilities that would exist in the real world. In order to gain a better perspective upon why this could end up being the case, it is worth looking at an example that, while not related to the issue of computer abuse, may nevertheless provide an interesting rationalization for some activities in this area. In her book discussing the French Minitel system,[70] Marie Marchand examines the success of one particular aspect, namely the message service (or *messagerie*) where users could conduct conversations through the electronic medium. Marchand describes communication using the messagerie as a "game of masks" where one can slip into, and hide behind, different identities at will. The fact of an electronic presence is viewed with an air of detachment ("one is there without really being there"), with the implication that an individual is more at liberty to behave as he or she chooses. Indeed, Guillaume views the computer screen as protection for the users in this context, as they may, if they wish, remain totally anonymous in a "position beyond responsibility."[71] This may be reasonable enough within the context of a Minitel or Internet Relay Chat (IRC) scenario, but an extension of this is that individuals may also feel less responsible for other activities within the electronic community, which they would not consider in other circumstances. For example, we may consider the traditional hacker activity of cracking passwords in order to obtain unauthorized access to someone else's system and files. Take the computer out of the equation and, regardless of the claimed motivation, the real world equivalent would be an act such as going into that individual's office and taking a crowbar to the filing cabinet; an activity that would be unlikely to appeal to the average hacker.

The motivation for many is simply the fun and challenge that playing with the system can bring. There is a lot to learn, and mastering the intricacies can deliver a great sense of achievement. This point is illustrated by the following quotations, taken from a letter written by a convicted hacker, Kevin Poulsen, to U.S. District Judge Manuel Real, explaining his fascination with hacking the telephone network:

> I knew that the telephone network reached into virtually every home and business in the country, and into every country in the world. It had existed decades before I was born, and would continue to exist long after I was gone. To me, a phone line was a connection to something omnipresent and eternal . . . I found the network to be a complex, fractal landscape; intricate and diverse . . . I think, in a way, part of me still saw the network as something mystical and arcane.[72]

Another factor to consider in terms of motivation is that, in some cases, the individuals concerned may be addicted to the experience in some way. Previous research has suggested that general Internet users (i.e. not specifically hackers) can become addicted to being online and can experience negative symptoms when they are not able to do so. This condition has been termed "Internet Addiction Disorder" and is linked to the Net's attractive qualities such as the ability to keep your real identity anonymous and operate as someone else (i.e. Marchand's "game of masks"). The basis for the theory comes from U.S. studies that have determined that, on average, one in ten users spend at least 400 minutes per day (i.e. over six hours) on the web. Edinburgh-based psychologist Dr. Keith Ashcroft makes a specific link to students, believing that they are particularly likely to be affected.[73] This is relevant in the hacking context, in that it can be observed that the general age group of students is the same as that of most hackers (particularly the stage at which people start hacking).

A recognized characteristic of many types of addiction is that, over time, a greater level of activity is required to achieve the desired level of satisfaction (e.g. alcoholics need to consume greater quantities of alcohol, gamblers bet larger sums of money, drug addicts often progress to harder types of drug). If the same is assumed to be the case with an online addiction, then it follows that people need to spend more time and do more things online to give them their "fix." It is somewhat natural, therefore, that a proportion will gravitate toward activities such as hacking – which for some may represent the ultimate expression of the combined power and anonymity that the Internet has to offer. Having said this, however, hacking is by no means the only way in which Internet addiction may manifest itself. More common associations can be made with aspects such as compulsive web surfing and over-involvement in online relationships.[74]

Some publications present a favorable image of hackers as pioneering explorers who are contributing to a worthwhile goal through their activities. Although it can be argued that, in some cases, the perpetrators may indeed be engaged in simple exploration of the computer network (and, therefore, feel that they are doing no real harm to anyone), it can increasingly be seen that hacking is being used as a means to achieve other ends. The aforementioned categories of hacktivists, cyber warriors and cyberterrorists, for example, clearly have different motives, which in all cases may be more than just innocently looking around. This kind of activity is far removed from that of the stereotypical teenage hacker operating alone in his bedroom, and the objectives may be more sinister than the straightforward mischief that he may perpetrate. The reports of such incidents are likely to cause further adverse effects on public opinion of technology as a consequence.

A classification of the hacker types described earlier against a variety of potential motivations is given in Table 3.1. Note that the column relating to "Old School" hackers makes reference to the original hackers of the 1950s and 1960s, and those who share their values today. The intention is not to cast them as criminals or system abusers, but to enable a contrast between their motivations and the other groups that are often classed under the generic label of "hacker." In each case, the most likely motivator for the class of hacker is also indicated by the emphasized tick mark.

As the table suggests, a single hacker will not necessarily have a single motivation that drives his or her actions. In this sense, hacking skills can be regarded as generic – able to be applied as appropriate to the needs of a hacker at a particular time. In the documented cases of hackers such as Kevin Mitnick and Kevin Poulsen (discussed later), the accounts suggest that mischief, challenge, revenge, money, and ego were seen to emerge as motivations at different points.

It can also be observed that some motivations may apply to different groups in different ways. For example, the motivation of "money" is indicated as applying to phreakers, samurai, warez d00dz, malware writers, and cyber warriors. For phreakers, this motivation is in the sense of being able to avoid paying for calls. Samurai and cyber warriors are both being paid to do a job. Warez d00dz may be in the business of selling on their pirated offerings. Finally, some malware writers, as we will see later, may distribute their creations in order to support some form of money-making scam.

In some cases, an apparent or claimed motivation may be just a front – a convenient excuse for the individual(s) concerned to hide behind and justify their hacking endeavors. Those mounting the most common forms of Internet attack, web defacements and denial of service, can often be seen to have adopted a cause to provide some ideological backdrop for their activities. However, tracking such activity over time, it can often be seen that the same hackers or groups have applied the same or similar methods against a variety of different targets, but citing support for different causes on different occasions. What one can reasonably draw from this is that they are either general malcontents, willing to protest at any opportunity, or that the causes being supported just provide them with a token rationale to explain their behavior if necessary. Some examples of this are illustrated as part of the discussion in later chapters, particularly in relation to the issue of hacktivism.

Appreciating the hacker perspective

To conclude the discussion of motivations, I shall reflect for a moment upon personal experience. Some years ago at college, we practiced some of the classic hacking tricks, using a Unix-based minicomputer system that was largely dedicated

TABLE 3.1 Hackers and their motivations

	Cyber-terrorists	Cyber warriors	Hacktivists	Malware writers	Old school	Phreakers	Samurai	Script kiddies	Warez d00dz
Challenge				✔	✔	✔	✔		✔
Ego				✔	✔	✔		✔	✔
Espionage		✔		✔					
Ideology	✔	✔	✔		✔				✔
Mischief				✔		✔		✔	
Money		✔		✔		✔	✔		✔
Revenge	✔		✔	✔				✔	

to use by the students on our diploma course. As we explored and learnt more about Unix, we were able to use the knowledge to rather less than productive ends. For example:

- We found that we could redirect the input from the keyboard to make the things that we typed appear on somebody else's screen. It was quite amusing to set this up, wait until someone was looking deep in thought working on a programming problem (or similar), and then hold down your return key so that whatever they were looking at quickly scrolled off their screen. The horrified expression on their face would normally make it worthwhile! The same technique could also be employed more subtly, such that when someone else was typing at their terminal, you could occasionally hit a character on your keyboard, making it appear on their screen and making them think they had made a typing mistake. They would then start trying to correct errors that did not actually exist.

- As well as typing, we found that we could also send whole files to somebody else's terminal. This could include, for example, sound files – so when the computer room was totally quiet you could cause someone extreme embarrassment by causing their computer to emit the sound of a flushing lavatory.

- Having obtained someone else's password, it was possible to log into their account and start killing their processes. So, if they were using a text editor, for example, you could remotely terminate the application and they would find themselves back at the Unix command prompt. Alternatively, you could kill their login process – rudely throwing them out of the system entirely and leaving them back at the login prompt. Unlike the other two escapades, this one could actually cause the victim to lose work if you terminated their session in the middle of it, so it was reserved for people that you did not like or, more typically, for organized competitions of "last man standing" using the system's guest account (i.e. all login as "guest" and see how quickly you could eject other people from the system).

It was all admittedly quite juvenile activity, but then we were only seventeen years old, so it seemed reasonably acceptable from that perspective. It was all done in the spirit of fun and adventure, often just to enable us to have a quick joke at the nominated victim's expense. Overall, it was just interesting that you could get the system to do such things – it did at least require you to learn a bit about how the system worked in order to be able to do it.

Whereas the above were simply little games that you could play on the spur of the moment, we also indulged in other, more involved, bits of trickery. One such method was the development of a password-capturing program. This form of attack is hardly novel, but it provides an example of a baseline hacker method that many have employed. The concept is simple, yet potentially very effective, and it represents a basic example of a Trojan Horse program – a category of malicious software that will be discussed in more detail in Chapter 5.

The basic premise of the hack was that someone would write a short program that simulated the appearance and operation of the normal system login prompt in order to fool other people into using it. When executed, the program would clear the screen and display what appeared to be the standard login prompt for the system. When the next unsuspecting user came to the terminal, they could attempt to enter their name and password as normal. When they did so, regardless of whether they typed it correctly, the system would respond with a "login incorrect" message. To the user, this would simply look like they had mistyped their password (a frequent enough occurrence for the average user) and, in most cases, they would not think much more about it. The system would then prompt them for the login information again and they could then proceed to successfully login as normal. Behind the scenes, however, the password catcher program was at work. When the user entered their ID and password the first time, the catcher would log the information and write it to a file. At a later time, the author of the program could inspect this file and see whose ID/password pairs they had managed to capture. Having logged the information, the catcher program would issue its bogus "login incorrect" message and then terminate the current session in which it was running. With the program having logged out, the genuine login prompt would appear onscreen, enabling the (normally unsuspecting) user at the terminal to attempt their login again.

Figure 3.1 illustrates what might be seen on the screen during the process, along with a description of what is actually happening at the different stages. It should be

```
1 ▶  Login: jsmith
     Password: apples

2 ▶  Login incorrect

3 ▶  Login: jsmith
     Password: apples

     ******************************
     Welcome to the college computer
     system
     ******************************
     %
```

1. The first "login" and "password" prompts are issued by the capture program. The information entered is logged to a file for later inspection.

2. The capture program issues the "Login incorrect" message and then logs out the active session.

3. Control of the terminal then reverts to the genuine login routine, which displays its own login prompt. The user can attempt to login again, and this time will be successful.

FIGURE 3.1 Operation of a password capture program

noted that, in a real world implementation, the password would be extremely unlikely to be visible on the screen. It is shown here merely for illustration purposes.

Sometimes, however, the aforementioned fun and adventure that we enjoyed through such activities did go too far. For example, the password catcher program managed to grab the "root" password ("root" being the system administration account on Unix operating systems, giving unlimited access within the system) – a fact that brought its existence to the attention of our system administrator. In return, some stern words were meted out to the perpetrators. It also had the knock-on effect that use of the system was more tightly controlled and monitored from then on. So, in a sense, we had left the legacy of a more restricted environment for those students that followed us in later years.

When a group of us moved on to university, such fun and games were not so easily tolerated. We found that something that would receive a warning and stern words at college would get sterner words and a temporary system ban at university. Upon reflection, the increased seriousness was justified, in the sense that the college system we had hacked was only really used by our group of students and a similar number of diploma students in the year below (probably about fifty people in total). By contrast, the university system was utilized campus-wide, with several thousand users requiring its services. As such, any problems could have far reaching effects.

Having had these experiences, it is easy to appreciate the factors that drive and motivate some hackers, as well as how they often find themselves breaking the rules. It was interesting and challenging to see what tricks you could play with the system and it was quite easy to stray over the line of what was legitimate behavior. It was not done maliciously and there was a genuine feeling that we were not doing any real harm – just having a bit of fun.

Elements of the hacker culture

Having established the sort of individuals that hackers are, the discussion now proceeds to examine aspects of the culture that they have established and which has developed around them. As we shall see, this includes the concept of a shared ethic, as well as means of linking together via groups, publications and gatherings.

The Hacker Manifesto

A significant and popular element of hacker culture is a brief text entitled *The Conscience of a Hacker*, which is more widely known and referred to as the *Hacker Manifesto*. This was written in 1986 by a hacker who operated under the pseudonym of "The Mentor" and who was a member of the notorious hacking group the Legion of Doom.[75] The full text is reproduced in Figure 3.2.

The Conscience of a Hacker

by
+++The Mentor+++
Written on January 8, 1986

Another one got caught today, it's all over the papers. "Teenager arrested in Computer Crime Scandal", "Hacker Arrested after Bank Tampering"... Damn kids. They're all alike.

But did you, in your three-piece psychology and 1950's technobrain, ever take a look behind the eyes of the hacker? Did you ever wonder what made him tick, what forces shaped him, what may have molded him? I am a hacker, enter my world... Mine is a world that begins with school... I'm smarter than most of the other kids, this crap they teach us bores me... Damn underachiever. They're all alike.

I'm in junior high or high school. I've listened to teachers explain for the fifteenth time how to reduce a fraction. I understand it. "No, Ms. Smith, I didn't show my work. I did it in my head..." Damn kid. Probably copied it. They're all alike.

I made a discovery today. I found a computer. Wait a second, this is cool. It does what I want it to. If it makes a mistake, it's because I screwed it up. Not because it doesn't like me... Or feels threatened by me... Or thinks I'm a smart ass... Or doesn't like teaching and shouldn't be here... Damn kid. All he does is play games. They're all alike.

And then it happened... a door opened to a world... rushing through the phone line like heroin through an addict's veins, an electronic pulse is sent out, a refuge from the day-to-day incompetencies is sought... a board is found. "This is it... this is where I belong..." I know everyone here... even if I've never met them, never talked to them, may never hear from them again... I know you all... Damn kid. Tying up the phone line again. They're all alike...

You bet your ass we're all alike... we've been spoon-fed baby food at school when we hungered for steak... the bits of meat that you did let slip through were pre-chewed and tasteless. We've been dominated by sadists, or ignored by the apathetic. The few that had something to teach found us willing pupils, but those few are like drops of water in the desert.

This is our world now... the world of the electron and the switch, the beauty of the baud. We make use of a service already existing without paying for what could be dirt-cheap if it wasn't run by profiteering gluttons, and you call us criminals. We explore... and you call us criminals. We seek after knowledge...

continued

FIGURE 3.2 *The Hacker Manifesto*

FIGURE 3.2 *The Hacker Manifesto* (continued)

```
and you call us criminals. We exist without skin color, without
nationality, without religious bias... and you call us criminals.
You build atomic bombs, you wage wars, you murder, cheat, and lie
to us and try to make us believe it's for our own good, yet we're
the criminals.

Yes, I am a criminal. My crime is that of curiosity. My crime is
that of judging people by what they say and think, not what they
look like. My crime is that of outsmarting you, something that you
will never forgive me for.

I am a hacker, and this is my manifesto. You may stop this
individual, but you can't stop us all... after all, we're all
alike.

                        +++The Mentor+++
```

The *Manifesto* is still widely accessible, some fifteen years after it was originally written. Ordinarily, this could be considered no great feat for a piece of literature. However, it is possibly more significant in the context of the technology field, where the pace of change frequently renders leading edge thoughts obsolete after a few years. In fact, the *Manifesto* probably has wider exposure now than it did at the time that it was written. A search on the web yields numerous links to sites reproducing the text. Indeed, a search for the term "hacker" followed by "manifesto" yields many more hits than a search for "orange book" followed by "security" (for the uninitiated, the Orange Book is the name commonly used to refer to the U.S. Department of Defense Trusted Computer Systems Evaluation Criteria, a significant publication in the IT security field which was published at roughly the same time as the *Manifesto*[76]). The author has conducted this search twice, once in August 1998 using the Infoseek search engine and then, more recently, in March 2001 using Lycos.* The search results are summarized in Table 3.2, which clearly suggests that the likelihood of being able to track down the *Hacker Manifesto* is far greater than being able to find the Orange Book.

This crude example suggests that the hacker perspective is more widely available than specific security guidelines. In addition, the *Manifesto* has found its way into

---

* These search engines were chosen because they allow the search to be refined using a second search term after an initial search has been performed (e.g. allowing a search for pages containing "hacker" and then allowing a search for those containing "manifesto" within the results returned). Infoseek was used for this in August 1998, but by March 2001 the Infoseek search engine had been replaced and did not allow the refinement of searches. As such, Lycos was used for the more recent results.

other forms of media outside the World Wide Web. For example, segments from it have been quoted in the MGM movie *Hackers*.[77] As such, the text cannot merely be dismissed as the views of one person and the material is worthy of further examination.

The *Manifesto* is clearly not using the interpretation of the term "hacker" that relates to the system and coding gurus described by Levy and others. The perspective is instead that of persons gaining unauthorized access to computer systems (i.e., the modern, mass media definition). That said, however, the *Manifesto* only presents a restricted view of a hacker – as largely a curious explorer, pursuing knowledge and intellectual challenge. Fundamentally, however, even unauthorized exploration of a system is equivalent to trespassing and may still breach commercial confidentiality or personal privacy. Parallels are frequently drawn between cyberspace and the physical world (e.g. discussion of concepts such as "community" occur in both contexts). If such comparisons are applied to notions such as property and privacy, then it is clear that the incursions that some hackers would argue are acceptable online would not be so easily justified in the physical world. For example, we could draw a parallel between an individual's web site and his/her home, or between a company's site and its high-street office or showroom. The hacker ethic would state that unauthorized entry into the system running such a web server would be acceptable as long as no damage is done. However, no one would be likely to be very tolerant of an intruder offering such excuses if found exploring in their home or office. Regardless of whether you agree with its sentiments, the views laid out in the *Manifesto* contradict the law in many countries.

The *Manifesto* also overlooks the fact that some systems or information may be protected from the general populace for good reason. There is a strong argument, for example, that military systems should incorporate sufficient security in order to prevent casual users from being able to browse or modify their contents. If everyone were to be allowed unrestricted access, then this would implicitly include potentially undesirable or dangerous groups, such as terrorist organizations. Therefore, if society were to insist that all IT systems should be totally open, organizations such as the military would effectively be prevented from putting a great deal of their

TABLE 3.2 Searching for the *Hacker Manifesto* and the Orange Book

Search Engine	Search terms	
	"hacker" followed by "manifesto"	*"Orange book" followed by "security"*
Infoseek (31 August 1998)	560	173
Lycos (19 March 2001)	8,613	0

information online for fear of the potential consequences. Military and defense related sites, such as the U.S. Air Force and the Pentagon, have actually proven to be an attractive target to hackers, with numerous incidents reported in the general media. A standard defense in such cases is often simple curiosity rather than some more sinister purpose. However, the sharing of knowledge is one of the underlying principles of the hacker community and, as such, even if the hacker effecting the break-in chooses not to use the information irresponsibly, others who gain access through him/her may not be so reliable.

Another motivation stated in the *Manifesto* is to enable the free use of services that would be "dirt cheap" were they not run by "profiteering gluttons." The main parties referred to here are telecommunications service operators, who provide the basic infrastructure through which hackers (and other users) are able to connect to remote systems. The observation that services could be cheaper may well be valid in some cases, especially where a key player is able to exploit a monopoly position. Over time, however, market forces (primarily the emergence of competition) or legislation often redress the balance and result in charges being reduced to a more realistic level. By contrast, it may be observed that the hackers and phreakers are paying *nothing* for the service in the meantime. Therefore, even if it eventually was to become "dirt cheap," it is debatable whether many would be willing to depart from this desirable situation (their moral justification for not paying could then maybe switch to "We have the skills to avoid paying, so why should we need to?").

In making its references to hackers, the *Manifesto* frequently repeats the phrase "They're all alike." However, evidence suggests that this is far from the case – from the perspective of both their motivations and intellectual capabilities. For example, throughout the text there is an implicit assertion of intellectual superiority on the part of the hacker and of being misunderstood and generally failed by society on this basis. Although many hackers *are* undoubtedly intellectually gifted, competent problem solvers and lateral thinkers, this categorization cannot be applied across the board. Furthermore, choosing to be a hacker does not automatically endow you with these characteristics. Many hackers succeed through sheer persistence, deter- mination and, in many cases, an exceptionally high boredom threshold. A successful hack is often the result of doggedly attempting to apply the same technique to multiple systems until a weakness is found. Furthermore, unwitting assistance is often provided by system administrators, who have left their systems vulnerable to attack through inadequate attention to, or understanding of, security (see Chapter 4).

It can, of course, be observed that the *Manifesto* does put forward some very positive views (e.g. advocating anti-racism and anti-war messages). However, you do not have to be a hacker in order to adopt these beliefs. Furthermore, the afore- mentioned assertion of intellectual superiority represents an attitude which itself could create a prejudicial society of a different type. Additionally, what the text plainly does not advocate is an anti-crime viewpoint. It is interesting to note that the seventh paragraph accuses society of cheating and lying, with the implicit interpretation to be made that such activities are incompatible with the hacker ethos. This, of course, tends to ignore the fact that many of the methods used by hackers to gain unauthorized access to systems, or their activities once having done so, would not be considered by most people to be fair and honest – e.g. tricking people into parting with passwords via social engineering (see Chapter 4); planting Trojan Horse programs to enable data gathering or provide a backdoor (see Chapter 5). Nowhere in the text does it make a statement about where to draw the line or where even hacker activity would be considered to be going too far. This has certainly been recognized in other hacker-originated material, which, while emphasizing themes such as free access to information, also advocates more responsible attitudes such as not inflicting intentional damage upon systems and not operating for personal financial gain. However, the promotion of such values does not always accompany the Manifesto and, therefore, many people will not receive the complete message.

The *Manifesto* cannot be criticized from the perspective of some of the general sentiments that it expresses – there are undoubtedly many parties who genuinely hold these beliefs. However, the problem is that the general dissemination of the text serves to invite and excuse a wider population. For example, it helps to excuse hackers who act with a complete disregard for others (e.g. breaching personal privacy or causing financial loss), and enables them to claim that their actions are compatible with the *Manifesto* or a wider counterculture.

Another basic problem with the *Manifesto* is that it can create a negative perception of the implications arising from information technology when, at the same time, we are living in a society in which our dependency upon IT is only increasing. Furthermore, there are numerous additional opportunities that are being offered by IT that have the potential to improve or simplify our existing practices. An example of this is the area of electronic commerce (or e-commerce). This represents a significant area of interest within the industry at the time of writing and various opportunities have been identified. However, there are still a number of barriers (both practical and conceptual) that must be overcome before e-commerce will be widely embraced by mainstream business or private individuals and two of the greatest concerns are security and privacy.[78] This can be illustrated using the example of credit card purchases, a form of commerce that is one of the most easily transferable to the online context, but also one in which a great deal of concern over security has been expressed.[79] Now, in actual fact, the use of credit cards over the Internet may be no less secure than the uses to which they are put in other scenarios. Most of us think nothing of providing credit card details over the telephone or handing over the card itself to strangers serving us in shops or restaurants. However, all of these activities expose our accounts to risk and, indeed, fraud and abuse is known to occur. Nevertheless, the Internet is still perceived to be less secure, and a likely reason for this is the public perception of hacker activity resulting from the level of exposure that it has been given in the mass media.

This section does not intend to imply that the *Hacker Manifesto* should bear the sole responsibility for promoting and endorsing hacker activity. Hacking occurred before the text was written and has developed in probably unforeseen ways since. However, the fact that the material suggests itself as a manifesto (i.e., something for a wider population to adopt and adhere to) means that its ultimate impact may be more profound.

The Hacker Ethic

The *Manifesto* is far from being the only document that has originated from hacker circles. It is actually predated by another text that is also widely reproduced on the web, namely *The Hacker Ethic*. Many professions and communities have established ethical codes by which their members are expected to abide. Such a code will typically identify core values and beliefs that individuals within the associated domain are expected to share and subscribe to. In some cases the codes are formalized – examples being the Hippocratic Oath within the medical profession and the Code of Ethics of the Society of Professional Journalists. In other cases, the code is much looser and can be considered to equate to rules of thumb more than hard and fast principles. It is the latter category into which the *Hacker Ethic* can be considered to fall.

Instinctively, of course, and particularly given their typical treatment in media reports, hackers are probably one of the last groups that one would expect to associate with the concept of ethics. However, the *Hacker Ethic* arose from the original hackers of the 1950s and 1960s at MIT and Stanford University, and the principles reflect their beliefs in the empowering and liberating nature of computer technology and its ability to overcome bureaucracy. The *Ethic* is described in detail by Steven Levy,[80] but the main principles are listed here in summary form:

1. Access to computers – and anything which might teach you something about the way the world works – should be unlimited and total. Always yield to the Hands-On Imperative!

2. All information should be free.

3. Mistrust authority – promote decentralization.

4. Hackers should be judged by their hacking, not bogus criteria such as degrees, age, race, or position.

5. You can create art and beauty on a computer.

6. Computers can change your life for the better.

When considered in isolation, without any accompanying understanding of the intended interpretation or the context from which they were derived, it is easy to consider several of these points to represent an implicit endorsement of unauthorized computer intrusion. However, it is important to recognize that the principles were established by hackers conforming to the original 1960s definition of the term – not by cyber criminals.

To some, the concept of computer security is totally alien in the context of the hacker ethic. It represents an affront to the ability to gain free access to systems or information and, therefore, activities such as unauthorized access, breaking of passwords, and piracy of software are justified (in the minds of the hackers at least) as a means of safeguarding their freedoms. In many cases, breaching the security is also considered to represent a symbolic stand against the organizations that would deny access to information or charge people for its use. This, however, is a fairly ideological viewpoint and it is not one that all hackers would genuinely subscribe to (some might happily use it as a flag of convenience though).

Given the nature of the abuse described in this book, the ethic is clearly applicable to only a subset of the hacker community and, in many ways, it is more suggestive of the original 1950s and 1960s definition of a hacker. Much of the advice promoted is not compatible with the public image of a hacker, as shaped by the media and presented by the dictionary definitions shown earlier. However, many who would associate themselves with the modern definition of the term "hacker" are happy to view and interpret the *Hacker Ethic* as a justification for their behavior. This has led some to question whether the modern hacker does actually subscribe to a particular ethical code at all.[81]

If the interpretation of "hacker" is restricted, and considered to exclude those individuals who some would classify under the terms Cracker and Black Hat, then some form of ethical code can still be seen to exist – which is in part illustrated by the fact that the activities of crackers, script kiddies and their ilk are regarded with dismay and contempt by other members of the hacker community. At the same time, there is a lack of a more widely applicable ethical code that the whole hacker community can be seen to follow – the drives and motives are too diverse. However, at the most basic level, there may still be an ethic in the sense of a principle that drives the participants. For many, the claim would be that hackers are driven by curiosity, exploration and the pursuit of information. The level of information being pursued may not necessarily appear meaningful to outside observers – it may just be to find out what is held on a system or to see how the system is configured, without having any intention to *do* anything with the information beyond this. For others, however, this interpretation is not applicable and their objective is to be seen to have had an effect of some kind. Defacing a system and leaving a tag on the web site shows other people that you were there. It may also help to spread a message for a wider cause that the hacker wishes to support. Whatever the motive, it is difficult to argue that an ethic of simple discovery or curiosity is in play. So, the most basic description that fits both scenarios could be more accurately stated as just being able to get access. However, doing this often involves gaining *unauthorized* entry to a system, which makes it difficult to argue that one is subscribing to an ethic – given that an ethic is defined as a "moral principle" and clearly the morality here can be questioned.

The bottom line, as with many of the issues in the discussion of cybercrime, comes down to diversity. It is impossible to make a clear statement that all hackers subscribe to an ethical code, but clearly a sense of what is right and wrong does guide the conduct in some cases.

Hacker publications

Hacker culture has spawned a myriad of publications, dedicated to various aspects of the underground scene: hacking, phreaking, virus writing, warez distribution – all are represented by some form of hacker-originated magazine.

The magazines themselves do not typically contain details about how to break into specific systems, or things like password lists, credit card numbers or other titbits of information favored by hackers – such things *are* often shared (or traded) within the hacker community, but in the more private surrounds of online chatrooms and bulletin boards. The magazines tend to focus upon sharing more general information, covering techniques, advice and opinions in relation to the hacking scene. Although some articles are relatively introductory, the magazines do not set out to teach readers how to hack – much of the information is too technical or too specific to be directly appreciated by the novice.

Many of the publications exist in electronic form and are published online (see, for example, the Packet Storm web site, at **http://packetstormsecurity.org/ magazines.html**, for a selection of such titles), while a more select number are also distributed in hardcopy form. Some titles appear in both formats and, in some cases (such as *40Hex*, a magazine aimed at virus writers), actually present a different range of articles in each medium (online publication, of course, allows a much greater quantity of information to be published at no extra cost).

The list below presents examples of just a small selection of past and present titles:

- *BoW Newsletter* – produced by the Brotherhood of Warez, focused on software piracy (now defunct).
- *fk* – f0rbidden knowledge, a hacking/phreaking e-zine, originating from a hacker group called SoS (Sons of Satan/Saviours of Systems).
- *HIR* – Hackers Information Report.
- *Phrack Magazine* – long-standing publication aimed at the phreaking community.
- *Vlad* – Virus labs and distribution.

The style of the magazines typically reveals the hackers to be a pretty liberal-minded bunch. Not only do various articles cover topics that are fairly close to the line from a legal perspective, but the manner in which they are written is also rather loose as well. Certain publications are quite often littered with profanity and obscene language that would typically be considered offensive elsewhere. As such, they are not really suitable for the faint-hearted.

A well-known and long-standing example is *2600 – The Hacker Quarterly*, which began in 1984 and publishes information on phreaking, accessing computer networks and the legal rights of hackers. The magazine itself is paper-based, but has an associated web site at **www.2600.com**. Unlike many others, *2600* is an example of a commercial publication and, in the U.S., it can be found on the shelves in many newsagent outlets. In other countries, its off-the-shelf availability may be more limited, but it is still available on a mail-order subscription basis (which can be made online via the magazine's web site). It is published in New York and edited by Eric Corley, a hacker who is better known online and in the magazine by his alias, Emmanuel Goldstein – a name taken from George Orwell's novel *1984*. In Orwell's book, Goldstein is the leader of the rebels and the designated enemy of the people because of his opposition to the society of Big Brother. This role is clearly that into which Corley sees himself fitting and much of the content of *2600* can be seen to reflect a freedom of information ethic (coincidently, 1984 was also the year in which publication of the magazine began).

A typical issue of *2600* contains a range of articles. Some of these are simply of an introductory or overview nature, addressing a particular type of system or security technology that may be of interest to the readership, but not containing anything that could really be considered insider information. By contrast, other articles adopt a more tutorial or advisory approach that may help to guide people in the exploration of systems. For example, the summer 2000 edition contained an article that described how one might piece together useful information about a target system.[82] The piece stated at the outset that its content would be of no relevance or interest to the script kiddie fraternity who purely wish to try out known vulnerabilities on any system possible. However, at the same time, the hints and tips it provides could be of immense use in helping such an individual to advance to the next level of proficiency as a hacker – not necessarily a desirable thing to encourage.

It should be noted that, in calling itself *The Hacker Quarterly*, *2600* is using the term "hacker" in its original sense, referring to a level of technical enthusiasm, proficiency and exploration. Although this interpretation is known to the regular readers of the magazine, it may not be so apparent to the casual observer. Therefore, from the latter's perspective (for whom "hacker" might have a different meaning), there may appear to be a generally available magazine, promoting activities to assist unauthorized system access and the like. This could, in turn, convey the implicit impression that engaging in such activities is acceptable – i.e. other people are doing it and writing about it, so why not me? Furthermore, while much of the information and advice presented could potentially be misused, the magazine does not include a global statement advising against unauthorized system access. Individual articles may include such a rider, but this appears to be at the discretion of their authors.

The lack of a generic advisory is not true with all hacker magazines however. For example, the following statements are taken from *Phrack* and *40Hex*:

> Keep in mind that *Phrack Magazine* accepts no responsibility for the entirely stupid (or illegal) things people may do with the information contained herein. *Phrack* is a compendium of knowledge, wisdom, wit, and sass. We neither advocate, condone nor participate in any sort of illicit behavior. But we will sit back and watch.
>
> *PHRACK MAGAZINE*

> Warning! *40Hex* magazine may contain source code that, if compiled, will generate a fully functional, possibly destructive virus. These source code files are distributed for research purposes only and are not intended to cause harm to computer systems. The management of *40Hex* magazine cannot be held responsible for incidental damage caused by the misuse of this source code.
>
> *40HEX MAGAZINE ONLINE*

From a certain perspective, of course, such statements can simply be seen as the magazines seeking to protect and disassociate themselves from the results of what people do with information they have published. However, having some warning is better than none at all. And it is certainly better than the stance adopted by some other publications originating from the underground. For example, early editions of the newsletter produced by the Brotherhood of Warez included the statement: "And Remember, Phone Fraud is Fun Fraud!"

As mentioned above, *2600* also commonly focuses on issues relating to the legal system and hackers' associated rights under it. The reasoning here is that the law is clearly something that many hackers are in constant danger of breaking and, therefore, it helps for them to have a good knowledge of relevant parts that may affect them. With this knowledge, hackers may be able to ensure that they get as close to the legal line as possible, without actually crossing it.

The implied message of some articles, however, is still a bit dubious. For example, the Spring 1999 edition contained an article entitled "A Hacker's Guide to Being Busted."[83] This recognized that hackers are generally at risk of having run-ins with the police and sought to clarify several aspects of the law so that they are aware of what the police are permitted to do. The text, written from a U.S. perspective, presented advice in relation to being stopped and searched in different scenarios (e.g. on foot, in a car, on the bus), as well as information about search warrants and Miranda rights (e.g. the right to remain silent and the right to have an attorney).

This, of course, is all fine in the sense that this information is not in any way a secret and everyone ought to have the opportunity to know their rights in order to avoid being treated unfairly. The problem is that the article was clearly not worded as if its aim was solely to provide advice to the innocent. For example, it made an advisory comment about how the wrong sort of clothing may draw unwanted police attention:

> Keep the chains and leather at home if you're going about doing things or carrying things you shouldn't.

Indeed, the overall tone of the article was not one of "Here is the law, be careful not to break it," but rather "If you are suspected of breaking the law, this is what the police can and cannot get away with doing to you." Of course, in a civilized society, lawbreakers are as equally entitled to justice and fair treatment as those who are innocent. However, from a common-sense perspective, it does seem rather odd to be advising lawbreakers how best to confound the efforts of those who are trying to stop them.

Of course, a counter-argument from the hackers' perspective may be that the law is wrong, having been formulated by people who do not properly understand the technology that they are attempting to regulate and protect. Hackers can consequently rationalize their actions from an ideological perspective, because they are only breaking a law that they do not believe in anyway. However, this sort of attitude and approach does not apply in a civilized society. What if the same view was to be taken by the perpetrators of other forms of crime, such as theft, murder, and child abuse? It just would not be tolerated at all. As such, simply disregarding the law is not an acceptable solution. Most laws have arisen as a result of previous experiences and events having occurred from which the public subsequently expect protection. For example, the U.K. Computer Misuse Act 1990 arose as a result of hacking incidents having occurred and there being no relevant existing legislation under which victims could seek recourse (of course, the fact that victims felt the need to seek recourse illustrates that they were not happy about their systems being breached and substantiates the need for a legal response). If the hackers disagree with the law, or the way it has been implemented and enforced, then there are more democratic means of addressing the point than simply breaking it. If the case is truly valid, then public awareness and lobbying campaigns could be used to highlight the perceived problems and request changes. Although this is certainly not a quick fix from the hackers' perspective, it would at least enable the merits of their argument to be aired to the people who their actions might otherwise affect.

Magazines and newsletters are not the only ways in which hackers publish information. As subsequent discussion of hacking groups will reveal, they also make materials available in a variety of other formats.

Hacker groups

Like many who share a common interest, hackers frequently organize themselves into groups for the purposes of sharing information, conducting hacking activities and even socializing. A number of hacking groups have come and gone over the years, and many groups are in operation today. This section briefly considers some of the groups, past and present, which have collectively played host to a number of hackers whose names are well known within their community.

Legion of Doom

Taking its name from a collection of comic-book villains, the Chicago-based LOD was one of many groups that sprung up in the 1980s. It actually began life as a phreaking group, changing its name to the Legion of Doom/Hackers (LOD/H) as members became more involved with computer hacking as well (the /H was ultimately dropped again later). The group was founded by a hacker calling himself Lex Luthor (also a comic-book name – the criminal arch-enemy of Superman) and was recognized as the home to many elite hackers of the time. Other LOD luminaries included Eric Bloodaxe, Leftist, Urville, The Prophet, and The Mentor (the latter will, of course, be recalled as the author of the *Hacker Manifesto*). It can be observed that by choosing names such as Legion of Doom and Lex Luthor, the hackers were doing very little to reassure casual observers that their intentions were not overtly criminal.

One of the most well known incidents involving the LOD was the theft of a document from a BellSouth computer, describing the operation of the 911 emergency system. An edited version was published in *Phrack* magazine, leading to arrest and a costly trial for the magazine's publisher, Craig Neidorf (aka Knight Lightning). However, the case was dismissed when it was established that the supposedly secret information could be openly purchased for $13.

In a move that would be emulated by some hacker groups that followed them, LOD produced a number of so-called "LOD/H Technical Journals" (the name being intended as a takeoff of the AT&T Technical Journal series, a well referenced source of information in the phreaking community). A total of five were produced – released somewhat sporadically between 1987 and 1993 (the last one being some three years after the original LOD had effectively been discontinued as a hacking group). The journals – which were actually presented as a series of online text files – contained a variety of technical information pitched at the hacker community, the nature of which was similar to that found in other hacker publications of the time, such as *2600* and *Phrack*. Subsequent groups have also gone down the path of producing materials for outside consumption, and have even extended the range of offerings to encompass not just written articles, but also things like security vulnerability advisories and software tools.

Originally founded in 1984, the LOD ultimately disbanded in 1990, as a result of a U.S. government crackdown on hackers. While some of its members were arrested during Operation Sundevil (a key element of the crackdown), others went on to create a security firm called ComSec. This particular company went bankrupt, but eventually re-emerged as LOD Communications Inc. – a company that can still be found today at **www.lod.com**.

Further details of the LOD can be found in Bruce Sterling's book *The Hacker Crackdown*, which particularly describes the effects of the U.S. government's harder stance on hackers and the arrests that followed. In addition, a history of the group, as presented by Lex Luthor, can be found in issue four of the LOD/H Technical Journal (see **http://packetstorm.securify.com/mag/lod/lod-4** for an archived copy).

Masters of Deception

Arriving on the scene with another grandiose and intimidating name, the New York-based MOD (also at some times known as Masters of Disaster) was founded by Mark Abene (aka Phiber Optik) – a hacker who was kicked out of LOD following a clash of egos with other members. As with LOD, the membership of MOD came to boast a variety of creatively named characters, including Acid Phreak, Scorpion, Nynex Phreak, Outlaw, Corrupt, Supernigger, Red Night, Seeker, Lord Micro, Crazy Eddie, Zod, Ella Cinders, and Plague.

Given its origins, it is perhaps not surprising that a fair proportion of MOD's efforts were directed in competition against LOD, and the two sides engaged in an online battle to be recognized as the most elite group. The MOD adopted the Latin motto "Summa Sedes Non Capit Duos," the translation of which means "The Highest Does Not Seat Two." This was basically intended as a reference to the battle against LOD and meant that there was only room for one group at the top. In pursuit of their objective, the group targeted a number of high-profile organizations, including the TRW credit-reporting agency, AT&T and the Bank of America. As well as hacking into databases, they also engaged in phone phreaking activities – creating their own party lines, listening in on other conversations and, of course, avoiding long-distance charges.

As with LOD, the activities of the MOD hackers effectively came to an end when a large number of them were arrested as part of the U.S. government's crackdown in the early 1990s. Five members of the group (Phiber Optik, Outlaw, Corrupt, Acid Phreak and Scorpion) were indicted in July 1992 on charges that they used their computers to access credit bureaus, other computer systems, and to make free long-distance calls.

A comprehensive account of the MOD can be found in Michele Slatalla and Joshua Quittner's book *Masters of Deception: The Gang That Ruled Cyberspace*.[84]

Chaos Computer Club

Representing an example of the relatively rare case of a high-profile hacking group from outside the United States, the Hamburg-based CCC was founded in 1984. Its members have included the late Wau Holland (a founder of the group), Steffen Wernery (co-founder), Christian Wolf, Obelix, Dob, Peter Carl, Hagbard Celine, and Pengo. The exploits of the group over the years have had a considerably political slant, providing public demonstrations of the weaknesses of technology. For example, in 1996, the group demonstrated security flaws in Microsoft's Active-X technology that undermined confidence in a number of Internet-based home banking initiatives that were about to emerge. The CCC had shown how Active-X flaws could be used to enable the transfer of funds without the need for a PIN. Later, in 1998, the group turned its attention to mobile phones, demonstrating the ability to clone the Subscriber Identity Module (SIM) card that holds details required for user identification and billing in GSM cellular networks.[85]

Although the above were significant, the CCC is probably best known for its links to an earlier incident – an international espionage case of the late 1980s, when several of its members were enlisted by the KGB to break into U.S. systems and obtain military secrets. Their efforts were detected by Clifford Stoll, the administrator of one of the affected systems at the Lawrence Berkley Laboratories, who then took a prominent role in monitoring their activities and tracking them down (he subsequently wrote an account of his experiences in a novel entitled *The Cuckoo's Egg*). Although they managed to penetrate a number of systems with surprising ease, the information that the hackers were able to obtain was actually not that sensitive. One of the hackers involved in this incident, Karl Koch (aka Hagbard Celine), is notable for having subsequently died by being dowsed in petrol and set alight. The circumstances surrounding the death were mysterious, and although the recorded verdict was suicide, others still suggest it was more likely to have been murder.[86]

Unlike LOD and MOD, the Chaos Club is still operational and some of their activities are discussed in the next chapter. Their web site is located at **http://berlin.ccc.de**.

L0pht Heavy Industries

Hailing from Boston, L0pht Heavy Industries was a group of grey-hat hackers that were variously described as anything from security watchdogs to notorious crackers. Indeed, with members going by names such as Mudge, Space Rogue and Weld Pond, they sounded pretty much the same as the hacker groups that had come before them. However, L0pht did not gain notoriety by hacking into sites themselves, but rather by publicly exposing security weaknesses in commercial software and through the tools that they made available for others to use. Their best-known creation in the latter respect was L0phtCrack, a utility for cracking passwords on Windows NT systems, which is described in the next chapter as part of a discussion of automated hacking tools. Another notable aspect of L0pht's history occurred in May 1998, when members of the group stated that it would take them only thirty minutes to render the Internet unusable for the whole country.[87]

They were not making a threat, however – the information was delivered during a testimony before the U.S. Senate Committee on Governmental Affairs and the hackers were presenting an analysis of the security weaknesses in the Internet's infrastructure and communications protocols.

L0pht's aggressive approach in publicizing security vulnerabilities was not to the taste of all commercial software vendors, but it should be noted that the group always worked on the basis of contacting the vendor first – giving them a chance to rectify flaws before they were made public. And, while their revelations might have been a thorn in the side of the vendors, their provision of free information was also of use to administrators interested in rectifying potential problems in their systems.

In January 2000, L0pht went fully legitimate and became the research and development division of the security firm @Stake Inc. A web search for "L0pht" still reveals many links to their pages, but attempting to follow them now takes you to @Stake's site instead. Several L0pht members, such as Count Zero (co-founder of the group) and Mudge (the co-author of L0phtCrack), have also become members of another group, the Cult of the Dead Cow.

Cult of the Dead Cow

Although it was founded in the mid-1980s, the cDc is a hacker group that did not really come to media prominence until the mid-1990s. As its name may suggest, the group is somewhat more bizarre than some of the others discussed here – a fact that is further confirmed by the homepage of its web site (**www.cultdeadcow.com**), which contains the following text as a warning to the potential audience:

```
This site may contain explicit descriptions of or advocate one
or more of the following:

adultery, murder, morbid violence, bad grammar, deviant sexual
conduct in violent contexts, or the consumption of alcohol and
illegal drugs.

Then again, it may not.

Who knows?
```

Indeed, the content of the cDc site is not strictly restricted to hacking and security materials. Alongside text files such as "The Tao of Windows Buffer Overflow" and "NetBIOS Attacks over TCP" are other works entitled "My Life as Santa's Rubber-Clad Love Slave" and "cDc's Guide to Sexually Transmitted Diseases." Clearly, the members and followers of the cDc do more than just spend all of their time sitting in front of computers.

As with the other groups discussed, a roll call of prominent cDc members throws up a number of weird and wonderful names: Grandmaster Ratte (the founder of the group), Sir Dystic, Count Zero, DilDog, and The Deth Vegetable. The cDc are a regular feature at hacker events such as DEF CON (discussed in the next section), at which they are known as much for their bizarre theatrical stage shows as they are for their software releases. To the world at large, however, the group's best-known contribution to the hacking scene is a remote administration tool, going by the rather unpleasant name of Back Orifice (BO) – originally released in 1998. Although it can be put to perfectly legitimate uses, BO is more typically found in the hands of hackers wishing to make a nuisance of themselves (as with L0phtCrack, a description of its capabilities is presented in the next chapter). It is largely as a result of BO that the group has garnered a fair degree of media attention in recent years – much of it negative and focusing upon the dangers posed by their software releases. In response to this, group member Sir Dystic offers the following opinion:

> It's all about marketing. The media like to portray the cDc as the bad guys but we're probably helping security businesses quite a bit by raising awareness.[88]

The hacking groups described above are merely some of the better-known examples. There are many other groups active in the computing underground and a more comprehensive list of links to their associated web sites can be found at **http://www.infosyssec.org/infosyssec/hgroup.html**. As with the groups discussed here, the motivations and ethics of the other groups can vary quite considerably.

Hacker gatherings and conventions

Although the most natural medium for hackers to convene together might appear to be online, there are also various scenarios in which they gather together in person. In some cases, these may be informal and private meetings between friends and associates. Other cases, however, may be somewhat more organized – for example, arranged meetings of members from particular hacking groups. Although this may initially conjure up images of dark-dealings and skulduggery, the reality is not necessarily as sinister as it may sound and what actually goes on at such meetings can vary considerably. In some cases, the gathering may have no direct connection to the act of hacking – the idea may just be to get together for social activities. This is illustrated by the following quotation from Low Tek, a hacker from the Atlanta chapter of the 2600 hacking group.

> Some of these guys here, I'll hang out at a club, go to a rave with, do the occasional drug . . .[89]

At other meetings, however, the act of hacking may take center stage. For example, the defacement of the U.K. Labour Party's web site (discussed in Chapter 4) was one of several online exploits that occurred during a gathering of British and international hackers on a Friday night in Manchester during late 1996. The social aspects of drinking and swapping stories were still there, but the hacking was the main event.

The venues for the meetings may also be pretty ad hoc. The aforementioned Atlanta 2600 hackers, for example, congregated in the food court of the Lenox Square shopping mall. The London chapter of the same group meet at the bottom of the escalators in the Trocadero Centre in Piccadilly Circus. Another U.K.-based branch, this time in Leeds, meet by the payphones outside the local train station. Like all other 2600-affiliated groups around the world, they meet on the first Friday of every month.

Hacker gatherings such as those mentioned above are typically localized events. However, they are by no means the limits of hackers' physical meetings. There are, in fact, a number of large-scale conference-type events aimed at (and organized by) the hacker community. Probably the best example is the DEF CON convention, which is held annually in Las Vegas (the name is taken from the U.S. military's five-level system for classifying the defence alert status). It describes itself as "an annual computer underground party for hackers" and attracts a varied audience from around the world. The first DEF CON event was held in 1993 and was attended by around 100 hackers. Eight years later, the number of attendees at DEF CON 00 was nearer to 5,000.

But if hacking is basically illegal, how do these people come to be gathering together, in public, in full view of the media? Well, of course, the plain fact is that the interpretation of hacking being made in this context is not illegal – although it is something that could be used illegally if an individual was so motivated. Hacking in this context is beating or circumventing security techniques or exposing new vulnerabilities – not explicitly advocating that people should go and actually break into real world systems. Underlining the point that it does not intend to provide a forum for fostering criminal talent, the DEF CON web site (**www.defcon.org**) says the following in its overview of the event:

> We are not trying to teach you to learn how to hack in a weekend, but what we are trying to do is create an environment where you can hang out with people from all different backgrounds. All of them interested in the same thing, computer security.

The focus on practical security issues can be illustrated by looking at a small selection of the topics addressed during the event. Some of the talks delivered at the DEF CON 8.0 were as follows:

- "Evading Network-based Intrusion Detection Systems."
- "Advanced Buffer Overflow Techniques."
- "Penetrating B1 Trusted Operating Systems."

- "The Citizen Hacker: Patriot or War Criminal?"
- "Federal Computer Fraud and Abuse Act."

Although such topics are clearly of likely interest to those interested in safe-guarding security, it could be argued that some of the titles are more clearly targeted at those interested in breaching it. In addition, DEF CON has also been the venue of choice for the unveiling of new hacking tools. For example, it was at the 1998 event that the Cult of the Dead Cow unveiled their now infamous Back Orifice tool (the capabilities of which will be examined in the next chapter).

Given that events such as DEF CON are used to showcase hacker tools, skills and techniques, it may not be surprising to learn that they are also frequented by undercover agents from various U.S. government agencies. However, the motives here are not simply to raid the place or to arrest everybody. Instead, the objectives are related more to the gathering of intelligence. Agents can see first hand the new tools that are being unleashed – tools that they may encounter in the field in the months to come. They can also keep an eye open for any rising stars within the hacking world – any individuals or groups that might come to represent a threat and could, therefore, be worth monitoring. In addition, at DEF CON 2000, another objective emerged – recruitment. Officials from the CIA, the Department of Defense and the National Security Agency were not only in attendance – they were on stage as part of the so-called "Meet the Fed" panel. The message to the assembled hacker talent was that they too could join and put their skills to good use in a legitimate context. Arthur Money, U.S. Assistant Secretary of Defense for Command, Control, Communications, and Intelligence, called upon hackers to become part of the government's efforts to secure the nation's networks.

> If you are extremely talented, and you are wondering what you'd like to do for the rest of your life – join us, and help us educate our people.[90]

Of course, even in the past, the hackers were by no means ignorant of the fact that agents were present in the crowds. Indeed, a tradition at DEF CON events is the "Spot the Fed" competition, in which any delegate who correctly identifies an agent wins an "I Spotted the Fed" T-shirt and the unmasked agent gets an accompanying "I Was the Fed" T-shirt to wear.[91]

Such support from the government agencies suggests that events such as DEF CON are almost mainstream. Indeed, the 2000 event was even supported by big names from the IT industry, with Dell providing equipment and Symantec providing speakers. By 2001, some participants were clearly beginning to resent the perceived departure from traditional hacker culture, and a photocopied brochure was distributed to delegates with the message:

don't pay for DC registrations . . . steal a badge . . . reclaim your culture . . . hack the exploiters . . . ignore the rules . . . don't buy anything.[92]

However, perhaps in keeping with the more corporate tone of the modern event, security guards were on hand to eject gatecrashers and control protestors. Those distributing the offending flyer were banned from the convention.

As regards the activities that delegates engage in at DEF CON, spotting federal agents is not the only challenge. In a challenge more oriented toward the skills that the convention seeks to promote, hackers engage in a "Capture the Flag" contest, in which they attempt to demonstrate their hacking prowess by hacking into specially designated machines (the objective being to compromise as many as possible). However, this is not to suggest that all of the goings-on at DEF CON are now entirely innocent. Somewhat more illicit activities at DEF CON 2000 included hackers taking over the internal TV system of the Alexis Hotel venue and eavesdropping on the conversations of Las Vegas tourists using a cell-phone scanner.

The existence of hacking groups and conventions should not be seen as a problem in itself. It can be considered to be analogous to the existence of organizations like gun clubs. Just because someone is a member of a gun club, it does not mean that they are likely to shoot other people with their gun. Likewise, to assume that all those who are members of hacking groups or attend conventions are then likely to set about hacking other people's systems is to assume that they have no sense of personal responsibility. Some may argue that there is no reason why people would want to learn hacking techniques unless they wished to apply them in practice. However, the gun analogy can be used again, in that many people are quite happy to practice and perfect their abilities to shoot paper targets, without then feeling the urge to unleash their skills for criminal purposes.

Hackers as celebrities

Hacking is, without doubt, one of the most recognized forms of cybercrime, and media interest in particular has brought it to the attention of the population at large. As a result, hackers can in some way be considered to be one of the celebrity groups that have emerged in the information age. More recently, they have been joined by dotcom entrepreneurs (who present a more positive image of what individuals can do with technology), and together these are probably the foremost groups that the general public now associate with the Internet.

This section considers the concept of celebrity hackers in both fictitious and real-world contexts. The former situation, examined in terms of how hackers have been portrayed in films, can be seen to have raised awareness of hacking, creating a certain image in the public mind. The real-world examples will consider actual cases in which particular hackers, and their associated misdeeds, have become so well known that their names have spilt over from merely being recognized in hacker circles to actually getting significant coverage in the general media.

Hackers in the movies

As a result of the media attention devoted to hackers and the mystique that surrounds the issue, filmmakers have identified that it represents a rich topic of interest to a potentially wide audience. The problem they face is that, although hacking exploits can be described in quite engaging terms using words, when you come to actually depict them visually they look . . . well, quite dull really. The idea of routing a network connection through various international systems before breaking into the Pentagon and stealing classified military secrets may sound exciting in the plot synopsis, but the reality could just involve a guy sat in front of a computer tapping a few keys and occasionally using the mouse. For added effect you could have him in a darkened room, with his face bathed in light from the monitor to give an impression of menace, but that's about it. As a result, directors frequently resort to fast-paced, lively, colorful, and entirely artificial interpretations for their on-screen hackers' interactions with their systems. They do not just type a few commands or click a few mouse buttons to move to the desired directory on a target system – they navigate their way through a 3D cyberscape, swooping and gliding toward their destination. In fact, about the only natural element of a computer interface that can seemingly be used to deliver any sense of drama is the status bar when a file is being copied (cue the scenes from films like *The Net* and *Hackers* when one of our heroes waits anxiously for the status to reach "100%" before the impending arrival of the villain).

There are numerous big-budget Hollywood films in which hacking activities have been sewn into the plot – particularly in more recent years. A few examples here include *The Net*, *Goldeneye*, *Mission Impossible*, *The Matrix*, *Clear and Present Danger,* and *Sneakers*. There are fewer pictures in which hacking is the main focus of the film, but there are nonetheless a couple of good examples – namely *WarGames* (1983) and *Hackers* (1995).

WarGames (1983)

The release of the 1983 movie *WarGames* was a seminal point in shaping the public perception of the computer hacker. The central character is David Lightman, a high school student and computer geek. Lightman learns of a forthcoming game from Protovision Systems and programs his home computer to "war dial" through the telephone numbers in the company's area code, recording all numbers that are answered by a computer modem tone. After hacking his way into a system that he believes to be Protovision's, he elects to play a game entitled "Global Thermonuclear

War." However, he then discovers that the computer he has contacted belongs to NORAD (North American Aerospace Defense Command) and that the "game" is real. Lightman then has to act fast to prevent the computer from completing the "game" and unleashing Word War III.

The story is essentially a race-against-time thriller, carrying with it an underlying message about the danger of relying upon machines rather than human intelligence. However, with its central plot concerning a teen hacker breaking into military systems, *WarGames* subsequently had a significant effect upon media reporting of computer abuse, with references frequently being made to it in hacker-related news stories. With the film having provided a reference point that the general public could understand, it was easier for the media to provide reports that people would be interested in. Arriving on the cinema screens at the same time as home computers were becoming affordable and popular, it is also likely that it gave ideas to many budding hackers (as well as establishing military systems as a suitable target for them).

For those wishing to get more information about *WarGames*, a good site on the web is **http://www-public.rz.uni-duesseldorf.de/~ritterd/wargames/logon.htm**. Better still, buy or rent the movie!

Hackers (1995)

Released in 1995, *Hackers* was one of the first movies since *WarGames* to feature hacking as its central theme. The main character is Dade Murphy, a young hacker of some renown, who is banned from using computers until his eighteenth birthday as a result of crashing 1507 computers on Wall Street with a virus when he was eleven years old. Moving to New York, Dade soon falls in with a band of other hackers who recognize him as one of their own. Within the group, all are veterans of the hacking scene, with the exception of the youngest one, who still needs to earn a hacker handle by demonstrating his skills to the others. So, seeking to prove his prowess, he hacks into the computer of Ellingson Mineral Corporation and makes a copy of a garbage file as proof of his accomplishment. However, unknown to him, the file contains information that proves that Ellingson's own security officer, a master hacker known as The Plague, has been up to no good – gradually siphoning off $25 million from Ellingson's financial transactions. The Plague reports the young hacker's intrusion to the Secret Service and he is pulled in, but not before the disk is hidden and then retrieved by the other members of the group – who then, of course, become targets themselves. In order to incriminate the others, and give the Secret Service a reason to chase them, Plague creates a virus and blames it on the hackers – a virus which will lead to an ecological disaster by capsizing oil tankers. The main thrust of the story then revolves around their efforts to clear their names, avert disaster, and ensure that The Plague and his accomplice are brought to justice.

In a rather overt interpretation of the competition that sometimes exists between hackers and authority, as well as amongst hackers themselves, an amusing side story involves a contest between the two lead hacker characters to see who can perpetrate the best hack against the Secret Service agent who has hassled their group. Their efforts include cancelling his bank card, creating fake traffic violation records and marking him as deceased in his payroll record.

In the early part of the film, the characters' hacking credentials are established by showing them doing a variety of things that viewers should identify with as being hacker-like. For example:

- Hacking into the school's computer system to alter class lists and reprogram the sprinkler system;
- Hacking into the local TV station (in order to be able to watch the programs that *they* want);
- Phone phreaking to get free calls;
- Getting high scores on video games.

It is interesting to observe that an analogous set of actions was also depicted in the scene-setting segments of *WarGames* – the David Lightman character hacks into the school's system to alter his grades, mentions his ability to avoid telephone call charges and is a bit of a wizard in the video arcade! The two films are around twelve years apart, and yet the actions portrayed to define the hackers are very similar.

Opinion in the real world hacker community was divided over the film. MGM's promotional web site contains quotations from hacker luminaries Emmanuel Goldstein (editor of *2600*) and Phiber Optik, expressing their support:[93]

> People who aren't hackers will enjoy the plot. People who are hackers will enjoy the message.
>
> EMMANUEL GOLDSTEIN

> It remains the most loyal compared to other movies recently released on the subject.
>
> PHIBER OPTIK

Other hackers were somewhat less enamored with the film and one chose to demonstrate his distaste by vandalizing the promotional site (a copy of which is retained as a link from the official homepage – along with the perpetrator's subsequent letter of apology).

Okay, but they're only movies

It could, of course, be argued that *WarGames* and *Hackers* are just movies and, therefore, do not have any significant bearing on hacking in the real world. However, by presenting an engaging story in which the hacker is the hero, a positive and exciting image is presented that is attractive to prospective newcomers. This is borne out by the comments of Emmanuel Goldstein:

> So every time a movie like "Hackers" comes out, 10 million people from AOL send us e-mail saying they want to be hackers, too, and suddenly, every 12-year-old with this sentiment instantly becomes a hacker in the eyes of the media and hence, the rest of society.[94]

It is worth considering further the way in which *Hackers* presented its topic and the impression that this may have conveyed to the people who saw it. Picking up on the Emmanuel Goldstein quotation from the film's homepage, it is true to say that the non-hacker audience would appreciate the plot, while hackers themselves would enjoy the message. However, it is less clear what the non-hacker audience would perceive to be the factual elements of the film. To the security-aware viewer, the film is clearly accurate in a number of ways and is peppered with references to reality, including the following:

- mention of the U.S. Department of Defense's Orange Book security evaluation criteria.
- discussion of the most commonly used passwords.
- reference, by content if not by name, to The Mentor's *Hacker Manifesto*.
- depiction of hacker techniques such as social engineering and dumpster diving (see Chapter 4).

However, there are also elements that are completely artificial. When they are online, the hackers in the film are not so much in cyberspace as they are in fantasy-land – with systems and user interfaces that behave almost totally unlike anything found in real life. At the same time, the film does not purport to be a documentary and, as with all things Hollywood, some dramatic license is to be expected. However, there is still an important difference. For example, when watching a western, Average Joe viewer will realise that, in reality, John Wayne and his six-shooter would probably not have single-handedly defeated the bad guys because, in reality, Big John would have run out of bullets and the baddies would not all have been such awful shots. Likewise, having watched a film like *Star Wars*, Average Joe would know that it was not real because we still launch space shuttles rather than Star Destroyers. However, for those unfamiliar with computing technology, it is difficult to pick the likely fact from fiction in a film like *Hackers*. The story is based in a contemporary setting, so nothing seems particularly unrealistic about that. We know that all of the core elements – such as computers, hackers and the police – exist in real life and there are established relationships between them (e.g. hackers break into computers and the police want to arrest them for doing so), so that aspect seems okay. The characters in the film seem a bit weird, but the media tells us that hackers *are* weird, so that seems to match up. They seem to be able to do and control a lot via their computers, but we know that computers are involved with everything now, so that too seems reasonable. So, although Average Joe may instinctively know that the dramatic license is in there somewhere, he cannot be sure where it is. Maybe it's just the story that is fictitious and everything else is accurately portrayed? You can see his dilemma.

The glamorization of hacking in the movies appears set to continue. At the time of writing, a new movie entitled *Swordfish* has appeared in the cinemas, in which a top computer hacker is enlisted to help steal $9.5 billion from a Drug Enforcement Administration slush fund. Although watching the film reveals that the hacker is somewhat coerced into participating in the plan (and is actually trying to go straight in order to avoid going back to prison), the tag line of the film, "log on, hack in, go anywhere, steal everything," conveys an immediate impression of hackers as intruders and thieves. So, again, what Joe Public is likely to perceive about hackers as a result will depend very much upon personal interpretation of what is likely to be fact and fiction in the film.

Having suggested that the film portrayals typically overstate the power and glamor involved when compared to average hacking incidents, it must also be acknowledged that there are *some* cases in which the reality is not that far removed from the fantasy. In some cases, the activities of real hackers may actually have been the inspiration for elements later portrayed in the films.

The real celebrity hackers

Over the years, the hacker community has spawned a number of genuine celebrity figures – real-life hackers whose activities have caused their names to become known not just within hacker circles, but also to a wider public through the mass media. In fact, their names may have become better known than the things that they have actually done. This section highlights three particular cases, which provide probably the best examples of celebrity hackers that have arisen to date. All of them have spent time in prison for their activities but, having been released, are now associated in some way with the preventative side of the IT security industry.

Cap'n Crunch

The first example of a celebrity in the hacker underground was probably John Draper, better known as Cap'n Crunch. Strictly speaking, though, Draper was not a hacker, but a phone phreaker. The genre of phreaking was introduced earlier in this chapter and you will recall that a key element was the use of Blue Box multi-frequency tone generators – in particular to generate a 2600 hertz tone to clear the current call and leave the switch open to phreaker control. However, although they were a key element of phreaker kit, Blue Boxes were not the only means by which the magical 2600 Hz tone could be generated. Some phreakers with perfect pitch found that they were able to manually whistle the tone into the handset. However, probably the most legendary story in phreaking history is that of how the means to generate the all-powerful 2600 Hz tone was given away with a breakfast cereal. The cereal in question was called Cap'n Crunch and in 1972 toy whistles were given away inside the packets. An innocent enough children's toy one would think and, indeed, it certainly was not the cereal manufacturer's intention to be providing anything else. However, the ingenious phreaker community quickly found an alternative use. It was discovered that, when one of the holes was glued up, the toy whistle would emit a perfect 2600 Hz tone. With this, the name of Cap'n Crunch found an initial link with the phenomenon of phone phreaking. It was soon to find another, longer lasting, link when John Draper, an engineer at U.S. company National Semiconductor, adopted it as his phreaker handle.

It should be noted that Draper does not actually claim the credit for discovering the phreaking application of the Cap'n Crunch whistle – he attributes this to some young blind phreakers, whom he claims had known about it for some time before him[95] (various members of the blind community found phreaking to be an attractive pastime, due to the entirely aural nature of the environment being explored). However, needing a handle within the phreaker community, he considered the name Cap'n Crunch to be appropriate, which led many people to assume that he was responsible for discovering the use of the whistle as well.

Phreaking had been going on for a while by the time that Draper entered the fray, but most people were unaware of it. However, the issue was widely publicized in October 1971, with the appearance of an *Esquire* magazine article that is now famous in phreaking circles, entitled "Secrets of the Little Blue Box."[96] Although the technical information that enabled phreaking had already been published in the AT&T technical journal (making it available to engineers and college students), coverage of phreaking activity in a mainstream magazine brought the issue to a much wider audience. As a result, more and more people began to experiment. The phone company had an increased incentive to take notice and arrests began to become more frequent.

Cap'n Crunch was a significant focus of the *Esquire* article and it is, therefore, not too surprising that Draper himself was arrested for his activities a few months after its publication. As a result, he spent some time in Lompoc minimum-security prison, where he found himself playing the role of teacher and advisor to a number of other would-be phreakers. It was not necessarily an occupation that Draper had that much choice over – it was more a means of survival. He found that by passing on his phreaking skills to the hardest of the hardened criminals amongst the other inmates, he could ensure an element of safety and protection for himself while on the inside. His classes covered topics such as blue boxing, bug detection and how to avoid having your calls tapped or traced. As a result of such tutoring, it is likely that by imprisoning Draper for his activities, the ultimate effect was that the problem of phreaking got worse. Whereas Draper applied his skills for exploration and occasional mischief, those whom he passed the knowledge on to would be more determined to make use of it for more overtly criminal purposes and personal gain.

It was not only in prison that the effects of publicity from the *Esquire* article were felt. Draper's celebrity was known to others in the technology field who would later go on to become even bigger IT celebrities themselves – namely Steve Wozniak and Steve Jobs, the founders of Apple Computer. Following the *Esquire* piece, Steve Wozniak made contact with him in order to get first-hand instruction on how to make a Blue Box – which Draper duly provided. Indeed, Draper was even an Apple employee for a short time during the early days of the company. Whilst there, he designed a new add-in card for the Apple II that could act as an automated telephone dialler and the ultimate Blue Box.[97] This card (known as the Charlie Board) never made it to commercial production – others at Apple were too wary of its potential for use in illegal activities. After a time, Draper left the company anyway – only to be arrested shortly afterwards for stealing $50,000 in telephone calls. Amongst the items in his possession was an Apple II with a Charlie Board installed. Cap'n Crunch went back to jail.*

It is, perhaps, a testament to Draper's celebrity status that the name of Cap'n Crunch still lives on to this day and can be found immortalized on the World Wide Web – a medium that was still decades away when Draper's exploits were at their height. Details can be found on various sites, but the most relevant is the Cap'n's own site at **http://www.webcruchers.com/crunch**. At the time of writing, he is working as a database software developer for ShopIP – a California-based security solutions provider of which he is the co-founder and Chief Technology Officer.

Kevin Mitnick

> I have 20 years' experience circumventing information security measures, and can report that I have successfully compromised all systems that I targeted for unauthorized access save one . . . I have gained unauthorized access to computer systems at some of the largest corporations on the planet, and have successfully penetrated some of the most resilient computer systems ever developed.
>
> EXTRACTS FROM KEVIN MITNICK'S WRITTEN TESTIMONY TO U.S. SENATE GOVERNMENTAL AFFAIRS COMMITTEE, MARCH 2000[98]

---

* When he later emerged again, Draper would resume his association with the Apple II, but this time on a legal footing as the author of the popular EasyWriter word processor.

A prime example of the celebrity hacker can be found in the person of Kevin David Mitnick, at one time known as "America's Most Wanted Computer Outlaw."[99] Born in 1964, Mitnick has been a hacker, and in and out of trouble with the law, since the early 1980s. At the time of writing, he had recently been released from prison and is on supervised probation. His name, more than any other, seems to be synonymous with the modern hacking scene (at least in terms of media attention).

So, how did Mitnick earn himself his "America's Most Wanted" moniker? The following is a list of some of the things that he is alleged to have done over the years:

- 1981 – Involved in a physical break-in at Pacific Bell's COSMOS (Computer System for Mainframe Operations) phone center. Sentenced to three months in the Los Angeles Juvenile Detention Center, followed by a year's probation.

- 1983 – Arrested by campus police at the University of Southern California for using a university computer to gain illegal access to the ARPANET. Sentenced to six months in a juvenile prison in California.

- 1984 – Arrest warrant issued after Mitnick, then working for Great American Merchandising, was accused of running unauthorized TRW credit reference checks.

- December 1987 – Convicted of stealing software from Santa Cruz Operation, a Californian software company and sentenced to thirty-six months probation.

- 1989 – Sentenced to one year in prison and six months in a counseling program for computer "addiction" following repeated unauthorized entries into systems at Digital Equipment Corporation's Palo Alto research lab in 1987–8. Digital claimed that he had stolen several million dollars worth of software (in particular, their VMS operating system) and had cost them $200,000 in their attempts to keep him out. It should be noted that Digital were valuing VMS based upon its development cost rather than the retail price, based on the fact that Mitnick was targeting the source code (which the company considered commercially sensitive).

- 1992 – Violated the terms of the probation following his 1989 conviction and went underground. Accused of stealing software from Motorola, Nokia and Sun, among others.

- December 1994 – Involved in stealing software, email and other files from a computer belonging to Tsutomu Shimomura, a computational physicist and computer security expert at the San Diego Supercomputer Center. Shimomura was outraged at Mitnick's intrusion and subsequently took an active role in tracking him down, in collaboration with the FBI and other victims.

- February 1995 – Kevin Mitnick is arrested in Raleigh, North Carolina, after more than two years on the run.

The above certainly represents a notable list of achievements and is suggestive of someone who does not learn their lesson very quickly. The cost of Mitnick's final hacking spree was placed at around $291.8 million (a figure based on the total of estimates provided by NEC, Nokia, Novell and Sun). NEC costed the software stolen from them at $1.8 million. Meanwhile, Nokia's estimate ran to at least $135 million, which included an estimate of $120 million in lost revenue due to new developments having to be delayed before being released to the market.

Having at this point established that Mitnick has been involved in a number of illegal hacking activities, it is worth considering the manner in which his case has been presented and publicized. Although one would instinctively expect that he would not receive a particularly positive press, many would argue that the media has been responsible for portraying a significantly exaggerated view of events. For example, the hacker folklore presented in the media claims that Mitnick's escapades also included a breach of the computer systems at NORAD. This, however, is something that Mitnick himself strongly denies[100] and it is not something for which he has ever faced formal charges. Indeed, NORAD themselves also deny that such an incident took place. Nonetheless, the story persists in the media. It is also frequently claimed that his face adorned FBI "wanted" posters as a result of his hacking activities. This is also untrue, although he did end up on such a poster from the U.S. Marshals Service in November 1992, in relation to the violation of his supervised release.[101]

One of the most frequent commentators on the Mitnick case was *New York Times* columnist John Markoff. Indeed, Markoff has co-authored two books relating to Mitnick. In the first, *Cyberpunk: Outlaws and Hackers on the Computer Frontier*, a third of the book is dedicated to the tale of Mitnick's early days,* in a section entitled "Kevin: The Dark-Side Hacker."[102] Although the book makes for an interesting read, such wording tends to color the reader's viewpoint from the outset. Indeed, in the further description that is presented as the book develops, Mitnick comes across as a vindictive and obsessive character, addicted to the (mis)use of computer systems and willing to exploit others in pursuit of his goals. The goals themselves are typically seen to relate to revenge or victimization, targeted against individuals or particular companies. The average reader will accept this as a true recounting of events, their rationale being that the book has, after all, been published, so therefore it must be accurate and trustworthy. However, Katie Hafner, the co-author of the book, has subsequently conceded that this characterization of Mitnick might have been unfair:

> It might have been a mistake to call him a darkside hacker . . . I hadn't spoken to him personally till after I wrote the book.[103]

---

* The other sections relate the stories of two other interesting security incidents, namely the activities of a group of KGB-sponsored East German hackers breaking into military systems and of Robert Morris Jr., the author of the *Internet Worm* in November 1988.

Of the people who have read the book, substantially fewer would have also read Hafner's second thoughts about it. From Mitnick's perspective, the published characterization would have only served to increase media coverage and attention toward him, creating an image that it would already have been difficult to escape from. Having said this, the fact that Mitnick continued his hacking endeavors (providing enough material for several further books focusing upon him alone) suggests that, at the time, he was not exactly trying to tread a totally innocent path anyway.

John Markoff's second book about Mitnick presents an account of the more recent events that led to his arrest and ultimate imprisonment in 1995. The book, entitled *Takedown – the pursuit and capture of Kevin Mitnick the world's most notorious cybercriminal – by the man who did it,* was written in collaboration with Tsutomu Shimomura, the administrator of the system into which Mitnick is alleged to have gained unauthorized access during the Christmas of 1994. This trespass prompted Shimomura to begin tracking him down. *Takedown* narrates the events that followed in the few weeks between Mitnick's Christmas break-in and his subsequent capture in February 1995. The story is written from Shimomura's perspective and presents a fairly detailed account of his dealings with law enforcement and other system administrators in their efforts to trace Mitnick. It is interesting to note that, in contrast to much of the other coverage that Mitnick has received, Shimomura's text at one point refers to him as an "anklebiter" – a description that contrasts somewhat with the image of him as America's number one cyber criminal.

An alternative account of the same period, which gives more of an insight into Mitnick's side of the story, is presented in Jonathan Littman's book *The Fugitive Game*. Like Shimomura's co-author John Markoff, Littman is a technology journalist with a particular interest in hackers and their activities. In contrast to the *Takedown* authors, however, Littman had established personal contact with Mitnick himself and the two would talk on the phone, with Mitnick giving details of his life and activities. Interestingly, this contact began before Mitnick's intrusion into Shimomura's system and continued throughout the time leading up to his capture. So, Littman's book gives more of an insight into the hacker's world, whereas *Takedown* is far more focused on the process of tracking one down. As such, the two books presented two sides of the same story and are both worth reading.

In addition to the books, the version of the story presented in *Takedown* was adopted as the basis for a Hollywood movie of the same name. It was actually filmed during 1998, but was held back from general release amid rumors that Mitnick had filed a lawsuit for defamation of character, due to the way in which he was represented in the picture (early versions of the script in particular portrayed him as being violent and dangerous, with fictionalized activities, such as hacking medical records and hitting Shimomura over the head with the top of a metal garbage can, being included for effect). At the time of writing, the film has only received a limited release – in France, for example, where it was released under the name *Cybertr@que*. It has not been released in the United States, the country in which it was made and in which the activities are set.

To add to his dubious achievements, Mitnick also found his way into the 1999 *Guinness Book of World Records*, listed under the heading of "Most Notorious Hacker Case."[104] The hacker magazine *2600* took particular exception to this on Mitnick's behalf, setting up a parody of the Guinness web site which dissected the text presented about Mitnick, and pointed out many inaccuracies in the description.[105] In fairness, many of these inaccuracies may have arisen as a result of conflicting media coverage of the affair in the first instance. What is more significant, however, is the fact that "Most Notorious Hacker Case" does not really stand up very well as a category for a world record. As *2600* also observe, the heading is entirely subjective – what may seem like the most notorious incident to me may not be viewed the same way by you. Other perspectives, such as "most widely reported hacker case," would have been better, in the sense that there would have been a chance of assessing the record against measurable criteria. Subsequent cybercrimes that have been listed in the context of world records have clearly taken this on board and the categories are now objectively based – e.g. "Fastest-spreading computer virus" and "Biggest fine as a result of Internet crime."[106] Another observation is that the general implication of establishing something as a world record is that it creates a target – something for others to potentially aspire to and attempt to beat. This impression is reinforced by the fact that the front of the *Book of Records* contains a general warning from Guinness World Records Ltd stating that attempting to break records or set new ones can be dangerous and would be done at the participant's own risk. Although common sense would suggest that one should not set out to break records associated with criminal activity, this may not be a barrier to some people. For those whose hacking exploits are driven by forces such as ego, competition and challenge, the establishment of a world record for hacking may simply be too attractive a gauntlet to pass up.

So, what of Mitnick's view of himself? It appears to largely conform to the stereotypical view that hackers have of themselves and their activities:

> I saw myself as an electronic joy rider . . . I was like James Bond behind the computer. I was just having a blast . . . I was an accomplished trespasser. I don't consider myself a thief.[107]

Many of Mitnick's victims would certainly take issue with this somewhat sanitized self-impression, citing that the nature of his activities were more insidious than mere trespassing. At the same time, however, Mitnick does now seem to have accepted that, although he did not consider his actions to be damaging or maliciously destructive, they were still morally wrong:

I do want to make a public apology . . . My past actions have invaded their privacy by getting into machines and getting into their code, and I do regret doing that stuff because it's wrong to do. But I was a kid having fun. I can't change the past, but . . . hopefully I can be forgiven.[108]

What does Mitnick think of his fame? He was asked this specific question during an online interview for ABCNEWS.com during May 2000, a few months after his release:

I've never intended to become a celebrity through my hacking activities. My motivation for hacking was the intellectual challenge and quest for knowledge . . . I believe I have support because of my unfair treatment by government prosecutors and the manipulation of my case in the media.[109]

The issue of how Mitnick's case was treated will be considered later, in Chapter 6.

Kevin Poulsen

Like many hackers, Kevin Poulsen started young and, aged around thirteen, he developed a fascination with the telephone system. Giving himself the handle Dark Dante, he began reading about the topic extensively, starting with resources from a local university library, before progressing to obtaining materials such as manuals and discarded equipment from the dumpsters outside phone company buildings. His search for knowledge led him into contact with other like-minded individuals and, ultimately, into unauthorized access of the phone company's computer systems.

By the time he was seventeen years old he had already run into trouble with the law and been raided by the Los Angeles County District Attorney's office for breaking into systems on the ARPANET. His age saved him on this occasion and he was not charged. At this point, he temporarily gave up his hacking hobby and got a job as a computer operator and programmer with government-contractor SRI International. However, even though he was working with computers, Poulsen did not find the work challenging and became bored. This, combined with discovering that his boss (a former phreaker) shared his passion for exploring the system, meant that it was not long before Poulsen found himself back on the other side of the law. In parallel with this, his technical talents had not gone unnoticed at work and he was elevated to what, from a hacker's perspective, was a somewhat more interesting role. He was given a security clearance and assigned the task of testing the security of government defense computer systems. It was, therefore, somewhat ironic that Poulsen's day job was to make systems and secrets safe from the sort of attacks that he himself was launching against systems by night.

As well as having his technical abilities, Poulsen was also skilled at picking locks – an attribute that he was also able to employ in support of his hacking. He and his friends were bold enough to physically break into phone company offices to steal manuals and other materials that would assist them in manipulating the systems that they hacked. The break-ins to systems and premises were discovered by the Pacific Bell telephone company in 1987. Poulsen was not charged, but his employers were informed of his activities and he lost his job. In spite of this, his hacking continued.

In November 1989, he was indicted on multiple counts of conspiracy, fraud and wiretapping. In addition to this, however, Poulsen was also suspected of engaging in more sinister activities. Further charges were leveled against him relating to embezzlement and the gathering of defense information – based on the security clearance that he previously held. Poulsen fled and, for the next seventeen months, became a fugitive. This, however, did not put a stop to his hacking exploits and, indeed, one of the most notable aspects of his story occurred during this period, when he used his skills to rig radio phone-in competitions by hacking into Pacific Bell's computer systems. Each week, the KIIS-FM station ran a contest in which the 102nd caller to phone in after a particular sequence of songs had been played would win a $50,000 Porsche 944-S2. On 1st June 1990, Poulsen hacked into the system and took control of the station's twenty-five telephone lines. In doing so, he was able to block out all calls but his own. He was then able to ensure that he dialled the 102nd call and claim a Porsche 944. He was also able to acquire himself a Hawaiian holiday via the same method. At the time, Poulsen considered this scamming to be a "victimless" form of crime[110] – however, in June 1994, he pleaded guilty to seven counts of mail, wire and computer fraud, money laundering, and obstruction of justice in relation to the radio scams and other incidents.

During the time that he was on the run, there was increasing interest in Poulsen and the nature of his illicit activities. Amongst the allegations were claims that he:

- snooped on FBI files relating to an investigation of the former Philippines President, Ferdinand Marcos.
- eavesdropped on personal phone calls of a Hollywood actress.
- plotted the theft of classified military information.
- reactivated old Yellow Page escort telephone numbers for an acquaintance who then ran a virtual agency.

Whereas Kevin Mitnick's escapades managed to get his face onto a wanted poster, Poulsen's analogous claim to fame is to have found an even wider audience – with his alleged offences being dramatized on the U.S. television show *Unsolved Mysteries*. However, it was not the kind of publicity that Poulsen particularly relished, as indicated by the following extract from a letter that he sent to Timothy Rogan of Cosgrove & Meurer productions, the producers of the program:

What I've read about the segment you've produced is that you intend on showing a Kevin Poulsen look-alike doing what the prosecutor has accused me of. You will be creating a crime for your audience and you will be showing "me" committing it. Even after I am eventually cleared of these ludicrous accusations involving national security, Ferdinand Marcos, etc., the images of "Kevin Poulsen" huddled over a computer stealing military secrets while cackling evilly will remain in the minds of your fourteen-million viewers. Adding an occasional "allegedly" to your report, or even reporting on my acquittal when it occurs, will hardly mitigate this. My life and career will be irrevocably damaged.[111]

In spite of the letter, the broadcast did go ahead, bringing his case into the homes of millions of Americans.

Poulsen was finally captured in April 1991 and, having been charged with national security violations, he was held without bail on the basis that he represented a danger to the community. Indeed, in December 1992 he became the first hacker to be indicted under U.S. espionage laws based on the charges that he had gathered classified defense information. His case also established another record, when he was ultimately sentenced to pay over $56,000 in restitution to the radio stations he scammed and spend fifty-one months in prison – the longest sentence issued for cybercrime. Significantly, however, the espionage charges that had prevented Poulsen from being allowed bail were dismissed – vindicating his long-term claims of innocence in this respect. The espionage claims are, nonetheless, one of the oft-quoted aspects of Poulsen's case and have added to his status as hacker celebrity.

Although he has not received anywhere near as much attention as Kevin Mitnick, Poulsen's is another case about which a book has been written by journalist Jonathan Littman, entitled *The Watchman – the Twisted Life and Crimes of Serial Hacker Kevin Poulsen*. However, Poulsen is clearly less than enamored with the end result and his web site describes Littman as a "compulsive muck-raker," accusing him of inventing quotations and making up facts for the book.[112] Luckily for Poulsen, however, it can be observed that the attention he received has ultimately not prevented him from again securing a legitimate career in the computing field – as a computer-crime writer and speaker. More details of what happened to Poulsen after his release will be considered in Chapter 6.

Other celebrity figures

It can be observed that, in technology terms, the cases described are all rather dated. The reason is that although there has been a massive increase in the use of Internet technology, and a corresponding increase in hacking attacks, analogous celebrity figures have not really emerged from the latest wave of hackers. Although there have been more attacks, the majority are down to script kiddies, who lack the skill or persistence to make their names well known. In the hacker underground of today, the groups are probably better known than specific individuals. Having said this, some people have still had a brief moment in the limelight during more recent years, for example:

- Ehud Tenebaum, aka The Analyzer, an Israeli hacker who was arrested for hacking into U.S. Department of Defense systems in 1998.
- Matthew Bevan and Richard Pryce – aka Kuji and Datastream Cowboy, two British hackers involved in hacking systems at the U.S. Air Force's Rome Labs in 1994.
- David L. Smith – the author of the Melissa macro virus in 1999 (see Chapter 5).
- Onel de Guzman – the alleged author of the Love Bug worm in 2000. Guzman was charged but then released and all charges dropped. (Again discussed in Chapter 5.)

However, the media attention that was focused upon these individuals, and others like them, quickly died away and their names did not create a really lasting impression. Having said this, the same is not always so true of the things that they were responsible for. Creations like Back Orifice, Melissa and the Love Bug are now landmarks in the history of IT security and these names may be recognized even if the names of the persons responsible are not.

In terms of ongoing celebrity figures, the closest are probably individuals like Sir Dystic, a member of the hacking group Cult of the Dead Cow, whose name frequently crops up as a spokesperson for the hacker cause in news reports and at security conferences. The name of Eric Corley (aka Emmanuel Goldstein) is also another one that occurs fairly frequently, but not on the basis of criminal hacking activities. Corley's role is again more as a spokesman for the hacker community and related issues such as freedom of information. In terms of out-and-out cyber criminal activity, no single figure has emerged in recent years to rival those discussed previously. In fact, at the time of writing, the media is still rather preoccupied with Kevin Mitnick's activities – despite the fact that he has not actually hacked anything for over six years. He is still cited as the archetypal hacker figure.

The potential downside of such focused attention is, of course, that other potential hackers may look at what individuals like Mitnick and Poulsen have done and perceive them as something of a role model. In spite of the fact that they had to endure prison sentences, both Mitnick and Poulsen have (from a certain point of view) ultimately done rather well as a result. Both have achieved a level of celebrity within the computer security field and both have been able to pursue related employment in the area on the basis of their past hacking exploits.

SUMMARY

This chapter has covered a wide range of issues relating to who hackers are and why they do what they do. One of the main points that comes out of the discussion is that, while the term "hacker" is often used quite liberally, the people to whom the label is applied are by no means all the same. Although there is certainly some evidence to substantiate the underlying stereotype that has emerged, there are also a number of distinct sub-categories that can be defined, which are closely linked to the motivations of the individuals involved.

The discussion has also illustrated that, contrary to the impression that is commonly presented, hackers are not all isolated loners. They are often members of a wider community, with groups, publications and gatherings dedicated to their interests. Moreover, with the existence of materials such as the *Hacker Manifesto* and the *Hacker Ethic*, there are obvious indications that, for many people, hacking is not just something that they *do*, but more like a way of thinking about both technology and society in general. Again, however, it is not possible to generalize and say that all hackers subscribe to these beliefs.

Hackers' views of themselves are often quite different from those of us that observe their actions or, indeed, find ourselves the victims of computer crime. Nonetheless, their activities can be seen to hold a fascination for a wide variety of people, leading to the emergence of the hacker as a celebrity figure in both fictional terms and in real life. In this sense, it is clear that the mystique or the power of hacking is attractive to an audience beyond those who are directly involved.

Having said all of this, an issue that has not yet been addressed is how hackers manage to get themselves into systems in the first place. This, in turn, raises the questions of what forms their attacks may take and why, when the problem of hacking is known about, such attacks are still successful. These issues are the focus of the next chapter.

Delving deeper – what hackers do and how they do it

THE PREVIOUS CHAPTER FOCUSED UPON PEOPLE WHO HACK AND WHY they do it. As the title suggests, this chapter proceeds to present more specific information about what hackers actually do and the methods by which they achieve it. However, in order to keep the material at a level that should be appreciable to a general audience, it will not look in any detail at the technical stages involved in any particular type of attack. It will instead present overview information about different forms of attack that are commonly encountered and the tools that can be used to facilitate them. Consideration will also be given to factors that frequently assist hackers in their endeavors, such as systems that continue to run older, more vulnerable versions of software. Finally, the discussion will illustrate that the attack methods employed are by no means of a purely technical nature – a factor that may surprise those with any preconceived ideas that all hackers are technical gurus.

Getting in and staying there

Before they are able to wreak the sort of havoc described in Chapters 2 and 3, hackers must be able to get into a system and obtain an appropriate level of access. As one might expect, some systems are far easier to penetrate than others and it basically comes down to how much attention the administrators have given to security. Key questions, then, are in what ways might a system be vulnerable and how might a hacker find out whether one is a good target?

Exploiting known vulnerabilities

In a surprisingly large number of cases, hackers find success breaking into systems not as a result of their own skills and initiative, but by exploiting well-known weaknesses that have been discovered and publicized by hackers that preceded them. These weaknesses are not restricted to a single system and may actually be exploited on a myriad of computers that run the same software. As such, being able to determine whether a particular weakness exists and, if so, knowing how to utilize it, can potentially act as a passport into many systems if the hole has not been plugged.

A common form of hacker reconnaissance is to perform a port scan on a target system. This can be done remotely over the network and enables a would-be attacker to see what ports are open to accept connections. The underlying principle here is that all Internet applications are made available via specific numbered ports (ports in this context are virtual connection points rather than distinct physical sockets on the machine). So, if a user on another system wishes to access an application on a particular host, the two machines will communicate by establishing a connection on the appropriate port. So, for example, Hypertext Transfer Protocol (HTTP) – the protocol used by the web – operates on port 80, while FTP, a common protocol for file transfer, operates on port 21 and so on. There are many other port numbers, each assigned to other Internet applications and services. However, most Internet hosts will only offer a small number of the possible services and, if an opportunistic hacker wishes to target the system, he needs to know which these are. Performing a port scan will indicate which ports are active on a specific system and thereby indicate the services it is running. Armed with this knowledge, a hacker may be able to exploit known vulnerabilities.

It should be noted at this point that hackers will not necessarily try to enter a system by the front door using a normal login account. Exploiting vulnerabilities of the target system is also a very common method of entry and, having established the services that are being run, a hacker can proceed to determine whether any of them can be used in this way. Different services (and different vendor implement-ations of them) will typically offer their own particular opportunities for compromise. However, it is possible to identify classes of attack that are common to a number of services and a good example here is the "buffer overflow" attack. A "buffer" in this context is a section of computer memory set aside for storing data relating to a particular application and, in simple terms, a buffer overflow attack is one in which a hacker deliberately sends input to an application that exceeds its allocated buffer size, causing program code to be overwritten. If the hacker's aim is simply to be disruptive, then the code could simply be overwritten with other arbitrary data, with the likelihood that the system will crash as a result. However, in order to use the overflow technique as a means of compromising and gaining access to the system, the hacker could be more creative and construct the input string such that it contains new executable code – which would then be executed in place of whatever the program originally did. So, by inserting their substitute code, the hacker has a foot in the door, with the opportunity to instruct the system to do their bidding. What the code can then do will strongly depend upon the nature of the program that has been compromised. A key point is that the replacement code will run with the same access rights and privileges as the original program and in many cases the targets of buffer overflow attacks are system services – running with full system access privileges. The consequence here is that any malicious replacement code will inherit virtually unrestricted access, with the capability to do anything within the system that an administrator could do. In this sense, the approach offers more potential for a hacker than compromising a normal login account, as most users would not have a sufficient level of privileges to enable access to the most sensitive parts of the system.

In truth, systems should not be vulnerable to buffer overflow attacks at all – if a program has been properly designed and implemented, with appropriate consideration for security issues, then it will incorporate suitable checks to ensure that the inputs it accepts cannot exceed the available buffer space. In reality, however, many programs simply do not do this and, indeed, various network applications and services have proven themselves to be vulnerable to this type of attack over the years and the problem can crop up in all sorts of places. As an example, the following quote is taken from a Microsoft Security Bulletin released in 1999 and relates to a vulnerability that was identified in the Windows NT Help system:

> The Windows help utility parses and displays help information for applications. The help information is contained in files of several types . . . and is stored by default in the WINNT\help folder. By default users can write to this folder. An unchecked buffer exists in the Help utility, and a help file that has been carefully modified could be used to execute arbitrary code on the local machine via a classic buffer overrun technique.[113]

This is an example that Microsoft themselves identified and rectified before anyone had managed to misuse it, with the bulletin claiming that there had been no reported incidents in practice. In other cases, however, buffer overflow vulnerabilities have frequently been used to facilitate system infiltration. For example, unchecked buffers that existed in early versions of the Unix *talk* and *finger* services were exploited to enable the remote penetration of network-based systems.[114] The *talk* service allows two users to participate in a text-based chat session, while *finger* allows someone to find out details about another registered user ID. The buffer vulnerabilities actually existed in the daemons* for the respective services (namely *talkd* and *fingerd*), both of which ran with root (i.e. full) privileges – thus they are examples of cases in which any substitute code would have enjoyed complete access to the system.

In hacking and security circles, taking advantage of a buffer overflow vulnerability is an example of an *exploit* – a general term for any unauthorized act that makes

---

* Despite the malicious-sounding name a daemon is *not* a classification of malware. The term actually refers to a program that runs transparently at the operating system level and remains dormant until invoked by the occurrence of specific condition(s).

use of a weakness in the system. However, this is far from being the only form that an exploit may take and there are many other categories that can be identified. An organization that has taken a key role in monitoring such vulnerabilities is the System Administration, Networking and Security (SANS) Institute – a collaborative forum through which system administrators and security professionals can share their knowledge and experience of security problems and related issues. Working in collaboration with experts from industry, academia and government, SANS has identified a list of the top ten Internet security vulnerabilities, a summary of which are presented below. It should be noted that a number of the vulnerabilities relate to specific implementation issues within systems software or utilities and, therefore, the exact nature of the flaws and how they may be exploited would not be meaningful to non-technical readers. For this reason, the descriptions in the list are limited to a fairly minimal level of information, but are still sufficient to indicate the general class of problem. Technical readers interested in obtaining more specific detail are referred to the full descriptions issued by the SANS Institute.[115] The key point is that each of these vulnerabilities can lead to successful exploits on the part of an attacker.

1. BIND vulnerability
   BIND (Berkeley Internet Domain) maps Internet hostnames (e.g. freeserve.co.uk) to underlying IP addresses (e.g. 141.163.169.32). Older versions of BIND have known security holes that hackers can exploit to determine the names and IP addresses (plus possibly operating system and machine type) of all the machines within an organization's internal network. Given this knowledge, they are in a more informed position to mount an attack on a specific system.

2. CGI Scripts
   Common Gateway Interface (CGI) is a means of displaying and reading input from forms on web sites. Web server systems typically come with example scripts to illustrate how to use them. However, because these scripts are not intended to remain on live systems, they often overlook security considerations.
   Consequently, hackers with knowledge of the standard examples are sometimes able to exploit them as a means for gaining wider system access or attack other sites if they have been left on an operational server. Unnecessary and unsafe CGI scripts should, therefore, be removed from systems to remove the risk of exploitation.

3. Remote Procedure Calls (RPC)
   RPC allows a program to be activated remotely from another system. This is often necessary in client-server network configurations, but many older RPC systems have vulnerabilities that can be exploited to enable full system access to be gained by unauthorized users. Therefore, if RPC is enabled, the latest patches should also be in place.

4. Microsoft IIS Remote Data Services
    Web sites operating on Windows platforms will typically use Microsoft's
    Internet Information Server (IIS) as their server software. However the Remote
    Data Services (RDS) component within IIS was originally vulnerable to buffer
    overflow attacks, which can allow a hacker to gain full control and remotely
    issue commands to the server. This allows all manner of unauthorized activity,
    including altering web content, disabling the server and recording keystroke
    data.

5. Sendmail vulnerabilities
    Originally designed as a graduate programming project, Sendmail has become
    the *de facto* standard for Unix-based email servers. However, its origins mean
    that security was never a prime concern and over the years it has continually
    been the subject of fixes and upgrades. The problem is the program runs with
    root (i.e. full) privileges and, therefore, if its security holes are exploited,
    Sendmail can be used to do anything else within the target system. Many
    systems unfortunately run (and are even still shipped with) older, unpatched
    versions of the program.

6. Sadmind and mountd
    Sadmind runs on Sun's Solaris operating system and allows an administrator to
    remotely administer systems on a network. Mountd enables remote file sharing
    on Unix-based systems. Early versions of both programs were vulnerable to
    buffer overflow attacks, allowing hackers to gain root access on the target
    machines.

7. Global file sharing
    File sharing between users is a useful feature of networked systems. However,
    it is possible to misconfigure the facility and inadvertently allow access to
    individuals outside an intended group. In today's context, network file sharing
    could potentially allow access by anyone on the Internet, leading to the risk of
    information being copied or modified on the local system.

8. Password mismanagement
    Passwords are the standard form of user authentication on most systems and
    yet classic problems exist in which accounts have either not been allocated a
    password or the password remains unchanged from a known "factory default"
    (e.g. the standard account used by maintenance engineers on Digital's VMS
    system was called "FIELD," with the default password "SERVICE"). Hackers
    know the defaults and will try them as a first line of attack. Systems are,
    therefore, vulnerable if they have not been changed.

9. IMAP and POP vulnerabilities
    IMAP and POP are email protocols that allow email access from anywhere on
    the Internet. Firewall systems (which are designed to block unauthorized and

unwanted Internet traffic) will usually allow these services to pass through and, therefore, if the email server software is not robust, hackers may use these protocols to bypass the firewall and reach the internal network.

10. SNMP vulnerabilities

SNMP is used to monitor the performance, status and availability of a network and can be used by administrators to remotely manage interconnection components such as routers and bridges. Although SNMP nodes are password protected by so-called "community strings," these are often left at the well-known default value of "private." In this scenario, hackers are able to take control of devices, shut them down or reroute the flow of network traffic. The integrity and availability of network access can, therefore, be put at risk.

In many cases (such as the Sendmail, Microsoft IIS, POP, and BIND flaws) the vulnerabilities are easily rectifiable, and appropriate patches have existed for some time – it just relies on people to install them. In some cases, the continued existence of unpatched vulnerabilities is not for want of trying by the vendors of the associated software. Microsoft, for example, has issued repeated advisories in relation to the RDS problem. It first became apparent in June 1998 and the company had issued a patch by the following month. However, the vulnerability (and the exploitation of it) remained in many IIS installations and continued to do so despite the company releasing subsequent advisories in both July 1999 and July 2000.[116]

The issue of vulnerabilities, and why they may remain unpatched, is one that will be returned to later in the chapter.

Owning a system

When a system has been successfully hacked, it is said to have been "owned" by the hacker(s) responsible for the attack. Having been owned, the computer and its contents are vulnerable to a number of undesirable eventualities. Although in some cases, hackers may simply be content with having beaten the security, there is often likely to be an objective beyond just getting in. Such potential objectives are many and varied, but could well include one or more of the following:

- Defacement of materials (particularly likely if the system is a web server, as highlighted later in this chapter) – typically including clearly visible messages stating the hacker's claim to have "owned" the system. If the motivation for penetrating a system is merely to acquire the associated bragging rights, then the more people who can see you've done it the better.

- Theft of information or software. This may be material that is proprietary to the targeted organization or just material for which the owned system represents a convenient source.

- Use the owned system as a cover for nefarious activities. If the activities are then traced, they will be traced back to the hijacked system rather than the hacker's own. Such activities may take many forms, including attacks on other systems, libelous emails, sending of threats and distribution of viruses. It may then be left to the legitimate owner(s) of the hijacked system to prove that they were not responsible.

- Utilization of the system as a storage repository, into which the hijacker may then place warez (pirated software) or other forms of undesirable or illegal material. As an example of this, in February 2001, a hacker from Sweden was discovered to have gained access to systems at Indiana University and used them as a repository for distributing gigabytes worth of MP3 music files. The university became aware of the misuse of their system when the amount of network activity dramatically increased as a result of other users downloading the files.[117]

- Outright destruction ("trashing") of content on the system. This is unlikely in most cases, but could be encountered in cases where the perpetrator is an immature script kiddie or where the motivation for the attack is revenge related.

Such eventualities are all undesirable and clearly some form of protection should be put in place to reduce their likelihood of occurrence. In order to do this, however, it is necessary to appreciate how they might originate. So how do hackers get into the position of being able to own a system in the first place? What techniques are employed to enable the system to be penetrated?

Using rootkits

In order to be able to claim true ownership of a system, a hacker must seek to obtain the highest available level of access privileges available within it. In all systems, this is the level granted to the system administrator, which is also commonly referred to as "root" privilege – the name being taken from that of the associated user account on Unix-based systems. Securing root access is a valuable prize and, as a result, a common tool in the hacker arsenal is something called a "rootkit." However, contrary to what its name may suggest, a rootkit is not used to enable a hacker to obtain root privilege – it is designed to help him to keep it.

Most hackers will typically gain their initial access to a system via a fairly low privilege account – such as one belonging to a standard user. Root access will then be obtained via the exploitation of a known system vulnerability (an issue that will be discussed in more detail later in this chapter). Having obtained root privilege (an accomplishment that is often more easily said than done), the hacker will not be keen to lose it and so requires a means of safeguarding their acquisition and hiding traces of their existence. Without this, the legitimate system administrator would soon be likely to notice abnormalities and batten down the hatches.

A rootkit assists by providing the means for a hacker to exploit his root privileges, while at the same time helping to hide his activities. All rootkits consist of several different programs, typical elements of which will include:

- Network sniffers, to enable the capture of network traffic such as passwords;
- Backdoors, provided by hacked versions of software such as the system login process, which provide the hacker with a convenient route back into the compromised system;
- Logfile cleaners, to remove traces of hacker activities from the system logs;
- Support programs to enable the concealment of hacker files and processes.

The last item here bears some further explanation. Such support programs will come in the form of hacked versions of operating system commands, which could otherwise betray the hacker or the rootkit's existence. For example, the Unix command *ps* (process status) can be used to list all active processes within the system. If rootkit components such as sniffers or log cleaners were running, then the command would ordinarily reveal their presence, alerting a legitimate system administrator to the penetration. A rootkit will, therefore, install a hacked version of the command in order to enable illicit activities to be hidden. Other commands can also be substituted in this way, such as *ls* (the command to list files in a directory), which can be modified so as not to reveal the existence of the hacker's files.

Rootkits are a recognized problem and, in response, other tools have been created (for system administrator use) to enable their detection. An example is a utility called *Tripwire,* which monitors the integrity of the system by looking for changes to key files (such as the commands mentioned above). It creates a database storing details such as the size and cryptographic checksums of the files to be monitored (a cryptographic checksum is analogous to an unforgeable fingerprint calculated from the contents of a file – any change to the content will mean that the checksum value will change). Any changes resulting from the installation of a rootkit will, therefore, be noticed when the system compares the current files against the database values. Such approaches are not foolproof, but can significantly reduce the vulnerability to rootkit utilization.

Note that a rootkit represents a classic example of a Trojan Horse – a category of malicious software that is described in more detail in Chapter 5.

Common forms of attack

In addition to well-known vulnerabilities that are targeted across many systems, there are also a number of general classes of attack that have proven to be particularly common. This section considers two particular examples of such attacks – namely web site defacements and denial of service – that occur very frequently in the Internet environment. The discussion then moves on to consider the fact that it is not always easy to be certain about what is going on and, in some cases, what seems like an attack may actually be something different.

Defacing web sites

With the increasing popularity and adoption of web technology by all manner of companies and organizations, the web has proven itself to be a rich target for hacker activity. The defacement of web sites represents a category of attack that has become very popular in the last four to five years, and is one that falls quite literally under the heading of vandalism implied by the title of this book.

Defacing a web site enables hackers to leave their mark in a very visible manner. While such an attack does not necessarily result in any breach of privacy, financial loss or even significant disruption to activity in order to overcome the problem (restoring the original page(s) from a backup will fix the damage, albeit without rectifying the security weakness that originally enabled access), it does have the potential to cause significant embarrassment to the affected organization. In addition, to the casual observer who logs into the site during the period in which it has been affected (or who subsequently hears reports about it in the media), the nature of the breach may look more significant. Even if the organization concerned does not hold its sensitive or business critical information on the same machine that houses the web server, Joe Public may not *realize* this. It may, therefore, be instinctively assumed that if, for example, the CIA's web site has been hacked, then all manner of secret intelligence information has also fallen into the wrong hands.

Survey results from the FBI and the Computer Security Institute (CSI) in the U.S. suggest that vandalism is the most common form of web-related security incident. In their 2001 survey, 23 percent of the 509 organizations that responded to the question indicated that their web sites had suffered some form of unauthorized access or misuse within the previous year. Of these, seventy-eight respondents were prepared to be more specific about the type of incidents they suffered and, in 90 percent of cases, they were found to relate to web site vandalism.[118] Further statistics that illustrate the increasing scale of the problem can be found on the web site of Attrition (**www.attrition.org**), a non-profit security watchdog group that has maintained an extensive catalogue of defaced pages. Figure 4.1 illustrates the total number of web site defacements reported per year, from 1995 to 2000 (as well as the total number observed up until 17th May 2001). It is clear that the problem has increased dramatically in the last couple of years, illustrating that once a technique gets known about, any sites that have not been afforded adequate protection are increasingly more likely to become victims. Numerous high-profile organizations have suffered such attacks, including the CIA, the U.S. Department of Justice, the U.K. Labour Party, the *New York Times*, and online auctioneers, eBay. Some of these, and some other examples, will now be considered and illustrated.

The U.K. Labour Party's web site was hacked in December 1996, as a result of a gathering in which fifty or so hackers set themselves a number of hacking targets to achieve. Defacing the Labour site was one such target. The attack involved the alteration of text and images on the site. For example, the image of party leader Tony Blair was replaced with a puppet of him, as used in a now defunct U.K. satirical show called *Spitting Image*. The pictures of other members of the shadow cabinet were replaced with pictures of The Muppets. The main banner on the site was changed from "new Labour. new Britain" to "new Labour. Same Politicians. Same Lies." In addition, extensive alterations were made to the text elements of the site. The result can be seen in Figure 4.2. The attack was claimed to be the beginning of a campaign of "socially responsible hacks," under the banner "hacking to be heard."[119] The main impact in this case was probably one of embarrassment on the part of the Labour Party.

A similar incident occurred around five months after the Labour Party hack, when the web site of the U.K. Conservative Party (who were then in government) was defaced by a group calling itself the Circle of Deception.[120] The text on the site was modified to offer the hacker's opinions about the government and also included the full text of the *Hacker Manifesto*. The image of the party leader, John Major, was altered to show him pictured in front of a swastika. The attack was again politically motivated and designed to cause embarrassment to the government.

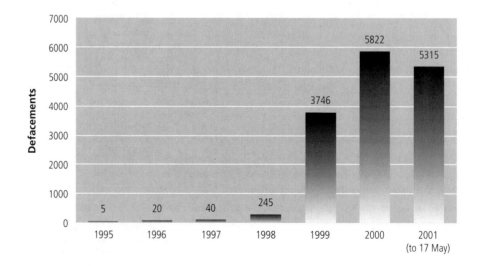

FIGURE 4.1 Annual web site defacement totals
(SOURCE: **http://www.attrition.org/mirror/attrition/annuals.html**)

In mid-September 1998, the *New York Times* web site fell victim to an attack by a hacking group calling itself HFG (H4CKING F0R GIRL13Z – an example of hacker-speak that translates to "Hacking for Girlies"). The attack was conducted in support of the then imprisoned hacker Kevin Mitnick. As can be seen from the figure, the resulting page contained some text written by the hackers, along with an image of the HFG logo, which itself incorporated partial photos of naked women. The site was affected for around twelve hours, during which time it was largely unavailable. In the initial instance, visitors to the homepage experienced variable results – some getting the intended *New York Times* version, while others got the HFG replacement (the latter prompting complaints from subscribers). As the day went on, attempts to access the site simply resulted in error messages, until it was restored to normal in the early evening. The overall effect was, therefore, a visible attack on a high-profile site.

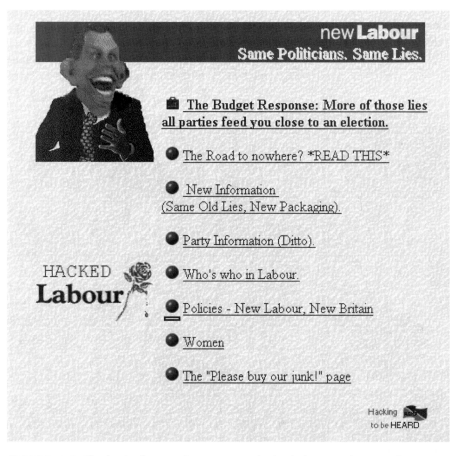

FIGURE 4.2 The hacked U.K. Labour Party web site (6th December 1996)

As the screenshot in Figure 4.3 shows, the hacked page made specific (and not very polite) reference to *New York Times* reporter John Markoff, a journalist whose columns for the *Times* had included a specific focus on the Mitnick case. HFG's view was that Markoff had become guilty of a conflict of interest. As a significant reporter of the Mitnick affair, he had been in a position to influence the public perception of the case, helping to shape the view of Mitnick as the number one hacker threat. He subsequently co-authored the book *Takedown* with security expert Tsutomu Shimomura (whose name is also mentioned in the HFG text) and then sold the film rights to it. In HFG's view, he was therefore capitalizing on the attention that he had given Mitnick in his earlier reports. The more general issue of media influence in relation to computer crime will be discussed in Chapter 6.

As well as the *New York Times*, the HFG hackers also attacked other web sites at around the same time period, leaving similarly modified homepages in their wake. The victims here included NASA's Jet Propulsion Labs, *Penthouse* magazine, the official MC Hammer web site, and a couple of sites belonging to Motorola. Archived copies of all the pages mentioned above can be found on the Attrition site (see **http://www.attrition.org/mirror/attrition/1998.htm**).

A more recent high-profile target was RSA Security inc., one of the main names in security products and research, which was hit in February 2000. The details of this

FIGURE 4.3 The hacked *New York Times* homepage (13th September 1998)

incident are somewhat different to the others described here, in that the content of the RSA web site itself was not altered – what actually happened was that traffic heading for the **www.rsa.com** address was redirected toward another system, which then presented a spoof version of the RSA site. However, anyone typing RSA's address into their browser would not have noticed the redirection, and so would have assumed that RSA had been directly hacked – so, in terms of perception, the end result was effectively the same as a standard defacement. The spoofed site is illustrated in Figure 4.4. The fact that RSA, a major supplier of security solutions, was hacked represents a significant scalp for the hacker (which was, of course, the motivation), and quite possibly a concern for customers of RSA's security products. If the company's own security cannot keep the hackers out, why should anyone else rely on their products? In reality, of course, RSA's site itself had not been breached, and the incident had no implications for the security of the company's various encryption and e-commerce solutions. The problem, however, is that the public may again not have appreciated any distinction.

FIGURE 4.4 The spoofed RSA Security web site (February 2000)

In late November 2000, a similar fate also befell web sites belonging to Network Associates, another notable name in the security industry and a supplier of products including anti-virus, secure email, and network analysis software.[121] The sites attacked were those relating to the Network Associates' Brazilian operations, and were actually hosted by a Brazilian ISP rather than the company itself (so, from a public relations perspective, Network Associates could rightly claim that its own systems were not actually penetrated). The activities were limited to the defacement of web pages, but from the hacker's perspective this was sufficient to consider that they had scored points against one of the industry big guns.

There are many more examples that could be cited (and more are occurring every day), but the cases above are considered sufficient to illustrate the nature of the problem. For those readers who wish to see more examples, the aforementioned Attrition site also has a vast range to look at. Having said this, by May 2001, the scale of the defacement problem had become so great that the Attrition team was no longer able to keep up with it. An advisory posted on the site explained that maintaining the defacements mirror had become "a near 24/7 chore,"[122] and that a single day could involve mirroring over 100 defaced sites. This, as they observed, was more than three times the total for 1995 and 1996 combined, and the task was too much for the small number of volunteers who were essentially running Attrition in their spare time. As a result of this, and the fact that hosting the resource had made Attrition themselves the targets of abuse and attacks, the decision was taken to discontinue the maintenance of the mirror. For interested readers, an alternative site can be found at **http://defaced.alldas.de**, which holds a mirror of defaced sites dating back to January 1998 and (at the time of writing) continues to be maintained.

In the documented cases, the web sites have been attacked and defaced in order to make a point. In some cases, this point may amount to little more than saying "ha ha, we own your site," whereas in others the objective may have been an attempt to draw attention to a more significant issue. In either case, the aim of the endeavor is to leave a visible message, and the breaches are discovered largely because the nature of the change is so obvious. However, the same techniques have the potential to be used for more insidious forms of attack, with information being modified in a more subtle way, in order to intentionally mislead the readers. Such changes could take much longer to be noticed than cases where hackers effectively advertise their presence all over a site's homepage.

In addition, although it was observed at the beginning of this section that organizations would not generally keep sensitive or business-critical information on the same machine as the web server, this is not always the case. For example, in June 2000, the U.K. Internet Service Provider Redhotant was hacked in order to expose security holes. The hacker in this case was an IT consultant, who claimed that he was acting in the public interest. He was able to break in with relative ease and allegedly gained access to Redhotant's customer database – containing details of more than 24,000 subscribers to their Internet service (including credit card information).[123] The lesson to be learned here is that there should be a physical separation between the system that runs public-facing web sites and those that hold sensitive information.

Denial of service

The previous section highlighted that vandalism and defacement are the most common forms of web-based abuse. Second in the rankings, according to the same CSI/FBI survey source, is denial of service (DoS) attacks – which the survey indicated were experienced by 78 percent of the respondents who disclosed the nature of their web-based security incidents. DoS attacks are popular with novice hackers, in the sense that they do not require any significant skill to implement (indeed, numerous tools are available to automate such attacks in software), but can nonetheless have dramatic and noticeable effects.

The principle of DoS attacks can be explained using a simple and well-known example, namely SYN Flooding, which takes advantage of a particular way in which Internet communications operate. The Internet is based upon a communications protocol called TCP/IP (Transmission Control Protocol/Internet Protocol). At the start of a TCP/IP communications session, the two machines wishing to communicate perform a handshaking operation, the purpose of which is to establish that both machines are willing and able to exchange data. The process begins with the originating machine (the *client*) requesting a connection to a system with which it wishes to communicate (the *server*). This is achieved by sending a SYN (synchronize) message. If the server is willing to accept the connection, it will respond with a SYN+ACK message to acknowledge the request. At this point the connection is termed "half-open." To fully open the connection, the client must respond with its own acknowledgment message (ACK), which indicates to the server that its message reached the destination. At the end of this exchange, both systems are assured that they are able to send and receive each others messages, and can begin passing data relevant to the service required (e.g. web browsing, file transfer, etc.). This handshaking process is illustrated in Figure 4.5.

Persons with malicious intent are able to exploit this process, by sending numerous SYN messages to a target server, but then not responding to the resulting SYN+ACK. This leaves the server connection in a half-open state. The problem with this arises from the fact that systems have a finite buffer for accepting connections, which will ultimately be filled up as more fake requests are received and then left half-open. The half-open connections will ultimately timeout and be cleared if they do not receive the ACK message necessary to complete them. However, new connection requests can easily be sent in such a way as to arrive more quickly than the existing half-open ones will timeout. This will ultimately overload the system, filling the connection buffer and preventing any further connections from being accepted.[124] Overloading of this nature does not prevent the target system from continuing to make outgoing network connections (nor, indeed, does it affect any incoming connections that are already in progress). However, there may be indirect effects as a result of the attack, and in some cases the system may run out of available memory or crash.

A number of strategies can be employed to combat attacks of this nature, but unfortunately none of them can completely eliminate the risk. A simple solution involves increasing the permitted number of half-open connections (by increasing the queue length) and reducing the timeout period. As such, false connections are cleared out more quickly, while also giving more opportunity for legitimate requests to be serviced. However, this approach also has its downsides. Increasing the queue allocation can result in large amounts of memory being required, while reducing the timeout can adversely affect remote users on slow links (whose legitimate connection attempts could timeout before their systems have responded). In any case, SYN flooding is far from the only category of DoS attack and subsequent methods have become substantially more sophisticated. For instance, the February 2000 incidents that targeted Yahoo!, eBay, Amazon, and others were examples of *distributed* DoS (DDos) attacks. A DDoS attack involves hiding software daemons on hundreds of computers, which then bombard other Internet sites with thousands of requests for information (the sites hosting the daemons typically do so unwittingly, the programs having been installed via stealth methods). As with traditional DoS attacks, the volume of incoming traffic serves to paralyse the target web sites. The distributed attack is more difficult to combat, as the malicious traffic comes in from many sources and, in addition, the daemons can give false addresses in their network packets, making them even harder to trace.

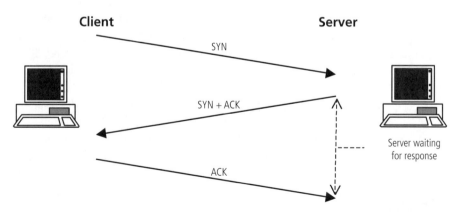

FIGURE 4.5 TCP/IP handshaking procedure

A further problem with DoS attacks is that the ability to launch them is now a feature of several cracker toolkits, such as HackTek (an issue that will be considered later in this chapter). Given that they can be automated in this way, the staging of such attacks does not require any skill or expertise on the part of the hacker (making them ideal for use by script kiddies). Indeed, it has been conjectured that around 90 percent of hacking is conducted by people using such methods.[125] This, of course, gives no cause for comfort – in the DoS context, the ease of the attack does not relate to the damage and inconvenience that can result.

Raising false alarms – a practical experience

The sheer range of companies and organizations now represented on the Internet and the web offers a significant number of high-profile targets for potential attackers. The example of the denial of service attack in February 2000 (previously highlighted in Chapter 2) provides evidence of the danger and, as a consequence of such reports, many organizations are sensitive to the threat of Internet-based attacks and take measures to guard against them. However, success here relies upon being able to accurately detect the signs of an attempted attack in progress and, as the next section illustrates, it is not always possible to reliably differentiate between attacks and other forms of network activity.

The risk of causing unintentional security alerts was illustrated during the course of a PhD research project within the author's research group. The project itself was unrelated to security but, nonetheless, one particular experiment resulted in attacks being perceived by other systems on the Internet. The experiment that caused the problems was intended to measure the average lifetime of a hyperlink on the World Wide Web. The discussion below summarizes the implementation of the experimental system and the aspects that served to cause problems. Some elements of the discussion are necessarily technical, but details have been generalized where possible (a more comprehensive description can be found in a related journal paper on the topic[126]).

In order to determine the average lifetime of a web link, it was necessary to collect a large sample of links at random. Each link would then be tested periodically, and the date and time would be recorded if and when the link failed (i.e. the resource pointed to by the link could no longer be found). The intended experiment comprised four different stages:

1. Compile a list of random servers.
2. From this list, compile a list of random web links.
3. Periodically determine the state of each server.
4. Periodically determine the state of each link.

However, only the first stage was ever reached, as several unanticipated side effects caused two unintentional security incidents to occur, which in turn forced the experiment to end prematurely. The side effects were a direct result of the design of stage one of the experiment interacting unpredictably with a server's firewall.

In stage one, a list of random web servers had to be compiled. This was achieved by randomly generating an Internet address and then attempting to connect to a web server at that location. If a response was received, the server's address and domain name were recorded as belonging to a web server. If no response was received, however, the machine was pinged* in order to determine whether the randomly chosen address was valid at all. If a response was received, the machine's Internet address and domain name were recorded as belonging to an Internet server (for potential use in another part of the experiment). If no response was received from the ping, then the address was noted as being dead, and played no further part in the study.

Although the experimental software was tested locally, it became apparent that the procedure was resulting in perceived security problems and, during the course of two months, two formal complaints were received from organizations whose systems had been randomly targeted. The details of these incidents, and the remedial actions that were taken, are described in the paragraphs that follow.

- Security incident one

  Figure 4.6 contains the text of an email received from the administrators of one of the randomly selected systems. It should be noted that elements of the figure have been edited to preserve the anonymity of the specific machines involved at the authors' site and of the affected remote domain (as such, organizational name references have been deleted and address elements have been replaced with "xx" where appropriate).

  From the perspective of the remote system, the activity of the program was considered to be comparable to that of port scanning tools (described later), which attempt to determine the Internet services that a remote system is running. However, in the context of the experimental study, the use of port 137 (the NetBIOS name resolution service) was not something that had been explicitly included in the program. It was, in fact, the default behavior exhibited by Windows NT Server (the operating system that was used for the experiment) when called upon to resolve an Internet address.

---

* Ping (Packet INternet Groper) is a useful program that lets you verify that a particular Internet address exists and can accept requests. However, although Ping and its associated messages are intended to be used for diagnostic purposes, they can also be used to mount a basic attack on a remote system by sending repeated Ping requests so as to overload the remote machine (causing denial of service for legitimate users). As such, many sites are now wary of accepting Ping messages.

Further, the "pinging of many addresses" (ping sweep) that was detected listed just two IP addresses that were pinged. Both addresses were selected completely at random, and were not part of the same sub-net, nor even looked as if they were remotely related. It was an unfortunate coincidence that both were pinged at the same time, and both happened to be owned by the same organization.

- Security incident two
The experiment was remounted, with NetBIOS support disabled on the originating NT system, and the ping configuration altered such that each ping packet had a timeout value of 1 second, and at most only six packets would ever be sent to one machine. The experiment was restarted, and for a time all went well. In fact, 700,000 different addresses had been tested over a period of two weeks, when a second incident occurred. Figure 4.7 presents the email message received in this case (note that the Internet addresses listed have again been altered in order to hide the identities of the machines involved).

The unfortunate situation in this case was the fact that the incident reported differed greatly from the behavior of the experiment under testing. 338 ping messages were allegedly received in five seconds, when the code was explicitly written to send only six. Indeed, the network traffic generated by the experiment had been extensively monitored before the experiment was restarted to ensure that no more than six packets were sent to any one machine. However, the email reported 338 such messages. Whether this was a fault in the experiment or in the firewall on the remote machine that reported the incident is impossible to determine, as further dialogue with the "victim" was not feasible.

```
We have detected unfriendly network activity, directed at our
machines, from xx.xx.xx.xx [xx.xx.xx.xx.uk]. The activity, which
began at 19:04 EDT (GMT-0400) on October 27, 1999 was a port scan
(137) and pinging of many addresses in our subnets (xx.xx.xx.xx,
xx.xx.xx.xx).

This type of activity is not desired on the [Deleted] domain and is
monitored frequently. Please advise your system managers and users
that this activity should stop immediately.

_____ -

[Deleted]
Computer & Network Security
```

FIGURE 4.6 Email received concerning first perceived intrusion

In both cases, the receipt of the complaint was immediately followed by corrective action and a written explanation of the experimental context. This was considered satisfactory and defused the possibility of further action. However, following the second incident, the decision was taken to discontinue this element of the research study.

Reflecting upon the experiences, it could be argued that in the first incident, the remote firewall software used was a little overzealous. The "incident" comprised one name resolution request to port 137, one HTTP request to port 80, and several ping messages on two separate servers with widely differing Internet addresses. It is debatable whether this should be considered to represent a threat. It should also be remembered that a contributing factor in the first incident was that the experimental software performed an unexpected task (i.e. a NetBIOS call) as a consequence of asking it to perform an intended function (i.e. a name resolution). In a sense, it

```
Intrusion Attempt Report


We have noticed the following behaviour originating
from IP addresses under your control:

ICMP denial of service attempt

The activity took place at approximately:

Dec 7 03:07 GMT

We consider this/these unauthorized attempt(s) to access
our networks as malicious in nature and hereby request that
you take steps to identify the person(s) involved and
arrange for this activity to halt immediately.

Here are some samples of the activity in question:

03:07:41.035397 xx.xx.xx.xx    xx.xx.xx.xx: icmp: echo request
03:07:41.036032 xx.xx.xx.xx    xx.xx.xx.xx: icmp: echo request
03:07:41.038980 xx.xx.xx.xx    xx.xx.xx.xx: icmp: echo request
03:07:41.039568 xx.xx.xx.xx    xx.xx.xx.xx: icmp: echo request
03:07:41.042556 xx.xx.xx.xx    xx.xx.xx.xx: icmp: echo request
03:07:41.043138 xx.xx.xx.xx    xx.xx.xx.xx: icmp: echo request

338 instances in 5 seconds

We further request that you reply back to us with the
Resolution achieved in this matter.
```

FIGURE 4.7 Email received concerning second perceived intrusion

could therefore be argued that the program author was the victim of an inadvertent Trojan Horse effect. Without this prior action occurring, it is possible that the respondent organization may not have perceived the subsequent pings to be part of a hostile attack.

In the second incident, ping messages were only sent for five seconds, which intuitively would not suggest that a Denial of Service attack was intended. It could be argued that this might have been an initial assault, designed to overload the firewall system and thereby enable exploitation of some other vulnerability. However, the fact that no further activity would have been apparent from the source machine should have provided an indication that this was not the case.

In both incidents, the ping feature had been disabled by the firewall (a relatively standard practice, which is intended to guard against ping-based DoS attacks). This meant that the experiment continued sending ping requests in an attempt to determine whether the randomly chosen Internet address was a live server or not, while the firewall silently monitored the requests, yet did not respond. In the absence of a response, the experimental software was unintentionally entrapped into appearing as a security threat. With hindsight, however, it can also be argued that, from a security perspective, the practical approach taken by the experimental study was ill conceived. To select an Internet address at random and then attempt to determine the state of the server can be seen to have the potential for mis-interpretation by a security conscious organization. From the organization's perspective, such a stream of traffic would have no obviously legitimate purpose and, therefore, by default would be regarded as suspicious. However, the fact that only two organizations flagged a problem during the period of the experimental study (during which over 700,000 random addresses were targeted in this way), gives a very strong indication that organizations are not monitoring their security to a consistent degree. If it is argued that the two complainant organizations were correct to interpret the network activity as attacks, then it could also be considered that the other organizations were failing in their network security strategy. This assertion must, of course, be offset against the fact that different organizations will be dealing with systems and data of different levels of sensitivity and, therefore, in some cases, the required level of security may legitimately be lower. Having said that, it is unlikely that in such a large sample only two organizations had data that they would consider sensitive.

In conclusion, it can be argued that all parties involved in the practical incidents described emerged as losers from their experiences. The researchers were unable to proceed with a potentially interesting experiment, while the remote organizations had effectively wasted resources in responding to false alarms. Before leaving this topic, it is useful to consider the question of how the security incidents would have been viewed if they were actually caused intentionally. Without doubt the launching of a ping-based denial of service attack would be viewed in a negative light and could easily result in criminal proceedings if the perpetrator were traced. However, the acceptability of an intentional and unauthorized port scanning of a remote system is a more contentious issue. Certainly, many system administrators adopt a similar policy to the organization that responded in incident one, viewing the scan as a hostile act. However, there has been at least one legal ruling (by the Norwegian Supreme Court) stating that probing of systems on the Internet, using techniques such as port scans, should not be considered illegal.[127]

Getting the tools to do it for you

One of the frequent benefits of information technology is that it can help to make complex tasks easier to perform by automating certain elements. Unfortunately, it is also possible to identify scenarios in which the automating properties of technology can be used to undermine the technology itself. An example here can be cited in terms of the identification and exploitation of computer security vulnerabilities. Although this was once the sole province of individuals with the appropriate technical skills, the ability to assess the protection of a system and, potentially, take advantage of any weaknesses identified, it is now frequently encapsulated within software tools that are publicly available on the Internet. Although the motivation of these tools is often to provide system administrators with an automated means of checking their systems, the public availability of the tools makes them an attractive facility for hackers with less benevolent intentions. Furthermore, a number of tools and pre-written attacks (often referred to as exploit programs) have been released by the hacker community itself, providing not only the means to automatically identify a vulnerability, but also to take advantage of it, to the detriment of the target system.

Chapter 2 discussed the distributed denial of service attacks that affected numerous systems in February 2000. Media reports at that time frequently mentioned the names of the tools that were suspected to have been used to mount the attacks (e.g. Tribal Flood Net, Trinoo, and Stacheldraht). Although this added to the completeness of the reports, it could also be argued that it provided a potential lead for those interested in conducting such attacks themselves. In possession of the names of the tools, an interested user could then do a web search and locate them for download fairly quickly (e.g. the author attempted an Infoseek search for "trinoo" and obtained a downloadable file after following two hyperlinks from the initial search results). This is not to say that the tools would then be instantly usable by a total IT novice – many of the distributions are program source code files, which a potential user would need to have the required knowledge and facilities to compile before use. However, the technical prerequisites here are significantly reduced when compared to the knowledge required to mount a comparable attack from scratch.

This section considers the threat posed by such automated analysis and attack programs. It begins by summarizing the evolution of such tools and then presents an overview of the different categories that can now be identified. The potential threat is then analyzed by considering the use of the tools by the hacker and system administrator communities. The latter aspect is supported by the results of a questionnaire study that attempted to assess administrators' awareness and use of the available software. The discussion concludes by considering the different approaches that may be used to control the problem.

An overview of analyzers and exploit programs

The concept of automated attacks can be traced back to programs such as password crackers and war dialers (the roles of which are summarized in Table 4.1), which have been around in some form since the early days of personal computing. The difference then was that the distribution of such programs (if indeed they were distributed at all) was quite limited. If a hacker had the need for such a program, then he would probably have had the skill to write one for himself – an upfront investment of skill and effort in order to reduce the level of mundane activity required later. It can also be noted that these tools were used to locate and assist in gaining entry to systems, rather than automating the exploitation of some vulnerability. Having gained access to a system, it would be down to the hacker's own creative talents to determine what happened next. This is in no way meant to applaud the hacker's subsequent actions or to suggest that they were any more legitimate because the hacker performed them without further programmatic assistance. The point is that the overall potential for damage was less because fewer people had the required knowledge and skills at their disposal to discover and exploit obscure vulnerabilities in operating system software and the like. With such knowledge now encapsulated in all manner of scripts and exploit programs, this is no longer the case.

Password crackers and war dialers take advantage of inherent characteristics of the implemented systems (i.e. that an alphanumeric string can be broken by brute force and that it is possible to distinguish between voice and data traffic) rather than exploiting unforeseen vulnerabilities. Some of the programs available today are in marked contrast to this, having been established specifically to identify and/or exploit bugs in software or potential holes in a security configuration for malicious intent. These newer tools provide the ideal platform for opportunity hackers – those who do not have the skill to break into a system themselves and may have no particular target in mind, but will happily attack a system if the vulnerability is there and the means is provided.

One of the first programs of the new breed to attract public attention was the Security Administrator's Tool for Analyzing Networks (SATAN), written by Dan Farmer and Wietse Venema and released in 1995. SATAN is a network-based vulnerability scanner that has the capability to identify a range of potential security weaknesses, including:

- systems that allow password file access from arbitrary hosts.
- systems in which remote shell access is possible from arbitrary hosts.
- FTP (file transfer) servers in which the home directory is writable by anonymous users.

The argument behind the public release of the tool, which is common to several others, is that the problems it can identify are not a secret. They have been documented in various sources, including advisories from organizations such as CERT (Computer Emergency Response Team) and CIAC (Computer Incident Advisory Capability), as well as in security handbooks. As such, the information necessary to exploit them is easily available for those with an interest in doing so. The question is whether putting it all together in an automated system is simply making it too easy (whereas obtaining the required information from documented sources and then manually using it to target systems at least required some effort and understanding). Of course, the authors of SATAN were not ignorant of its potential for misuse, as illustrated by the following quote from their Frequently Asked Questions web page:

> We realize that SATAN is a two-edged sword – like many tools, it can be used for good and for evil purposes. We also realize that intruders (including wannabees) have much more capable (read intrusive) tools than offered with SATAN. We have those tools, too, but giving them away to the world at large is not the goal of the SATAN project.[128]

It should also be noted that, although SATAN detects and reports vulnerabilities, it does not actually exploit them. Furthermore, it offers tutorial explanations of the problems and what can be done to rectify them – reinforcing the point that it is offered from the perspective of assisting the administrator in strengthening the system rather than for use by a hacker to disrupt it. Nonetheless, SATAN's release was met with a mixed reaction from the IT and security industry, with many expressing the view that it was inviting trouble.[129] The choice of name was, of course, hardly helpful in promoting a safe image either.

SATAN falls into the category of vulnerability scanner and there are now various other tools of a similar nature. In addition, there are several other categories of tool that may also be of use to both system administrator and hacker communities. Table 4.1 presents a summary of these, indicating some of the better-known examples of available programs in each case. There are, of course, some other categories of program that have no legitimate security analysis purpose whatsoever, for example the aforementioned denial of service tools. These programs have clearly been

TABLE 4.1 Categories of security analyser tools

Category	Description	Example programs
Vulnerability scanners	A program that can probe a network and identify systems connected to it. Once identified each system is investigated to assess its susceptibility to attack. Typical vulnerabilities may include known weaknesses or bugs within operating systems, Internet servers or application software.	Titan SATAN SAINT SARA
Remote administration	A program that allows a user to remotely monitor and control a target system. If used by a hacker, the program may be installed via stealth methods (e.g. as a Trojan Horse). The remote user may be able to capture passwords, download/alter/delete files, access emails and even corrupt system files.	Back Orifice 2000 NetBus BackDoor-G SUB7
War dialers	A program that dials a list of telephone numbers either in sequence or randomly. Once a modem carrier tone is detected the phone number is logged for further investigation.	Toneloc PhoneSweep
Port scanners	A program that probes specific systems (or a range of network addresses) and identifies the Internet services that they are running (e.g. web, file transfer and emails servers). Once a port is identified it may be possible to exploit known weaknesses of a service or determine further information, such as the target operating system, which may reveal further vulnerabilities	Nmap Strobe Ncat
Sniffers	A program that enables the capture of all network traffic transiting the machine on which it is located. This can be used to directly grab plain-text passwords (e.g. as sent by programs like email clients) or to gather encrypted versions for later cracking. Sensitive data may also be captured from other forms of network traffic, such as email messages.	Ethereal Supersniffer WinSniff tcpdump
Password crackers	A program that attempts to break an encrypted password string. Passwords are gathered in an encrypted form, either from a copied password file or by eavesdropping on the network. Once captured, the program can compare the encrypted string against a dictionary of pre-encrypted words to find a quick match. Failing this, a brute force attack attempting all combinations can be launched.	Crack John The Ripper L0phtCrack

created with a malicious intent and it is not possible to offer even the shaky defense of legitimacy that can be given for other hacker-originated tools. Their only use to system administrators is in running a self-test to ensure that a system is not vulnerable to such attacks.

With many of the tools identified in Table 4.1, the problem is not so much that they exist, but that they are so freely available. Why should the average Joe, with no system to administer, be permitted to have the same access to a vulnerability scanner as someone responsible for IT assets worth thousands of dollars? Making scanners freely accessible is analogous to saying that anyone should have the freedom to go around and try the doors and windows of your house, and be free to determine whether or not you have left them properly secured.

An open invitation to hackers?

Having established the range of tools available, the discussion will now proceed to consider their relative merits in practice by assessing the extent to which hackers and administrator audiences can make use of them. In relation to the first group, it could be argued that if a technically competent hacker wishes to get into your system, then he/she will be able to do so regardless of assistance from analyzer and exploit programs. One of the main concerns, therefore, is how greatly these tools open up the playing field for relatively unskilled novices. Although some tools still require a fair level of technical competence to install, run and interpret their output (enough at least to scare away the casual newbie looking for a quick result), others provide a truly automated, point and click approach to assessing and exploiting vulnerabilities (effectively enabling anyone to go around doorknob rattling on potential target systems). The use of such methods would generally be frowned upon by the hackers of the previous generation. To quote John Draper (Cap'n Crunch):

> True hackers don't learn from books. They work with very little information and go out and find things on their own, instead of learning it from someone.[130]

The ease of current tools can be illustrated by considering the use of a program called Back Orifice 2000 (BO2K), which provides a means for remote administration of a target system (Back Orifice is chosen as an example here as it has been around for some time and to show the process of attack, therefore, reveals nothing new. In addition, most security conscious organizations should already be protected against it via standard malware-detection software). BO2K is the latest incarnation of the Back Orifice tool that was originally launched in 1998 at the DEF CON hacker convention in Las Vegas. The name was a pun on Microsoft's BackOffice suite (which, at the time, was the company's collective name for its range of database, messaging and network servers) and, indeed, the program was specifically intended as an attack against the (in)security of Microsoft's offerings. As briefly mentioned in Chapter 3, it was written and released by the hacking group Cult of the Dead Cow (cDc), whose allegation was that, in its attempts to make PCs easy to use, Microsoft had neglected the issue of security and left significant holes that could be exploited. Back Orifice was designed to provide an illustration of this and, at the time of its release, was described by its author (a cDc hacker known as Sir Dystic) as an attack on Windows 95. However, to the computer novice or the technophobe, the fact that Microsoft has made its systems easier to use is hardly something that it seems reasonable to criticize the company for. Indeed, in an ideal world, systems would be easy to use and should not *need* security, as everyone could be trusted to behave themselves. In making their point, and making the software freely available, the cDc has illustrated exactly why security is necessary in the first place.

The Back Orifice 2000 tool consists of two main elements, a client application and a server application. The client, running on one machine, can be used to monitor and control a second machine running the server. The use of BO2K, therefore, requires that the server program be installed onto each target machine. This could be done explicitly by an administrator wishing to use it to conduct remote administration duties, but it more typically arrives as a Trojan Horse, attached to an email message or similar, and relies upon installation by an unwary end user. Once installed, anyone with the other half of the BO2K software (the administrator tool) can control the victim's PC from anywhere on the Internet. The remote user can surreptitiously do a multitude of things to the victim's machine, some examples of which include.

- executing any application on the target machine.
- logging keystrokes from the target machine.
- restarting the target machine.
- locking up the target machine.
- viewing the contents of any file on the target machine.
- transferring files to and from the target machine.
- displaying the screen saver password of the current user of the target machine.

The cDc promotes BO2K as a legitimate remote administration tool – their web site describing it as "the most powerful administration tool available for the Microsoft environment, bar none."[131] However, while the above features could conceivably be of use to a system administrator wishing to remotely monitor and control a machine within his/her network, it can also be seen that the facilities would represent a significant security risk if placed in the wrong hands. cDc hacker Count Zero consequently defends the tool as follows:

Back Orifice is a powerful tool, and yes, it can be easily used for malicious intent. But that's true of ANY powerful tool . . . software, hardware, machines . . . and it doesn't mean BO should not have been released. Should all knives be outlawed because they're used to commit crimes?[132]

From a certain perspective he is right of course. It is possible to utilize a great many useful tools – in computing and other domains – for dangerous and malicious purposes. What the above sentiments overlook, however, is the fact that the risk of this occurring can be minimized by ensuring that the tools are appropriately designed and distributed. Consider, for instance, Count Zero's example of knives. No, you do not outlaw the use of them but, at the same time, there are many kinds of knife – some more dangerous than others – and you do not freely hand out machete knives to people if you simply want them to be able to eat a meal. It is a question of fitness for purpose. The point here is that BO comes endowed with capabilities that invite misuse and several of its features suggest that it is by no means limited to a legitimate role. For example, one would expect that a legitimate remote administration tool would only be installed by the system administrator responsible for the associated machine. So, a clear problem in the case of BO2K is that someone else can distribute it using stealth methods. Furthermore, BO2K supports some additional capabilities that were not present in the original version of the tool. These include the abilities to remotely activate microphones and cameras on the target system – enabling direct monitoring of the remote environment. Unlike the features listed above, these are unlikely to be features that a genuine administrator would wish to utilize. From the perspective of a mischievous or malicious attacker, however, they provide a significant opportunity to invade the privacy of the remote user. The BO2K web site includes a statement about the product's legitimacy and acknowledges that script kiddie hackers have previously used the Trojan Horse capabilities as a means of damaging systems. However, it goes on to describe the risk as "a fact of life with a tool that has the ability to be silently installed."[133] What it does not acknowledge, however, is that BO did not have to be endowed with this capability to enable its effective use as a legitimate system administration tool.

There is a tutorial on the BO2K web site that provides a user with step-by-step guidance for installing the application and configuring both the client and server elements. Furthermore, there is an automated installation wizard that minimizes the amount of the user interaction required to initially set-up the application. As such, the installation of the program is certainly not beyond the capabilities of a novice user. The simplicity is further illustrated by the user interface that is presented when running the application. This allows commands to be issued to the server via simple mouse and menu interactions, as illustrated by the anonymized example in Figure 4.8.

To again quote Sir Dystic, speaking in relation to the original 1998 release of the tool:

We made the software easy enough for an eight-year-old to hack with and we think it could do serious damage.[134]

These sentiments again do little to support the wisdom of the cDc's cause. In fact, the impression is quite the contrary, and allowing the open availability and free distribution of the tool seems highly irresponsible. Furthermore, the fact that it is Open Source (i.e. the underlying program code is made available for inspection and modification) means that appropriately skilled misusers can easily add further undesirable features and create their own custom version if they wish to. The cDc's accompanying claims that the program also has a role as a legitimate remote administration tool are, not surprisingly, seldom seen as the most prominent points about the software. In fact, almost everything about the tool – its origins, its name and its surreptitious method of distribution – suggest that its legitimate use is the last thing that was intended or expected.

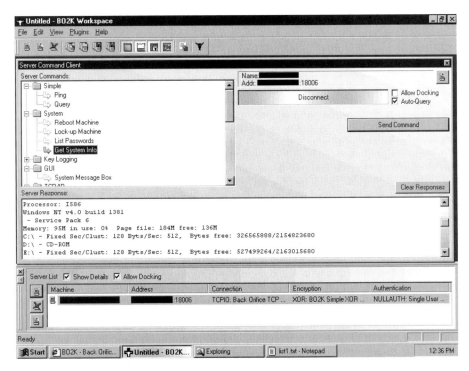

FIGURE 4.8 The Back Orifice 2000 administration tool

Back Orifice is by no means the only example of a tool that has arisen from the hacker community as a potentially double-edged sword. The last chapter made reference to the hacker group L0pht Heavy Industries and their password-cracking tool L0phtCrack. As previously observed, password crackers are not, by definition, a bad thing and can actually be used to improve security. An appropriately authorized system administrator could use them to determine whether any users had selected weak passwords and were, thereby, leaving their account and the wider system vulnerable to compromise. In this context, the program would be more accurately described as a password-auditing tool. In the wrong hands, however, the same tool could be used to facilitate unauthorized entry.

Originally released in April 1997, L0phtCrack was not the first example of an automated password-cracking tool (the Crack utility for the Unix operating system had appeared several years earlier), but it was one of the first to target systems running Windows NT. At the time, NT was Microsoft's flagship corporate-level operating system, and the only offering in its range that claimed to offer anything substantial in terms of security, so the emergence of a tool specifically targeting the NT platform was considered noteworthy.

L0phtCrack offers several mechanisms for actually obtaining password information. The first is to get it from the registry of the target machine – which can be done locally or over the network if the user running the program has sufficient privileges. The second approach is to take a copy of the SAM file* of the target machine – which, again, requires appropriate access to the system in order to make a copy. The final method is to packet sniff the local network and grab password data as it is sent between machines (e.g. when a user makes a connection into another machine on the network). With this approach, it is possible to cast the net a bit wider and capture password information from other users within the same organization. However, capturing the raw password data is not the end of the story – the whole reason for needing a *cracker* is that the information is encrypted rather than being stored or transmitted in clear-text. The role of the tool, therefore, is to find strings of characters that, when encrypted, produce a matching value to the captured password. The tool, again, supports a number of techniques in this respect. The first is a straight-forward dictionary-based attack. Here the captured password values are compared against a set of pre-encrypted common possibilities – in L0phtCrack 2.5, the version tested by the author, this dictionary contained 29,156 entries. If a user has selected one of these as their password, it will be found very quickly. This is followed by a hybrid attack, which targets cases in which users have taken a common dictionary word and simply added on some additional characters in the hope of making them less vulnerable to attack (e.g. passwords such as "apple23" or "route66"). The final

---

* The SAM (Security Accounts Manager) file contains the encrypted user account information, including passwords.

avenue of attack is a brute force approach, whereby every possible character combination is tried until a password match is found. By default, L0phtCrack uses just alphanumeric characters (A–Z and 0–9) in its search, but it can be configured to try a range of special/punctuation symbols as well for cases where more secure passwords have been chosen.

As with Back Orifice, the tool presents a clear, easy to use, menu-driven interface and it is very simple to install and get the password cracking underway within just a couple of minutes. The operation of L0phtCrack is shown in Figure 4.9, which illustrates the process of cracking passwords obtained from a local system registry. As well as the simple interface, a number of other factors can be observed to explain what is going on in the figure:

- the target system has five registered user accounts: Administrator, Guest, and three others that have been anonymized in the figure.
- of these, all but the Guest account have passwords.
- the Administrator account has a short password (less than eight characters) and was actually decoded within seconds during the dictionary attack phase.
- the cracking has now progressed to the brute force phase (trying all possible character combinations) and is operating at a rate of almost 1.8 million tries per second.
- the characters remaining to be cracked are shown as "?" symbols – as the cracking process proceeds, these are gradually replaced by the actual characters from which the passwords are comprised.
- a few characters of the remaining passwords have already been determined and the program estimates that the process will be complete in another twelve and a half hours.

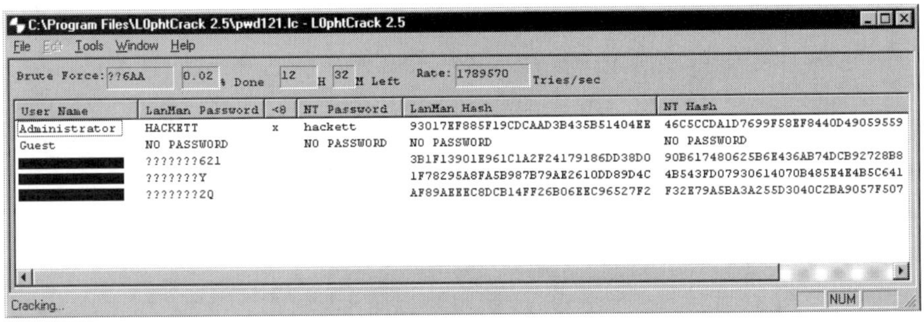

FIGURE 4.9 L0phtCrack password cracking

The time taken to crack the passwords will depend upon how well the users have selected them. Passwords based upon common words, and consequently found in the program's dictionary, can be cracked within minutes. If a brute force attack is required, then the speed will depend upon a number of factors, including the lengths of the passwords that users have selected (longer passwords take longer to crack) and the range of characters that they have incorporated into them (e.g. passwords containing just alphanumeric characters will be found quicker than those that also contain some punctuation characters, as fewer character combinations have to be tried). A further factor is the speed of the machine running the program. The accompanying documentation suggests that a brute force attack run on machines with processors ranging from Pentium 166 to Pentium II/450 should take between twenty-four and seventy-two hours.[135] Current machines are much faster than these, so the cracking time is also considerably reduced.

From this discussion it can hopefully be appreciated that L0phtCrack represents a fairly powerful tool and it could well be seen as a danger if placed in the wrong hands. So what was said about it when it was released? Here is an example:

> If you have an NT network, and you have that network connected to the Internet, you're in deep trouble.[136]

This kind of observation might well be expected to have come from a security expert commenting upon the threat posed by the program. In actual fact it comes from Mudge, one of the authors of the tool, speaking at the time of its launch. He went on to say that "the next version is going to blow Microsoft out of the water." These statements suggest a great deal about the probable motives behind the program and indicate that the preservation of security was not the overriding priority. As with Back Orifice, the desire to have a stab at Microsoft appears to come across as the more pressing objective. Nonetheless, it can perform a useful security function and system administrators do commonly use it (or similar tools) for the purposes of auditing their users' password choices (as some survey results presented later in this chapter will illustrate). In addition, although it could represent an asset to hackers, it must also be pointed out that L0phtCrack does not go as far in assisting them as something like Back Orifice. For example, it cannot be installed somewhere by stealth methods like BO2K, and a user requires an "administrator" level privilege in order to run it on a target system. As such, in order to be able to use L0phtCrack, the hacker has to have a good level of access to the system beforehand, or to have obtained a copy of the password file by other methods in order to run the cracker on his own system.

As an aside, it can be noted that as well as producing its own tools, the L0pht group also produced add-on enhancements for the cDc's Back Orifice program (it is worth remembering at this point that the membership of these two hacker groups overlapped). For example, L0pht produced BOTool, a so-called "Professional Plug-in" that enabled users to more easily view and edit the Windows file system and registry, via a graphical interface. Their claimed rationale, of course, was to improve BO's potential as a remote system administration tool, rather than to further simplify the task for crackers wishing to use it to compromise other systems.

Returning to a general level of discussion, it can be conjectured that a significant barrier to the illicit use of such tools is not only the moral standpoint but also the fear of getting caught. If presented with the necessary means to mount an attack, as well as a 100 percent guaranteed assurance that they would not be found out, it is likely that many more users would consider taking the opportunity to indulge in some form of mischief. However, in the past, in order to scan or probe a remote machine for vulnerabilities, it was necessary to do so from your own system – introducing the possibility that the attempt would be traced if the target site was vigilant regarding its security. Although accomplished hackers could employ means to cover their tracks and hide their location, novices would not have this capability. Recently, however, the landscape has changed and there are now web-based tools available that enable the security of remote sites to be scanned via an intermediate web server. The consequence of this is that, from the perspective of the target system, the scan is coming from the web server system and cannot be so easily traced beyond that. Therefore, the attacker is able to remain anonymous, shielded behind the web server that performs the scan on his/her behalf. An example of such a web-based vulnerability scanner was reported to the Windows NTBugtraq mailing list on 14 August 2000.[137] The posting was made by Daniel Docekal, the editor of Czech IT newspaper *Svet Namodro* and concerned vulnerabilities identified in web sites running on Microsoft's Internet Information Server and using Active Server Page (ASP) technologies. The message explained that, as a result of the bugs, people could potentially gain access to password information, source code of scripts, and database files from the affected servers. The possession of such information could then open the way for a more significant breach of security. In order to enable the easy identification of the vulnerabilities, an automated tool was made publicly available on the *Svet Namodro* web site. Although the intention was to allow concerned administrators to test the vulnerability of their servers, the completely open availability of the tool was effectively a security risk in itself, enabling anyone to go to the site and enter the URL of a server that they were interested in scanning. The page did caution users to only use the tool against their own servers and applications, but this clearly would not have prevented them from doing otherwise. The site also claimed to log IP addresses to enable any misuse to be traced. However, this issue may be clouded where people connect to the server via an ISP, in which IP addresses are normally assigned dynamically for each session. In addition, it assumed that either the target site or the *Svet Namodro* server could determine that misuse was actually occurring. Reports suggested that Docekal was appalled that thousands of sites were still vulnerable several days after the test had been made available.[138] However, this may be a somewhat naïve assessment, as it tends to assume that the administrators of the aforementioned sites are all subscribers to the NTBugtraq list or a similar information source that may also have picked up the story. In addition, as later discussion highlights, there are a variety of reasons why system administrators may not be able to respond to security issues as quickly as one may hope or expect.

Other web sites offer what could be considered a more secure scanning service, whereby you can log in and get the server to scan the security of the client machine that your connection originates from. This is still useful from the perspective of an administrator or a security-conscious end-user, in that it allows their own system security to be assessed, while preventing an assessment of any third party's security from being made (thereby removing the potential to assist in attacking someone else). Examples of such services are:

- Shields Up! From Gibson Research Corporation (see grc.com), which enables the Internet connection security of Windows-based systems to be analyzed.
- HackerWhacker (see hackerwhacker.com), which enables the scanning of TCP and UDP ports, SMTP email server vulnerabilities and web server CGI weaknesses.

Both services output a report, indicating any potential weaknesses that are identified and are advantageous in determining the baseline vulnerability of a system. The details can be gathered without having to breach the security of the target system or spy on it for a prolonged period. Furthermore, the same level of information is effectively available to *anyone* who can determine the target machine's Internet address and so these tools can give administrators an insight into what hackers will also be able to see. The downside is that, with the analysis locked to the machine from which the user is accessing the web site, the administrator would be forced to move from machine to machine in order to check multiple clients on a network. The wider issue of administrator use of security analyzer tools is discussed in the next section.

Analyzers as tools for system administrators

In order to investigate the extent to which system administrators are aware of and utilize analyzer tools, a questionnaire was devised and distributed to fifty IT managers (the names of the organizations contacted were obtained from databases of the top 100 companies according to a *Financial Times* survey). Although the responses were anonymous, the response rate was expected to be very low due to the sensitive nature of the subject matter. The survey yielded a total of twelve usable responses (24 percent of those contacted), while several further companies replied that they were "unable to divulge any information on this subject for security reasons." Table 4.2 summarizes the extent to which administrators were aware of different information sources for security vulnerabilities.[139]

The respondents were also asked to indicate their awareness and use of different categories of analyzer tool, with specific examples being indicated that can be freely obtained from the Internet. Table 4.3 summarizes the results in relation to this issue.

A significant point that can be immediately observed from the results is that, in all but one of the cases, less than half of the respondents are aware of the specific tools listed (and, in many cases, the proportion of awareness is nearer to a third or less). Even allowing for the fact that security may be only one of their responsibilities,

TABLE 4.2 Administrators awareness of security information sources

Source	Awareness (%)
Web pages	66
Microsoft security alerts	50
Bugtraq or other mailing lists	58
Internet newsgroups	66
Internet Relay Chat channels	58
Magazines (*Phrack*, *2600*, etc.)	41

TABLE 4.3 Administrator awareness and use of specific tools

Category	Tool	Awareness (%)	Use (%)
Vulnerability scanners	SATAN	41	25
Remote administration	Back Orifice	66	8
	NetBus	41	8
	BackDoor-G	8	0
Port scanners	Nmap	41	25
	Ncat	16	16
	Strobe	25	0
Sniffers	NTSniff	25	0
Password crackers	Crack	33	0
	L0phtCrack	41	33
	Ntcrack	33	16
	John the Ripper	25	0

one would instinctively expect administrator awareness of tools such as password crackers and vulnerability scanners (which have received a fair degree of attention in the computing press) to be higher than that suggested. Comparing the results in Table 4.3 with those from Table 4.2, it must be questioned whether the relatively high percentages that claimed to be aware of web and newsgroup information sources are actually using them effectively.

It can be observed that, in the vast majority of cases, the proportion expressing awareness is substantially higher than that in which the tools are actually used. In some cases, this can probably be explained by the fact that administrators are aware of tools that are not appropriate to their own systems (e.g. a Windows NT administrator may be aware of SATAN, but unable to use it as it requires a Unix platform). In other cases, such as Back Orifice and NetBus, one would not routinely expect system administrators to make use of them, other than to possibly evaluate their capabilities and the level of threat that they represent.

When considering the survey percentages it is important to remember that they are based upon a small sample group and, therefore, they may not be fully generalizable to a larger audience. However, as will be seen from the discussion below, there are a number of reasons that would also suggest that low awareness and usage figures should be expected.

The argument is often offered that making tools with security analysis capabilities publicly available is a valid means of improving security, as system administrators have an equal opportunity to download and utilize them for defense as hackers do for attack. However, the general consensus amongst the respondents was that the hacker community was getting more benefit from the freely obtainable tools than the administrator audience. Indeed, although the equal availability argument is theoretically true, the practical situation is quite often not as clear-cut as might be implied. The following factors should be kept in mind:

- Hackers have a greater level of motivation to obtain and utilize the tools, as doing so will directly assist their cause. For a system administrator, the use of an analysis tool has the potential to increase their workload if problems are exposed that need to be followed up. This is likely to act as a disincentive, particularly if they already have a significant workload.

- For system administrators, security will be only one of their responsibilities and, therefore, will only command a proportion of their available time. Conducting routine maintenance tasks and responding to user-related issues are likely to represent significant jobs in themselves. The most likely security issues to receive attention are password management, data backup and anti-virus measures. Some of the constraints are discussed in more detail below.

- Hackers may get to learn about the availability of new tools quicker than system administrators. The nature of hacker communities means that word may spread amongst them. By contrast, system administrators are more likely to find out about new tools via formal sources than by word of mouth. Their best chance of quick notification is likely to be via a security-related email list or discussion group, but administrators are only likely to be members of such lists if they are already reasonably well attuned to security.

As a result of these constraints, administrators sometimes take a step that may, upon first inspection, appear rather strange – namely, hiring in hacker expertise to target it against their own systems. As will be discussed further in Chapter 7, this expertise will normally come in the form of what are termed ethical hacking services (offered by so-called White Hat hackers). These are basically the good guys, who have the skills to break a system, but are only using them in order to help improve security. However, in some circumstances, the administrator may find a Black Hat (bad guy) hacker offering to help instead.

Why do vulnerabilities persist and what can be done?

Even though many exploits are based upon vulnerabilities that have been known for some time, the problem is a difficult one to keep on top of. The issue is not so much the availability of technical solutions to the vulnerabilities identified, but the administrative overhead involved in actually addressing them. Many software makers routinely release patches that enable known bugs and vulnerabilities in their products to be rectified – in some cases this happens before particular weaknesses have become publicly known, while in others it is in response to a problem being reported. As a result, the situation in many cases is that simple maintenance activity by system administrators is all that would be required to plug the holes. However, despite this, the problems clearly remain. The SANS Institute has identified several reasons why this may be the case:[140]

- 1.2 million new computers are added to the Internet every month.
- there is a lack of security experts to address the problems.
- the number of vulnerabilities continues to grow and there is no priority list for dealing with them.

These are not the only problems. The frequency with which new security vulnerabilities are reported can have the effect of desensitizing people to the dangers involved. Elias Levy, a moderator for the Bugtraq vulnerability mailing list, offered the following opinion at the same time that a new weakness was discovered in Microsoft's Internet Explorer 5.5 web browser:

> The security holes happen so frequently that people are now starting to gloss over them.[141]

From the system administrator's perspective, the main requirement is to ensure that the system remains operational and available – this is what the users expect and complaints will quickly occur if this is not the case. So, unless installing a patch is explicitly required in order to maintain system availability, the task is likely to be given a lower priority. Indeed, looking at the number of warnings that are issued, it is easy to see how administrators might downgrade the importance of responding to them immediately. The problem of volume can be illustrated by considering the security bulletins issued by Microsoft in relation to its product range (e.g. operating systems, Internet servers and application programs). When vulnerabilities are identified, the company works to develop a solution and then issues an advisory bulletin when a software patch or upgrade is available for download. The graph in Figure 4.10 summarizes the number of such bulletins issued per month, between January 1999 and March 2001.[142] Obtaining the bulletins is easy – they can be accessed on Microsoft's web site or they can be emailed directly to registered users as they become available.

It can be seen from the graph that the number of security bulletins issued ranges from two per month up to eleven per month (the average was seven per month over the twenty-seven month period). This might not be so bad if the associated patch was being installed on just a single system, but in some cases an organization's IT and network configuration may dictate that the administrator must go around and update a number of individual systems in turn (which could obviously become time consuming). In some cases, the number of systems may run into the thousands, whereas the administration team may number less than ten. Relating this to the average of seven patches per month (and assuming ten administrators and 1000 machines, each requiring all patches), this could lead to

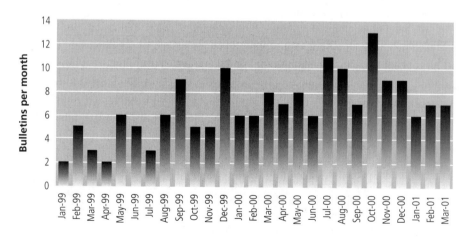

FIGURE 4.10 Microsoft security bulletins (January 1999 to March 2001)

each administrator having to patch about twenty-three machines per day. It should also be remembered that these bulletins are only those related to Microsoft products. Where an organization's IT set up is based upon a heterogeneous, multi-vendor configuration, security advisories from other sources would also have to be taken into consideration. It has been estimated that as many as 100 new software vulnerabilities may be reported each month.[143]

So, in view of all this, it can be appreciated that administrators might start out with good intentions, responding to each advisory as it arrives. However, this could quickly become burdensome and so the decision may be taken to batch them up and respond to them on a less frequent basis. Although this makes good administrative sense, it is less sensible from a security perspective. Once an advisory has been issued, the information about the associated vulnerability is available to anyone – and any hackers who were not aware of it before will certainly have access to it from then on. As such, any systems in which the weakness has not been addressed are exposed to a greater level of risk than before the advisory was made.

The risk of publicizing new vulnerabilities too quickly is recognized by the U.S. government's Computer Emergency Response Team (CERT). Although the organization publicly discloses details of all software vulnerabilities and flaws that are reported to it, this is not done immediately upon receipt of a confirmed problem. Instead, CERT allows the developers of the associated software a forty-five-day grace period in which to rectify the issue (e.g. by releasing a patch), before making a public announcement. This approach is good in the sense that responsible software companies should have been able to provide a solution for their users by the time the majority of would-be exploiters then get to know about the vulnerability. However, this still does not overcome the problem of organizations and administrators being unaware of the patches that are released or not having sufficient time to deal with them.

So what is the effect of not installing the available fixes? According to Attrition.org, 99 percent of the 5,822 web site defacements that occurred during 2000 were as a result of failures to patch known vulnerabilities for which the fixes were already available.[144] The actual number of defacements went up 56 percent, from the previous figure of 3,746 reported or uncovered in 1999. A further interesting estimate in favor of installing patches comes from the Honeynet Project (**http://project.honeynet.org**), which suggests that almost 80 percent of unpatched servers would not survive for more than three weeks before being compromised in some way by Internet attackers. Despite this, Alan Paller, the director of research at the SANS Institute, does not feel that the problem of vulnerabilities and exploits will disappear:

> The exploits will always be there and be growing. When the vendors take
> responsibility for making sure their customers actively know about the vulnerabilities
> and make updates as easy as anti-virus updates, we'll all be a lot safer.[145]

A number of options can be considered as potential top-level responses to the threats posed by automated analysis and attack tools as a whole. Unfortunately, it is quite easy to identify potential flaws in each case.

- Criminalizing the illegal use of security analyzers and vulnerability scanners. This is essentially the approach taken as part of the Draft Convention on Cyber-crime, proposed by the Council of Europe[146] (discussed further in Chapter 6). Article 6 of the Convention relates to "Illegal Devices" and prohibits the unauthorized creation, distribution and use of programs that may assist in illegal access, system interference, etc. However, this proposal has caused concern in the security community, as it will also cause difficulties for those wishing to conduct legitimate activities to identify and overcome weaknesses in their own systems.[147] The key issue that the Convention is seeking to address is clearly the *illegal* use of such tools. However, if the distribution of the tools is restricted to prevent hackers from getting hold of them, how are legitimate administrators meant to do so?

- Payment-based availability. Having to pay to obtain the tool is likely to be a disincentive to the casual hacker. However, given the scale of software piracy, it is very unlikely that this would be a barrier for long and cracked copies of desirable tools would be circulated in warez communities.

- Making the accessibility of the tools registration-based, such that users have to provide personal details before downloading them. This is already the case with some tools, such as L0phtCrack. Unfortunately, of course, there is nothing to stop people providing bogus information or, indeed, from still using pirated copies.

- Incorporating technical restrictions into the tools. For example, only enabling a vulnerability scanner to target machines in the same network domain – to limit the potential for misusers to scan remote systems. However, this still cannot eliminate internal misuse of the tools within an organization.

The flaws identified mean that, while these measures may help to reduce the problem, none of them represent a complete solution. It can also be observed that these methods will only apply in cases where tools originate from sources that are motivated by improving security. Where tools originate from the computing under-ground, the opposite motive is more likely to be true, so the considerations above would become irrelevant.

When considering each of the tool categories separately, the possible counter-measure options are clearer. For example:

- Standard anti-virus software is able to detect the presence of code relating to systems like Back Orifice and NetBus.

- Other software can be used to detect the activity of vulnerability scanners. For example, Courtney and Gabriel were two tools that could be used to detect and monitor SATAN probes (see http://ciac.llnl.gov/ciac/ToolsUnixNetMon.html). Such functionality is now a feature of modern Intrusion Detection Systems. Alternatively, attention can be diverted away from sensitive systems via the use of honeypots (special software that is designed to fool hackers by appearing to be legitimate servers/services, while enabling their actions to be tracked without damage to real systems).

- Packet sniffers can be foiled by encrypting sensitive network traffic and/or by detecting and disabling network cards operating in promiscuous mode (a mode in which they can accept traffic destined for other systems).

- The threat posed by password crackers can be significantly reduced if an organization follows appropriate password procedures (e.g. ensuring that passwords are based upon non-dictionary words and are at least eight characters long, using a combination of alphanumeric and special characters if possible). This forces the cracker to revert to time-consuming brute force attack methods (i.e. trying each possible character combination in turn).

This suggests that, although there is not a universal quick fix for the automated attack problem, it is possible to incorporate effective safeguards against the individual categories.

The discussion above has largely considered controls that relate to the user community. It is also worth noting that a significant proportion of the tools work by making use of known bugs in operating systems, Internet servers and the like. It can, therefore, be argued that if vendors paid sufficient attention to security in the first place then such opportunities would not exist. Indeed, this is often the defense used by some authors to justify the public release of their tools (often with the accompanying intention of naming and shaming the associated vendor, to reinforce the point that action needs to be taken). For example, this was the claimed motivation with Back Orifice, where even the name was intended as a side swipe at Microsoft's Back Office suite. However, the obvious flaw in this approach was that Microsoft users, rather than the company itself, suffered as a result of the tool being shared.

So, unless dramatic changes are made, it seems probable that the problem of security vulnerabilities will not only remain, but will become worse. The reasons for this are twofold. Firstly, as new software emerges, offering more complex functionality, the potential for unforeseen vulnerabilities is almost inevitable. Secondly, the increasing proliferation of Internet systems means that computers incorporating such vulnerabilities will be more widespread, thereby offering more opportunities for automated analyzers to be used. In terms of the aforementioned dramatic changes that would help to avoid this undesirable scenario, possibly the most important is for software vendors to afford significantly more attention to security during the design, development and testing of their products. From a commercial perspective, security does not appear to be as important an investment as activities such as marketing. However, it should be recognized that attention to the issue in advance could then avoid undesirable bad publicity later, which could otherwise serve to undermine marketing efforts and product image.

It should also be recognized that even with an improved effort to focus on security, some vulnerabilities may still slip through into released products. As such, contingency measures are still needed. From the vendor's perspective, this requires fast response in order to offer a remedy, in the form of patches and upgrades. Current evidence suggests that many vendors are already responsive in this sense and do act quickly to make solutions available. Possibly the more significant aspect at this stage is ensuring a response from the user perspective. The successful misuse of vulnerability scanners and exploit programs is based upon the fact that known security holes have not been addressed – holes that have sometimes been recognized for years. It is, therefore, necessary to make the user community more receptive to the fact that software updates may be required and that, in most cases, they are already available.

Using less technological approaches

Although the previous discussion in this chapter has focused exclusively upon software-based approaches for compromising systems, it is important to note that a hacker's repertoire of skills will not all necessarily be computer-based. A number of non-technical methods are often successfully used as a means of facilitating access to systems and some examples are discussed in the sections that follow.

Social engineering

Social engineering (sometimes also referred to as "human engineering" or "gagging") relates to obtaining information or intelligence through deception. A hacker with good social engineering skills will be able to trick people into giving him confidential information or doing things on their behalf to facilitate a breach of security. Use of the techniques is by no means limited to the hacking fraternity – other people with a need to uncover confidential information, such as private detectives, may also make use of it in order to obtain something they need – but it has a history of successful use in this context. The technique relies upon a combination of helpfulness and gullibility on the part of the end user. The object of the exercise is generally to acquire information that will be of use in gaining access to a system or specific resources within it.

Traditionally, the telephone has been the main mechanism by which social engineering exploits have been mounted. The hacker will pose as someone in need of information or assistance, which the targeted user is in a position to provide. Popular roles for the hacker to assume in this context are someone from the computer support staff or a new user who is unfamiliar with the system and, therefore, in need of help. The following is an example of the former scenario, involving a fictitious dialog between a hacker and a user at the equally fictitious Barcminster Bank.

Hacker:	Good morning. I'm calling from Macrohard. We handle the IT maintenance contract for Barcminster Bank. Could you spare a few moments of your time?
User:	Yes, okay.
Hacker:	I need to do some remote administration on your systems, but I'm having problems with the service engineer login account. I need to login so that I can clear some jobs from your process queue.
User:	What do you want me to do?
Hacker:	It would probably be easiest for me to do the work, but I need to be able to login first. Could I quickly login under your account so that I can reset mine?
User:	Do I need to logout first?
Hacker:	No, that's okay. All I need is your username and password.
User:	Okay, my username is "jsmith" and the password is "apples."
Hacker:	Great. I'll login now and fix the problem. Thanks a lot for your help.

Of course, such an attempt will not always be successful and will depend upon the hacker's delivery as well as what he or she says. If the caller does not sound suitably professional and authoritative, then the user is likely to become suspicious. In addition, requesting information such as a password may well be too blatant – some users will at least be security aware enough to realize that they should not be parting with this information. As such, the shrewd hacker will often ask for more subtle elements of information that they could piece together to achieve the same ends.

If the hacker is prepared to do a bit of advance planning, the chances of success are increased. The bluff will be more convincing if they know something about the organization in which the target user is working (for example, if the intention is to pose as someone from the organization's computer supplier or Internet service provider, it is easier to do so if you actually know who that supplier or provider is). The basic reliance here is that the user will assume the caller is legitimate because they appear to be well informed. But how would you find out such information without seeming suspicious? Well, actually with relative ease. The hacker could phone up the target organization a few days in advance of the main assault and claim, for example, to be conducting a telephone survey on behalf of a randomly chosen Internet Service Provider. He could then ask a few innocent questions about who the target's current ISP is. Most users would not see such an enquiry as threatening and would, therefore, be likely to volunteer the information. In possession of this, the hacker could then phone again a few days later, claim to be from the correct ISP and then request information that could enable unauthorized access to be achieved.

An alternative to the telephone approach is to use email. Figure 4.11 gives an example of the sort of message that might be sent in order to fool the user into helping to open the door.

A few modifications could be made to the basic message in order to make it even more convincing and persuasive. For example, it could address the subscriber by name (e.g. "Dear Mr. Jones"), engendering a feeling of familiarity and, hence, greater trust on the part of the recipient. Further investigation on the hacker's part could determine the name of the local system administrator. The message could then be made to look more authentic by mentioning that he or she has been advised of the situation and supports the request.

A final example of social engineering is provided by security expert Bruce Schneier, who describes an incident in which a hacker posted flyers on a company bulletin board, purporting to provide the new help-desk telephone number. The phone number was, in fact, the hacker's own and he was then the recipient of calls from the company's unsuspecting employees, from whom he was able to social engineer passwords and other useful information in return for help.[148]

As previously mentioned, social engineering partially relies upon the gullibility of

```
Dear Subscriber

I am writing to advise you that XYZ-ISP has recently suffered a
breach of security in which the passwords of our subscribers may
have been compromised.  As a result, we have decided to allocate a
new password for each subscriber in order to avoid the possibility
of further unauthorised access.  I would therefore be grateful if
you could change to the password below as soon as possible.

Recommended new password: POLBIK23

Thank you for your co-operation.

Yours sincerely
John Smith,
System Security Administrator
```

FIGURE 4.11 Example of a potential social engineering email

users. They should, therefore, be made aware of the threat and cautioned against divulging information such as passwords or acting upon email instructions such as those above.

Dumpster diving

One person's rubbish is another person's treasure. The idea of dumpster diving is basically to go through the trash that an organization throws out, on the lookout for any information that may be useful in compromising security.

The practice originated with phone phreakers, who would go to phone company offices and trawl through skips outside the premises in the hope of finding technical information. Discarded copies of things like phone company manuals proved to be a rich source of technical information – providing more insight into potential targets and ways of manipulating them. But why resort to raiding the garbage? Typically because it may have represented the only reasonable means of obtaining the information. Most of it was not openly available and the phone company would not provide it on request. So, other than stealing it or befriending a telco employee, getting a junked copy was about the only choice. This is not to suggest that the activity is actually legal – just because something has been thrown out by its original owner does not mean that it is free for the taking. Under the law, the contents of a dumpster may actually belong to the disposal company that has provided it, so taking things out that you did not put in could be regarded as theft of their property.

So how does dumpster diving relate to hackers in general and what might they hope to find? To answer this it should firstly be noted that phone companies are not the only possible targets and, indeed, phreakers are not the only potential beneficiaries. The activity is mentioned in the published accounts of how hackers like Kevin Mitnick and his associates gathered information. As such, if wishing to target a particular organization or system, dumpster diving could be a useful means of preliminary fact-finding. Depending upon how careless the target organization has been with its disposal of sensitive material, it may be possible to find all manner of useful information in the trash. Things like the aforementioned old manuals could give details of the hardware and software technology that the company is using. Armed with this information, the hacker may be able to use it in several ways. For example, if you know that a particular operating system is in use, a technical attack can attempt to target its known vulnerabilities. Alternatively, a social engineering attempt could utilize the information to make the attacker appear more knowledgeable about the organization's systems (and, hence, sound more convincing). On the other hand, materials of this nature could just be collected in order to broaden the hacker's knowledge and range of available resources for later use.

Other useful finds may include confidential paperwork, copies of correspondence, and other items that may give clues to the operations of the target organization or its systems. In some cases, the link between the material disposed of and its ability to be used by a hacker may not be immediately obvious. Even something as innocuous as an internal telephone directory could be useful – it will typically contain a list of employees, possibly their full names, and sometimes grouped by department. With this information, it would be possible, for example, to phone someone up and social engineer them more effectively – using the basic knowledge of the organizational structure and possibly the names of some key individual(s) to enhance your credibility ("Hello, I'm calling from Macrohard. Mr. Smith in your IT department gave me your number and suggested I should call . . .").

These opportunities will not always be available, of course. Conscientious companies will have a policy to shred or incinerate any waste materials that contain confidential or otherwise sensitive information, rather than just disposing of it in a casual manner. Others will account for the risk in other ways – such as CCTV monitoring of their waste disposal areas and/or other physical protection measures. However, it is probable that the majority do not have the facility for this and others may not even have given it a second thought. As such, dumpster diving may remain a useful technique for those determined hackers who do not mind getting their hands dirty.

Hackers as lock-pickers

Dumpster diving is all very well, but the things that a hacker is likely to find most valuable are often those that are not thrown away and still reside inside the target organization. Getting access to them may, therefore, require physical penetration of the site – which some may consider is straying over the line of what they consider acceptable. However, it will not necessarily be seen as a barrier in all cases and the extreme end of hacker techniques encompasses activities that are closer to those of traditional burglars. For example, during the annual congress of Germany's Chaos Computer Club (CCC) in December 1999, workshops and competitions relating to lock-picking were a big hit with the attendees (with toolkits and practical "how to" information being made available). This highlights a certain synergy between the world of lock-pickers and the hacker community, which is further reinforced by the fact that Steffen Werney, a co-founder of the CCC, is also the president of a spin-off Hamburg lock-picking club. Furthermore, Werney's attitude toward lock-picking is very similar to that exhibited by hackers when justifying their breaches of security, claiming that "The only problem is the [lock-making] industry, which is selling such bad stuff."[149] On the face of it, the argument offered may seem plausible and, indeed, the lock-pickers may claim to be helping the public at large by illustrating the vulnerability of the protection that they are currently using. However, it overlooks a number of counter-arguments that may be applied from the perspective of the lock-makers and the public, for example:

- the existing locks may be sufficient to repel the vast majority of opportunist criminals.

- making better "stuff" may increase the cost of the product to a point where it is not commercially viable in a mass market.

- many people may be satisfied with the current level of risk/cost compromise.

Are the lock-pickers providing a sensible service by providing tuition to people who might not otherwise have even considered it? By then having such a "skill," some people may be encouraged to want to put it to use (and, for this type of skill, there are more illegal opportunities for doing so than legitimate ones). Effectively, the lock-pickers are increasing the level of risk by actively sharing their knowledge through providing guides and tools. If the motivation was really that of concern for the protection of the public at large, then a more appropriate route would be to enter into a dialogue with the lock manufacturers to highlight the weaknesses and, thereby, determine their point of view.

It is easy to spot similarities here with the common arguments relating to the pros and cons of system vulnerabilities being highlighted by hackers. At this level, there is a clear analogy to be made between physical locks on doors and the passwords that protect access to systems. Both represent a barrier that needs to be passed in order to gain access. There are also parallels between lock-picking kits and the vulnerability exploitation tools discussed earlier in this chapter. In most cases, hackers will content themselves with targeting the system-oriented protection measures but, for the more determined, it is clear that physical attacks and intrusions are not out of the question.

SUMMARY

The discussion in this chapter has really only scratched the surface of the tools and techniques that hackers are able to employ. Nonetheless, it is clear that the various activities can represent a major problem for both the administrators of systems and the general users who wish to access them, with the effects of incidents like web defacement and denial of service being felt by more than just the people within the target organization. Methods of attack can take many forms and can be utilized by hackers of varying levels of ability. Taking advantage of some of the common vulnerabilities in systems may still require a reasonable degree of technical knowledge and competence. By contrast, some forms of attack can be so heavily automated that complete novices can initiate them, but still cause very significant impacts as a result. As such, the problem that is posed by hackers is certainly not one that can be dismissed lightly.

If the illicit activities of hackers are to be thwarted, then a major element of responsibility falls upon the administrators of individual systems. The discussion has demonstrated that they often face a significant problem here due to the sheer volume of security patches and advisories that need to be heeded in order to keep a system secure. While there are a variety of tools that administrators can use to assist them in assessing their protection, these are equally available to the hacker community and can be deployed to the detriment of security. From this perspective, the maintenance of security and the prevention of cybercrime can be regarded as an ongoing battle, in which each side strives to regain the advantage. Although specific vulnerabilities may be addressed, the underlying problem of hacking will not disappear, so the only solution is constant vigilance.

Although significant discussion has been devoted to the issue, it is important to remember that hacking is only one face of the cybercrime problem. As the next chapter will illustrate, major threats can also come from other directions, with the ability to cause far more widespread impacts than a single hacker could possibly achieve.

Manifestations of malware

HAVING FOCUSED EXCLUSIVELY UPON HACKERS IN THE PREVIOUS TWO chapters, some may find it surprising to learn that the most widespread form of cybercrime actually comes from another direction. Recalling the statistics presented back in Chapter 2, however, it is clear that computer viruses have been the most common form of incident in recent years. Viruses are one form of a more general type of threat – namely the problem of malware. This chapter outlines the different forms that it may take and considers examples of incidents that have occurred in practice.

What is malware?

The term "malware" is a concatenation of "malicious software." The basic concept is that attacks on a system can be conducted completely under software control. On this basis, it can be observed that we have already encountered some forms of malware in earlier discussion. Denial of Service tools and exploit programs, for example, could both be considered to fall into this category. For the purposes of this discussion, however, a more specific focus will be made. Although both of the aforementioned programs are clearly malicious forms of software, it can also be observed that they are *tools* used by hackers – so the overall category of attack is still a hacking incident. By contrast, other forms of malware can be considered to constitute an attack category in their own right and, in certain cases, the attack can be automatically distributed from system to system, thereby affecting multiple targets. Human involvement is still required in the initial instance (i.e. to create and begin the distribution of the malicious code) but individual attacks can subsequently occur without the need for the instigator's further involvement.

A useful starting point for a discussion of malware is to attempt to get our use of terminology right. This is something that media reports often fail to do and, as a result, some of the different names are sometimes incorrectly used in an almost interchangeable manner. At one level, it may be argued that such concern over the use of accurate technical terminology is being unnecessarily pedantic – after all, the end result is often largely the same in the sense of disruption to operations and damage to systems and data. However, from another perspective, this is like saying that murder is the same issue as manslaughter in the sense that people are killed in both cases. Clearly the crimes are of a different nature and one is more serious than the other, and so it is with the different classes of malware. For the purposes of this initial discussion, we will identify four top-level classifications as the basis for further consideration. The categories in question are *viruses*, *worms*, *Trojan Horses,* and *software bombs*, each of which will now be defined in the sections that follow.

Viruses

The virus is, without doubt, the most recognized malware term from a public perspective and is sometime used (erroneously) as a catch-all term to encompass all forms of software-based abuse. Although they may come in many forms, viruses can generally be defined as follows:

> a non-autonomous set of routines that is capable of modifying programs or systems so that they contain executable copies of itself.[150]

The description of viruses as non-autonomous refers to the fact that, in order to spread, they must attach themselves to some form of host before they can spread any further. Through this process of modification, the virus "infects" files or disks and can then spread further as they are used or shared.

In addition to the concept of infection, two other issues that are inextricably linked to viruses are *replication* and *payload*. In order to maximize its potential for infection, a virus requires a good replication strategy – a means for it to spread between different systems. In the early (i.e. pre-mainstream Internet) days, the most common mechanism for the transmission of a virus was the sharing of floppy disks between systems (which could occur, for example, when people take documents to and from home on disks or share them in the office with colleagues). Today, however, network-based transmission is a more common route, with viruses being concealed in downloaded materials or, most likely of all, received via email. In general terms, there are three ways in which a user can inadvertently trigger the infection of their system:

- booting a PC from an infected medium (e.g. a floppy disk).
- executing an infected program.
- opening an infected file (e.g. a document or spreadsheet).

Needless to say, nobody would willingly allow any of these means of infection to take place. As such, viruses are typically concealed within materials that a user will more readily accept. Examples here typically include email attachments, pirated copies of software, and shareware/public domain programs.

If all it did were replicate then a virus would not necessarily represent that much of a problem. The real problem is that, having infected a system, a virus will attempt to do more than simply replicate further and will typically activate a *payload* element that causes unexpected and potentially harmful activity when it is executed. As some of the later examples will illustrate, the payload activity may take many forms – ranging from the harmless but irritating display of messages on the screen to the trashing of data or the manipulation of other programs within the system. An example of the former is illustrated in Figure 5.1, the effect of the payload in this case being the display of a crude animated ambulance along the bottom of the screen, accompanied by a siren sound. This, however, is an early DOS-based virus and, unfortunately, most modern viruses have more malevolent effects. It is important to note that the payload element will very rarely manifest itself the instant that a virus infects a system. To do so would effectively undermine the replication strategy, as the virus will not have had the opportunity to spread further before being detected. As such, the most successful replicators are often those viruses that lay dormant for a fairly long time before invoking their payloads.

Although the concepts of replication and payload are common to all classes of virus, there are various sub-classifications that can be made based upon how the viruses are implemented and what they actually infect. The principal groupings are summarized below.

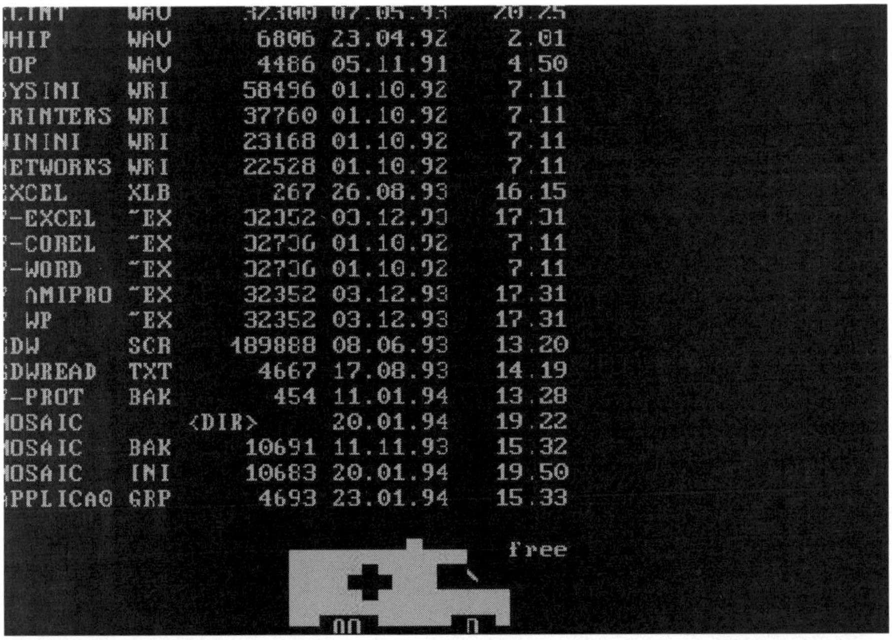

FIGURE 5.1 The effect of the Ambulance virus

- Boot-sector viruses. These infect systems by copying their code to either the boot sector on a floppy disk or the partition table on a hard disk. During startup, when the machine is switched on or rebooted, the virus is then automatically loaded into memory. Once there, it can infect any non-infected disks accessed by the system. The exchange of floppy disks between systems then enables the virus to spread further.

- File (program) viruses. These attach themselves to, or replace, executable programs (e.g. .COM and .EXE files on PCs). File viruses infect other programs when they are executed in memory. In some cases, other programs will be infected when they are opened, whereas in others the virus simply infects all of the files in the directory it was run from.

- Macro viruses. Some computer applications contain macro languages to help users automate tedious or repetitive tasks. Although they are intended to provide a useful facility, macro languages can be misused to implement viruses that can infect other documents and perform unwanted effects (e.g. corruption of document content, initiation of email messaging). Macro viruses are typically spread through the exchange of files from applications such as word processors and spreadsheets.

There are a few other terms that are often encountered in the context of viruses, which are also relevant to mention:

- Multipartite viruses are those that utilize a combination of techniques to infect a system, including the infection of documents, executables and boot sectors.

- Polymorphic viruses attempt to evade detection by continually mutating to avoid leaving a detectable signature. Many anti-virus programs attempt to find viruses by looking for certain patterns of code (known as virus signatures) that are unique to each virus – the occurrence of this code within a scanned file will indicate that it has been infected with the associated virus. As polymorphic viruses spread and infect new files, they encrypt themselves differently – such that they do not leave a consistent signature and it is more difficult for anti-virus software to detect them. A small portion of the virus decrypts the rest of the virus code when it is activated.

- Stealth viruses are those that attempt to hide evidence of their existence, in order to avoid detection. For example, if a virus has infected an executable program, the size of the file will almost inevitably have been altered as a result. A stealth virus may attempt to conceal this by reporting the original, uninfected file length. This can be achieved by the virus intercepting disk-access requests.

Viruses are, without doubt, the most recognized and commonly encountered form of cybercrime. A whole subset of the computer security industry has arisen in response to the virus threat, with companies such as McAfee, Sophos and Symantec doing their main business through anti-virus products. Furthermore, now that the genie has been let out of the bottle, the problem will never disappear. The situation is rather neatly summed up by the following quotation, taken from the U.K. National Computing Centre's Business Information Security Survey 2000:

> Computer viruses are now an everyday part of life and a reality that we have to live with, even tying up resources when only a hoax. Though we have the technology for their early detection and for limiting their impact they still manage to slip through the net.[151]

Worms

Like a virus, a worm is another form of replicating malware. The key difference when compared to a virus is the independence of the worm – it does not need to attach itself to a host (e.g. file or disk boot sector) in order to facilitate its transmission and replication. The earlier definition of virus included the property "non-autonomous" to highlight the reliance upon some form of host. A worm, by contrast, can be defined as:

> a set of programs or routines that are capable of independently, or with the help of an unsuspecting user, propagating throughout a network.[152]

So if it does not infect other programs, what is the problem with a worm? The key issue is that the replication of a worm may result in significant consumption of both computer memory and network resources, thereby leading to a degradation of performance.

Some definitions also suggest that a worm lacks the payload element of a virus. However, this really depends upon what you consider the payload to be. As later examples show, some worms now replicate by sending emailed copies of themselves to all of the contacts in your PC address book. The infection of your friend's systems, and the associated embarrassment that this brings to you as the originator of the message that did it, could well be considered to represent a payload!

The distinction between viruses and worms is the one that often becomes the most blurred, particularly in media reporting of cybercrime. A case in point is the Love Bug worm (described in detail later in this chapter), which television news reports and newspaper articles typically referred to as being a virus.

Trojan Horses

Taking their name from the hollow wooden horse that the Greeks used to conceal their soldiers in order to invade Troy, Trojan Horses are programs that appear to perform a useful or harmless function, but also contain hidden functionality that is unknown to the user. This functionality is intentionally implemented and will typically cause unwanted and often damaging effects for the unwitting user. The fake login program described in Chapter 3 was an example of a Trojan Horse, as it is doing something fundamentally different to what the user believes.

Although they can all result in unwanted end results, Trojans differ from viruses and worms in two key respects. Firstly, although their authors typically intend for them to infiltrate many systems, the process of replication is not automated. Instead, the spread of the program generally depends upon its perceived attractiveness and relies upon manual download and distribution. For example, a Trojan program may be given a name such as "sex.exe," which many users would find attractive or intriguing and, therefore, willingly run on their system to find out what it does. This leads to a second significant difference from the malware previously discussed – Trojans are quite likely to be introduced into a system with the user's explicit consent.

From a certain perspective it can be argued that any program that has been unknowingly infected by a virus is also a Trojan Horse, because running the program results in unanticipated consequences as a result of the virus payload. However, strictly speaking the program should not be classified as a Trojan, as the unwanted code was not originally implemented within the host program. A true Trojan is one that has been specifically written or modified to include a hidden function.

Also worth a mention at this point are backdoor programs. These are a specific type of Trojan that enable infected machines to be accessed remotely, by incorporating both client and server components within the software. An example would be a program such as the Back Orifice tool, discussed in the previous chapter.

Software bombs

The final category of malware considered here is the software bomb. A bomb is essentially malicious code, hidden within a program, which is set to activate under particular conditions. Software bombs can be split into two sub-categories, namely time bombs and logic bombs. The term "time bomb" refers to code that is set to trigger after a period of time has elapsed or when a specific date or time is reached. By contrast, a logic bomb is triggered by the occurrence of a specific event (or event series) within the system. A classic example of the latter would be the unauthorized inclusion of code within a payroll system to watch for the removal of a specific employee's name. Based on the assumption that such removal represents the firing of the employee, the code could be set to perform a malicious action, such as deletion of files, as a form of revenge or even blackmail by the employee.

In the other malware categories discussed so far, it can generally be argued that the aim is to affect as wide an audience as possible in order to gain notoriety. In the case of viruses and worms, this process will be automated and transparent, as part of the normal exchange of information. With Trojan Horses, the spread relies upon the attractiveness of the host program in which they are hidden. Software bombs differ in that they are more likely to be specifically placed within a particular target system, with the aim of having an equally specific effect upon it.

It can be argued that bombs are not necessarily standalone categories of malware, as they are often utilized in the realization of some of the other approaches. For example, a program containing a time or logic bomb element could also be considered to be a Trojan Horse, as it conceals unexpected and unwanted functionality from the user's perspective. Similarly, a virus might use a bomb element as the trigger for the activation of its payload. However, the software bomb category is denoted separately here as they may be implemented independently of these other malware contexts. Neither Trojan Horses nor viruses *have* to incorporate a bomb element and program authors may incorporate a bomb into their software in other contexts.

When the bomb technique is used in isolation (i.e. not as part of the underlying mechanism within a virus etc.), the author's motivation is likely to be specifically related to the target organization or system, as opposed to simply wanting to cause a widespread effect. This does not imply that the motive is any less malicious (indeed, in some cases, it may be more so), but it will certainly be more focused.

In considering this issue of motive, it should also be noted that the techniques associated with bombs are not restricted to malware-related usage. In implementation terms, they are the same techniques that, for example, can be used to prevent an evaluation or shareware version of a piece of software from working after a prescribed period of time or a set number of uses. Therefore, the classification of the code as a bomb is more to do with the motivation of the author than the actual software techniques employed.

Due to their more confined impact, significantly high-profile examples of bombs are more difficult to identify and, as such, they do not receive significant focus in the examples presented later in this chapter.

Motivations of the malware writers

So why would someone knowingly create and release a disruptive or destructive program like a virus? In considering this question it is important to recognize that the writers of malware do not necessarily fit the mould of the hackers that have been discussed in previous chapters. Virus writers cannot, for example, hide behind the claim that they are simply trying to explore the system in the same way that many hackers do. Having said this, their attitude is often no different to hackers in the sense that they do not consider their actions to be wrong. For example, the following is a quotation from Onel de Guzman, a self-confessed malware writer who is alleged to have created the infamous Love Bug worm (discussed later in this chapter). The worm exploited vulnerabilities in Microsoft's Outlook email program and de Guzman's view is that Microsoft is consequently to blame for the incident, as its software was open to abuse:

> For programmers like us, it is not wrong . . . I'm the user, I buy the product. If I use it in a wrong or improper way, why should I be blamed?[153]

It is difficult to sympathize with this viewpoint, which is like saying that because you have bought a car it gives you the right to go and crash it into everyone else's, and that the car manufacturer is really to blame because the car did not prevent you from doing so. It is, nonetheless, probably quite typical of the mindset that prevails and provides a sufficient basis to reassure an individual that they are justified in their actions.

The possible motives could typically be placed into one or more of the following categories:

- to see how far their creation can spread or how much attention it can attract (the former often influencing the latter).
- to cause damage or disruption (an aspect that could itself be motivated by factors such as revenge or ideology), which may take the form of a targeted attack against an individual, an organization, or a regime.
- to achieve a feeling of power or superiority over those who fall victim to the creation (the aliases of past virus writers, such as Dark Avenger and Black Baron, suggest some attempt to boost their own ego and sense of importance).
- to use the malware as a tool to leverage some form of personal gain (e.g. the AIDS Trojan Horse, discussed later in this chapter).
- to give people a lesson in security, by providing a practical illustration of security weaknesses to users and vendors.
- to merely conduct an experiment and see what can be achieved with modern software, networking technology, etc.

In addition to the above, some cynics might also suggest that a further possible motivation is to create and sustain a market for anti-virus products* – a suggestion that associated software vendors would probably take issue with. There are certainly a sufficient number of new virus strains emerging independently for anti-virus companies not to have to worry about creating their own. In reality, the most common

---

*Personal experience has shown that asking this question of any sufficiently sized audience always elicits at least one response supporting this view.

motivation is probably the first one, and viruses and worms in particular are often analogized to electronic graffiti in which the author's motivation is to see their "tag" spread across cyberspace. It can be seen, however, that the motivations listed are not mutually exclusive, so other factors may also feature in parallel with this. It can also be noted that, whereas the last two points listed may be genuine reasons in some cases, in others they may just be token justifications by which the individuals concerned attempt to rationalize their disruptive activities.

If the author's aim is to be able to trace the spread of his or her creation (and then garner some personal satisfaction from knowing the extent that it was able to replicate – as opposed to just releasing it and assuming it must be doing some harm somewhere) then its methods or effects must be notable enough to warrant it gaining some industry and media attention. In the early days, simply writing and releasing a virus was enough to make people sit up and take notice – it was a new phenomenon that had not been encountered before. Then, as the concept became more commonplace, something was needed to sufficiently distinguish a new virus from the other strains for it to receive mainstream attention. An example of a successful strategy in this respect was the time bomb effect, as exemplified by the Friday 13th and Michelangelo viruses, which had the then notable feature of being programmed to trigger on specific dates (the former's target date being evident from its name and the latter targeting 6th March – the anniversary of the painter's birth). As a result, the media had something to hook onto – namely the countdown to the activation date and speculation about the damage that would result. By the time the dates arrived, the actual effect of the virus would largely be secondary – from the author's perspective, the creation would have achieved the desired fame and attention. Indeed, both viruses are much more notable for the hype that surrounded them than the actual damage that they caused.

As time has moved on, however, and the number of virus strains has soared, it takes something a bit more special to ensure that the virus will come to the attention of the masses. As a result, virus writers can be seen to be continually pushing the envelope in terms of the methods and effects that their creations employ. This aspect is illustrated by a number of the examples presented later in this chapter.

The evolution of viruses

Although many readers may assume that, by their very nature, computer viruses must have originated from cybercriminals, the true origin is actually quite different. The idea was first formally proposed in an academic research paper written by Fred Cohen – a student of Professor Leonard Adleman, a well-known name in the IT security field and most notable as one of the creators of the RSA encryption algorithm in 1977. Cohen's first paper on the topic, entitled "Computer Viruses – Theory and

Experiments,"[154] was published in 1984, and was followed by a dissertation in 1986, as part of a doctorate in electrical engineering from the University of Southern California. The original paper described the concept of a virus and presented details of an experimental implementation that Cohen himself had created the previous year. However, while the description of the functional concept is credited to Cohen, it was actually Adleman that came up with the name "virus" – something that he feels was influenced by his interest in AIDS research at the time.

So what, you may ask, did a respected cryptologist and his research student think they were doing by developing something that represents such a serious threat to security? In actual fact, Adleman and Cohen did not commence their research with the idea of creating a malware mechanism and were aiming toward something that would have the potential to improve computing technology (Cohen, for example, describes the concept of benevolent viruses, which could reproduce to perform useful tasks such as large-scale distributed computation).[155] However, they also saw that the resulting findings had the potential for abuse and felt it appropriate to warn people of the threat. To quote Professor Adleman:

> We discussed the implications and ethical complexity of the situation and concluded that viruses were inevitable . . . We also believed that as part of academia, it was our duty to publish our findings.[156]

For a time after Cohen's paper, others were dismissive of the computer virus concept and the idea was not taken seriously. However, the genie was out of the bottle and, within a couple of years, real viruses were emerging. From that point, the problem has only ever got worse. Figure 5.2 illustrates some key stages in the evolution of computer viruses. From the starting point of Cohen's experiments in 1983, it presents a timeline of when significant forms of virus first appeared "in the wild." Early examples of specific viruses in each category are indicated in parentheses.

TIME		
	1983	Fred Cohen creates experimental virus
	1986	Boot sector viruses arrive (e.g. Brain)
	1987	File viruses appear (e.g. Jerusalem)
	1991	Polymorphic viruses (e.g. Tequila)
	1996	Word and Excel macro viruses (e.g. Concept, Laroux)
	1999	Self-distributing email viruses (e.g. Melissa)

FIGURE 5.2 The evolution of the computer virus

As indicated in the figure, 1996 witnessed a fundamental change in the virus world, with the emergence of a new variation of the problem – the macro virus. As previously mentioned, these are implemented using macro languages that are now found in many popular applications. The most common macro virus platform is provided by Microsoft Word – the word processor application within the Microsoft Office suite. The macro language in this case is Visual Basic for Applications (VBA), which provides the facility to automate a variety of actions, both within Word and in relation to other applications. In the Word context, opening an infected document will typically cause the virus to infect the user's NORMAL.DOT template. This is the standard template that Word uses to create new documents (and other templates) and so, once it has become infected, the virus will automatically spread to all other documents and templates as they are opened in the system. Furthermore, unless another document is specified at start-up, NORMAL.DOT is also opened by default when the Word application is launched – meaning that the virus will be present from the outset every time the application is run. As such, any new documents become carriers of the virus.

Placing the virus within a document rather than within a program serves to significantly extend the potential for widespread distribution and infection. There are two key reasons for this. Firstly, individual documents are far more likely to be exchanged between users and systems than would be the case with executable programs. Secondly, if the host application in which the macro runs is available on several operating systems (e.g. different Windows variants, Macintosh, etc.), then it serves to make the virus platform independent as the infected template will load up happily on the different versions. As such, whereas Mac users would previously have been safe against virus strains developed under Windows (and vice versa), the macro variety has the potential to spread between the two types of system if they share compatible document formats.

With macro variants joining the other strains, the overall rise in the number of viruses has been staggering. Anti-virus vendor Sophos stated in July 2001 that around 66,000 viruses were known to exist,[157] and that a staggering 6,127 new strains had emerged in the first six months of 2001.[158] This has significant implications for those trying to keep on top of the problem. For example, anti-virus software vendors must provide updates to their detection packages to enable them to deal with new virus strains that have emerged since the last release. Whereas these updates used to be issued on a quarterly basis, the rate of release for new viruses now means that weekly updates are more appropriate (use of the Internet actually facilitates the provision of updates on a daily basis).

While an overall total of 66,000 viruses seems worryingly large, it should also be noted that only a small percentage of them actually manage to make it into widespread circulation. The majority of the strains are only known to exist within the confines of anti-virus research centres – they have not been encountered in a real-world environment. Such varieties are, therefore, referred to as exotic viruses. If, however, a virus is actually reported as being encountered in practice it is referred to as being "in the wild." The concept of "in the wild" viruses is widely used by anti-virus software vendors, and their products aim to detect any viruses that are classified in this manner. Since 1993, anti-virus researcher Joe Wells has maintained the definitive list of viruses considered to be "in the wild" at any given time. Wells collects reports from anti-virus experts around the world in order to compile the WildList (see **http://www.virusbtn.com/WildLists/**). This is a well-known resource and anti-virus products are consequently expected to score 100 percent success in detecting the viruses listed. A virus is considered to be in the wild (and, therefore, eligible for inclusion in the list) if it has been verified as being encountered by a minimum of two WildList participants during the relevant survey period.

To illustrate the difference between the number of viruses known and those in the wild, it can be observed that the average number "in the wild" during the twelve-month period from November 1999 to October 2000 inclusive was 196. This figure is based on averaged totals from the eleven releases of Joe Wells' WildList during this time (there was no list for March 2000). What can also be seen during this period, however, is an overall upward trend in the number of "in the wild" viruses, starting from a low of 162 in November 1999 and reaching 213 by October 2000 (with a twelve-month high of 217 having been reached in July). This is illustrated in Figure 5.3 and the overall trend provides further support to the view that the virus problem is getting worse.

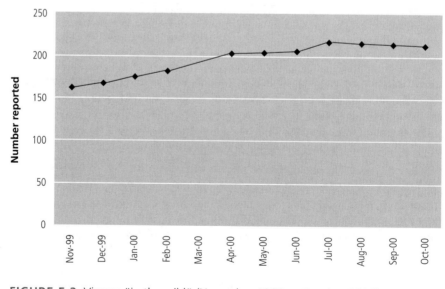

FIGURE 5.3 Viruses "in the wild" (November 1999 to October 2000)

Viruses are now regarded as an inherent part of the IT experience. This can be illustrated via a real-world example. The Microsoft Hotmail system (the popular web-based email service previously mentioned in Chapter 2) incorporates a facility for an email recipient to run a virus scan on any file(s) that a sender may have attached to a message before the files are downloaded. Thus the risk of infection is removed from the user's machine, as any file downloaded can be certified as safe before commencing (with the obvious reliance that the Hotmail virus detection software is up to date). For a time, the slightly strange thing about this facility was that the virus scan was offered to the user as an option (i.e. for any attachment, the option to "Scan for viruses" or "Download without scan" could be chosen). From the security perspective, it would clearly be better (and safer) not to offer the choice and to automatically scan files before downloading them. This point was obviously considered by Microsoft, because the situation changed in May 2000 and the scan is now automatic. It could be argued that an advantage of the previous arrangement was that, by making the action to perform a scan explicit, it served to reinforce the dangers posed by viruses (which, in turn, may have helped to encourage users to consider the possibility that they may be downloaded during other online activities and, hence, encourage the use of anti-virus software on the local machine). How-ever, of the two approaches, having the automatic scan is undoubtedly better and, in the manner it has been implemented, the user is still made aware of the fact that it has taken place. The scan result is explicitly reported before an attached file can be downloaded, and the associated pages are accompanied by prominent placement of the logo for the McAfee anti-virus product that has been used. This is preferable to making the process totally transparent to the user (which could easily have been done), as the issue of the virus threat is still highlighted.

Notable malware incidents

Having provided the general definitions and background information about the problem, the discussion now proceeds to describe a variety of incidents that have occurred in recent years. It begins with a range of virus and worm examples and then proceeds to consider a few notable Trojan Horse cases toward the end.

The Melissa virus

One of the most significant macro virus incidents to date occurred in March 1999, with the release of a Word 97 macro virus called Melissa.[159] Although macro viruses had been around for several years by this point, Melissa was distinguished by the nature of its payload, which used Microsoft Outlook as a means of distributing copies of itself to other victims by sending them infected documents as email attachments. This was made possible by the VBA macro language, which allows the functions of one Microsoft application to be accessed and controlled from within another – enabling the whole process of creating and sending emails to be automated without further user intervention. This method of malware distribution is by no means uncommon now (as a later example will also show), but Melissa represented the first occasion in which it had been used to such effect.

The spread of the virus commenced when its author posted an infected document onto the Internet newsgroup "alt.sex" (a discussion group containing sexually oriented content). As an enticement to get other users to download it, the message posted along with the document claimed that it contained passcodes to various pornographic web sites. Downloading and opening the document, of course, unleashed the virus and, from that point, it was able to spread itself to other potential victims automatically – by emailing them copies of itself in infected documents.

Having used the topic of sex as a means of hooking the attention of its initial victims, Melissa's subsequent approach was also cunning in that it employed further elements of social engineering to encourage recipients to open the infected documents. The title of the email they received would have read as follows:

Important message from *username*

where *username* was the name of the person whose email address book had been hijacked in order to send the message. Given that the recipient user's name was found in the originator's address book, it would generally be the case that the two knew each other, and, therefore, the recipient would assume the message to be from a trusted source. In addition, the text of the email message also aimed to bait them into opening the infected document. The text read as follows:

Here is that document you asked for ... don't show anyone else ;-)

A naïve user would be encouraged to open the document on the basis that the sender seemed to think they had asked for it and also because it was obviously important (the message title said so!). Furthermore, the request not to show anyone else, along with the winking emoticon, implies some potentially interesting content – another incentive to have a look. In actual fact, the content of the document could well have been interesting – it could, in fact, have been anything, because the virus sent out whatever document the sender was working on at the time. As such, confidential or sensitive material could have been sent to the victim's friends and associates.

Unlike some later variations of the approach, Melissa imposed some restrictions upon the extent of its emailing activities. Firstly, the messages were only sent to a restricted number of recipients – namely the first fifty entries in the victim's Outlook address book. Secondly, emailing was only done once – the first time that an infected document was opened on the system. On subsequent occasions, the virus could determine that it had already sent emails by checking a flag that it set in the Windows system registry. In spite of these limits, however, the replication method was still very effective – each infected computer could potentially infect another fifty computers, which could, in turn, infect another fifty computers, and so on.

In addition to the Outlook email distribution, there was also a second payload element that triggered during a particular minute every hour. The specific minute varied and was based upon the current date (e.g. on the 20th of the month, the payload was triggered at twenty minutes past the hour). Opening or closing a Melissa-infected document during the appropriate minute caused the following sentence to be inserted into the text:

> Twenty-two points, plus triple-word-score, plus fifty points for using all my letters. Game's over. I'm outta here.

In order to protect itself, Melissa attempted to hide its activity by disabling macro-related menu options in Microsoft Word – thus preventing users from being able to list the macro code in a document and manually check for infection. It also disabled Word options that would otherwise aim to protect against macro virus infection. With the threat of macro viruses now recognized, Word is able to prompt the user before doing things that may allow them to spread. For example, if the NORMAL.DOT document template has been modified, then the system will ask the user whether they wish to save the changes to it. Similarly, when opening a document that contains macro functions within it, Word will warn the user of the potential danger and ask whether they wish to continue. If the document is not from a trusted source or is not expected to contain macros, then the user can elect to play safe and disable them. However, Melissa (in common with other macro viruses) disabled these safeguards and suppressed the warning message – leaving the user potentially unaware of the problem.

It can be seen from the above that the technical aspects behind the implementation of Melissa were multi-faceted, with mechanisms to both promote and protect itself. At the end of the day, however, the most significant thing about Melissa was not its implementation, but its impact. The virus spread to systems worldwide and, in the United States alone, affected 1.2 million computers in one-fifth of the country's largest companies. It was consequently estimated to be responsible for losses running into hundreds of millions of dollars as organizations disabled their email access and took corrective actions.

It is somewhat unusual for the creator of a virus to be traced and brought to account, but, in the Melissa case, the author was actually found and arrested within a matter of days. He was identified as a result of the original posting to alt.sex having been traced to a hijacked America Online account. Working with the FBI, America Online determined that the culprit had logged in from New Jersey and on 1st April 1999, less than a week after the original posting, and the police arrested David Smith, a thirty-year-old computer programmer from Eatontown. In December 1999, Smith pleaded guilty to state and federal charges against him and his plea agreement acknowledged that Melissa had caused damages in excess of $80 million.[160] The state recommended a sentence of ten years and fines of up to $150,000, whereas the federal charge carried a maximum sentence of five years and a fine of $250,000.

A footnote to the story occurred in early 2001, almost two years after the original Melissa incident. It may be recalled that one of the general characteristics of macro viruses is that they have the potential to be cross-platform (i.e. spreading between different types of systems, such as Windows PCs and Macs). However, at the time of its original release, the main impact of Melissa was felt by members of the Windows community, due to the linkage between Word and Outlook that was made possible by VBA. Although the Melissa macro could also infect Word documents on the Mac, it had very little impact because Mac users did not have a full version of Outlook for their systems (the more restricted Outlook Express was all that was available at the time, which lacked the Visual Basic support required for the macro to initiate emails and spread itself further). However, in January 2001, a public beta version of Outlook for Mac was made available and shortly afterwards reports of Melissa infections started to occur in relation to Mac systems. It was conjectured that, with the macro finally able to take advantage of the required Outlook features, documents that had long been infected with Melissa were able to start demonstrating their side-effects.[161]

Prior to Melissa, the most widespread Internet security incident had been a worm program released by Cornell University student Robert Morris in 1988. Morris had written his worm as an experiment, with the aim of seeing how far it was able to spread itself. Unfortunately, an error in his code caused the worm to replicate far faster than he had planned and, as a result, it effectively crippled all the machines that it infiltrated, by tying up their processing and network resources.[162] The impact of the worm was significant – with around a tenth of the systems on the Internet being affected (which, at the time, equated to around 6,000 systems) and costing some $15 million to bring them back to health.* The impact of the Melissa virus, of

---

* At the time, the worm was combated by an ad hoc collaboration between various security experts, who managed to devise a means of eradicating it from infected systems. However, the incident was a catalyst for the formation of a more formalized approach, the Computer Emergency Response Team (CERT), to deal with future security incidents. It is interesting to note that one of the organizations that participated in the fight against the Morris Worm was the National Security Agency (NSA), and the chief scientist of its National Computer Security Center was Robert Morris Sr. – the father of the worm's author!

course, dwarfed these figures, and in 1999 it was the most significant malware incident to have hit the Internet. However, this dubious achievement was soon to be beaten …

Love bytes

This incident occurred on 4th May 2000, and is an example from which I can quote some limited personal experience. Mid-way through the morning, I received a phone call from a colleague in my university to say that he had received a strange email message that appeared to be a love letter. The title of the message was "ILOVEYOU" and it had an attached file entitled "LOVE-LETTER-FOR-YOU.TXT.vbs." Being rather astute, my colleague realized that a ".vbs" extension on the attachment meant that the file was a Visual Basic Script (basically, a series of instructions that the computer would proceed to execute if the attachment was opened). This is not the normal format in which someone would write a love letter, so my colleague decided that he ought to exercise care in dealing with it. Sensibly, he disconnected his machine from the network and proceeded to have a look at the contents of the file. He was quickly able to determine that the file contained anything but a love letter and was actually an executable script that appeared to invoke email activity and corrupt files on the local machine. The attached file was a worm program and executing it would have enabled it to spread to numerous other systems. My colleague did not run it, but quite evidently many other people did – by mid-afternoon, reports of the worm had appeared on various online news services. By the end of the day, it was headline news on television. Notable victims included the U.K. Houses of Parliament, NASA, the Pentagon, Vodafone AirTouch, and the British Broadcasting Corporation.

So how did it work? As described above, the worm arrives as an attachment on an email message, masquerading as a love letter (as shown in Figure 5.4). As with the Melissa virus before it, this represents a bit of social engineering on the part of the worm's author, in the sense that many recipients would be quite flattered to receive such a message, or at least inquisitive to determine more details, thus increasing the likelihood that the attachment would be opened. The name of the attached file, "LOVE-LETTER-FOR-YOU.TXT.vbs," is unusual in the sense that it appears to have two file extensions (i.e. ".TXT" and ".vbs"). This is also rather cunning in the sense that many Windows systems would have been configured differently to that of my colleague and would have hidden the file extension. In such situations, this would mean the suppression of the ".vbs" part, which identifies the file as a Visual Basic Script. What the user would then see would simply be "LOVE-LETTER-FOR-YOU.TXT," which suggests itself to be an innocent text (".TXT") file. Again, this increases the likelihood that users will be happy to open it without suspecting a malicious intent.

Then comes the technical bit of what the worm does when someone actually opens and runs the attached file:[163]

- It saves three copies of itself on the host PC, in the system directory (as files MSKernel32.vbs and LOVE-LETTER-FOR-YOU.TXT.vbs) and in the Windows directory (as Win32DLL.vbs).

- It creates appropriate start-up commands to ensure that the program is executed whenever the machine is switched on or reset.

- It attempts to download a file called WIN-BUGSFIX.exe (a password stealing Trojan Horse program) and randomly selects one of four web addresses from which to obtain it. If the Trojan is successfully obtained, a Windows registry entry is created that then runs the program every time the system is started up. All of the web addresses were hosted by a Philippines-based Internet Service Provider, which has since removed them.

- A copy of the love letter email, containing the worm attachment, will then be sent to all addresses in the user's Outlook address book. This is in contrast to the Melissa virus approach, where only the first fifty address book entries were targeted, and resulted in far more widespread distribution.

- Any script files on the PC's drives with the extensions ".js," ".jse," ".css," ".wsh," ".sct," and ".hta" are overwritten and renamed as ".vbs" files (such

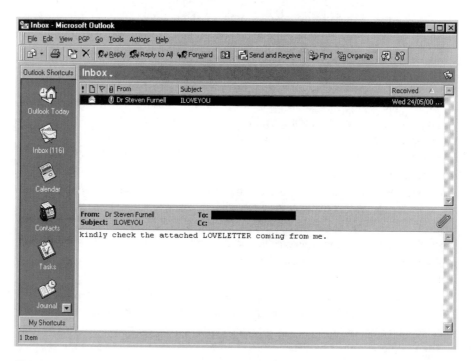

FIGURE 5.4 An unwanted expression of affection

that any attempt to invoke the previous scripts would then invoke the worm script instead). This would offer another means of replication, particularly if the affected machine was a web server and remote users downloaded a page containing a reference to one of the overwritten script files. In addition, any JPEG image files or MP3 music files are renamed to become ".vbs" files.

- Any Internet Relay Chat (IRC) related files are overwritten to cause a LOVE-LETTER-FOR-YOU.HTM file to be sent to anyone who joins an IRC channel in which the client is participating. This represents a further means of spreading the worm.

As can be seen, the above actions invoke a number of further means for the worm to spread to other systems, accounting for the rapid pace at which it spread around the world. Reports estimated that the Love Bug had been received by around 70 percent of computers in the U.K., and the worldwide effects of the worm were estimated to have caused at least $7 billion in damage,[164] mostly in terms of lost work time. It is somewhat astounding that the actions of a 10K file could have such as massive impact upon so many users, across a network the size of the Internet.

The worm was found to have originated in the Philippines and twenty-four-year-old college drop-out Onel de Guzman was ultimately suspected of having been the person responsible. The authorities were alerted to de Guzman when teachers from the local Amable Mendoza Aguiluz Computer College warned them of similarities between the worm and an Internet password-stealing program that he had submitted as a college thesis (the college rejected the thesis and de Guzman did not graduate). At the time, the investigation was already looking in de Guzman's direction, having traced the worm to the flat that he was sharing with his sister and her boyfriend (the boyfriend, Reonel Ramones, had initially been arrested as a suspect on 8th May, but was released due to lack of evidence and the spotlight then turned toward de Guzman). Evidence pointed to de Guzman having written and distributed the worm and, indeed, he admitted that he may have released it by accident (although he did not admit to creating it). In spite of this, in mid-August 2000, the Philippine government decided to drop all charges against de Guzman, because the laws under which he had been charged did not apply to hacking (being more related to traditional crimes such as fraud). As Peter Toren, a former prosecutor in the Computer Crimes and Intellectual Property section of the U.S. Department of Justice observed:

> As long as there are governments that don't take these crimes seriously, it's going to be very difficult for other countries to really protect their computers.[165]

The Philippines is a developing country, not in any sense part of the technological elite and the Love Bug represented the first computer crime case for Manilla's

National Bureau of Investigations. The parliament of the Philippines have since introduced a bill to make cybercrime illegal, but its introduction in June 2000 was too late for use against de Guzman, who had already been charged. Public opinion in the Philippines, however, was very much toward the side of the Love Bug's author. Indeed, he was considered by many to be a national hero, responsible for putting his country on the map for its technological capabilities,[166] and was apparently inundated with job offers from around the world as a reward for his illicit activities. However, in perhaps a more positive move, de Guzman decided that he would prefer to return to education and complete his studies:

> Of course I want to go back to finish school. I'm thinking of a new thesis proposal, but this time it would not be controversial, it would be educational … There will be no more Trojan horses that can be used only by hackers. This time it will be a program for all … When I log onto the Internet, I think I won't go to the hacking sites anymore. After what happened with my thesis proposal, I'm going to change things … I've learned my lesson.[167]

Unfortunately, the Love Bug was not the end of the story. As is often the case, the attention it attracted served to stimulate other budding malware writers to unleash their wares – in this case using the Love Bug's Visual Basic Script as their starting point. A number of these were simply renamed versions of the same thing, whereas others also altered the functionality of the code. In neither case was the approach particularly creative, and probably represented script kiddies getting in on the action, by hitching a ride on the original author's work. By 19th May (roughly a fortnight after the initial outbreak), around thirty variants of the Love Bug had been identified,[168] with names such as "Very Funny," "BugFix," "Mother's Day," and "Virus ALERT!!!." All were based upon the same distribution method, with vaguely similar effects. It can be noted that some of them (such as "BugFix" and "Virus ALERT!!!") rode on the back of the publicity surrounding the Love Bug and encouraged users to run them by purporting to provide solutions to the original problem (the latter having an attachment called "protect.vbs"). This is clearly a rather cruel trick, but malware writers are not renowned for the fairness of their methods.

As with the Melissa virus before it, the Love Bug was able to take advantage of the automation facilities within Microsoft's Office application suite. The central element in this case was again Microsoft Outlook, the email client and personal information management system. With the Love Bug, the vulnerability exploited was the ability to run software automatically (and transparently to the user) when an email attachment is opened. Of course, providing a platform to facilitate the replication and transmission of malicious software was not the original motivation of the Microsoft programmers who conceived the Outlook automation features. Their objective was to incorporate additional functionality into their applications and improve their usefulness. However, it was inevitable that such a powerful facility could be misused and a number of voices could be heard in the aftermath of the Love Bug incident suggesting that Microsoft was to blame for releasing software with security vulnerabilities that were so easy to exploit. It was pointed out that the default configuration of an application such as Outlook should not permit programs of dubious origin to be run invisibly and unchallenged. It is relatively easy to sympathize with this point of view – Microsoft is the dominant player in most areas of desktop computer software, with millions of dollars at its disposal to direct toward product development and testing. It also has a dedicated security team assigned the task of identifying security weaknesses in products before they are released (see Chapter 7, "Hackers for hire"). As such, it would certainly seem to be something that they should have been aware of.

On 22nd May 2000, eighteen days after the Love Bug's emergence, Microsoft announced the intention to release a patch for Outlook to provide protection against this and other similar types of virus or worm (the patch was ultimately available for download from Microsoft's web site from 8th June). Outlook's functionality was changed such that files of an executable nature (e.g. ".exe," ".vbs," ".bat," etc.) could no longer be accessed, while still allowing the opening of other forms of attachment, such as documents and images. The application was also modified to watch out for other programs attempting to access the user's address book (as used in the Love Bug's primary replication mechanism). Such occurrences now cause a warning window to pop up, asking the user whether or not to allow the action to proceed. This is clearly an improvement from a security perspective and draws the user's attention to programs that would not be expected to exhibit such behavior. However, there are some occasions when legitimate programs will attempt such activity and these will also cause the warning to pop up. In these cases, the pop-up message will waste time and potentially cause unnecessary concern to the user. This is essentially the price to be paid for the additional security safeguard. As Microsoft themselves observed, this relates to the need to maintain an appropriate balance between product openness and security.[169]

Ultimately, therefore, Microsoft was seen to be acting to improve the security within its product range. However, it was shortly to be reminded that the security of products is not the only consideration. Within six months of the Love Bug hitting other companies around the world, Microsoft was to find itself the target of …

"A deplorable act of corporate espionage"

On Wednesday 25th October 2000, security staff at Microsoft noticed that something strange had been happening with their systems. New user accounts were being created and passwords were being sent out of the company to an email account registered in St. Petersburg, Russia. Subsequent examination of system log files revealed that the passwords had been used to compromise user accounts and enable access to the source code of Microsoft products – something normally restricted to the company's own staff or external parties who have signed strict contracts beforehand. Moreover, the evidence initially suggested that the activity had been going on undetected for about three months. Without a doubt this was a serious breach of the company's security.

Numerous media reports suggested that the company's systems had been breached by a worm program called Qaz,[170] which had probably arrived as an attachment to an email message sent to an employee. By the time of the Microsoft incident, Qaz had been known about in security circles for some months and its method of operation was already documented. In its standard incarnation, the program is disguised as a file called Notepad.exe (i.e. it appears to be a copy of the Windows Notepad application – so in this sense it can also be considered to be a Trojan Horse). When this is run, the genuine Notepad application is renamed and replaced with the worm's version. The new version contains a backdoor, which allows the remote attacker to perform operations on the target system. The program also modifies the Windows registry, so that it automatically runs every time the computer starts up the operating system. As part of its replication strategy, it also attempts to spread itself onto other machines through shared drives in the same local network. When installed, the worm sends a notification to the attacker, with the Internet address of the infected machine. This facilitates the use of the backdoor, through which the attacker is then able to run or upload files.

Naturally enough, Microsoft were not best pleased about the breach and described it as a "deplorable act of corporate espionage." At the same time, they also wished to provide reassurance that the situation was not devastating to the company's products. Company President Steve Ballmer made a specific point of stating that the source code had not been altered:

> I can assure you that we know that there has been no compromise of the integrity of the source code, that it has not been modified or tampered with in any way.[171]

However, what he did not wish to point out was that the integrity of the code was only one of the issues to be considered. What about the confidentiality of the product under development and, more importantly, its functional design? If the source code is the blueprint of the product, then whoever has stolen it will be in a privileged position, compared to many others outside Microsoft, to know exactly how that product works and whether there are any opportunities to exploit vulnerabilities. Microsoft, unlike many other notable names in the IT industry, does not generally subscribe to the concept of Open Source distribution for its products (i.e. making the source code publicly available). Despite the fact that the source code of some products, such as the Windows NT operating system, is available outside the company, this is done on a license basis, with Microsoft ultimately retaining control over who gets access. Although there are clear commercial reasons behind the restricted access (e.g. preventing others from being able to freely take elements of the code, modify it and produce competing products), the relatively closed nature of the code means that a lack of scrutiny may allow errors to go unnoticed. Certainly the frequency of Microsoft's own security bulletins (highlighted in Chapter 4) suggests that products are released with exploitable security flaws, which are only noticed and addressed some time after widespread distribution has taken place. This, of course, is not intentional, but even with a team of developers and testers it is difficult to ensure that a system is completely bullet-proof when a finite release schedule is imposed. In addition, the source code relating to products such as the Windows operating systems and the Office application suite has evolved over time rather than being rewritten with each release. As such, they contain a large amount of legacy code, originally written by developers who may have long since left the company. This makes it more difficult for the development team to keep track of things and make sure that it all works as intended, with no unforeseen weak-points left exposed. Microsoft is by no means alone in this respect, but it does have a unique position in the industry due to the ubiquity of its products (Windows, for example, is found on 90 percent of desktop systems and Office is the most widely used range of productivity software). Therefore, if a Microsoft product is vulnerable to attack, the majority of IT users can be considered to be at risk. As such, by keeping the source code largely to itself, Microsoft is uniquely responsible for ensuring that its products are as secure as possible. This can be contrasted with an open source approach (such as that taken with the increasingly popular Linux operating system), in which enthusiasts can openly see the source code, and collaborate together to extend and enhance it. Not only does the increased developer base help to progress the evolution of the product, it can also contribute to security and reliability thanks to an increased number of people analyzing the code and thereby identifying and correcting any mistakes.

In reporting the Qaz incident, certain elements of the media were astounded at the fact that a company of the stature of Microsoft could apparently be breached so easily – assuming it to be at the forefront of security technology. This view contrasts dramatically with the view of large elements of the security industry (and, indeed, the hacker community), who regard the attention to security within Microsoft's products to be somewhat dubious. However, if the facts reported were correct, then the media did have a point and it raised a number of interesting questions regarding several aspects of the company's operational security.

- How did the arrival of the Qaz worm go undetected? It had been known about since around July/August 2000 and could be spotted by up-to-date versions of standard anti-virus software, so why did it remain unnoticed in Microsoft for up to three months? A potential explanation for this is that software developers often disable the operation of anti-virus programs, as they can degrade the performance of the computer. Even so, this does not really excuse the fact that the program went undetected for so long. Temporarily disabling virus detection is one thing – not running it at all is quite another.

- Why were the unusual access patterns not spotted earlier through auditing and inspection of log files? The creation of new user accounts is a fairly visible activity – if the breach was only noticed because of this, then it would be conceivable that other less obvious intrusions could have gone unnoticed.

- If Microsoft is so concerned about the proprietary nature of its source code, why was it located on an Internet accessible host?

- Were Microsoft's employees not cautioned against casually opening and running potentially dubious attachments on unsolicited email messages? This question is particularly pertinent, given that the Love Bug incident had occurred only a few months earlier.

Microsoft defended its security team and pointed out that, given the scale of the assets requiring protection and the attractive target that the company represents to hackers, it could generally be considered that protection was being maintained very well. A company source was quoted as follows:

> Microsoft is a huge company, with thousands of desktops and many servers. We have a security team working 24 hours a day to keep people out of our systems, and I have been told that there are real attempts to enter the systems, on average, hundreds of times a week . . . Given that, I'd say the security guys are doing a good job. No, they aren't perfect, but they're human and so we don't expect them to be perfect, either.[172]

So who was responsible for the Qaz attack? The St. Petersburg email address naturally suggested a Russian connection, but this could equally have been a front. Media reports were unclear and a range of potential suspects was identified, including the Russian Mafia or some other branch of organized crime, an individual with strong anti-Microsoft feelings, anarchists, or a disgruntled Microsoft employee. In short, nobody knew, but it seemed that everyone was prepared to hazard a guess. So which product(s) had been compromised? Well, the media reports were not very clear on that either. Microsoft was certainly not making any specific comments. However, the strong implication in many reports was that the code to Windows itself had been taken – effectively the crown jewels of the Microsoft empire, as the media described it. Microsoft's other leading product, Office, was also named in several reports. Despite the lack of concrete details, the significance of the breach was certainly not lost on the media. It made front-page news in the U.K.'s leading broadsheet (heavyweight newspaper), *The Times*, which opened its article with the statement that "Microsoft was facing the collapse of its reputation."[173] In its editorial piece the same day, U.K. tabloid stalwart The *Mirror* stated that the "stolen codes" could be used to undermine Microsoft-based systems around the world and concluded that "The implications are truly terrifying."[174] So, while both the perpetrator(s) and the long-term impacts of the incident were unknown, the public would likely be left with the lasting impression of devastating consequences.

A few days after the initial media frenzy, subsequent reports scaled back the estimates of how long the hacker had actually had access to the system. Rather than three months, Microsoft stated that the period was in fact twelve days – its earlier estimate had been made when the duration of the attack was unclear and it was considered better to over-estimate the extent of the problem. Twelve days was, of course, still plenty of time for hackers to see confidential information, but the fact that they were noticed and (to some extent) monitored was a better reflection on Microsoft's security. In addition, although it still did not identify the nature of the source code that was accessed, the company did state that it related to a product that was "years from release" and was not a version of Windows or Office.[175] This, of course, was in marked contrast to the implications and speculation in earlier reports. Finally, as far as Microsoft's statements were concerned, the role of the Qaz worm in the breach was not confirmed either.[176]

Considering this further evidence, the overall impression is of a less significant breach of security (by no means trivial, but less damning than initially supposed). Although the security industry would have kept a keen and watchful eye on the situation, it is likely that the public at large could have missed these later details, as the subsequent reporting was very low-key by comparison to the original headlines. It can, therefore, be observed that Microsoft did themselves no favors by making the incident public with an over-estimate of the scale, as this is the part that people are likely to remember.

Some observers, such as ex-hacker Kevin Mitnick, still retained doubts over Microsoft's version of events. Speaking to the Software Development 2000 Conference and Expo East in Washington during the week following the incident, Mitnick suggested that, despite Microsoft's claims that no source code had been copied, it still could have been transferred in compressed format. Mitnick summed up the situation quite well with the comment: "It's hard to tell if you're getting the straight story."[177] At the end of the day only the attacker(s), and possibly Microsoft, knew the full story.

In the absence of a definitive, agreed version of events, it is not surprising that many chose to adopt the worst-case view of the situation. This is illustrated by a report released two months after the incident by the Center for Strategic and International Studies, a Washington-based think tank, which used the Microsoft breach as an example of the threat posed to national security by cybercrime. Sticking with the view that the breach had allowed access to a future version of Windows, the report drew the following conclusion:

> A profound concern to both private and public entities becomes whether or not any of these products will be trustworthy once they are released . . . With most military and government systems powered by Microsoft software and more generally reliant on COTS [commercial off-the-shelf software], this recent development can pose grave national security-related concerns.[178]

Microsoft were, understandably, unhappy about such comments and accused the report of sensationalizing the incident and misrepresenting the facts.[179] However, given the confusion caused by the earlier reporting of the incident and Microsoft's own statements on the matter, it is difficult to argue with the stance adopted by the report. The negative outcome from Microsoft's perspective illustrates the importance of appropriate public relations to manage the impact and perception of cybercrime incidents. It also provides an example of why, if given the choice, many organizations prefer not to publicize incidents that they have experienced (an issue that will be considered in later discussion).

So what difference did it all make to the global hordes of Microsoft-dependent users? Did people suddenly decide to stop using their Microsoft software and switch to another supplier? Well, no. In most cases people went back to work or switched on their home PC, booted up Windows and thought very little more about it. For some managers or administrators it may have been a wake-up call, providing the necessary impetus for them to set about addressing security in their own systems. At the same time it may have had exactly the opposite effect for many others – the rationale being that if the mighty Microsoft cannot protect itself, we surely don't have a hope of doing so, so why should we waste money trying? Those in the latter group may also have looked at Microsoft's share price and noted that, despite the high level of adverse publicity, it had not been affected (which was in marked contrast, for example, to the hit that it took in response to the publicity surrounding the anti-trust ruling earlier in the year). So, the impression one could justifiably form is that the market is not really bothered by a security scare – presumably not considering it to be a likely threat to future profits. Depending upon the exact nature of the breach, this view could, of course, be entirely wrong, and it is a worrying indication that some elements of society may now be becoming too blasé about security.

Approaching Armageddon

Malware such as Melissa and the Love Bug have been significant in terms of the extent to which they spread and the headlines that they grabbed as a result. In terms of their actual ill-effects, however, they were relatively limited. Although the Love Bug undeniably resulted in billions of dollars of estimated consequential losses, the data it destroyed was limited to MP3 music files and JPEG format images – neither of which are likely to represent business critical data in most situations. With appropriate backups, the affected systems were recoverable. The Melissa virus, for all its notoriety, did not actually destroy anything at all. By contrast, around the same time that Melissa was doing the rounds in 1999, another lesser-known virus was also highlighted in the media. The virus in question was called CIH, but is also often referred to as Chernobyl, as in early versions its payload was set to trigger on 26th April, the anniversary of the Soviet nuclear disaster of 1986 (a subsequent version of CIH was released that will trigger on the 26th day of any month). The name CIH was derived from the initials of its author, a twenty-four-year-old man called Chen Ing-hau. The virus was first discovered in Taiwan in June 1998, but did not trigger for the first time until 26th April 1999.

The payload of CIH is what sets it apart from other viruses and, in actual fact, it has two elements. The first overwrites the hard disk with random data, starting from the beginning of the drive and using an infinite loop until it causes the system to crash. The system will then be unable to reboot from its hard disk and the data it contained will most likely be irrecoverable (other than from backup copies). Although this is obviously a very nasty payload, it does not fundamentally set CIH apart from other virus strains that preceded it. The second element of the payload, however, is where things start to get really interesting. This aspect attempts to take malicious advantage of a feature of modern PCs – namely a flash programmable BIOS. The BIOS is the Basic Input Output System and is located on a chip inside the PC. As the name suggests, the BIOS contains basic information that tells the PC how to deal with input and output (e.g. how to read from a disk and display text on the screen). In older systems, the content of the BIOS was fixed in hardware and could not be changed. However, in newer systems, BIOS chips have been made flash programmable (which means they can be overwritten while the chip is still installed inside the PC), enabling easier updates to systems and avoiding the need to replace the chips themselves. CIH takes malicious advantage of the flash capability and attempts to corrupt the data stored in the BIOS. With the BIOS data gone, the computer does not know how to do anything. There is no option to reboot from an uninfected boot disk (as might be the lifeline to overcome other viruses) as the computer cannot get that far into its start-up sequence. You literally have a £1,500 corpse on your hands, which requires hardware repair to enable it to be used again.

At the time of writing, the impacts of CIH have not been as widespread as for other virus strains. When it triggered for the first time in April 1999, it was estimated that it caused over $250 million in damages in Korea, having infected around a million computers.[180] Meanwhile, corporate users elsewhere in the world were largely unaffected, possibly because their anti-virus software was already in place and up-to-date, having been prepared in response to the threat of the Melissa virus. However, to dismiss the problem on this basis is missing the point. CIH demonstrated the ability to render a system totally unusable without a hardware fix. To any user, corporate or domestic, this represents a more significant disruption to activities than simply reinstalling software and data. The latter could normally be done in-house, assuming the availability of software installation disks and data backups. However, overcoming the BIOS problem would almost certainly require intervention from external specialists – further prolonging the time to recover. What has yet to be done, but will inevitably happen (it may have already happened by the time you read this), is for someone to develop and release a virus with the destructive power of CIH combined with the replication capabilities of something like the Love Bug.

Unsuspecting children catch worms online

All of the incidents discussed so far have largely been notable because of some aspect of their technical implementation. However, the following example stands out for a different reason, this time relating to its target audience – namely children. With the level of media coverage associated with incidents like Melissa and the Love Bug, even the most isolated IT user should have got the message about the problems that malware can cause. Following these two incidents in particular, many more users are now aware of the hazard represented by email-based viruses, and would hopefully think twice about opening and executing an attachment on an unexpected or suspicious email. As a result, malware writers face greater problems in successfully distributing their wares (increasing the challenge and, hence, the perceived kudos from actually succeeding) and are consequently dreaming up more inventive approaches.

An example of one such approach appeared in June 2000, with the emergence of a worm program called "Pokey," based upon the popular Nintendo-originated children's craze Pokemon.[181] For the uninitiated, Pokemon is short for Pocket Monster, and is a Japanese cartoon series involving a range of colorful little creatures, which are caught and trained to fight each other. The series, and its associated marketing machine, caused a phenomenon with children, spawning a whole range of associated products – trading cards, video games, cuddly toys, feature films, and many other forms of merchandise. As such, children were keen consumers of any Pokemon-related material that they could get hold of. The main Pokemon character is called Pikachu – a yellow teddy bear-like creature – and is the most popular with the young audience. It was this character that the authors of Pokey used as the basis of their dissemination strategy. The worm arrives as an email with the title "Pikachu Pokemon" and the message "Pikachu is your friend." This is accompanied by an attachment that appears to be a Pokemon animation, a major attraction to encourage the young fans to double-click on it. When they do, of course, the worm's payload is unleashed. Pokey's effect is rather devastating for the infected computer, causing the destruction of the Windows and System directories on Microsoft Windows-based PCs. With the system files gone, the only option is to reinstall the operating system – a task beyond the capabilities of many adult PC users and almost certainly too much for the poor Pokemon trainer who had unwittingly caused the problem.

In practice, Pokey did not have a major impact and spread relatively slowly (being largely confined to the United States). A possible reason for this is that children with email access are currently the exception rather than the rule, particularly outside the U.S. The delay was fortuitous, allowing time for anti-virus vendors to create and incorporate detection within their products – thus further lessening the potential for widespread damage. The anti-virus experts said that this was the first time that a worm or virus had been specifically targeted at children. However, now that the idea has been aired, it is unlikely to be the last. So now, not only do parents and teachers have to worry about their children accidentally accessing undesirable online materials such as pornography, but also the possibility that they may be inadvertently tricked into downloading a virus or other malicious software.

Can't talk now, my phone has a virus

The scenarios and examples considered so far have all been concerned with the introduction of malicious software onto a standard PC platform. However, processing and communications capabilities are now increasingly found in non-PC devices, such as mobile phones and set-top boxes for digital TV. As such, the potential exists for these to be targeted by viruses and other forms of computer abuse (and, as experience in the PC domain has shown, if the possibility is there, it is inevitable that someone will exploit it).

There is already evidence of virus writers recognizing the existence and potential of mobile phones, and then incorporating this into the payloads of their creations. An example of this was reported in early June 2000, with the release of a virus named "Timofonica."[182] The virus utilized the same basic replication method as the Love Bug, which had occurred a month earlier, using an attached Visual Basic Script to send copies of itself to all of the email contacts in the victim's address book. In this instance, the host email message contained critical comments about the Spanish telecommunications operator Telefonica and invited readers to open the attachment to discover details of the company's dubious commercial practices. This, of course, was the hook to stimulate the recipient's interest, and doing so unleashed the payload. It was Timofonica's payload that established a relationship to mobile phones, as one of its actions was to send messages to a Short Message Service (SMS) gateway. SMS messages are a standard feature of GSM mobile phone networks, allowing users to exchange text messages of up to 160 characters. An SMS gateway is a computer server that allows messages to be sent from a normal PC and then relayed on to a nominated mobile handset. Timofonica exploited this facility in order to send SMS messages to thousands of randomly chosen subscribers on the Spanish Movistar service. The addresses to which the message were sent were composed of known prefixes for the service's subscribers (namely 609, 619, 629, 630, 639, 646, 649, or 696), followed by a randomly generated six-digit number. The total number of messages sent was dependent upon the size of the user's Outlook address book – one randomly addressed SMS was generated for each entry. Finally, a further aspect of the Timofonica payload, unrelated to the mobile context, was the corruption of both the CMOS* and boot information on the target PC.[183]

It is important to remember that the Timofonica virus itself was not transmitted wirelessly. Neither did it result in widespread damage or losses in the same way that the Love Bug was responsible for. Nevertheless, the fact that wireless devices were being targeted as an aspect of the payload was an illustration of how they could be drawn into the sphere of malware activity.

Another example occurred a couple of months later, on 9th August, which gave a further foretaste of future problems. This incident was focused in Japan and involved the country's popular i-mode mobile phones (i-mode is a mobile Internet access method, analogous to the WAP standard that is now common in Europe and the United States). i-mode phone users were affected by a prank that had been embedded within an online quiz about relationships. When contestants took part in the quiz, they were posed a question that asked whether they would drink from a girlfriend's half-empty cup, knowing that she had a slight cold. The script was configured such that if they answered "yes" their phone would automatically dial "110" – the Japanese police emergency number. The police reported receiving 400 fake calls in one day as a result.[184] In this case, the prank was not based on a virus or a worm, as it did not spread itself between phones independently and was simply downloaded from a central source. It was, in fact, an example of a Trojan Horse, but the mischievous payload gives an indication of the sort of inconvenience that could be caused via mobile platforms. Although media reports did not suggest that there had been any knock-on problems, it should not be overlooked that making fake calls and wasting police time in this manner could have prevented timely attention from being given to genuine emergency situations – the ultimate consequence of which could have been far more serious.

In addition to these phone-related incidents, there are also examples of malware emerging that target Personal Digital Assistant (PDA) platforms – pocket and palm sized devices running operating systems such as PalmOS, EPOC, and Windows CE. Although these again are not actually being spread automatically by wireless

---

* CMOS stands for Complementary Metal Oxide Semiconductor, and in this context refers to a small amount of battery-powered memory that the PC uses to hold the date, time, and system setup parameters.

communication, they do provide further evidence that mobile devices are being targeted by malware writers seeing the opportunity to cause problems. The most popular PDA platform to date has been PalmOS, and it has consequently been the main target for PDA malware, with several Trojan Horses having emerged. Two early examples were Liberty Crack and Phage, both of which had the effect of removing third-party applications from target devices when they were executed. The Liberty Crack Trojan purported to provide a crack for *Liberty* (a PalmOS-based GameBoy emulator), enabling the free shareware version to be converted into a full version of the product without payment. What it actually did, of course, was remove other applications. Although potentially damaging, the effect of this early example was limited – Liberty Crack had no way of automatically replicating itself to other systems. However, subsequent cases, such as Phage, began to add replication capabilities, albeit in a very limited manner when compared to their desktop PC counterparts. Phage appeared as a program icon on infected PalmOS devices and, when run, had the effect of blanking the screen. However, unlike Liberty Crack, it had virus-like properties in that it was able to spread from one Palm application to another. In addition, the sharing of files from an infected PDA (e.g. via infrared beaming or via a desktop docking station) provided a means for Phage to spread between different devices. In this case, the overall impact and potential damage was still low – resetting the PDA and restoring from a backup would remove the problem. However, it did represent an indication that the PDA malware scene was evolving.

The emergence of malware on PDAs also has significance for mobile phone users, as the functionality of the two devices is currently converging, with the consequence that many future mobile phones will be based upon operating systems inherited from the PDA domain. The consequence of using such operating systems is that they are generally more open than the previous proprietary mobile phone OS devised by individual manufacturers, in order to facilitate and encourage application development by third party suppliers. Whereas the inner workings of manufacturer-specific systems may have been known to few outside the company, a typical PDA operating system will be more fully documented and described for external software developers. This openness facilitates easier and more widespread software development, but it also serves to deliver a more accessible platform for virus writers.

These trends and the incidents previously described have convinced anti-virus companies that the appearance of a truly wireless virus strain is only a matter of time. To quote Vincent Gullotto, the director of Network Associates' AVERT labs, speaking at the time of the Timofonica incident:

> We can't say when specifically … it could be a year, it could be six months, it could be two years … My guess is yes, at some particular point [it will happen].[185]

This is hardly an encouraging prognosis, but it is difficult to disagree with.

The AIDS virus Trojan Horse incident

The last section introduced some examples of Trojan Horse incidents affecting mobile phone and PDA users. The remaining examples now stay with the Trojan theme, including the following example of a rather old incident, which provides a particularly good illustration of the problem.

In December 1989, a major money-making scam was perpetrated by Dr. Joseph Popp, a zoologist from Cleveland, Ohio. His plan essentially involved extortion, but the method by which he chose to attempt it involved the large-scale distribution of a Trojan Horse program. He created a database application, purporting to contain information about the AIDS virus and how to assess an individual's risk of contracting it. This was placed on diskettes and then mailed to around 20,000 recipients on a worldwide basis, along with an accompanying instruction leaflet. Of course, this apparently benevolent act was not what it seemed. The first indication of this was that the nature of the advice presented in the database was quite farcical. Some illustrative examples are listed below:

- "AIDS can be prevented by avoiding the virus"
- "Buy condoms today at a pharmacy when you leave your office"
- "Insist that your sex partner be mutually faithful to the relationship."

Upon seeing this, most users would have already been aware that they had installed a dud as far as useful AIDS data was concerned, making it unlikely that they would have returned to the program very often after the first attempt. However, that was not the point. The program only needed to be installed on the system in order to unleash its Trojan effects. Once this was done, hidden directories and files were created on the host computer and a counter was concealed in one of the system start-up files. When this counter reached 90, the Trojan caused the encryption of data on the victim's hard disk, and presented the user with a message containing Popp's demand for money. This ordered victims to send $378 to a Post Office box in Panama City, in return for which they would be told how to restore access to their data.

It should be noted that the instruction leaflet distributed with the diskette did actually contain an indication that this was no normal piece of software. A couple of key quotations are as follows:

> PC Cyborg Corporation also reserved the rights to use program mechanisms to ensure termination of the use of the program . . . these mechanisms will adversely effect other program applications.

> You are advised of the most serious consequences of your failure to abide by the terms of this license agreement: your conscience may haunt you for the rest of your life . . . and your computer will stop functioning normally.

In fact, during Popp's pre-extradition trial in Cleveland, his lawyers attempted to cite this as evidence to suggest that prospective users had been warned not to use the software if they did not intend to pay, and that, therefore, the corruption of the hard disk was a valid measure to guard against unauthorized use. However, this would be software license protection in the extreme and, unsurprisingly, it was not accepted as a valid defense. Although the users were warned that they would be expected to pay, the database had arrived as unsolicited mail, so it was not until after they had installed the software that they could determine what they might be paying for. Of course, having installed and used it, and experienced the poor quality of the information on offer, there was little chance that they would consider it worth paying for.

The ethics of Popp's methods are highly questionable. Beyond the fact that he was attempting to extort money from his victims, one must also consider the community that he targeted in order to do so. The disks were sent to Europe, to the subscribers of a magazine called PC Business World.[186] Although this list contained people from various backgrounds, it can be assumed that the database would have been of most interest to those from the medical profession. Indeed, another specific group to whom disks were sent was the delegate list from a World Health Organization (WHO) conference on AIDS. As a result, the software would have been loaded onto systems in hospitals and other healthcare establishments. The consequence of the ensuing data loss could, therefore, be extremely serious – the affected systems could conceivably have contained patient records and other data that might pertain to clinical care. The unavailability of such data could lead to care decisions needing to be made without relevant information being available, which could in turn lead to risks for patient safety.

The scam prompted an investigation by the Computer Crime Unit at New Scotland Yard, and the trail was quickly traced back to Popp. He consequently was extradited from the U.S. and sentenced to stand trial in London. However, he exhibited rather strange behavior while on remand (wearing a condom on his nose and putting hair curlers in his beard, in the belief that they would ward off radiation sickness). As a result, he was released in November 1991, after the court decided that he was mentally unfit for trial and he was required to leave the country. However, justice was ultimately served when Popp was brought to trial a year later in Italy, and a Rome court sentenced him to two-and-a-half years in prison.[187] Popp's case is notable because he was the first cyber criminal to be extradited to face charges, and from a U.K. perspective, because his was the first British case of someone being tried for writing malicious code.

Perpetrating the scam had been an expensive business for Popp, with costs of £14,000 to cover the diskettes, instruction leaflets, envelopes and stamps relating to the mailshot. However, the potential reward was far in excess of this. In theory, if the plan had been successful, he could have amassed over $7.5 million in license fee payments from the 20,000 recipients of his diskettes (assuming that everyone had installed the database and then paid up). In reality, however, no one at all actually sent any money to the Panama PO box. Had they done so, and the crime had been successful, then the indications are that Popp had not intended for it to end there. When the FBI raided his home in Ohio, they found one million blank diskettes, which suggested that Popp had intended to use the proceeds from his first mailshot to fund a second one on an even larger scale. Luckily, he did not get this opportunity.

The Moldovan porn scam

In December 1996, a Trojan Horse was used to perpetrate a scam that specifically targeted Net users on the hunt for pornographic images. Web sites offering porno-graphic content can always rely upon attracting a fair share of attention from certain members of the online community, and so using such material as the basis for a scam was a good way to guarantee some revenue. This is essentially the same principle that sits behind things like premium rate telephone sex lines, where the attraction of erotic material is used to entice people to call premium rate numbers.

In late 1996, as now, there were numerous Internet sites offering adult content, but in this incident three new web sites had been established that claimed to provide free images – namely **1adult.com**, **beavisbutthead.com**, and **sexygirls.com**. From these names alone there was nothing that really set them apart from the hundreds of other web sites that also offered materials of an adult nature. Somewhat unusually, however, before being able to display any images, users were required to download a specific application in which to view them. Typically, photographic images (even those from pornographic sites) are downloaded in formats that are supported as standard by web browsers. As such, the need to have a new application may have been seen by some as an indication that something suspicious was going on. In other contexts, however, downloading new software and plug-ins for browsers is not that unusual, so more trusting users may have thought little of it. They would have been wrong, of course, because in this case the viewer was actually a Trojan Horse …

Once downloaded, the program performed several hidden activities. Firstly, it muted the sound from the computer's speakers in order to prevent the user from being able to hear any subsequent sounds of modem activity. Having done this, it hung up the current connection to the user's local Internet Service Provider, and instructed the modem to dial a number in Moldova (a small country in Eastern Europe). The call was then forwarded to an ISP in North America, which enabled the Internet session to continue.[188] The user would then be reconnected to the adult web site and one of the desired images would appear. From the user's perspective, the disconnection and reconnection operations would have happened entirely transparently, and they could happily continue browsing the Internet … or inspecting the newly acquired photograph. All the while, of course, they would now be paying for an international call – at a rate of more than $2 per minute. The long-distance connection was maintained when the user left the viewer program and even when they attempted to close their Internet session. Only powering off the computer or the modem would actually terminate the call. As a result, the call charges to the Moldovan number began to accumulate.

The motivation for the Trojan was not just to maliciously incur costs for the unwitting users – it was to actually make money for the creators of the program. The basis of the scam related to the way that international call charges are split between the telephone operators involved. Although from the subscriber's perspective they only pay a single charge (per call) to their long-distance service provider, what actually happens is that their provider will then pay a share of the charge to the foreign telecoms provider whose network has been called. In this case, the routing via the Moldovan number yielded revenue for the Moldovan telecoms provider. This provider was not, however, the originator of the scam – the perpetrators were found to be two companies and three associated individuals from New York. They earned money by being paid a portion of the revenues received by the Moldovan telephone carrier to whom the international telephone numbers were assigned.

In due course, the affected subscribers began to notice something amiss – particularly when phone bills started to appear with call charges to Moldova totalling hundreds, or even thousands, of dollars. In addition, fraud control groups at the U.S. long-distance phone companies also noticed the operation of the scam. In six weeks, around 800,000 minutes of call time was logged from the U.S. to Moldova – many times more than usual and, hence, very noticeable to those monitoring the patterns of phone activity for signs of fraud or other unusual behavior.[189] These factors triggered an investigation by the Federal Trade Commission (FTC), which traced the registrations of web sites concerned. The investigation resulted in $2.4 million in refunds being agreed with the companies and individuals concerned. It was estimated that over 38,000 people had been caught out by the scam.[190]

The underlying lesson in this case, as with many other Trojan Horse incidents, is that we as users should not blindly trust software that we are sent or can be downloaded freely over the net, unless we are sure of the legitimacy of the source.

Causing problems without writing code

All of the previous incidents described in this chapter have relied upon the originator of the malware actually writing their own code. Although admittedly in some cases the coding work was not that challenging (such as with the numerous Love Bug clones that sprung up as a result of people modifying the original script), there was nonetheless some requirement for the malware creators to be code authors. However, as this section will show, this is by no means a prerequisite for causing a malware alert. There are utilities that will write the code for you, and there are some forms of virus that do not involve any program code or script at all.

Malware creation tools

In the same way that hackers have automated tools to assist them in their endeavors, so too do malware writers. While hacking tools often provide the means to attack and penetrate a system, malware tools provide the means for new strains to be created and unleashed by total novices. As with automated DoS and cracking tools, the problem with malware toolkits is that they make the task of releasing a virus or worm so easy that a complete novice could do it. Additionally, unlike some of the categories of hacker tool, there is no legitimate security role that can be claimed for these programs. Whereas an administrator could use a scanner or a password cracker to test the security of their own system, there is no corresponding use to which they could put a home-grown virus.

Virus creation toolkits are not a new idea, and a number of programs (such as Virus Creation Laboratory) have been around since the early 1990s, offering operation via pull-down menus and a selection of payload options. The difference now is the mass audience that they are made available to via the Internet. They can now be located via a simple web search*, enabling someone who simply reads or hears of their existence to locate one in a matter of minutes. Numerous kits are available (one typical web site, for example, listed fifty different choices – other observers have put the total at over 100), with names such as the following:

- Instant Virus Production Kit.
- Kaos.
- MuTation Engine 1.00a.
- SiCem virus creation utility.
- VBS Worm Generator.
- Windows Virus creation kit.

Taking the example of the Vbs Worms Generator, it is possible to see just how easy it makes the process of creating a potentially harmful piece of malware. The whole thing is remarkably simple. To begin with, the program has a user-friendly

* A quick search on MSN yielded several links to appropriate web sites within the first fifteen hits.

interface, with the same familiar look and feel as other Windows applications. It also comes complete with a small help file to guide the creation process. The main interface is depicted in Figure 5.5, which enables the creation of a custom-designed worm program with just a few entries and mouse clicks.

The author of the program, who goes by the alias [K]Alamar, claims to be seventeen years old and to come from Buenos Aires in Argentina. In the program itself and the text file that accompanies it, [K]Alamar suggests that the software is intended for educational purposes only, and that he accepts no responsibility for any damage caused by files created using it.

Having downloaded and installed the program, the actual creation of a worm can literally be done in under a minute if you already know the options you want to choose. The characteristics of the new worm are specified on a step-by-step basis, as follows:

1. Give the worm a name and identify the author (clearly, the latter would involve using an alias rather than entering your real name).

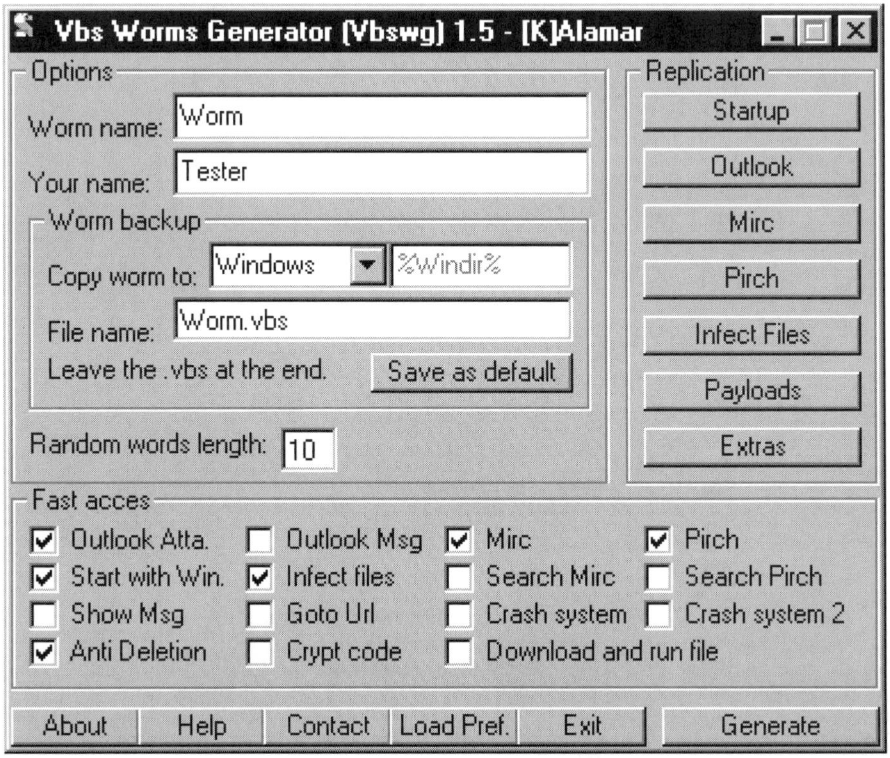

FIGURE 5.5 The main control interface of Vbs Worms Generator 1.5

2. Select a method of replication. Figure 5.6 presents an overview of the mechanisms offered as options within the toolkit, as described on the "readme" text file that accompanies the tool (spelling mistakes are as they appeared in the file). As can be seen, a worm can send copies of itself to users listed in Microsoft Outlook address books, affect users of Internet Relay Chat channels, and can overwrite selected types of disk file.

3. Choose up to four actions from a selection of potential payloads for the worm to carry out (and the day and month that it should do so), as follows:

   – Message: the worm will display a message box containing text specified by the user (the default is "You are stupid!").
   – Open web address: opens up a user-specified web address.
   – Crash System: the worm will repeatedly attempt to create 1Mb variables until the system runs out of memory – causing it to crash.
   – Crash System 2: the worm repeatedly launches notepad applications until the system again runs out of resources and crashes.

```
Outlook Replication:

Send as attachment: It uses the same function that all the vbs's,
js's or any other kind of worm,+ it sends a message, that you can
define, whit te worm attached to every preson in the user's address
list.

Send in html code: The worm is added to the html code of the
message, so, when the person views it, they'e infected!

Mirc replication:

Search for mirc.ini(what means that the mirc is there) in the most
commons floders(programfiles\mirc, c:\mirc, c:\mirc32) and if it
is found, the worm create "script.ini" in that folder, that script
make the mirc sends the worm to every person that join to a
channel.

Pirch replication:
Same as mirc, but for pirch (i haven't tested the script cause i
haven't got pirch, please someone test it and tell me if this
work).

Infect Files:

The worm will search for all the hard drives (and the network
drives too, i think) for files whit the extencion that you want(in
this version only .vbs and vbe are searched) and copy overwrite him
whit itself.
```

FIGURE 5.6 Replication options offered by the Vbs Worms Generator

Having done this, the new creation is ready to be released to the world. However, to make things better (for the worm), the toolkit also provides other features, such as the ability for the worm to conceal itself from anti-virus software using encryption. Also worthy of note is that [K]Alamar invites comments from users (to quote the readme file that accompanies the program, "Any idea?, contact me and i will add it!"), and an option is available on the main control page for sending email messages to him.

So, although everything is made incredibly easy, would a worm created with such a program have the same chances of success as one that was hand-coded? Alarmingly, the answer appears to be "Yes," as a worm created using this very toolkit was responsible for a widely reported incident in early 2001. A worm called "OnTheFly" was released by a twenty-year-old Dutchman operating under the same name, and spread like wildfire. The reason for its success was that it was distributed in an email that claimed to contain pictures of Russian tennis star Anna Kournikova (which led the media to christen it the Kournikova virus). The media attention devoted to the worm was so great that it frightened OnTheFly into giving himself up to the authorities – he was apparently unprepared for the worm to spread so quickly or create an incident of such scale.[191]

Hoax viruses

With the increased public awareness of viruses, it was inevitable that someone would hit upon the idea of exploiting this as a basis for hoaxing other people. The idea of the Hoax virus basically involves making up a warning about a scary-sounding, but non-existent, virus strain and then sending it out to other people and asking them to pass the word on to all their friends. The method takes advantage of people's goodwill and of how quickly messages can be spread on the Internet.

On the surface, the idea just sounds like someone's idea of a joke – albeit one in rather poor taste – which does not really result in any harm. However, due to people's paranoia about viruses, it can lead to large amounts of unnecessary concern and a similar degree of wasted time for system administrators having to respond to false warnings. Figure 5.7 illustrates an example of one of these messages (the so-called "Win a holiday" hoax, which was originally circulated in 1998), which the author has personally received on numerous occasions.

As can be seen, the text is worded in a way that purports to be helpful, and includes enough information to convince the average user that it is something they ought to be concerned about. To the casual reader, it also includes elements that suggest its legitimacy, by making reference to well-known technology companies such as Microsoft and America Online (AOL). As such, it is not surprising that many well-meaning, but misguided, individuals happily comply with the request to share the information with their "online friends," thinking that they are being helpful. In reality, of course, they are unwittingly perpetuating the hoax. The approach is analogous to spreading a virus via social engineering. The replication in this case is occurring via human intervention. It can still cause significant inconvenience and wasted time as people pass on the message, and system administrators become inundated with emails from people who are just trying to be helpful. This is effectively the payload of the virus.

There are many such messages in circulation and, as of late May 2001, Symantec Corporation had details of 118 hoax viruses on its web site.* However, it can be observed that this number is very small when set against the number of genuine virus strains that have been catalogued. In addition, hoaxes are not being unleashed with the same frequency as the real thing (an earlier examination of the Symantec site in May 2000 found the list of hoaxes to number eighty-two, and so the number of hoaxes that emerged in the subsequent twelve months was only thirty-six).

Some people have seen the humor in the hoax virus situation and have created spoofs in the style of the typical hoax virus warnings. Figure 5.8, which describes the fictitious "Badtimes virus" (a spoof on a genuine virus hoax called "Good Times," which originally surfaced in 1994), provides a good example. This makes such outrageous claims that, hopefully, not even the most naive user would take them seriously (having said that, Symantec include it in their list of virus hoaxes, so someone might have believed it!).

```
Subject: VIRUS WARNING !

Dear all,

If you receive an email titled "WIN A HOLIDAY" DO NOT open it.  It
will erase everything on your hard drive. Forward this letter out
to as many people as you can. This is a new, very malicious virus
and not many people know about it.

This information was announced yesterday morning from Microsoft;
please share it with everyone that might access the Internet.
Once again, pass this along to EVERYONE in your address book so
that this may be stopped. Also, do not open or even look at any
mail that says "RETURNED OR UNABLE TO DELIVER". This virus will
attach itself to your computer components and render them useless.
Immediately delete any mail items that say this. AOL has said that
this is a very dangerous virus and that there is NO remedy for it
at this time. Please practice cautionary measures and
forward this to all your online friends ASAP".
```

FIGURE 5.7 The "WIN A HOLIDAY" hoax virus warning

*See **http://www.symantec.com/avcenter/hoax.html.**

This consideration of hoax viruses concludes by highlighting another example in which, like Badtimes, people were just using the whole virus issue as the basis for a bit of a joke, but it also serves to illustrate what can happen when people simply do not get the joke at all! In 1995, *Datamation* magazine published an April Fool's Day

```
Subject:  VIRUS WARNING _ VERY VERY NASTY


VIRUS WARNING: KEEP READING

If you receive an e-mail entitled 'Badtimes', delete it
immediately. Do not open it. Apparently this one is pretty nasty.
It will not only erase everything on your hard drive, but it will
also delete anything on disks within 20 feet of your computer.

It demagnetises the stripes on ALL of your credit cards. It
reprograms your PIN access code, screws up the tracking on your
VCR and uses subspace field harmonics to scratch any CDs you
attempt to play. It will recalibrate your refrigerator's coolness
settings so all your icecream melts and your milk curdles. It will
program your phone autodial to call only 0898 sex line
numbers.

This virus will mix antifreeze into your fish tank. It will drink
all your beer. It will leave dirty socks on the coffee table when
you are expecting company. It will replace your shampoo with
engine oil and your engine oil with orange juice, all the while
dating your current girl/boyfriend behind your back and billing
their hotel rendezvous to your Visa card.

It will cause you to run with scissors and throw things in a way
that is only fun until someone loses an eye. It will rewrite your
backup files, changing all your active verbs into passive tense
and incorporating undetectable misspellings which grossly change
the interpretations of key sentences.

If 'Badtimes' is opened in Windows95/98, it will leave the toilet
seat up and your hair dryer plugged in dangerously close to a full
bath. It will also molecularly rearrange your aftershave/
perfume, causing it to smell like dill pickles.

It will install itself into your cistern and lie in wait
until someone important, like your boss or girlfriend, does a
serious number 2, then block the s-bend and cause your toilet to
overflow. In the worst case scenario, it may stick pins in your
eyes.

PLEASE FORWARD THIS WARNING TO EVERYONE YOU KNOW.
```

FIGURE 5.8 The "Badtimes" hoax virus spoof

article that presented details of what it claimed were a number of new viruses that had recently been discovered "in the wild." These were listed under the serious-sounding heading "Virus Threat Gains Momentum." Here are a few of the descriptions:[192]

- Clipper*: Scrambles all of the data on a hard drive, thereby rendering it useless. The National Security Agency knows how to restore the data but refuses to tell you how to do it.
- Clinton: Designed to infect programs, like other viruses, but then eradicates itself when it can't decide exactly which program to infect.
- Lecture: Deliberately formats your hard drive, destroying all of the data, and then scolds you for not catching it.
- SPA**: Examines programs on your hard disk to see whether they are properly licensed. If illegally copied software is detected, the virus seizes the PC's modem and automatically dials 911 and asks for help.

It can hopefully be seen that these definitions were intended to be humorous, as the descriptions do not exactly sound like typical virus behavior. The article appeared alongside a range of other spoof stories in the magazine's "Cutting Edge" column, which had been entirely given over to April Fool jokes for that issue (a tradition that dated back to 1957, as the magazine's editorial actually explained). As the further examples below illustrate, the other stories were similarly unbelievable and included details of:

- a hacker sting in which the authorities caught a group that had been responsible for using the Hubble space telescope to spy on a nudist colony and had re-routed telephone calls from the White House to the fictitious Marcel Marceau University (described as an institution for mimes).[193] For any readers aware of cybercrime history, a further clue to the fabricated nature of the story was given when the article referred to the incident as "Operation Moon Angel" (a spoof of the genuine Operation Sundevil raids of 1990 that had been conducted against suspected hackers across America by the U.S. Secret Service).
- a press conference in which the CEO of chip manufacturer Intel blew a raspberry at the assembled journalists and suggested that they should have stuck with the

---

* Clipper was the name of a controversial encryption chip proposed by the U.S. National Security Agency, which contained a backdoor to allow law enforcement to easily decrypt any messages.

** At the time of the article, SPA stood for Software Publishers Association, which has since become part of the Software & Information Industry Association (SIIA).

original mathematically flawed version of the Pentium processor instead of upgrading to one in which the bug had been fixed.[194]

- a group of Californian surfers launching a petition to ban the use of the term "surfing the Internet" because "The dudes who claim they're surfing the Net are really holed up in the dark in front of computers. Man, that's something true surfers can't relate to."[195]

- a group of virus writers in Romania announcing plans to set up a company called VirusSoft to sell viruses. The leader of the group was claimed to be a legendary virus writer called Vlad Impaler.[196]

Unfortunately, despite the fact that the whole column was an April Fool joke and that anything more than a cursory inspection of the material suggested it to be nonsense, some people still accepted the virus stories as fact. Notable amongst the believers were a couple of U.S. professors with an interest in computer crime, who read the article and proceeded to quote the virus examples in their own publications.[197] The details were subsequently cited as real world examples in papers presented to the FBI and the Academy of Criminal Justice Sciences. In addition, mention of the spoof viruses also appeared in the FBI's Law Enforcement Bulletin in an article from the same authors entitled "Computer Crime: An Emerging Challenge for Law Enforcement." More informed sources pointed out to the FBI that the viruses were actually jokes and reference to them was consequently removed from the Bureau's web site. However, the printed version of the article had already been sent to 55,000 subscribers, probably serving to perpetuate the myth even further.

This incident serves to illustrate a worrying combination of gullibility and inadequate research. The fact that the stories were readily believed – not just by the professors, but also by the parties who accepted and published their papers – illustrates how easily people seem to accept outrageous claims relating to computer crime. This may in itself be the result of a great deal of media hype about an issue that relatively few people really understand. From an academic perspective, the fact that the original material from Datamation was consumed and reproduced verbatim, without any further verification of the facts, serves to indicate a lack of rigor on the part of those claiming to offer expert opinion. It must be remembered, of course, that no further supporting evidence could possibly have been found because the stories were made up. What could have been found, without much difficulty, was the admission, in the same issue of the magazine, that it was all a joke – to quote the editorial: ". . . *Nor did anything else happen as reported in this issue's Cutting Edge . . . .*"[198] However, it can be noted that the unsuspecting professors also believed the story about the Hubble hackers, and presented details of that in their later articles as well.

Future directions for malware

To date, the biggest impact of malware has been in the business domain. There are probably two main reasons for this, both related to the fact that the business environment offers an open route for the mechanisms by which malware spreads. Firstly, the business world frequently involves the exchange of documents and other files between different systems – providing a means for infected materials to pass from machine to machine. In earlier days, this exchange would occur via the sharing of disks. Nowadays, however, it is equally likely to occur over a network. The network, and specifically the Internet, represents the second reason why business has been more prone to malware incidents, because to date there has been a greater likelihood of business IT users having an Internet connection and receiving risky materials via email or the web. Of course, once malware has found its way into a business, the effect is likely to be felt across a number of systems, rather than the single computer that would typically be found in the home.

As a result of the impacts having centered around organizational users, the general public may still consider themselves largely immune to the problems. In spite of seeing the statistics about malware or reading the media reports of particular incidents, people may have considered themselves at least one step removed from the issue, even if they were computer users at home. However, the discussion presented in this chapter has illustrated that more recent malware developments are likely to affect non-business users – relevant examples being the viruses targeting mobile devices and those aimed at children. As such, there is a greater likelihood that the average user will ultimately get some first-hand experience of the problems. In addition, increasing Internet access from PCs in the home will expand the routes available for the spread of more traditional forms of malware. Finally, as the home PC is increasingly accompanied by other Internet access devices, such as digital televisions, set-top boxes, and video game consoles, it is conceivable that further forms of malware will become specifically focused at the home market. Although it would be foolish to speculate about what the precise effects might be, it can be observed that all of the aforementioned devices include a significant dependence upon software in their operation. It is, therefore, not difficult to imagine ways in which this could be used to mischievous effect if malware was able to enter and compromise the device's normal operation. In addition, devices such as the set-top boxes may contain personal details, such as the subscriber's bank account or credit card number for online purchasing, which could again be considered more vulnerable to attack if devices were directly accessible on the Internet. It was as a result of concerns over Internet security that the British satellite television broadcaster BskyB chose to establish its own proprietary environment for its interactive digital television information, entertainment, and shopping services, rather than providing Internet access for its subscribers.[199]

It can also be confidently forecast that malware will become more sophisticated in traditional PC environments. The worm and virus incidents of recent years have already demonstrated how techniques have evolved to take advantage of the newer facilities available to them (e.g. the use of automated email distribution methods). In terms of future advances, anti-virus experts predict that rogue programs will become more difficult to detect. For example, it has been suggested that the techniques viruses use to conceal themselves will become smarter, advancing from current polymorphic techniques to fully metamorphic approaches – whereby the virus is able to alter itself each time it is passed on.[200] This will render them invisible to detection via standard signature-based methods, placing a greater reliance upon heuristics that are able to identify virus-like activity and behavior.

Another example, which has already surfaced in early forms, is the multi-platform virus. It has already been observed that macro viruses like Melissa have the potential to cause infections across different operating systems if the same host applications are being run. However, it has also been shown that it is possible to create a cross-platform virus that infects executable (program) files. The first known example of this came to light in late March 2001, with the release of the W32.Winux virus. This has the capability to infect files on both Windows and Linux operating systems – the two most likely candidates to be found on an end-user's desktop. Up until this point, file viruses would exclusively target a single operating system, and Windows was undoubtedly the target of choice, as it has the highest installed user base and, hence, largest potential for impact. Indeed, by the time Winux arrived, it was estimated that the total number of viruses targeting Linux was less than ten.[201] The ability to target multiple operating systems with a single virus would, however, be attractive for the virus writer looking to cause maximum disruption or damage. In the case of Winux, the virus could replicate under the main desktop flavors of Windows (95/98/Me/NT/2000) and under Linux. It achieved this by infecting .EXE files (Windows executables) and .ELF files (the Linux equivalent). Nonetheless, the specific threat from Winux was considered to be very small – it neither spread quickly nor carried a particularly destructive payload. The significance, however, was in providing a proof-of-concept that would doubtless give ideas to other virus writers, who could potentially use the cross-platform technique to more harmful effect. This is not an idle speculation – evidence has shown that once a malware program pioneers a particular technique, numerous strains will follow that attempt to build upon it (the Melissa and Love Bug cases provide good examples, with numerous viruses and worms having subsequently appeared that utilize the similar replication methods, but combine them with different payloads).

With observations like these in mind, it is clear that, with the help of advancing technologies and their evermore-inventive creators, viruses and other forms of malware will continue to evolve and will represent an ongoing problem for users at all levels.

S U M M A R Y

With the exception of the wry smiles that may have been prompted by some of the hoax virus tales, the discussion in this chapter has painted a relatively bleak picture. This is not without justification – malware-related incidents, in particular viruses and worms, are the most prevalent forms of cybercrime. These self-replicating categories of malware can be pretty indiscriminate, infecting any systems in which the opportunity arises. This can be contrasted with hacker attacks, in which (a) the perpetrator will generally be making a conscious decision to target a particular system and (b) the time and effort involved to stage the attack will be longer – thus limiting the number of systems that could feasibly be affected in any given period. Having said this, there are a number of things that can be done to protect systems and reduce their vulnerability. With proliferation of viruses via email and other downloadable methods, the fact is that you are now likely to be significantly safer if you do not use the Internet. However, for many people this would be impractical … and much less fun. Luckily, a combination of security technology and appropriate vigilance by individual users can provide significant protection. Anti-virus software companies are now very experienced in providing inoculations to known viruses, and have proved themselves capable of rapid response when new strains arise. For example, Symantec Corporation released a definition to enable the detection and repair of systems infected by the Love Bug on 4th May 2000 – the same day that the worm itself first appeared.[202] The fact that anti-virus software exists, however, is not in itself a solution to the problem. Users have to be educated to realize that they need them, and protection relies upon having an *up-to-date* package installed. The last point is particularly important to remember. If you are a PC user and are reading this safe in the knowledge that you installed a new anti-virus program six months ago, then the unfortunate fact is that you are not safe at all. The rate of release for new strains, and the speed at which mechanisms like email allow them to spread, means that weekly or even daily updates are not out of the question.

In conclusion, the malware problem certainly does not look like it will ever go away, but it can tentatively be suggested that the issue is manageable if the appropriate precautions are taken.

Societal impacts of cybercrime

THE PREVIOUS THREE CHAPTERS HAVE FOCUSED QUITE HEAVILY UPON particular categories of cybercrime and the impacts that have resulted in a number of specific cases. However, there are also cumulative effects that influence a wider population than those organizations or individuals that find themselves the victims of incidents. For example, the occurrence and reporting of cybercrime will undoubtedly have some effect upon the attitudes and awareness of the general public. This, in turn, may color their views regarding the acceptance of information technology and the new opportunities that it presents to them. From another perspective, knowing that computer crime and abuse is occurring will mean that people expect some form of legal protection against it, as well as appropriate punishment for those responsible. The issue consequently has major impacts upon the laws and legislation that are appropriate to the modern age. With these points in mind, this chapter explores some of the various impacts that cybercrime has upon the citizens of the information society.

Implications for society at large

The most obvious impact of cybercrime is felt by its victims (or even potential victims). This raises the question of how ready individuals and organizations are to accept the fact that the issue is relevant to them. When a significant proportion of the population is still not at ease with technology, the widely reported incidents of computer abuse can do nothing but give the information society a bad reputation (or, indeed, worsen an already bad one – given that, in the eyes of many, computers are already perceived as job-slayers and the creators of a technological elite). It is off-putting enough for novices to be faced with the task of learning to use IT (along with overcoming the associated burden of terminology and jargon), without feeling that they are entering an unfriendly world where others will deliberately set out to damage their systems.

The greatest IT opportunities to emerge in recent years, for organizations and end users alike, have been the Internet and the World Wide Web. The Internet represents a fundamental advance in terms of communication, and the sharing of information and resources. The subset of the Internet represented by the web is many things to many people: information source, shop window, marketplace, entertainment venue – the list goes on. Many organizations and individuals can, therefore, see benefits that the Internet and the web offer to *them*. However, along with the good things that they may have heard or read in recent years, some of the most memorable headlines have come from incidents such as Melissa and the Love Bug. From the perspective of an organization debating whether to invest in IT or Internet connectivity, such bad publicity may count against the decision – potentially harming their future compet-itiveness and productivity as a result.

Even restricting the discussion to existing Internet users, it is likely that the majority have very little appreciation of the online world in which they participate. They use their email systems to communicate and this may be the full extent of their knowledge. They do not understand how the system works, and quite legitimately they have no wish to. They may also have little or no appreciation of the other groups with whom they share cyberspace. It may not be apparent to them that hackers have established their own communities on the Internet. The fact that hackers have far more of an appreciation of the virtual world in which they are operating than most other users makes them better placed to take advantage of it. While a detailed understanding of technology is not necessary in order for individuals to be able to prosper in the information society, it is important that there is adequate awareness and confidence. In his 1994 book *The Virtual Community*, Howard Rheingold makes the crucial point that potential opportunities offered by technology can only be realized by an informed population.[203] As such, an awareness of the problems, some potential solutions and the associated laws is not only prudent, but increasingly essential.

The need for awareness is never more relevant than when you become the victim of cybercrime. However, it appears that the issue is currently regarded somewhat differently to other forms of crime. For example, one would instinctively assume that, if an organization suspects, or discovers concrete proof, that it has become the victim of a cybercrime, then it would report the incident to the police. However, it has been estimated that as few as 5 percent of computer crimes are ever actually reported.[204] There are three general reasons why this may be the case. Firstly the organizations concerned may not consider the incidents to be significant enough to warrant concern or further action. A second potential reason is that the victim may lack confidence in the ability of the authorities to deal with the matter, and may feel that there is little to gain by getting them involved as few cases result in convictions (e.g. the chances of prosecution for hacking in the U.S. are claimed to be one in 10,000[205]). However, research suggests that the third explanation is the most likely – namely, that organizations do not wish to report crimes as they are concerned about the adverse effects that widespread knowledge of such incidents could have upon their business.[206] Organizations are generally keen to avoid adverse publicity, as this may risk losing the confidence of the public or their shareholders. In addition, certain incidents could (if publicized) lead to a risk of legal liability. From a more personal perspective, those responsible for maintaining security may prefer to hush things up rather than report an incident in order to avoid potential ridicule by peers. The result of all this is that, in many cases, incidents are not willingly reported.

It is, of course, easy to appreciate the company perspective in these situations – particularly in cases where the loss or disruption is ultimately perceived to be negligible or, at least, manageable. It may simply not be worth the effort, or indeed the risk, for them to report an incident. At the same time, those that keep quiet can be considered to be helping to hide the extent of the problem – which ultimately makes life more difficult for the rest of us. If the overall extent of the problem is underestimated, it will certainly receive less attention than it actually deserves. This may be manifested within individual organizations (where those in charge may still focus their attentions upon more traditional threats such as burglary), as well as at higher levels, such as the level of funding allocated by governments to cybercrime prevention initiatives.

Certain incidents are, of course, of such high profile that the organizations concerned have little chance of keeping them quiet (e.g. the hacking of Microsoft), or the effects are so widespread that people are not ashamed to put their hands up and admit to having been affected (e.g. the Love Bug incident, where many big name organizations were mentioned in media reports). Although these incidents act as periodic wake-up calls to organizations at large, the impression that comes across is of the cybercrime problem being one of occasional, isolated occurrences rather than a continual issue to be aware of. Such attitudes will not be acceptable if the information society is to fulfill its full potential. With the computer as the very hub of operations, any nefarious activities will have to be policed effectively if the society is to succeed. There should, therefore, be the same moral obligations to assist in the prevention and punishment of offences that are encouraged in conventional society.

Public attitudes and awareness

With so many high-profile cybercrime incidents having been reported in the media, some form of public reaction is to be expected. However, while various surveys have previously assessed the *level* of cybercrime (as indicated in Chapter 2), they have not considered the wider issue of how it may be affecting public perceptions of information technology. This is a significant issue in the context of the information society, particularly in scenarios where public trust and confidence are required to ensure wide-scale acceptance of technology. The Internet already has a general reputation for being insecure, which may ultimately limit its acceptance by the general public and lead them to less flexible solutions. As such, it is useful to determine more specifically how cybercrime incidents are perceived and the possible effects that this may have. To this end, a survey was conducted to assess the attitudes and awareness of the general public, as well as the influence the media has over individual views and perceptions of computer crime and abuse. The survey was distributed to a wide range of individuals and organizations, and was made available in both printed and online versions. A total of 175 responses were obtained as the basis for the analysis that now follows.

Survey respondents

The survey demographics showed a male dominance in all age groups, with 80 percent of the total respondents being male. There was also a bias toward younger members of the population, with 42 percent aged between sixteen and twenty-four, 32 percent between twenty-five and thirty-four, 19 percent between thirty-five and forty-nine, and the remainder over fifty. With 74 percent of the respondents aged below thirty-five, it is clear that the vast majority of the responses were likely to be from people who had "grown up" with IT to some extent.

A high number of responses were received from people employed in the technology field (with 103 out of the 175 responses claiming to be from the computing, communications or engineering domains). Academically over 70 percent of the respondents claimed to hold A-Levels (final school exams) or above, with 44 percent having a degree-level education. This represents a generally high level of academic achievement and reflects the fact that the distribution of a large proportion of surveys occurred via academic channels.

The vast majority of respondents had considerable familiarity with IT, with over 98 percent having used a computer for over a year, 88 percent using a computer at work, and 84 percent using one at home. In terms of the level of use, the results indicated that, in both home and work environments, over half of the respondents used their systems for four hours per week or more. The respondents were also asked about the availability of Internet access, with 88 percent claiming to have it at work, and 48 percent having access at home. The latter statistic indicates that the respondent group was clearly ahead of the U.K. average in terms of Internet adoption, as the penetration into U.K. homes at the time was considered to be around 14 percent.[207] Such considerable exposure to IT placed the respondents in a good position to offer opinions about computer crime and abuse, as they were aware of the technology and its implications. However, the composition of the respondent group did tend to preclude an assessment of how non-IT aware members of the public might have been affected by media presentation of cybercrime issues.

Personal misuse practices

Before asking the respondents about a variety of computer abuse issues, the survey attempted to gauge their own morals. This was achieved by obtaining their views regarding three types of dubious practice, namely the use of unlicensed software, unauthorized use of IT facilities, and the sharing of passwords.

The issue of software piracy is a recognized problem for the IT industry, and various initiatives have been established to monitor and control the problem. An example is the Business Software Alliance (BSA), an international organization established in 1988 and now representing the interests of leading software developers from sixty-five countries. Its activities include educating users about the issues of software copyright, and directly fighting the problem of piracy. In recent years, the BSA has taken a firmer stance on the use of unlicensed software in the workplace, with initiatives such as Crackdown 99 – a four-month campaign in which many small-sized U.K. organizations were contacted to request information about their software-licensing status.[208] Despite such efforts, the responses to the author's survey revealed that the use of unlicensed software was still rife, at 30 percent. In addition, 20 percent of respondents claimed they did not know the status of the software they were using, and 12 percent declined to answer this question. However, this was overshadowed by 61 percent of domestic users with unlicensed software, although again 18 percent declined to answer.

The results indicated that 75 percent of those using computers at work used their equipment for non-work related activities. Although this type of activity is classed as abuse according to the categorizations of bodies such as the U.K. Audit Commission, it may well depend upon the policy of individual organizations as to what extent it is permissible. However, the level to which such illegitimate activities occur may well be of interest to employers.

In terms of passwords, 21 percent of the 151 respondents who used computers at work claimed to have used another person's password or account without their consent or knowledge. This is especially of concern as, in a later question, 55 percent of these people were then amongst the 65 percent of respondents who considered the act of viewing someone else's data to be a serious act of computer abuse (although how they can reconcile their views and their own actions is questionable). Finally, despite the obvious risks, 29 percent of respondents claimed that other people knew their password(s). Issues relating to password-based authentication are discussed in more detail in Chapter 8.

Opinions on computer crime and abuse

In general terms, over 80 percent of respondents felt that computer crime and abuse was a problem. Although this represents the vast majority of respondents, it is surprising that the figure is not higher still. The fact that a fifth of respondents do not perceive cybercrime as a problem suggests that they either have an extremely lenient view of the activities or do not recognize the significance of IT in modern society.

A more detailed evaluation of respondents' views began by asking them to assess the seriousness of a range of potential abuse scenarios. As can be seen from the results in Table 6.1, most acts of computer crime were rightly considered to be of serious concern. However, a number of interesting observations can also be made. Firstly, it can be noted that only theft of computer equipment was considered to be entirely criminal, with no respondents considering it to be acceptable. Secondly, the incidents that were most readily identified as being "very serious" were those with a clear analogy in the real world (i.e. theft, sabotage and, to a lesser extent, fraud). By contrast, a surprisingly high proportion of respondents expressed indifference or no concern about issues such as unauthorized copying of data or software, or viewing someone else's data. This indicates that many people may have little appreciation of issues such as privacy in an IT context, and draws into question whether they would be able to make informed decisions about their own use of technology. The responses regarding unauthorized copying of software tie in with the earlier results observed in relation to personal misuse practices.

Respondents were asked a number of questions in relation to computer hackers, which represent one of the most "hyped" forms of abuse in the mass media. When asked to describe their image of a hacker, the strongest single view that emerged (from 30 percent of respondents) was solitary, young, male, and lacking social skills – which is, of course, the stereotypical image previously discussed in Chapter 3. No other strong view was apparent from the other 70 percent of responses, with many respondents giving their opinions of what hackers *do* rather than the type of people

TABLE 6.1 Views on computer crime and abuse

	Very serious %	← %	Indifferent %	→ %	No crime %
Viruses	71	17	9	1	2
Viewing someone else's data	29	37	25	4	5
Altering someone else's data	80	15	3	0	2
Theft of computer equipment	82	15	3	0	0
Unauthorized copying of software	18	22	36	13	11
Unauthorized copying of data	24	35	26	6	9
Computer fraud	70	20	9	0	1
Sabotage	90	6	3	0	1

they are. With regard to the popularity of the stereotypical image, it should be noted that although this is often still the case, the use of hacking skills is no longer the sole province of the lone teenager in his bedroom to whom this image is normally applied. For example, there is evidence to suggest that hacking skills are being applied in organized activities such as information warfare and cyberterrorism (see Chapter 7). Such activities are beyond the scope of the loner portrayed by the stereotype, and suggest that some people need to reappraise their views of what hacking may mean in modern society.

The respondents were also asked whether they considered hacking to be acceptable (71 percent claiming it is not), an invasion of privacy (80 percent claiming it is), and theft (52 percent claiming it is). It can be noted from these figures that there were surprisingly large proportions of respondents who did not appear to be taking a negative view of hacker activity. To further determine perceptions of hacking and attitudes toward the hackers, the survey asked for opinions of why people hack, the results of which are shown in Table 6.2. This clearly illustrates that the majority of respondents can identify with hackers having multiple motivations.

It is interesting to consider in more detail the views of the 29 percent of respondents who felt that hacking *is* acceptable. Of this group, the views expressed regarding the motivations for hacking were generally benign (i.e. for the thrill of it, out of curiosity, and to "beat the system"). However, more than half of them still considered hacking to represent an invasion of privacy – which seems contradictory to it being acceptable.

The respondents were asked whether they considered that acting via a computer was likely to make the hackers feel less responsible for their actions. The basis for this is that it is often conjectured that many hackers would not contemplate undertaking analogous activities in the real world to those that they undertake online. The general opinion of the respondents was that this is the case, with 61 percent giving a positive response (23 percent did not agree, while the remaining 16

TABLE 6.2 Perceived motivations for hacking

	Yes %	No %	Don't know %
Out of curiosity	82	11	7
To make money	62	21	17
For the thrill of it	93	1	6
To "beat the system"	94	1	5
For malicious reasons	68	16	16

percent were unsure). In reality, however, it can be recalled from earlier discussion that hardcore hackers have no qualms about committing physical theft or breaking and entering in order to assist them in their hacking endeavors.

While the respondent's views on hacking showed that such activities are considered unacceptable, their attitudes toward suitable punishment were not so clear. When asked if confessed or convicted hackers should be allowed to work in the computing field, 59 percent said they should, with only 25 percent suggesting they should not. This reaction is generally supported in the IT industry, with security companies employing hackers as consultants to provide an alternative viewpoint when evaluating and implementing security systems (see Chapter 7). A similar response was found when the respondents were asked if hackers should be allowed to have a computer at home – again 59 percent had no problem with this. However, when compared to the responses regarding the use of computers in work, a slightly lower proportion (23 percent) was firmly against the idea of allowing access at home. This viewpoint appears to be counter-intuitive, in that computer access at home would be more likely to be unsupervised and, as such, there is more chance for the hacker to revert to undesirable behavior. The generally lenient views of the respondents are in stark contrast to decisions made in certain highly-publicized hacking cases, where the convicted hackers' access to computing equipment has been severely restricted in both employment and domestic contexts (as discussed later in this chapter).

The survey also attempted to assess awareness of relevant legislation. Given that the majority of respondents were expected to be from the U.K., the survey targeted two specific acts of parliament; namely the Data Protection Act and the Computer Misuse Act. The Data Protection Act is relevant from the perspective of requiring organizations to implement appropriate security to protect the data that they hold, whereas the Computer Misuse Act provides a means for them to deal with people who have breached that security (the specific provisions are discussed later in this chapter). As such, people should ideally be aware of both. However, the survey results revealed that awareness of them is variable. While 76 percent of respondents had heard of the Data Protection Act, an act that has received much publicity, awareness of the Computer Misuse Act was much lower, with only 46 percent of respondents having heard of it. This raises the question (particularly amongst such an apparently IT literate response base) of how many people realize that computer abuse is actually illegal, as opposed to just being morally or ethically wrong. In the absence of this knowledge, some individuals may easily enter into abusive activities, while victims may not realize that they have a legal recourse (an observation that links back to the earlier discussion of the proportion of cybercrimes that are not reported).

Media influence

Earlier chapters have conjectured that the media has a significant role in shaping people's appreciation of the cybercrime issue. In order to gauge the extent of media influence, the respondents were first asked to indicate whether they could recall reading or hearing about *any* computer crime incidents in the news. The vast majority (81 percent) responded positively to this point. To determine the media's role in more detail, the respondents were presented with a list of cybercrime related headings (encompassing people, groups and viruses), and asked to indicate which they had heard of. The majority of entries referred to issues that would have received media attention several years before the survey and were, therefore, considered to represent a good test of the extent to which media reporting left a lasting impression. The five headings used, the explanations of them (which were not shown to the respondents), and the respondent awareness observed are listed in Table 6.3.

The results give a clear indication that the general public can recall the occurrence or reporting of specific cybercrime incidents. This, of course, does not prove that the respondents recalled the incidents accurately, or the extent to which they understood any technical issues involved, but it can be concluded that the media has some success in increasing long-term awareness of computer abuse issues. It is clear from the results that virus incidents are the most easily recalled. This is particularly significant in the context of the two virus examples that were mentioned in the associated question. At the time of the survey, both viruses were already several years old and were no longer active "in the wild." In addition, even at the time of their original release, neither had actually caused much damage. As such, the fact that they were still remembered several years later is a testament to the long-term effects of media reporting, and possibly the extent to which both viruses were originally over-hyped.

The fact that viruses are the most easily remembered class of incident may be attributed to the effects that they can have upon the public at large. Whereas the activities of hackers can often be dismissed as being "someone else's problem," the indiscriminate nature of viruses and their potential for direct impact upon an individual causes more people to take notice. Another possible contributor to the high positive response may have been that the word "virus" was included in the two associated headings presented to respondents. This may have helped some people to classify and, thereby, recall the Michelangelo and Friday the 13th incidents, or it may have prompted them to respond positively simply because they recognized the term "virus" (even in the latter case, the figures still serve to give a general indication of virus awareness).

With regard to the hacking-related incidents (i.e. Chaos and Mitnick), the awareness was significantly less than other categories. However, the proportions are still considered significant for a number of reasons. Firstly, unlike the virus items, the list presented in the questionnaire did not give any indication to the respondents about who or what the entries might be (i.e. they simply said "Kevin Mitnick" and "Chaos Computer Club" and asked for an indication of awareness). Secondly, neither of the cases are directly related to the U.K. (where most of the survey respondents came from) and, as such, have received little coverage outside the technical press.

When asked to describe their view of the way that the media treats IT crime issues, the respondents' answers were generally critical, with the comment that the

TABLE 6.3 Awareness of publicized computer abuse incidents

Heading	Description	Respondent awareness (%)
Chaos Computer Club	The German hacking group that has been responsible for breaking into (supposedly) secure systems on a worldwide basis.	25
Kevin Mitnick	The notorious U.S. hacker who has been involved in a range of hacking incidents. At the time of the survey, Mitnick was awaiting trial in relation to his most recent arrest for hacking into more than a dozen organizations, including Fujitsu, Motorola, Air Touch, MCI, Pacific Bell, and Sun Microsystems.	22
WarGames	The 1983 Hollywood film in which a teenage hacker almost triggers a nuclear war. Passing reference to the film is frequently made in mass media reports of hackers, increasing the likelihood of respondents having heard of it.	55
Michelangelo virus	One of the early viruses to gain the attention of the mass media (in 1992). The payload of the virus was programmed to activate on Michelangelo's birthday (6th March), affecting both floppy and hard disks.	70
Friday the 13th virus	Another early virus, which affected .COM files on the target PC and was activated, as the name suggests, if the day was Friday 13th. The virus is now very rare, but it again received media attention when originally introduced, making it potentially memorable to respondents.	71

media glamorizes such cases appearing many times. Many of the respondents also considered that the media trivialized the reporting of computer crime issues, reflecting a perceived distinction between the reporting of "common" crimes and those that are IT-related. In the context of the information society (with IT forming a core feature of communication, commerce, leisure, and many other activities), the attitude of the mass media toward reporting IT-related issues will become more important. If the media continues to glamorize computer crime cases (as some respondents perceived), then public opinion may turn to favor the offenders (previous discussion has, of course, already established that some hackers have been elevated to celebrity status through their activities). Furthermore, it is possible that the public may be influenced into accepting computer crime as an unavoidable part of modern life. This could result in a tolerance of computer crime in much the same way that individuals accept that in certain areas, the more common forms of crime occur frequently. Similarly, if those reporting computer crime treat such cases as being regular occurrences, public perception could be adversely affected and the uptake of promising technologies, such as electronic commerce, may suffer.

Public awareness of computer crime and abuse is a double-edged sword. On one side, some level of awareness of issues such as viruses is essential (even amongst domestic users) in order to ensure that appropriate precautions may be taken. On the other side, the focus should not be such that people are scared away altogether (which could easily be the effect upon those who are already uncomfortable with IT). It is clear from the results that awareness of computer crime amongst the respondents is high, and it can be suggested that the media has played a significant role in this. Therefore, in order to better gauge the potential for media influence, a brief investigation was also conducted to determine the level to which computer crime and abuse issues are mentioned in the media and the manner in which they are presented. In order to achieve this, an electronic search was conducted of articles that had appeared in two of the main U.K. broadsheet newspapers (and their associated Sunday editions) over the two-and-a-half years directly preceding the survey. The newspapers in question were *The Times/Sunday Times* and The *Guardian/Observer*, and the search string "comput* AND (virus* OR hacker* OR hacking)" was applied to the full text of all archived articles. This was intended to locate any articles containing the word "computer" (or a variation), as well as references to either hacking or viruses. The articles retrieved were then manually filtered to remove those that still did not relate to the subjects under investigation. This yielded the results shown in Table 6.4 and it can be seen that, on average, cybercrime issues are mentioned twice a week in each of the newspapers sampled.

It should be noted that these results did not all relate to reports in which hacking or viruses were the headline news, but rather where mention of one or both issues was made in a news-reporting context (which included both main stories and side references to the issues). However, the results are still considered to provide a valid indication of the extent to which computer crime and abuse issues pervade our current society. It is also worth noting that the search would only have trapped reports in which hacking or viruses were mentioned alongside the word "computer" (which was considered the most likely context and was used to avoid, for example, the inclusion of stories about medical viruses in the results). As such, other stories relevant to computer crime and abuse (e.g. computer-based frauds) may have gone unnoticed.

Having established the extent of reporting, the other consideration of interest was the manner in which crime and abuse cases were presented. An effective way of assessing this was considered to be via the headline banners of the reports (which are specifically intended to draw readers' attention and are likely to be amongst the best remembered elements of the story). With this in mind, the following list presents examples of some specific headlines identified from the newspapers above:

- "Red faces at the Pentagon as hackers drop in on the military" (*The Times*, 4th March 1998).
- "Hackers can cripple Internet in 30 minutes" (*The Times*, 21st May 1998).
- "Virus terrorists plot to upstage millennium bug" (*The Times*, 27th January 1999).
- "E-mail virus sparks world alert" (*The Times*, 31st March 1999).
- "Sabotage by computer hackers costs big business billions" (*The Sunday Times*, 4th April 1999).
- "Hackers from hell cast a wide net to take their revenge on the FBI" (The *Guardian*, 29th May 1999).

It is clear that several of these have a rather sensationalist tone and, indeed, reading the full articles often reveals the headlines to be somewhat misleading. This leads to questions about what the motives of the media actually are, and many (particularly in the hacking community) would argue that the objective of much press coverage is more to scare the readers than it is to inform them. If this is the case, then the wisdom of this approach is debatable. On one hand, recalling such strong headlines may help to convince people that they ought to do something about their

TABLE 6.4 Articles mentioning computer crime and abuse

	1997	1998	1999 (Jan–Jun)
The Times/Sunday Times	101	91	69
The *Guardian*/The *Observer*	61	89	58

own security. However, from another perspective, it is likely that they serve to increase people's fear or mistrust of technology. Furthermore, over-glamorized reports may actually serve to encourage other computer abusers, eager to attract a similar level of publicity for themselves. Another interpretation of much media coverage is that the commentators do not actually appreciate the intricacies of the issues that they are reporting, and so run the risk of making superficial or inaccurate reports. A final observation is that the sample headlines were all taken from broadsheet newspapers. In general terms, these are considered to house more responsible journalism than tabloid publications, and it can be assumed that the coverage in the latter (which influence a larger proportion of the population) would have been more sensationalist.

The way in which the media sometimes portrays the perpetrators of computer crime is also somewhat questionable. Later discussion will consider the 1993 case of Paul Bedworth, a teenage hacker acquitted on three counts of conspiracy under the U.K. Computer Misuse Act on the basis of claimed computer addiction. Although Bedworth was acquitted, the fact that he was a hacker, and gained unauthorized access to other people's systems, was not in doubt. However, the description of Bedworth and his activities in the newspaper reports at the time made reference to him as "the boy genius" and "a hi-tech wizard"[209] – casting him in a rather more positive light than one might have considered his actions deserved. As such, from the perspective of discouraging others from following in his footsteps, it can be argued this did not necessarily send out the right messages.

One of the concerns about media treatment of computer crime is that it may influence the public's willingness to adopt new technology such as the Internet. Although the survey did not address this issue directly, some related observations can be made. Of the sixty-nine respondents who claimed to have Internet access at home, 91 percent still expressed very serious concerns about three or more of the issues highlighted in Table 6.1. This suggests that their awareness of computer crime was not a barrier to their use of the Internet and that the benefits were perceived to outweigh the potential risks. However, it can also be noted that people without domestic Internet access expressed a similar level of concern over the security issues, and it may be conjectured that this is one of the factors preventing their uptake (however, the survey results did not provide conclusive evidence to support or refute this theory).

Although the overall results suggest that the media has been successful in terms of informing people that computer crime exists and instilling an awareness of the different types of incident, it seems to have done a relatively poor job of raising awareness of the possible corrective actions. This is illustrated by the relatively low awareness of 1990's Computer Misuse Act when compared to general awareness of computer misuse. In this sense, media reports may not be performing such a useful service as might otherwise be the case, and they are likely to have a scare-mongering effect upon those who are less familiar with the area. The need for a more responsible and informed approach by the media is, therefore, evident.

Electronic commerce – an example of society's need for protection

It is interesting to note whether views and attitudes about cybercrime affect people's acceptance and adoption of new IT opportunities. This can be considered by examining one such area – namely that of electronic commerce, which has been one of the major buzzwords in IT over the last few years. The U.K. Department of Trade & Industry defines the e-commerce concept as follows:

> using an electronic network to simplify and speed up all stages of the business process, from design and making to buying, selling and delivering.[210]

It may be argued that e-commerce is not a new phenomenon, with related activities such as Electronic Data Interchange (EDI) having occurred since the 1970s.[211] However, this referred to essentially business-to-business transactions, operating within a closed environment. The difference now is the use of the Internet as an enabling technology, making e-commerce services directly accessible to the average person – which is referred to as business-to-consumer e-commerce. Businesses communicate with customers and partners through many channels, but the Internet is one of the newest and, for many purposes, one of the best. It is fast, reasonably reliable, inexpensive, and universally accessible. Originally the presence of businesses on the web could be analogized to a shop window approach – where you could see what products or services were available, but you could not actually purchase them directly. This has now changed, and the web is being put to more varied uses with the names of sites such as Amazon.com (online bookstore) and eBay.com (online auctions) being part of the everyday vocabulary for many Net users.

In order for the Internet to be accepted as a viable e-commerce platform, it is necessary to establish a foundation of trust amongst the participants. Trust is, of course, also important in the context of traditional commerce, and has been developed over time through the formation of appropriate policies, procedures, and practices to safeguard transactions and company assets. However, a comparable safety net is not yet fully established for electronic commerce over the Internet. Furthermore, because of the global nature of the Internet as a public network, the issue of trust has even greater importance than in traditional commerce because:

- the party being dealt with may be unknown.

- it is not possible to have full control of the data during its transfer (for this reason, some people use the web to locate products, but prefer to place their order via telephone or fax).

- the other party might be at a different and unknown physical location, and might have different rules and legislation.

An example of the need to establish trust is the experience of the credit card operator Visa in relation to Internet-based transactions and instances of fraud. In the early days of web-based e-commerce it was reported that, while only around 2 percent of their credit card transactions were conducted via the Internet, this accounted for about 50 percent of disputes and discovered frauds.[212] The publication of such statistics is unlikely to improve public confidence in e-commerce or the Internet environment in general. In addition, there is a lack of harmonized legislation in the field. As a result, there is no significant practical experience within the legal system and/or case law that may be used for reference in settling disputes.

In order to investigate the consumer perspective, a small survey was conducted amongst members of the general public in order to assess attitudes, awareness, and expectations in terms of security in an e-commerce environment. A total of 100 questionnaires were distributed in paper form, along with an online version that was made available and publicized on the author's web site. This yielded a total of thirty-eight responses to paper surveys and twenty-six online results (the survey population in this case was different to that of the cybercrime awareness study described previously). This final total (i.e. sixty-four responses) was considered sufficient to at least gain a general appreciation of end user opinions.

As with the cybercrime survey, the vast majority (83 percent) of respondents were male, with a bias toward the younger end of the population (45 percent were aged between sixteen and twenty-four, 51 percent between twenty-five and thirty-nine, and the remainder forty or over). The respondents generally appeared to be IT literate, with 61 percent claiming to use a computer both at work and at home.

The full set of respondents were asked whether or not they had purchased online and were asked to indicate their reason(s) why. A total of 42 percent claimed to have purchased online, with the main reason being the attractiveness of the offer (55.5 percent of cases). In addition, 85 percent of respondents who had purchased online also cited some other reason. These included fast response from the retailer, access to international shopping and a wider range of products, and that online purchase was the only option available to them. Of the 58 percent who had not yet purchased online, the main reasons were concerns over insecure communications (51 percent), potential untrustworthiness of the vendor (43 percent), and no need to buy online (46 percent). These results suggest that the issues of trust and security are currently preventing a significant proportion of individuals from becoming involved in e-commerce activity.

The respondents were also asked whether they had any concerns about doing business via the Internet. While a small proportion (11 percent) claimed to have no concern, the majority of respondents cited at least one concern. The biggest problem was perceived to be communications security, cited by 61 percent of respondents. Use of personal information by the vendor (55 percent), vendor authentication and credibility (52 percent), and vulnerability of the vendor's internal network (33 percent) were other suggested concerns. The fact that the figures relating to communications security and vendor credibility are higher than the corresponding figures from the previous paragraph suggests that a proportion of the respondents who *are* currently purchasing online are doing so in spite of their concerns.

Having previously established that the majority of respondents possessed credit cards, a later question attempted to assess their opinion of using it in different contexts. The scenarios considered were face-to-face transactions, via a third party (e.g. a waiter in a restaurant), over the telephone, and via the Internet. The respondents were requested to rate the perceived security of each, using good, medium, or poor rankings. Table 6.5 presents the findings from this aspect.

Overall it can be seen that the Internet fares worst – an observation that is particularly revealing, because in terms of the actual protection afforded to the card details, the Internet is probably safer than both the third party and telephone options. Indeed, in contrast to the earlier figures from Visa, more recent findings from the U.K. Association of Payment Clearing Services (APACS) suggested that Internet activities account for a very small proportion of payment card fraud. Of the £3.5 billion card purchases in the U.K. during 2000, fraudulent activity amounted to £190 million (5.4 percent of the total turnover). Of this, only 4.75 million (2.5 percent) related to Internet-based losses. This strongly suggests that traditional card fraud is still the dominant danger. As an aside, however, it can be observed that there are some classes of Internet activity that are more prone to fraud than others. Evidence suggests that users of "adult" web sites and participants in online auctions are the most likely to fall victim to some form of incident. In relation to the former, MasterCard conducted a European survey that established that half of all electronic fraud is conducted by the providers of adult web sites. The victims here can be seen to be safer than average targets for fraudsters as, in many cases, they are unlikely to complain to their card provider or to the police about being defrauded, because to do so would also require an admission about the type of site they were accessing. With regard to online auctions, the Internet Fraud Watch has estimated that, during 2000, they accounted for 78 percent of all online frauds,[213] with an average loss per victim of $326.[214] In fact, ever since they came to prominence, online auctions have represented the most common form of Internet fraud, topping the lists in 1998 and

TABLE 6.5 Perceived security of credit card transactions

	Face-to-face	Via a third party	Over the telephone	Via the Internet
Good	36	9	8	9
Medium	22	34	26	25
Poor	2	18	25	27

1999 as well. Why is this the case? Even though most of the sites hosting such auctions have reputable names and are providing the service in good faith, the system can often be undermined. The anonymity of claimed sellers and the potentially international distances separating them from the buyers serves to complicate the normal checks that both the auction convenors and the participants can make to ensure the legitimacy of the lots.

Returning to the results of the e-commerce survey, the respondents were finally asked to indicate their expectations regarding the measures that Internet commerce sites should take in relation to customer privacy. As expected, this produced a strong response, with 87.5 percent indicating that they would expect comprehensive information regarding the site's security and privacy policy. Use of personal information was also a key consideration, with 81 percent wanting a chance to choose whether it could be used for purposes other than the conduct of the transaction (e.g. addition to mailing lists).

It is interesting to assess more closely how respondents' security concerns affected their attitude to shopping online. Of the 47 percent of credit card holding respondents who were online shoppers, 92 percent had some form of security concern. The fact that this concern has not prevented them from engaging in the activity suggests that, from the customer perspective, the benefits of online shopping clearly outweigh the risks. Figure 6.1 illustrates the specific security concerns expressed by the respondents, with the results having been sub-divided according to whether or not they were online shoppers.

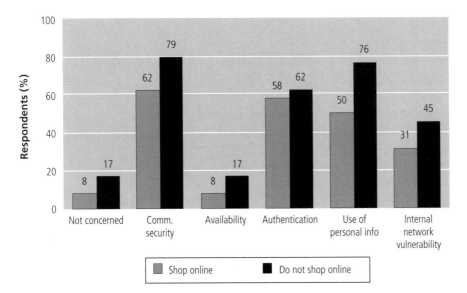

FIGURE 6.1 Online shopping in relation to security concerns

As the figure shows, respondents who do not shop online exhibited a greater level of concern in all categories, and it can be conjectured that actually participating in online commerce would remove some of their doubts. However, it is also important to avoid making the assumption that their security concerns are the only reasons these respondents do not shop online. Various other factors, such as the lack of an Internet connection at home, or simply not having encountered the need to do so, could be equally valid explanations. This is illustrated to an extent by the fact that, even amongst the small number of respondents with no concern about security, the majority are still not online shoppers.

As well as the consumer viewpoint, it is also relevant to consider the perspective of businesses themselves. In the U.K., it has been suggested that businesses may be waiting for the "right time" to engage in e-commerce. Possible reasons for this include a belief that consumers lack an understanding of e-commerce, especially on the issue of security and privacy,[215] and a perceived lack of understanding and support from government on the legal and liability issues. A good illustration of commercial attitudes from a security perspective is provided by the results of the 1998 KPMG Information Security Survey,[216] in which respondents were asked to assess a range of business issues in terms of their importance and likely impact upon the organizations. Electronic commerce was considered to be the most important issue (cited by 23 percent of organizations), ahead of other areas such as mobile computing and the Year 2000 issue (which was, of course, still a major concern at the time). However, the same survey discovered that many organizations using the Internet are not aware of the associated risks.

The earlier figures from Visa indicated the problem of fraud online. This is supported by the findings of a joint survey of 132 online merchants conducted by CyberSource Corporation and Mindwave Research.[217] Their findings indicated that 83 percent of respondents found online fraud to be a problem, and 61 percent were taking more precautions as a consequence. Another significant finding was that many merchants did not realize who would be considered liable for the costs of online frauds. In common with purchases made by telephone and mail order, Internet orders are categorized as "card not present" transactions. In these situations, it is actually the merchant that is expected to bear the cost of claims resulting from fraudulent activity. However, the CyberSource/Mindwave findings found that 28 percent of merchants did not realize this, and were either unsure of who would be liable, or considered that it was the responsibility of the credit card company.

As more people gain access to the Internet, the potential for business-to-consumer e-commerce can only increase. However, the issue of security is likely to remain a concern in the short term, as an environment of trust has yet to be established. This is not necessarily because of a lack of confidence in the security technologies themselves, but because, in many cases, people are not sufficiently aware of the possible protection that exists. This is supported by the results of the survey conducted, which shows that even current online shoppers are concerned about security problems. In addition, there are more people who do not shop online at all because of security worries.

This discussion, and that in the previous section, has established that the threat of cybercrime does have an impact upon average members of the public. However, the societal impacts extend beyond this, and as the next few sections will indicate, there are significant implications for those trying to formulate and enforce the law.

Policing the problem

> To protect the honest law-abiding citizen, law enforcement must keep pace with advance in computer and telecommunications technologies.[218]

The above quotation, from former U.S. Attorney General Janet Reno, illustrates the realization that the police have a significant responsibility to ensure that they are up to date with the latest technologies. However, from the investigator's perspective, the issue of investigating cybercrime has become much harder. Not only has the range of potential attacks increased, but the dramatic increase in desktop computing capabilities has also influenced the magnitude of the investigator's task. For example, whereas a typical computer in 1990 would hold an average of around 3,000 files, their modern equivalents hold around 25,000. So, whereas copying the contents for analysis would have taken one to two hours a decade ago, it is now more likely to take four to six (i.e. the best part of a working day).[219] Furthermore, the resulting volume of information also represents more of a burden when it comes to analysis.

Not only has the job become more demanding, there has also historically been a lack of people available within the police force who actually have the skills to do it. The general feeling internationally is that the law enforcement community has been caught out by the pace of technology and criminal advancement and, as a result, has had to rely upon private sector skills and resources to compensate in many cases. An example of the limitations can be seen in the U.K., where, until recently, there was no nationally-recognized body to whom cybercrime could be reported. Up until April 2001, the nearest thing was the Computer Crime Unit (CCU) at New Scotland Yard. However, rather than being a nationwide outfit, the CCU is part of London's Metropolitan Police Service, and without prior knowledge of its existence it is not exactly obvious that the unit is there at all (even the Met Police web site, which one might consider a natural place for victims of IT crime to look for help, has only a passing mention of the CCU and a contact telephone number). With a limited staff and a single geographic base, the CCU was not ideally placed to handle computer crime incidents with a national or international element to them. Nonetheless, the unit has been the U.K.'s main contact point for IT crime, and has been successfully involved in a number of high-profile international investigations.

The U.K. situation finally changed in September 2000, with the announcement that the Government was to establish a £25 million National Hi-Tech Crime Unit (NHTCU), which began operation in April 2001. At a national level, the role of the NHTCU is to investigate "attacks on the Critical National Infrastructure; major Internet based offences of paedophilia, fraud, or extortion; information from seized electronic media; and gather intelligence on cybercrime and cybercriminals."[220] Local police forces support this work by investigating crimes committed on computers and assist with requests for information from abroad. The formation of the new unit represents part of the U.K. Government's commitment to establishing a positive environment for e-commerce, and followed a September 1999 report that promised to "improve the technical capability of law enforcement and establish an Internet Crime Unit."[221]

The NHTCU comprises representatives from a number of other U.K. agencies, including HM Customs, the Association of Chief Police Officers, the National Crime Squad and the National Intelligence Service. Although again based in London, the Unit has an increased size and coverage compared to the CCU. When the new unit was announced, it was stated that it would have a main staff of around forty investigators, and that, in addition, there would be links to local police forces, with up to forty-six further officers distributed around England and Wales.

The NHTCU is not the only organization to have been formed in response to the threats posed by new technologies. On 20th December 1999, the U.K. government had previously announced the creation of the National Infrastructure Security Co-ordination Centre (NISCC), the role of which is to co-ordinate activities to protect the Critical National Infrastructure (CNI) against electronic attack. The CNI is defined as:

> Those parts of the United Kingdom's infrastructure for which continuity is so important to national life that loss, significant interruption, or degradation of service would have life-threatening serious economic or other grave social consequences for the community, or any substantial portion of the community, or would otherwise be of immediate concern to the Government.[222]

Consequently, IT systems in each of the following sectors are considered to represent part of the infrastructure requiring protection: central government, emergency services, energy, financial, health, telecommunications, transport, and water and sewerage.

The composition of NISCC is based upon a collaboration between the Home Office, Government Communications Headquarters, the Security Service, the Ministry of Defence, and the Police force, with staff drawn from these various sources. The center works with the organizations that operate CNI systems to identify the critical systems and ensure that they are afforded an appropriate level of protection. It also acts in an advisory and response role, providing warnings about incidents and assisting with response in serious cases. In pursuit of its aims, the NISCC operates a number of schemes that are intended to assist government departments and CNI organizations. The Unified Incident Reporting and Alert Scheme (UNIRAS) receives reports of electronic attack incidents and disseminates appropriate alerts to other users. It also provides a helpdesk service in relation to security incidents, and co-ordinates responses to serious incidents through the center's Electronic Attack Response Group (EARG). This group provides practical assistance to CNI organizations or government departments that experience electronic attacks, with the ability to call upon appropriate technical and security resources according to the nature of the incident.

The NISCC is very similar in concept to the U.S. National Infrastructure Protection Center (NIPC), a multi-agency facility established by the Clinton administration in 1998. The NIPC is a $64 million facility, employing some 500 staff across the country, with representatives taken from existing agencies such as the Secret Service, the CIA, NASA, the National Security Agency, the Department of Defense, and several others. The role of NIPC is to "detect, deter, assess, warn of, respond to, and investigate computer intrusions and unlawful acts" that threaten or target U.S. critical infrastructures such as telecommunications, energy, banking and finance, water systems, government operations, and emergency services.[223] The NIPC guards against criminal threats, as well as the dangers posed by information warfare and cyberterrorism – two issues that will be considered in the next chapter.

Although policing and protection initiatives are moving in the right direction, there are still questions over whether appropriate levels of resources are being directed at the cybercrime problem. For example, although the formation of the NHTCU represents a significant advance in the U.K. cybercrime policing, it has nonetheless been criticized by security experts as being of limited capability. Craig Whitney from Internet Security Systems offered the following opinion:

> It will be able to catch the low-hanging fruit, the easy pickings, the people that are
> not very good at covering their tracks. £25m is a drop in the bucket when you
> compare it to the amount that the industry spends as a whole on security.[224]

The U.K.'s efforts are not alone in attracting criticism. In the U.S., for instance, Gartner Group Inc. suggests that around 97 percent of all law enforcement funding for cybercrime is spent on about 300 federal agents (which represents less than 0.1 percent of the 600,000 agents that are funded in total). Furthermore, of the estimated $17 billion in federal discretionary spending that is directed toward law enforcement, only £10 million goes toward training, staffing, and support relating to cybercrime. This represents less than 0.1 percent of the total spending. As a result, Gartner concludes that the majority of Internet crime goes unpunished, and that cyber criminals know that they have little to fear from law enforcement.[225] The situation in most other countries is not substantially different and, if anything, is likely to be worse.

Legislating against computer crime and abuse

Policing the issue is, of course, the front line legal response, and must be supported by appropriate cybercrime laws that can be enforced. Many developed countries have now introduced relevant legislation to address the problem of cybercrime and associated activities. As an example, the discussion below will examine the U.K. Computer Misuse Act 1990, which can be considered reasonably representative of the issues that other countries have also taken into account when enacting cybercrime laws.

Prior to the introduction of the CMA in 1990, the need for specific legislation to deal with computer crime had already been highlighted in the U.K. by a high-profile incident that had been widely reported in the media a few years earlier. This related to the hacking of British Telecom's Prestel service – a mainframe-based videotext system that subscribers dialed into via modem connections. In 1984, two hackers, Robert Schifreen and Steve Gold, gained unauthorized access to Prestel user IDs and passwords, giving them access to a variety of associated user accounts.[226] A particularly notable aspect of the case was that the hackers had been able to gain access to an electronic mailbox belonging to Prince Philip, the Duke of Edinburgh. The Prestel account had been allocated to the Duke when he officially opened the service for BT in the late 1970s and, in reality, it was unlikely that he actually made any use of it. However, this did not prevent it from being used to draw public attention to the case, and it was this aspect that was most readily reported in the media – both at the time and in the years since. Schifreen and Gold ultimately notified Prestel's management of the security holes that they had been able to exploit and offered to help to fix them. However, rather than take up this offer, Prestel called in the police and the hackers were arrested in April 1984. However, given that the U.K. had no specific legislation in relation to hacking, Schifreen and Gold had to be charged under an existing law. The prosecution cited the Forgery and Counterfeiting Act 1981 on the basis that, in order to masquerade as other Prestel users, the hackers would have had to type in the passwords without their owner's permission – an electronic analogy to forging their signatures. The case went to trial and they were convicted at Southwark Crown Court in April 1986. However, the two hackers appealed and, after legal proceedings lasting a total of three and a half years, and costing almost £2 million, the original ruling was ultimately overturned in the House of Lords – the Lord Chief Justice considered that the Forgery Act was not intended for computer misuse offences. Given the publicity that had surrounded the case, and that the final verdict had effectively set a precedent that made hacking of this kind acceptable under U.K. law, a more appropriate and reliable alternative was clearly needed.

The activities of Schifreen and Gold were far from the only hacking incidents to occur during this period, and during the latter part of the 1980s, studies into the U.K. legal system's ability to cope with computer misuse were carried out by both the Scottish Law Commission (in 1987) and the Law Commission for England and Wales (in 1989). Both identified categories of misuse that were not properly addressed under existing laws, but which nonetheless required sanctions under criminal law. The recommendations and findings of the reports led to a Private Members Bill being passed through the U.K. Parliament, which in turn led to the enactment of the Computer Misuse Act 1990. This came into force at the end of August 1990 and established three new offences, as summarized in Table 6.6.

The Section 2 and Section 3 offences are considered "arrestable offences" – meaning that an individual may be arrested without warrant by a police officer if he or she has reasonable suspicion that they have committed that type of offence. As

TABLE 6.6 The U.K. Computer Misuse Act 1990

	Section	Example targets	Penalty
1	"Unauthorised access to computer material."	People who browse through other peoples' systems. Persons who exceed their authority within a system to which they have access.	Up to £2,000 fine and/or up to six months' imprisonment.
2	"Unauthorised access with intent to commit or facilitate the commission of further offences."	Persons gaining unauthorized access to a system in order to commit a further offence (e.g. theft).	Up to five years' imprisonment and/or an unlimited fine.
3	"Unauthorised modification of computer material."	Any action with intention or effect of impairing system operation or causing destruction/alteration of data (e.g. propagation of a virus).	Up to five years' imprisonment and/or an unlimited fine.

the table suggests, these offences are considered more serious than the Section 1 offence.

The CMA is now fairly widely referenced and recognized by U.K. organizations with major IT investments. For example, a web search for the words "Computer Misuse Act 1990" will yield a number of references to it – a fair proportion of which seem to exist on university web sites, where the text of the Act has been reproduced in order to inform students regarding the acceptable use of the computer systems (students perhaps being a population of users more in need of a reminder than others!). Having said this, individual awareness is probably somewhat lower, as was illustrated by the results of the survey presented earlier in this chapter.

The CMA was not the first example of cybercrime legislation, nor indeed is it the most recent. Some countries have only recently recognized the issue in law and others have still to do so. This introduces a problem of inconsistency, which is considered later. Firstly, however, it must be recognized that having the relevant legislation in place is only really the first step at the national level. As the next section will discuss, the effective enforcement also requires that the problem it sets out to police is properly understood at the various levels below the legislature.

The problems of enforcing the law

The law is undoubtedly right to try to protect us from the activities of hackers, and at a theoretical level, things like the CMA seem to be fairly clear-cut and sensible. However, those enforcing the laws frequently seem to have problems striking a balance in terms of the action to take. It is possible to identify a variety of general scenarios in which the outcomes of cybercrime cases seem to reflect as badly upon the law enforcers as they do on the hackers. This section outlines such scenarios, drawing upon examples of past cases (it should be noted, however, that some examples are indicative of early experiences in the investigation and prosecution of cybercrimes, and as such, the same problems would not necessarily arise today).

Firstly, there have been a number of examples of cases in which law enforcers and the courts have shot themselves in the foot by pursuing the wrong targets or attempting to press unrealistic charges. This, unfortunately, serves to undermine their credibility, while also conferring more legitimacy onto the hacker's claims that their activities are misunderstood. Some documented examples of such cases are outlined below.

- Attempting to charge *Phrack Magazine* editor "Knight Lightning" with illegally publishing proprietary material from the BellSouth telephone company. The material in question was a document relating to the control of the 911 emergency system, which had been stolen by "Prophet," a hacker from the

Legion of Doom. Prophet circulated his prize, providing a copy to Knight Lightning, who published an edited version in *Phrack*. BellSouth claimed that the document was worth $79,449, but when the case went to trial, the defense were able to show that this information and more could actually be ordered directly from Bellcore (Bell Communications Research) – for $13.[227]

- Seizure of computers from Steve Jackson Games, a creator of non-computer based simulation and role playing games, as part of the search for copies of the BellSouth E911 document. This gained a lot of bad press, as the official reason given for the seizure was that the investigators believed that one of Jackson's new role playing books, entitled "Cyberpunk," was actually a manual for committing computer crime (the text of the book was stored on the seized systems).[228]

- The 1988 arrest of Kevin Mitnick on charges of "causing $4 million damage to a Digital Equipment Corp. [DEC] computer" and "stealing a highly secret computer system," when the actual cost was nearer to $160,000 (and only then when taking into account the cost of tracing the security vulnerabilities that he had been able to exploit).[229]

- In the case of his more recent arrest in 1995, Mitnick argues that the claimed damages that led to his conviction and five-year imprisonment were actually based upon the research and development costs of the software he accessed, rather than its actual value. Indeed, he claims that federal officials specifically requested these costs instead of the amounts associated with any real damages, thereby significantly inflating the apparent seriousness of his crime (for example, it was alleged that Sun Microsystems lost $80 million as a result of Mitnick downloading the source code to its Solaris operating system – which is actually sold for $100).[230]

Having said this, these faux pas are not necessarily that well known or publicized outside of hacker circles, and have, therefore, probably done little to harm the image of the law in public eyes. More worrying from the public perspective, however, may be the second category of problem scenarios – high profile cases of genuine abuse where the law has failed to secure a conviction. Examples here include the following:

- The U.K. court's acquittal of hacker Paul Bedworth, accepting the defense of computer addiction (discussed in the next section). This was not dissimilar to the grounds on which Kevin Mitnick's lawyers had previously been able to mount a successful defense.

- The U.K. court's inability to bring AIDS database author, Dr. Joseph Popp, to trial for his activities (although, admittedly, this was not for a lack of trying, and he was ultimately convicted in Italy).

- The case of Kuji and Datastream Cowboy, two British hackers who had hacked into a U.S. Air Force installation known as Rome Labs in 1994. When initially discovered, the incident was widely cited in U.S. defense circles to illustrate the dangers posed by terrorists' use of worldwide computer networks, and the two hackers were suspected of being international spies. However, after a three-year investigation, crown prosecutors in the U.K. informed the judge that there was insufficient evidence to justify the cost of a trial, and that there had been no threat to national security.[231]

- Failure to prosecute suspected Love Bug author Onel de Guzman (as discussed in Chapter 5).

The third and final problem scenarios are cases in which convictions were secured against the correct people, but where the sentences seemed overblown and did not seem to fit the crime when examined in detail (giving the accused and other hackers a platform from which to complain about unfair treatment). The best examples here are the long sentences and subsequent restrictive release conditions faced by Kevin Mitnick and Kevin Poulsen (discussed later in this chapter). These cases again may not represent too much of a concern to the public at large, on the basis that the correct people got punished and, if they felt the punishment was too harsh, they should not have broken the law in the first place. However, as the next section will indicate, unfair and unjust sentences could arise because law enforcers and the courts do not have as good an understanding of cybercrime as they do about more traditional offences, and so cyber criminals could find themselves the unfortunate victims of misconceptions and exaggerated claims.

As one might expect, the hacker community has been particularly vociferous in its objection to the sentences bestowed upon people like Mitnick and Poulsen. Their point can, however, be illustrated by considering the figures presented in Table 6.7, which list the average sentences meted out in the U.S. for a range of other offences, unrelated to cybercrime.[232]

These figures have actually appeared on Kevin Mitnick's web site, drawing a negative comparison with his own sentence of five years for unauthorized access to corporate computer systems and copying proprietary software. Of course, Mitnick was hardly innocent of the crimes for which he was convicted, but the point here is that, in other cases, hackers have received considerably less severe sentences for crimes that are essentially similar. Many would argue that the sentence Mitnick received reflected the threat that he posed rather than the damage that he actually did. Certainly, with the access to systems that he was able to obtain, he could have been more destructive if he had a mind to. If someone was to stab and injure someone else with a knife, we would not charge them with murder simply because the victim could have been killed. Yet, to a degree, this seems to be the logic that prevails with high-profile cases such as Mitnick's. It is easy to see the dilemma that faced the authorities. The sentence had to justify the amount of time, effort, and money that had been spent trying to track him down. It also had to be a sentence befitting the amount of media coverage that the case had received. However, given the previous observation that the likelihood of even being prosecuted for hacking in the U.S. is 1 in 10,000 (and the odds of being imprisoned are even less),[233] it can be questioned whether the sentences of hackers such as Mitnick (and Poulsen) are genuinely fair, or whether they are effectively part of a "show trial" approach, resulting from the hacker's own celebrity.

From another perspective, however, Mitnick can consider himself to have got off lightly. In China, for example, the authorities have been known to take a much more hard-line view of hacker activities. A reported incident from 1993 highlights the execution of a convicted hacker, Shi Biao, for a £122,000 theft from the Agricultural Bank of China, at which he was an employee.[234] Biao's execution was intended as a warning to others. However, it appears that some people take a lot of warning and there have been subsequent incidents of a similar nature. For example, in December 1998, two further Chinese hackers were sentenced to death, this time for stealing 260,000 yuan from the Industrial and Commercial Bank of China.[235] The money was recovered, but this did not affect the outcome for the hackers.

Although appropriate sentencing of convicted cyber criminals is an important issue, there is also an argument that whatever is done at this stage is not likely to have much of a benefit for the case in question. To quote Ronald Noble, the secretary-general of Interpol:

TABLE 6.7 U.S. national average length of imprisonment for 1997
(SOURCE: U.S. SENTENCING COMMISSION)

Crime	Average sentence
Auto theft	1 year, 9.9 months
Manslaughter	2 years, 10.2 months
Assault	3 years, 1.9 months
Embezzlement	7 months
Larceny	1 year, 2.4 months
Fraud	1 year, 6.9 months
Burglary/Breaking and entering	2 years, 4.8 months
Money laundering	3 years, 5.1 months
Forgery/Counterfeiting	1 year, 3.9 months

It's the kind of crime where you want to work on prevention because the prosecution comes too late and the cost outweighs by a thousand-fold or a million-fold what you can expect to recover from the individual or individuals involved.[236]

As such, one of the main advantages of a cybercrime prosecution may simply be to serve as a warning to others, and guard against the occurrence of future incidents. In this context, the harsher the sentence is seen to be, the better the potential deterrent to other would-be criminals. This does not, of course, mean that the approach is fair on those individuals who are held up as the examples. To quote Phiber Optik, the founder of the hacking group Masters of Deception, who was jailed for his various system intrusions:

I am really pissed off. The judge said he was sending me to jail to send people a message. Couldn't he figure out some other way to send it?[237]

Understanding the issues involved

This is the price we pay when people with no understanding of technology are the ones in charge of regulating it.[238]

The above quotation reflects the view of Emmanuel Goldstein, the editor of hacker journal *2600*, and is a commentary on what he views as unnecessarily restrictive laws on the use of technology. It is true that technological changes seem to be occurring faster than either the law or the general population are able to appreciate. Consequently there is a strong argument that we should not attempt to impose controls and legislation upon a society that is not yet fully understood. However, we must at least be sufficiently prepared to take action when necessary. Unfortunately, there have been signs in recent years that this is not the case. For example, even with the formation of the specialist units discussed earlier in this chapter, the level of specialist computer-crime training and expertise in law enforcement is often rather low. An example of this is provided by the views of Tsutomu Shimomura, the security expert involved in the capture of Kevin Mitnick, who makes frequent statements suggesting his exasperation with the technical capabilities of law enforcement personnel during his account of Mitnick's chase and capture.[239] However, having appropriately skilled officers or agents introduces another problem. It is not unusual for those who have established knowledge and expertise in cybercrime investigations to capitalize upon it by leaving law enforcement and joining the world of private consultancy, where the same skills can command higher salaries. As such, the police constantly risk losing many of their most competent cybercrime investigators to the commercial marketplace. Furthermore, computer crime cases are often perceived as being less interesting to investigate than more traditional forms of police work,[240] making it difficult to attract new blood into that line of policing.

Patrolling the cyber beat is not the only problem. It can also be observed that, even where legal provisions do exist, the judiciary frequently do not possess a sufficient understanding of information technology to appreciate the crucial details of cases put before them. Those passing judgment in cases may not appreciate the seriousness or significant implications that a computer intrusion may have, their views having perhaps been influenced by media reports that portray hackers as merely harmless pranksters. In the U.K., for example, after a two-and-a-half year investigation, one of the first prosecutions under the Computer Misuse Act ended with the defendant, Paul Bedworth, being acquitted on the grounds of computer addiction. Bedworth, who began hacking in his early teens, was charged with penetrating a variety of systems, including ones belonging to the FTSE 100 share index, the European Commission and a Belgian cancer research charity. He was arrested in 1992, after an eight-month investigation into the hacking activities of a hacking group calling itself 8LGM (for Eight Legged Grove Machine), and was charged under the CMA. However, after a three-week trial, Bedworth walked free in March 1993 on the basis that he was hooked and could not stop himself from hacking (an expert witness, Professor James Griffith-Edwards of the Institute of Psychiatry, testified that Bedworth had a clinical addiction to using his computers). As observed in Chapter 3, the premise of addiction does not appear to be unreasonable, but it does not excuse the fact that the activities conducted were known to be wrong. The police criticized the verdict at the time, expressing concern that it would lead other hackers to think that, by claiming they were obsessed, they would be able to escape punishment. It has since been suggested that because the unauthorized access was made to and via a computer system (as opposed to physical property), it was not viewed in such a serious manner, and that a more IT literate jury would have had difficulty in accepting the line of defense that was offered. It should also be noted, however, that Bedworth's co-defendants – two student hackers known as "Pod" and "Gandalf" – were convicted and sentenced to the maximum prison term.

Although the Bedworth case dates back to 1993, the general feeling is that little has really changed in terms of the court's ability to deal with computer-related evidence, and a lack of computer literacy is still recognized as a problem. In 2000, the Computer Evidence Taskgroup, established by the British Computer Society's Legal Affairs Committee to examine the current practice and procedures for dealing with computer evidence, highlighted several problems in relation to its handling by the police and the courts.[241] Some key points were identified as follows:

- criminal courts are generally unfamiliar with the subject of computer evidence.

- courts regularly underestimate the technical complexity of cases that involve computer evidence.
- the mishandling of computer evidence "quite frequently" leads to prosecutions having to be abandoned.

The taskgroup strongly recommended the establishment of a code of practice for handling, securing, and preserving computer evidence. It was also suggested that the composition of the court ought to be given special consideration in computer-related cases. It was recommended that there should be either a jury of laypersons with an appropriate court-appointed IT expert available to them, a judge and a technical assessor, or an entire jury composed of technical specialists. Any of these scenarios should considerably reduce the potential for confusion and misunder-standing.

The situation in the United States does not appear to be substantially different, as illustrated by the following assessment:

Law enforcement officials have been frustrated by the inability of legislators to keep cyber-crime ahead of the fast moving technological curve.[242]

Such apparent weaknesses will obviously have to be overcome as an increasing proportion of crime becomes technology-related. In the meantime, it is worrying that we are so dependent upon technology, yet frequently appear ill-prepared to deal with problems.

The situation amongst the lawmakers is not too different. For example, although governments have begun to sit up and take notice of the Internet crime issue, some have observed that they are debating and making decisions about things that they fundamentally misunderstand. They can all too easily see the problems posed by incidents such as distributed denial of service attacks and email viruses, but they do not understand how the Internet works, which complicates their ability to legislate any solution. To many politicians, the Internet shares a basic similarity with the telephone network. Both are seen to provide a global communications infrastructure, allowing electronic connections between two endpoints. Given this conceptual resemblance, surely the same principles can be applied in terms of policing and control? Well, actually no, because (as indicated back in Chapter 1), the underlying systems work very differently. However, it is not difficult to see why such misassumptions might arise – particularly given that the entry point to the Internet for typical domestic users is via the telephone line. The politicians know that, with normal voice calls, it is possible to tap and trace the phone line. As such, from an observer's viewpoint, there does not appear to be an appreciable difference when accessing the Internet – any remote user or system is ultimately being called on the phone. However, in the Internet context, the actual telephone call is only being made to one place – to the Internet Service Provider (ISP), whose computer then provides subscribers with their gateway into the wider Internet. Furthermore, every time someone dials up the ISP they are typically allocated a different Internet address, which they hold only for that particular session. As such, if you are starting from the point of a remote system that has been attacked, it is much more difficult to trace things back to their source, and the co-operation of the ISP will be required (which has implications for the privacy of its subscribers).

Tapping the network at an intermediate point is not feasible. The routers within the network (which direct data packets to their desired destination) are not designed to take notice of where the packets are coming from, and the fact that packets can travel via different routes would further complicate the monitoring. Equally, logging the traffic passing through the network would represent a massive overhead, storing terabytes of data – most of it unnecessarily. Finally, actually doing anything with this volume of data would also be difficult, as searching it would be no small undertaking. As such, although the politicians and law enforcers might like to have such control, the network that they are trying to police does not lend itself to letting them have it.

Ignorance about the technology being dealt with can also cause irrational decisions to be made, and misconceptions to arise, about the individuals involved as perpetrators of cybercrime. A number of such misconceptions can be cited in relation to the case of Kevin Mitnick, which influenced his treatment while in prison.[243] For example:

- he was denied the use of a laptop computer to prepare information for his defense, based on the concern that he would be able to use it to continue his hacking activities (which would be impossible as long as the machine provided to him was not equipped with a modem).

- he was placed into solitary confinement, as it was feared that he could convert his walkman into a transmitter and thereby bug the prison warden's office.

- it was rumored that he could use phone phreaking techniques to launch nuclear missiles by whistling into a telephone, creating concern over his access to even this sort of device.

Not only did such concerns cause Mitnick to be viewed with undue suspicion; they also caused him to be treated unfairly and denied facilities that he could reasonably have used without representing a threat.

From the discussions above it can be seen that problems relating to a lack of understanding can manifest themselves at various levels in the legal process. However, as previously indicated, these are not the only difficulties to be faced, and equally significant problems are apparent when considering the fact that the crimes themselves frequently transcend national boundaries. As the next section will show, this leads to problems relating to the differing laws that exist in different jurisdictions.

Global inconsistency

Back in Chapter 1, it was observed that the current population of the Internet is in excess of 369 million users, and that (with a couple of exceptions) this exceeds the individual populations of any country on Earth. With a physical population of this size, it would be inconceivable to allow it to evolve without some form of regulation and without a defined set of laws under which to operate. However, this is effectively the situation being faced by the Internet. Although there are various bodies associated with administrative and engineering issues (e.g. the assignment and structure of domain names), there is no overall body that defines the rules that Internet users are expected to abide by. The consequences of this can manifest themselves in both positive and negative ways. For example, one of the great advantages of the World Wide Web is that it allows anyone to freely publish things on it. This brings great benefits and flexibility to both organizations and individuals in their ability to share and access information. At the same time, there is no control over the actual content of what is published, which can lead to various effects, such as a profusion of information that many people would regard as low quality, harmful or obscene. From a practical perspective, the sheer volume of information now makes it very difficult to search the web in an effective manner. This is not to suggest that there is not also a great deal of useful and high quality material on offer, or to advocate any form of censorship function for the web. The point is that the openness of the web, in common with the wider Internet, can be regarded as a great enabling technology, but may also be considered to represent its Achilles heel.

The downside of the open and unregulated Internet can also manifest itself in terms of cybercrime. As many of the examples discussed so far have illustrated, its effects can easily cross national borders. This becomes problematic when you realize that, although the effect of the crime will typically be the same in different countries, the ability and willingness to mount a legal response is extremely variable. For example, at least 60 percent of countries that are members of Interpol lack the appropriate legislation to deal with Internet and other computer-related crimes. Sinrod and Reilly provide a good assessment of the current situation:

> While the major international organizations, like the Organization for Economic Co-operation and Development (OECD) and the G-8, are seriously discussing co-operative schemes, many countries do not share the urgency to combat cyber-crime for many reasons, including different values concerning piracy and espionage or the need to address more pressing social problems. These countries, inadvertently

or not, present the cyber-criminal with a safe haven to operate. Never before has it been so easy to commit a crime in one jurisdiction while hiding behind the jurisdiction of another.[244]

The previous example of the Love Bug provides a case in point. As highlighted in Chapter 5, the suspected Filipino author of the program was not required to face sentencing for his alleged actions, and indeed, was regarded as something of a hero by certain elements of the population. By contrast, had the same crime been committed in another country, such as the United States or the U.K., the author would have had to face the full force of the law. Unfortunately, the issue of establishing globally agreed and recognized laws for something like cybercrime is fraught with problems. In some cases it is not simply that the law in a particular country has not managed to keep pace with the laws that have been passed elsewhere (as was then the case in the Philippines), but that there is a fundamental difference of opinion over what is considered acceptable. This can be easily illustrated using an example unrelated to the Internet or computer crime – namely the age of consent defined in different countries (i.e. the age at which it is considered legal for persons to engage in sexual activity). In the U.K., the accepted age is sixteen. In some parts of the U.S. the threshold is eighteen. By contrast, in The Netherlands the legal age is just twelve. So, there is six years' difference between the two extremes and, in all cases, these are countries that could be generally classed under the heading of "western democracies." Bringing other countries into the equation serves to blur the issue even more – the upper limit is increased to twenty-one and virtually every other age in between is featured as a legal age of consent in one country or another.[245] It should also be noted that this just relates to heterosexual activity – when gay and lesbian liaisons are also taken into consideration the issue becomes even more varied (the same countries often define different age limits to those for heterosexual sex, and some even consider it illegal). So which country's laws are correct? Which should be selected as the global standard? It is, of course, impossible to say, because it is a matter of perspective and cultural acceptability. And here we are dealing with a fairly fundamental issue of everyday life. If the bounds of acceptability are so widely different over an issue such as this, one can imagine that getting clear agreement in relation to cybercrime offences and associated penalties is hardly likely to be a straightforward matter. Andy Jones, a group manager at the U.K.'s Defence Evaluation & Research Agency, makes the following pertinent observation in relation to the scale of the task that is faced:

> The law of the sea is the best simile you can find – that took 40 years to ratify. We don't have 40 years to get this right. We don't have four years.[246]

As Sinrod and Reilly identified, the cybercrime problem has prompted discussion amongst the Group of Eight (G-8) industrialized nations. In October 2000, a three-day cybercrime conference was held in Berlin, attended by specialists from the G-8 community. German Foreign Minister Joschka Fischer indicated that, in Germany alone, the losses from cybercrime account for 100 billion marks per year. His counterpart at the Interior Ministry, Otto Schily, added to this by explaining the international nature of the problem:

> The worldwide data networks jump over all borders, and so Internet criminals do not stop at our national boundaries . . . Of the criminal activity registered by Germany's crime agency in 1999, 80 percent had traces leading to the United States, Canada, Japan, Australia and Russia.[247]

The current concepts of legal jurisdiction are based upon lines drawn on maps, and generally relate to an age when someone had to be physically present in order to commit a crime. Computer networks have basically turned this situation on its head – in a manner that governments in general seem to have been largely unpre-pared for. It has been apparent since at least the 1980s that the problem of cross-border computer crime existed, and it did not take much imagination to see that it could only increase as network communications became more mainstream. However, here we are, at the beginning of a new millennium, and a solution does not seem substantially closer. In the years to come, the problem will undoubtedly be solved – in the meantime, however, we remain in a vulnerable state, where cyber criminals have a realistic hope of evading legal accountability for their actions. Even as agreements are established, it is easy to imagine that some countries will sign up more quickly than others, leaving the latecomers with a role as potential hacker havens in the interim.

Until the situation is resolved, law enforcers are forced to take somewhat elaborate measures to draw out the cyber criminals if they are based in a location where jurisdiction and relevant laws do not apply. An example is provided by the case of U.S.-based Bloomberg Business News, which became the target of attempted extortion by hackers based in Kazakhstan. Having become the victim of system infiltration, the company received emailed demands for $200,000, in return for which the hackers offered information about how they were able to get in. Bloomberg enlisted the help of the FBI, but while they were able to trace the location of the perpetrators, they were unable to arrest them there. As a result, the would-be extortionists were lured to London in August 2000, where the FBI was able to mount a sting operation in collaboration with the Metropolitan Police, and then begin proceedings to extradite them to the United States.[248] Although the operation was effective, it would clearly have been a lot easier for the FBI to have been able to contact law enforcement representatives in Kazakhstan and have the hackers arrested there directly.

Although the need for more geographically wide-ranging measures are recognized, attempts to extend computer crime legislation beyond a national level illustrate the complexity of the issue (in fact, even achieving national harmonization may be a challenge in some cases – for example, in the U.S., different states have different laws in relation to cybercrime, which vary in terms of both scope and resulting penalties). For example, at the time of writing, the Council of Europe (CoE) is working on a Draft Convention on Cyber-crime,[249] which proposes an international treaty to address cybercrime problems. An overall aim of the convention is to make it easier for law enforcement bodies to collaborate on computer crime investigations that cross European borders. In addition to the forty-one members of the Council of Europe, officials representing the United States, Canada, South Africa, and Japan were also involved in the development of the treaty, and other countries will be invited to sign up to the final version. However, several aspects of the proposals have the potential to cause difficulties for those engaged in entirely legal activities. For example, Article 6 of the draft is perceived to be a problem, in that its effect may also complicate legitimate security procedures. The associated text is presented in Figure 6.2 (note that the Articles 2 to 5 referred to in the text relate to "Illegal Access," "Illegal Interception," "Data Interference," and "System Interference" respectively).

```
Article 6 - Illegal Devices

Each Party shall adopt such legislative and other measures as may
be necessary to establish as criminal offences under its domestic
law when committed intentionally and without right:

a. the production, sale, procurement for use, import, distribution
   or otherwise making available of:

1. a device, including a computer program, designed or adapted
   [specifically] [primarily] [particularly] for the purpose of
   committing any of the offences established in accordance with
   Article 2 - 5;
2. a computer password, access code, or similar data by which the
   whole or any part of a computer system is capable of being
   accessed with intent that it be used for the purpose of
   committing the offences established in Articles 2 - 5;

b. the possession of an item referred to in paragraphs (a)(1) and
   (2) above, with intent that it be used for the purpose of
   committing the offenses established in Articles 2 - 5. A party
   may require by law that a number of such items be possessed
   before criminal liability attaches.
```

FIGURE 6.2 Article 6 of the Draft Convention on Cyber-crime

Article 6 is intended, amongst other things, to criminalize the use of the software tools such as those discussed in Chapter 4, which hackers may utilize in scanning and breaching target systems. However, this has served to upset the security community, in that it will also cause difficulties for those wishing to conduct legitimate activities to identify and overcome weaknesses in their own systems.[250] The key issue that the Convention is seeking to address is clearly the *illegal* use of such tools. However, if the distribution of the tools is restricted to prevent hackers from getting hold of them, how are legitimate administrators meant to do so?

The provisions of the draft convention also prompted other worries. For example, in a letter to the Council of Europe dated 18th October 2000, members of the Global Internet Liberty Campaign (GILC) expressed concerns on a number of counts. Specifically, they considered that the treaty:

- "is contrary to well established norms for the protection of the individual."
- "improperly extends the police authority of national governments."
- "will undermine the development of network security technologies."
- "will reduce government accountability in future law enforcement conduct."[251]

The original GILC letter had thirty signatories, from a variety of privacy and Internet rights groups from around the world. Examples included the U.S.-based Electronic Frontier Foundation and the Electronic Privacy Information Center. In addition, the online letter offered an option for other interested organizations to email their support and have their names added to a separate list below the original signatories. Organizations such as the U.S. Association for Computing Machinery and the U.K. Foundation for Information Policy Research were added in this manner.

As well as objecting to the provisions of Article 6, the letter also took issue with other aspects, such as the requirement for Internet Service Providers (ISPs) to retain records about their customers' activities. This, it was claimed, would represent a risk to the privacy of innocent individuals and would actually go against the European Commission's own Data Protection Directive. Another concern from the ISP perspective was that the convention would potentially render them liable for the content of third-party material hosted by their systems. As the GILC members observed, this could have a significant impact upon the free flow of information and would run contrary to the current open ethos of systems such as the web. If ISPs are forced to protect themselves against being taken to court for hosting undesirable material, then it would effectively force them into applying some form of monitoring and censorship controls. This would not only be extremely burdensome for the ISP, but it would also dramatically reduce the freedom that individuals currently have to publish information and send messages on the Internet.

There have also been suggestions that individual countries are attempting to utilize the treaty as a means to obtain powers that they have been unable to enact through domestic legislation. To quote David Banisar, a U.S. attorney and senior fellow at the Electronic Privacy Information Center:

> When the U.S. government cannot get a controversial policy adopted domestically, they pressure an international group to adopt it, and then bring it back to the U.S. as an international treaty – which obliges Congress to enact it.[252]

For their part, officials from the CoE and the U.S. Department of Justice indicated that much of the concern was a result of people misunderstanding the intended meaning of the treaty's text, pointing to a need for further clarification. They stated that there should be no impact on legitimate security testing activities, and suggested that the privacy concerns were probably no different to the sort of issues that could arise from other international treaties.[253]

The criticisms above are not intended to suggest that the CoE have got it all wrong and that the treaty is not well intentioned in its attempt. However, the situation does illustrate very clearly the difficulty in attempting to apply regulation to a previously open medium without eroding the existing culture. The issue of privacy represents a substantial topic of debate in its own right and many commentators have expressed concern that, if too much power is granted, at national or international levels, then personal privacy could be put at risk. This issue is considered as part of the discussion in Chapter 7, which examines existing powers and methods of communications interception.

Did the crime, did the time – what next?

Previous discussion has already highlighted the apparent severity of the prison sentences meted out to certain hackers. In some cases, however, being released from prison is not the end of the story and it is worth briefly looking at this situation from the hacker's perspective. Chapter 3 discussed the cases of Kevin Poulsen and Kevin Mitnick – two hackers whose activities attracted significant attention from law enforcement and high-profile commentary in the media. Given this history, it is unsurprising to discover that they continued to attract some level of attention after their respective releases from prison. It can be seen that their later experiences share a number of similarities, as highlighted in the discussion below.

After spending over five years in prison, Kevin Poulsen was freed on 4th June 1996. Once released, he began a three-year period of supervised release, during which time he was initially banned from owning or coming into contact with a computer (thus possibly setting the precedent for the Mitnick case that followed). Poulsen felt that this complicated his chances of employment, as illustrated in the following extracts from a June 1996 letter to his Probation Officer, Marc Stein:

The court also prohibited me from owning or possessing a computer, or seeking employment that would allow me access to a computer, without your permission. You explained that The Court's use of the word "possession" was a reference to a legal principle called "constructive possession" . . . By way of example, you stated that I was in possession of the computer in your office by virtue of the fact that I could reach over and take it.

I asked you for permission to seek employment that would allow me access to computers. As you know, my employment history is good, but consists entirely of computer work. This is the only area in which I have any marketable skills. You declined to give me permission, but suggested that the cash registers at McDonalds might be acceptable despite their computerized nature. You used a video rental store as an example of a work environment that would not be acceptable because of its high-tech equipment.[254]

After a year, however, this restriction was relaxed and Poulsen was granted permission to use a computer at home for word-processing. However, the system had to be modem-free – in order to prevent any chance of unauthorized excursions into cyberspace. Just to make sure, his probation officer also required him to submit his monthly phone bill for inspection, to ensure that no computer dial-ups had taken place.[255] It was another year and a half before he was permitted to access the Internet. In the interim, Poulsen was able to capitalize upon his position as an ex-hacker denied Net access and began to give media interviews in which he contrasted his situation with that of an increasing proportion of his fellow countrymen, for whom Net access was now becoming an everyday thing. As a result of this exposure, Poulsen got his first foothold back in the world of legitimate IT-related employment, working as a columnist for the ZDTV web site.

Poulsen's supervision ended 4th June 1999, and he has since pursued a number of opportunities in the security field. As a freelance journalist he has written a weekly column for ZDTV's *Cybercrime* (see **http://www.zdtv.com/zdtv/cybercrime/**). In May 1999, he spoke at the Senior Information Warfare Applications Course at Maxwell Air Force Base, Alabama, and then in July 1999 was a speaker at the DEF CON 7 hacker convention in Las Vegas (sharing the platform with U.S. computer crime attorney Jennifer Granick). At the time of writing he is the editorial director for SecurityFocus.com, the IT security industry's leading online information portal for businesses and security administrators. As such, Poulsen's is considered to be a credible voice in the computer security field – with the fact that he has been a hacker actually adding weight to the opinions he is able to offer.

Amongst the materials that Poulsen has written, it is somewhat ironic to find articles commenting about Kevin Mitnick's case[256] (which are, naturally enough, written from a fairly sympathetic perspective). By the time Poulsen was completing his supervised release, Mitnick was still in the early stages of his prison term.

Following his arrest in 1995, he spent almost five years in prison and was finally released on 21st January 2000, having received credit for time served and good behavior. However, while Mitnick was no longer imprisoned, he was quite clearly not yet a free man – like Poulsen before him, he first had to complete a further three-year probation period under supervised release. The terms of the release were more severe than Poulsen's and placed a three-year restriction upon his access to both computer systems and wireless communication (reflecting that both technologies had been involved in his downfall). At the time of writing, Mitnick is not permitted to own such devices, nor is he permitted to use them as part of his employment. In fact, the only technology he is permitted to own is a landline telephone. To a degree, one can sympathize with this viewpoint, as prolonged access to the technology could encourage a resumption of his hacking endeavors. However, the terms of the release do not end there. Mitnick is also barred from taking employment with any company that has computers or computer access on its premises. Consider for a moment the practicality of this in our modern society and you will realize that it rules out a significant number of potential employment opportunities. It would certainly seem to rule out any form of white-collar employment (and, for that matter, many opportunities for pursuing further education should he wish to). The terms are not just saying that he should be banned from any job where he comes into direct contact with technology, but rather any job where the employer possesses it. Mitnick's own view is, of course, that the terms are unrealistically restrictive, as illustrated by the following quotations:

> The supervised release restrictions imposed on me are the most restrictive conditions ever imposed on an individual in U.S. federal court, again according to the research of my defense team. The conditions of supervised release include, but are not limited to, a complete prohibition on the possession or use, for any purpose, of the following: cell phones, computers, any computer software programs, computer peripherals or support equipment, personal information assistants, modems, anything capable of accessing computer networks, and any other electronic equipment presently available or new technology that becomes available that can be converted to, or has as its function, the ability to act as a computer system or to access a computer system, computer network, or telecommunications network.[257]

> The requirements mandating I can't touch a computer or cell or cordless phone are akin to telling a forger not to use a pen or paper. There is no way I can earn a living when I get out. I couldn't even work at McDonald's. All I could do is something like gardening.[258]

Having said this, pursuing a traditional job was not the only means by which Mitnick could make a living. As previously mentioned, his name has become well known as a result of his exploits and the degree of media exposure given to his case.

Consequently, it was not long after his release before a number of media-related opportunities began to present themselves. It soon became clear, however, that the conditions of his probation would complicate matters. For example, he received an invitation to speak at the Net Trends 2000 conference in Salt Lake City during April 2000.[259] The fact that he was invited to deliver a keynote speech indicates that the conference organizers believed that he would be a good crowd-puller for their event. However, the terms of his release restrict him to a seven-county area of Southern California, outside which he cannot travel without the permission of the court. The U.S. District Court of California refused to grant permission in this instance, thus preventing Mitnick from being able to share his wisdom. He did, however, manage to find a way to participate in *2600* magazine's H2K convention, a couple of months later. He achieved this by phoning in from his home rather than attempting to attend in person. However, even this resulted in the threat that he could be sent back to prison.[260] One thing his probation officer did permit him to do during this period was to testify about computer crime before a U.S. Senate Committee.

Speaking engagements were not the only offers that Mitnick received. He was also invited to write articles about computers for an online magazine. However, it was initially considered that taking up such offers would violate the terms of his release, which, as well as barring his use and ownership of technology, also prohibits him from acting as an adviser or consultant to computer-related businesses. As a result, Mitnick's probation officer summed up the official position regarding the opportunities that have been presented to him since his release:

> In regards to the numerous requests you have received concerning writing and critiquing articles and speaking at conferences, we find it necessary to deny your participation and recommend that you pursue employment in a non-related field.[261]

Many would agree with this view and argue that placing such restrictions upon Mitnick are entirely appropriate. After all, why should he be able to place himself in a position where he can profit on the basis of his previous criminal activities? A possible answer is that by sharing his knowledge in the right circles it could be used to positive effect – for the improvement of security. Moreover, as Net Trends and H2K indicated, there is clearly a demand from people to hear what he has to say, and being asked to speak before a Senate Committee implies that the opinions are considered likely to be worthwhile. As for getting paid for his efforts, Mitnick is no different to anyone else in terms of having to support himself. In addition, he did have the issue of paying compensation to his victims to consider. Here, however, it can be considered that he got off somewhat lightly. As a result of his apparently limited employment opportunities and the expectation that he would be forced to take a minimum wage job, the judge set the restitution that he was required to pay at just $4,125 – not bad for a hacker who had been accused of causing damages amounting to many millions. Mitnick was able to make the payment in relatively short order.

On 26 June 2000, Mitnick returned to court in Los Angeles to seek clarification over the terms of his probation, with the result that the judge insisted the employment opportunities offered to him be reviewed. The following month, the U.S. Probation Office announced that he would be permitted to pursue several offers of employment – including speaking engagements, security consulting, and written articles in the technology field. Mitnick duly took the opportunity and several keynote speaking roles followed (e.g. at the Infrastructures for E-Business Conference and the Software Developers Expo 2000). At the time of writing, he produces a monthly column critiquing Internet and computer-related articles for the online magazine Contentville.com, and is also a talk radio host on KFI 640 AM – Los Angeles, with a show focusing on technology and Internet issues. It can be noted that although he writes for Contentville, Mitnick's technology ban means that he cannot actually view his own work on the site. Furthermore, even though he is now permitted to write articles, the terms of his probation still restrict how he does so. Rather than use a word processor, as most journalists would do in the modern age, Mitnick must use a manual typewriter or dictate the contents of the column over a landline telephone. The following statement is taken from the footnote to one such article and is presumably included to provide reassurance that Mitnick has not broken the terms of his probation:

> He wrote this article on an IBM Quietwriter 8 typewriter. As part of his terms of supervised release, Mitnick is prohibited from possessing or using computer-related equipment, personal digital assistants, web-enabled television sets, or any other electronic equipment that can be converted to or has as its function the ability to act as a computer system or to access a computer system, computer network or telecommunications network.[262]

It is interesting to note that, since the relaxation of the restrictions upon him, Mitnick's web site has been modified to include details of how to make requests for speaking engagements. He is represented by the United Talent Agency and the web site description markets him as "the world's most famous hacker."[263] In this sense, he is clearly an example of a hacker who has turned his skills to commercial advantage. The next chapter will begin by considering hackers who have found commercial rewards in other ways.

SUMMARY

Even if you have not been a victim of cybercrime, the issue can still be seen to have indirect effects upon the type of society we live in. For those people that use computer systems, and the organizations that own them, the threat of cybercrime has clear impacts in terms of the need to introduce measures to guard against compromise. At the very least, most users now have to accept the presence of things like anti-virus software on their systems – a requirement that would not be there at all if it were not for the activities of cyber criminals. Other users may have to contend with more significant restrictions, such as limitations upon their Internet access, which some organizations have imposed for fear of their systems becoming the targets of abuse from unwelcome outsiders.

From a societal perspective, however, the impacts of cybercrime go far beyond peoples' everyday use of IT. The issue receives a significant degree of attention in the media and, as such, even if you have not experienced it first-hand, you will doubtless have read or heard about someone who has. This serves to heighten public awareness and, from the survey results presented, it is evident that the vast majority of people can recall cybercrime incidents and perceive the general issue to be a problem. Of course, an increased awareness of the problem can have knock-on effects in terms of shaping peoples' attitudes and increasing their concerns about information technology. As a result, the new opportunities that are emerging, such as electronic commerce, may be stifled as a result of concerns over cybercrime and security in general.

With the threat being perceived at all levels, it is not surprising that governments have increasingly felt the need to introduce initiatives for the policing and prevention of cybercrime. Although this is meant to be a constructive step, it can actually be seen to have both positive and negative implications for the law-abiding citizens of the information society. On the plus side, they have increased protection against cybercrime, as well as a means of legal recourse if they should happen to become the victim of an incident. On the downside, the introduction of legislation could ultimately restrict what they are able to do online, which effectively reduces the freedom and openness that have previously made the environment so attractive. Having said this, the legislation and policing of cybercrime are clearly issues that have yet to be fully resolved. The problems observed in relation to misunderstandings and the lack of international harmonization are symptomatic of an area that is still evolving. In time, therefore, it is possible that these points may be ironed out satisfactorily, in a manner that does not unduly restrict or penalize those who are making legitimate use of IT systems.

Commercial and political evolution

THE MAJORITY OF INCIDENTS THAT HAVE BEEN EXAMINED SO FAR CAN clearly be seen to represent examples of cybercrime, and in these cases few would dispute that the perpetrators were in the wrong. However, this chapter considers a range of scenarios in which the same (or similar) techniques are used, but where the context would not necessarily be regarded as cybercrime. Indeed, the first section discusses the concept of ethical hacking, where hacker skills are employed in order to test and improve the security of a computer system. Few, if any, observers would argue about the legitimacy of this approach. Subsequent examples, which include sections focusing upon hacktivism, information warfare, and cyberterrorism, are less clear-cut, but the perpetrators would doubtless find support for their activities in certain quarters. The underlying theme is that, in these contexts, the techniques and technologies are being used to pursue commercial or politically oriented objectives and, by virtue of this, are seen as having a more legitimate basis that does not automatically cast the perpetrators as criminals.

Hackers for hire

Despite the claimed security of many systems and products, it is often uncertain whether a system will actually stand up to an assault until someone actually tries it. It is obviously undesirable for this person to be an uninvited hacker, and as such, security-conscious companies are often keen to test their protection for themselves. A market consequently exists for what is known as "ethical" hacking, whereby hacking skills and methods are applied against a system by persons who can be trusted not to use any discovered weaknesses for illegitimate purposes.

The provision of ethical hacking services is frequently an internal company function in larger organizations. For example, Microsoft has a dedicated group known as the Rapid Exposure Detection (RED) team, who represent the first line of defense against genuine hackers from the outside world.[264] The role of the team is to identify security vulnerabilities within software systems at the development stage, and suggest a solution before systems are released and can be exploited by hackers.

This is little more than you might expect from the world's largest supplier of desktop operating systems and applications, but what options exist for an organization that does not possess the personnel or financial resources to support such an internal facility? One approach that can be considered is to engage the services of external hackers to test your security for you. Although this may sound unusual, it is an approach that is often pursued by security vendors wishing to publicly demonstrate the effectiveness of their products. To this end, they effectively lay down the gauntlet to the hacker community by establishing competitions in which hackers are challenged to use their skills to beat the system.

While such competitions might at first glance appear to be mere marketing ploys on the part of the vendors, it is important to recognize that submitting a product to such a trial is not a move that would be entered into lightly. The vendor has to have a significant degree of confidence in the product beforehand because if it was easily beaten, it would stand little chance in the marketplace as a result of consequent bad publicity – arising from hackers, or more likely, competing vendors. So, by staging such competitions, the companies concerned are visibly demonstrating their faith in their products – which is, of course, further endorsed if the product manages to withstand the assaults that are then wreaked upon it.

In January 2001, for example, *eWEEK* magazine organized a hacking challenge called OpenHack III in which hackers were openly invited to demonstrate their skills by attempting to penetrate and corrupt a fictitious Internet Service Provider (ISP) and e-commerce web site that was set up especially for the competition. The challenge was sponsored by Argus Systems Group, an Illinois-based security solutions provider, who also provided underlying software in the form of their PitBull intrusion prevention system. To make the competition more attractive, participants stood to gain more than just hacker kudos – four tests were incorporated as part of the challenge, with a $50,000 top price for being the first to complete all of them. The competition ran for seventeen days, during which time 5.25 million attack attempts were logged, and it was estimated that somewhere between 100,000 and 200,000 individual hackers took part.[265] Despite this, however, none of the OpenHack III tests were passed and the prize money remained unclaimed. In *eWEEK*'s two previous OpenHack challenges, in September 1999 (assessing Windows NT and Linux security) and June 2000 (assessing five operating systems, an e-commerce platform and multiple intrusion detection approaches), the systems had been successfully hacked.

The fact that hackers failed to win in OpenHack III was largely attributed to the protection that had been provided by Argus's PitBull system. During the course of the competition, hackers had been able to exploit various application vulnerabilities and even gain root access on the target systems, but PitBull still prevented them from completing any of the challenges. This outcome, and the associated publicity, was clearly good news for Argus Systems, who could consequently point to substantial evidence for the security of their product. Although standing up to attack for just over two weeks does not prove that a system is invulnerable, it does provide a good indication of resilience. The system was subjected to an intense period of analysis and attack, with hackers motivated by an obvious reward. From the vendor's perspective, the argument would be that if hackers with this opportunity and incentive were not able to get in, then the system should represent sufficient defense against casual attackers.

In the OpenHack scenario, the important point to realize is that the penetration attempts are being openly invited. However, there are other contexts in which hackers may offer their services for the apparent benefit of security, which may have different implications for those concerned. One potential situation is where a hacker has already breached security on a system and then volunteers to help plug the holes – typically in return for a fee or some other form of payment in kind. An example of this is illustrated in Figure 7.1, which shows the homepage of a hacked web site in which the hacker has left a message for all to see, volunteering to fix the hole (which he appears to claim to have given prior warning about) and indicating that he is available for hire. It should be noted that the image has been modified to preserve the anonymity of the victim and the email address of the hacker, as neither are crucial to the example in this case.

In this case, the price to be paid is not financial, but to continue to allow the

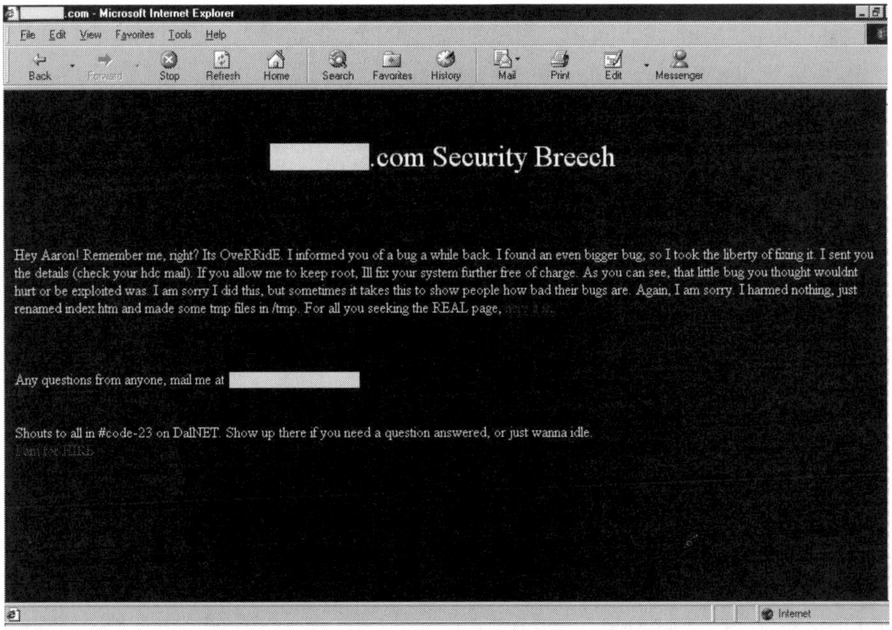

FIGURE 7.1 A hacker offers assistance in fixing a security vulnerability

hacker to have "root" access (i.e. all access privileges within the system). This hardly seems like a sensible idea, as it would open the door for further blackmail at some later time. However, at least in this particular case the hacker seems to be volunteering the information about the breach and making the offer to help of his own volition. Alternatively, hackers have been known to offer help in situations where system administrators have discovered their activities and it represents a preferable alternative to facing prosecution.

Using or hiring hackers in this way can be considered to have a number of advantages. First, as a member of the hacking community, the hacker may have a number of advantages when compared to some security professionals, including familiarity with the latest hacks and the ability to gain access to information from other hacker contacts. In addition, the hacker's personality and motivation (i.e. driven by the challenge and enjoyment of beating the system) may lend itself better to the task of uncovering further vulnerabilities than a standard security consultant, who may simply be working through a checklist of known potential holes. In short, the system will be subject to a more realistic penetration attack, conducted by exactly the sort of person who might otherwise be trying to break in. All of this may help to ensure a comprehensive identification of system vulnerabilities and appropriate corrective measures. Furthermore, the service may work out cheaper than if hiring outside consultants for an equivalent period of time. These methods are considered attractive by numerous organizations, and it has even been speculated that U.S. Department of Justice has looked to recruit hackers in order to conduct penetration tests on its networks[266] (the DoJ having suffered security breaches in the past, including the defacement of their web site in August 1996[267]). However, it is difficult to argue that this represents a genuinely positive contribution by hackers – if they did not exist at all, the penetration testing service would not be needed either.

It should also be noted that the advantages mentioned above only represent one side of the story, and there are also a number of significant points on the downside. Firstly, several of the points above assume that the individual concerned is actually competent to do the work, as opposed to being a relative novice or script kiddie who has got lucky and managed to breach the system. In addition, there is also a significant question regarding the trustworthiness of the individual who is volunteering to help. In the scenario where the hacker has breached security and then makes himself known, it can be argued that the organization is effectively being held to ransom – the hacker is already able to access the system, so what might happen to it if his offer of "assistance" is turned down? In addition, although the fact that security has been breached is an illustration of a problem that needs to be rectified, the hacker has already contravened computer misuse legislation in making the point. Is a lawbreaker the right person with which to trust your security? In the alternative situation, in which the hacker has offered to help only after being caught, it must be considered that his only motivation is to save his own skin.

If the hacker is inherently untrustworthy, how can the quality of the work be relied upon? The system may ostensibly appear to be secure, but the hacker may have left himself backdoors so that he can return later. This could simply be to enable ongoing access to a desirable system, but could also be for more threatening purposes (e.g. so as to be able to extract more money from the organization at a later date if required). In either case, the chance of the hacker's continued presence would be an unwanted extra.

If he considers himself to be a member of a wider hacking community, the hacker may have feelings of loyalty to his peers. Therefore, if the vulnerability of the target system has already been made common knowledge, he may not wish to close all the doors to his friends. It should be remembered that the idea of completely securing the system is contrary to the hacker ethic that there should be free access to systems and information.

Although it was observed that the service might be cheaper than professional consultants, this may also be reflected in terms of the quality of the overall package that is delivered. It is unlikely that a casual hacker would be in a position to offer much in terms of a meaningful warranty for the work undertaken. As such, in the event of things going wrong or the work turning out to be substandard, the client organization may have little useful recourse. Another aspect that may be lacking is documentation of what has actually been done.

Ethical hacking

In view of the various points above, the idea of engaging a casual hacker may be unappealing. However, this does not rule out the opportunity of conducting penetration testing, and an alternative is to consider assistance from companies offering what are termed ethical hacking services. Ethical hackers (also known as White Hat hackers) perform penetration testing against target systems, to determine whether they would stand up to a genuine hacker attack. Although it could be argued that in-house IT/security staff could conduct such testing, this is unlikely to provide a realistic evaluation. These people are responsible for the day-to-day administration of the system and are already familiar with the organization, the system, how it has been configured, and where protection is expected to reside. This risks their assessment being less objective than that of an outsider, and may lead them to make assumptions or overlook aspects that might otherwise be considered. It can also be assumed that, if in-house staff has configured the security in the first place, then they will have done so to the best of their ability. As such, their attempts at penetration testing may still be limited by the extent of their own knowledge.

So how does the use of ethical hackers compare with enlisting the help of an outside hacker who has already penetrated the system? A first, and fundamental, difference is that with ethical hackers it is the target organization that makes the first move – it is their decision to test security, rather than having the issue forced upon them by an uninvited guest. Another key point is that the hackers have prior authorization to probe and attempt to breach the target system. A third issue, which is particularly relevant from a business perspective, is the perceived credibility of those being hired. Although the ethical hackers are also external to the organization, they are typically based on a more reliable commercial footing. Indeed, a number of recognized and reputable companies now offer such services, including such names as PricewaterhouseCoopers[268] and IBM. For example, ethical hacking is one of the services offered by IBM's Global Security Analysis Lab (GSAL), a group based at the company's Watson Research Center in New York and Zurich Labs in Switzerland.[269] Of course, commercial companies like these will often offer traditional security audit and risk analysis services, which can lead to a comprehensive report regarding any potential vulnerabilities discovered. Why then would commissioning penetration tests be a preferable option? The main point is that the results would be far more persuasive. Risk analysis basically says, "This is what *could* happen." A penetration test says, "This is what *did* happen" and provides a direct and tangible demonstration of what someone else could do. Armed with such proof, it is easier to justify any expenditure or changes necessary to improve the security of the compromised system.

The financial side of the arrangement with ethical hackers may also be preferable. Some will only charge a fee if they have been able to successfully breach the system – meaning that if the client has already managed to provide adequate protection for their systems, then they will not have to pay out again for the privilege of being told so. If the hackers break in, however, their fee may reflect the level of penetration that they were able to achieve.[270] In this sense, the client will face an uncertain level of cost – dependent upon how secure their systems are to begin with. Some may, therefore, prefer to agree a set fee upfront, irrespective of whether any vulnerabilities are identified.

The expected boundaries of the tests will be formally established at the outset, with the target organization specifying whether any systems should be particularly targeted or, alternatively, left alone during the penetration attempts. In order to be realistic, however, they would probably be advised against the latter aspect, as a genuine hacker assault would not be constrained by such rules. Once the client has signed the contract, the hacking team will have the freedom to breach the system. In some circumstances, the operational staff and others using the system will not be made aware in advance that hacking attempts are going to take place. This will again increase the realism of the attack and will enable the penetration team to gauge how effective the organization's current intrusion detection mechanisms may be. Another issue is whether the hackers are permitted to conduct their penetration attempts in an obtrusive manner – where they may result in disruption to the target's day-to-day operations or actual harm to the systems under analysis. In most cases, clients would shy away from this level of testing, but those truly wishing to determine the full effects of a breach may allow such activity in order to accurately measure the impacts (on the understanding that any damage to systems could then be reversed and things restored to normal afterwards).

So, what do the ethical hackers do once they have got the green light? One would instinctively expect that they would apply hacker techniques and attempt to breach security by any means possible. However, some commentators have criticized the practice employed by some companies claiming to offer ethical hacking services, whereby they simply use off the shelf software to test the system on the client's behalf (i.e. they are apparently not bringing much in terms of their own specific expertise).[271] In other cases, the attempt will be much more comprehensive, assessing not just the computer network, but also the surrounding infrastructure of people and buildings. In this context, the concept of ethical hacking is extended to what can be referred to as a "tiger team" approach. The name "tiger team" comes from U.S. military circles, and has been used for many years to refer to teams of paid professionals who are brought in to test the security of military bases and the like, and then report on any weaknesses that they were able to find. The name has subsequently been generalized to apply to similar types of specialist testing in non-military scenarios. The use of a tiger team increases the realism of the security test, widening the range of methods used to encompass techniques such as social engineering and physical intrusion (which, as earlier discussions have identified, determined real-world hackers are not afraid to use). Tests of this nature give an indication of the effectiveness of security measures beyond those that IT staff are directly responsible for. Issues such as the effectiveness of building security and reception personnel, and the willingness of general employees to divulge company information, can also be assessed.

The contract will also specify the manner in which the hacking team is expected to present or demonstrate its findings to the client. They may, for example, make minor changes within the system(s) that they were able to penetrate (e.g. leaving "got here" messages in particular locations, such as directories or web pages). Alternatively, the host company may not want any actual changes to be made and may ask instead that the hackers present a catalog of the sensitive material that they were able to access. A standard objective for the hackers will be to demonstrate the ability to breach the administrator (or root) account on the system – effectively giving the penetrators complete access and control over the compromised system. The hacking team will typically document the vulnerabilities uncovered, the level of system access that these facilitated, and whether the breach of security was subsequently noticed (enabling both the current security configuration and the vigilance of the organization's administrators to be assessed).

So who are the ethical hackers and where do they come from? It is not necessarily a case of Black Hat hackers suddenly developing a conscience and deciding to provide a legitimate service. The firms or departments offering the services are quite often staffed by ex-military or secret service personnel, who have had relevant experience in their previous careers. Indeed, the companies offering the services quite often make the specific point that they do not hire hackers, even if they claim to be reformed. In some cases, however, reformed hackers have actually established their own security consultancy companies. For example, Matthew Bevan (aka Kuji, one of the two hackers involved in the Rome Labs hacking incident that was briefly mentioned in Chapter 6) has since become the Technical Director of Tiger Computer Security, a U.K.-based company that boasts the use of real world hackers to conduct its penetration tests for clients.[272] There are also other examples of hackers going commercial. In January 2000, L0pht Heavy Industries, the underground hacker group responsible for the password cracking tool L0phtCrack (described in Chapter 4), merged with e-commerce security firm @Stake Inc. in order to act as the company's research and development arm.[273] The more established consultancy providers, however, caution against the reliance upon these sources. To quote Fred Rica from PricewaterhouseCoopers:

> Many ex-hackers, also known as "gray hats," have entered the security consulting arena. This has created alarm and confusion among organizations as to whom they should turn to provide these very sensitive services.[274]

Rica's view seems to be generally echoed by the information security professionals surveyed as part of the 2001 CSI/FBI Computer Crime and Security Survey. Asked whether their organization would consider hiring reformed hackers as consultants, 67 percent of the 524 who responded said "no" (16 percent said "yes" and the remaining 17 percent were unsure).[275]

The fact that an organization may feel the need to consider hiring in hacking skills, ethical or otherwise, provides an indication of the extent to which in-house systems administrators are now playing a constant game of catch-up with the hacker community. Indeed, there are now courses available that administrators can attend in order to learn to think like the enemy.[276] During these courses, they can gain first-hand experience of using the tools and techniques practiced by real hackers, as well as obtaining details of relevant countermeasures. Although such training courses appear to be a logical means to enable administrators to fight abuse, there is also an argument that being an effective hacker is something that cannot simply be taught (i.e. it is more like a state of mind). As such, the lessons will not be effective against all classes of hacker – only those that similarly do things by the book. So, whereas the administrators may then be able to repel the script kiddies, they may still have difficulty in dealing with the more dedicated and creative die-hards who may use less predictable methods of attack.

From a certain point of view, the idea that administrators should need to be educated to think like hackers at all is rather bizarre. The concept of "know your enemy" is one thing, but if there are well-known vulnerabilities in a particular operating system, service, or application, then many would consider it reasonable for a system administrator to keep abreast of the situation. The reality is, unfortunately, symptomatic of the fact that many system administrators are unaware of the intricacies of IT security, and of those that are, many do not have the time to routinely maintain their knowledge of the latest vulnerabilities and attacks while also dealing with the routine tasks required to keep their systems running. The idea of having a dedicated security administrator (or, indeed, a team) may well be practical for larger organizations, but for administrators in small to medium sized organizations, security is often one consideration amongst many. Hackers, by contrast, can devote themselves whole-heartedly to discovering or learning the weaknesses and then exploiting the knowledge that they have obtained.

Hacktivism

Earlier discussion has identified that ideology frequently represents a motivation for computer hackers. They have a point to make or an ax to grind and they see cyberspace as the ideal location to place their soapbox. This type of action is commonly referred to as hacktivism – using computers and hacking as a tool for social change. Indeed, some of the previous examples in this book have already illustrated some hacks perpetrated in the name of hacktivism (e.g. the 1996 defacement of the U.K. Labour Party web site; the Timofonica "virus" protest against the Spanish telco Telefonica). This section presents some further examples of hacktivist activity, considering the motivation for the actions and the likely value of the attempts.

Online fuel protester hits strange targets

In September 2000, the U.K. was rocked by fuel shortages and widespread public protests about the level of fuel tax imposed by the government. Motorists had been unhappy for some time that they had to pay more in tax than their counterparts in the rest of Europe. So, when an OPEC-originated rise in the worldwide price of oil caused another two pence per litre to be added to the price at the pumps, the motorists of the U.K. decided that enough was enough. Led by farmers and road hauliers, whose line of work meant that they had been hit hard by rising fuel costs, protests and blockades were staged at oil refineries and fuel depots around the country, with the result that delivery tankers were unable to transport anything but fuel destined for the emergency services. Within a few days, the pumps around the whole country were running dry, with around 90 percent of filling stations reported to be out of fuel. People in rural areas were cut off, hospitals complained that lives were being put at risk because their staff could not get into work, and without deliveries to replenish them, supermarket shelves were beginning to run out of certain stocks. In the midst of all this, a hacker was at work.

The hacker in question went by the handle of Herbless and had decided to mount his own protest in support of the fuel crisis. To this end, he attacked some 450 popular web sites and replaced their homepages with one of his own design, as illustrated by the anonymized example in Figure 7.2. Amongst the many sites affected were an online jobs register, an opticians, a ceramics and pottery company, a web design and consultancy firm, a golf equipment supplier, and a company involved in the buying, selling, and repair of clocks. Although these examples are just a small proportion of the sites that were attacked, they serve to illustrate the significant diversity of organizations that Herbless targeted. They also illustrate that he was not particularly discerning in his selection of the victims.

In addition to fuel price protest, the tail end of Herbless's replacement page also included the following advice aimed at the administrators of the systems that he breached:

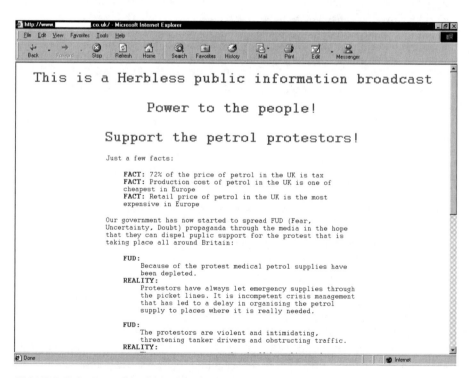

FIGURE 7.2 One of Herbless's fuel protest pages

Admin: Learn how to change passwords. Hint: SQL server doesn't just do SQL. Your old index has been backed up. Email me for details of the exploit used.

In doing this, the implied message is that Herbless is actually trying to be helpful in fixing their security vulnerabilities. However, if people like him were not there trying to exploit them, then the vulnerabilities would not be problems in the first place.

Although he attempted to provide a justification that would sit well with the public mood (i.e. protesting about fuel prices), this incident is exactly the sort of thing that gets hackers a bad name. Herbless was certainly making a point and getting attention, but who were his targets? Examples such as an opticians and a jobs database are hardly the sort of organizations that spring to mind as having any responsibility for fuel prices! As such, in having their customer web sites defaced, they were just innocent victims – the same as the members of the general public who perceived that they were being overcharged at the pumps.

So how did Herbless justify his actions? The following quote was attributed to him in news reports:

If I see something that I believe is wrong or unjust, then I speak out about it.[277]

This sounds reasonable enough, and in a free society, merely speaking out would not be a problem. Unfortunately, Herbless's actions were more akin to spray-painting his views on any available wall. Herbless in fact protested about so many things (as well as fuel prices, he hacked into sites to protest for the right to freely distribute music on the Internet,[278] about the UKUSA surveillance agreement,[279] and about the dangers of smoking[280]) that one suspects that he was either permanently discontent or just using the various causes as flags of convenience under which to excuse his hacking.

Another quotation attributed to Herbless:

Breaking into a site, stealing confidential information, deleting data and other abuses are not ethical. I do not condone such behaviour.[281]

On the face of it, these appear to be praiseworthy sentiments, but they rather overlook the fact that Herbless's own actions involved breaking into sites and committing abuse. In every case that he replaced an organization's homepage with his own, he compromised the integrity of their server. Furthermore, the reinstatement of the correct pages resulted in lost time for the associated webmasters. This is not to mention the confusion and bemusement for customers attempting to access the affected web sites. In compromising their sites, Herbless was conveying more than his explicit message about petrol prices. In the customers' minds he was probably raising questions about Internet security – "If this company's web site has been compromised, can they be relied upon?" – which could have resulted in harm to their business. At the very least, anyone looking to obtain information from the site would not have been able to do so while Herbless's page was there instead, as he did not provide any sort of onward link to the genuine homepage. As for the longevity of Herbless's modifications, although most of the affected sites rectified the problem in relatively short order and restored their intended pages, others were still displaying Herbless's version over a week later. If anyone had repeatedly tried to visit such a site during this period, then the continued display of the protest page would have potentially reinforced the impression that a serious breach of security had occurred.

On 19th September, Herbless struck again in relation to the fuel tax issue. In this instance, he attacked web sites belonging to HSBC Holdings, and as well as making some points about the fuel tax, took the opportunity to educate his readers in the ways of hacktivism. He called upon hackers to "take up this challenge; to work together" and suggested that "A distributed hacker network can be put in place very easily in two months" to aid further fuel protests. This provides a great excuse for those looking for a convenient reason to justify a bit of mischief, as well as conveying a rather menacing message to the casual reader accessing the site in order to utilize HSBC's online services. Continuing his public-spirited advice, Herbless also highlighted a number of "Things to keep in mind" when pursuing a hacktivist agenda:

Don't hack charity or small-business websites. You should know why not.

Don't delete data. This is not the spirit of hacktivism, and is tantamount to destruction of property.

Try to target widely used or very profitable sites. Things like the stock exchange are ideal.

Try to make sure it is very easy to see why the hacked sites have been hacked.

Try (without doing any permanent damage) to make the hack "stick" as long as possible.

Don't steal confidential information for any purposes. This is a protest, not espionage.

Check your hacks for spelling and grammar. Dum speeling missstakes stewpid look.

Coming from Herbless, the first, third and fourth points were astonishing bits of advice. Here was a hacker who had targeted the web site of a small ceramics and pottery company in order to protest about fuel tax, cautioning others against picking the wrong sort of target!

At the same time that Herbless was targeting all and sundry, another online fuel protestor staged the same kind of attack against OPEC, the Organisation of Petroleum Exporting Countries. As indicated earlier, OPEC was responsible for the rise in underlying oil prices that had preceded the price rises at U.K. pumps, and as such, many considered that OPEC was ultimately to blame for the situation. It was not known whether the perpetrator of the attack on their web site was an individual or a group of hackers, but the name "fluxnyne" was left as the calling card. The homepage of the OPEC site was altered to incorporate the following message:

> I think I speak for everyone out there when I say you guys need to get your collective asses in gear with the price of crude.[282]

Although in no way condoning fluxnyne's actions, at least the organization being targeted was the one perceived to be to blame for the problem being protested about. Even then, though, who was to say that fluxnyne had got it right? OPEC members highlighted the fact that the people of western nations were probably feeling the effects of their governments' fuel tax policies more than they were the underlying price of crude oil. This was certainly the viewpoint of the protestors at the U.K. fuel depots, and the placards that they were waiving blamed the government rather than OPEC.

In the cases of fluxnyne and Herbless, the hackers were using the Net as a platform for protests, but targeting an issue that was not linked to it. However, as the next example shows, there are also cases in which the Internet is directly related to the issue giving rise to hacktivist activity.

The Condemned Network – hacking for a noble cause

The majority of the discussions so far have clearly cast hackers and hacking in a negative light. However, there are situations in which the issue can become blurred, such as when the motivation for hacking is to combat a problem that would be widely accepted as more serious. Such an example can be cited in the fight against child pornography. The Internet is widely known to have established a significant role for itself as a platform for distributing pornographic material, with "sex" representing one of the most popular terms entered into web search engines (see **http://searchenginewatch.com** for evidence of this). Indeed, in many cases where individuals have been diagnosed as having an Internet addiction, the reason relates to the compulsive use of adult-oriented web sites and "cyber porn."[283] Unfortunately, the extreme end of this activity on the Internet includes the provision of an environment for paedophiles to distribute and exchange their materials – something that certain media reports have been quick to seize upon in their attempts to demonize the Net. Indeed, along with computer crime, child pornography has now become one of the recognized evils of the Internet – and not without good reason. It is possible to find newsgroup discussion forums with names such as "dadsanddaughters," "childpornonly" and "babyrape." Investigators have claimed that the Internet may be acting as a catalyst for the mainstreaming of such material, as paedophiles are able to make easy contact with like-minded individuals and consider this a validation of their perversion.[284]

It is not surprising that many people are outraged by such use of technology and have chosen to do something about it. Media reports have included reference to hackers who have dedicated themselves to the eradication of child pornography on the Internet.[285] Examples of online organizations formed to combat child pornography include the "Condemned Network" (http://www.condemned.org) and antichildporn.org (http://www.antichildporn.org), both of whom have, in the past, advocated the use of hacking to help remove the problem from the Internet. To quote from the web site of the Condemned Network:

> The Condemned Network . . . was established in early December 1999 to actively oppose and eradicate the existence and advertising of child pornography online –
> www.condemned.org/about.php

At the time, their use of the term "actively oppose" encompassed the use of hacking to achieve the objectives. Their methods included the use of buffer overflow attacks to take offending servers offline, as well as the use of known exploits to enable access to the systems themselves. Having penetrated a system, the Condemned volunteers would erase the contents of the hard drive, ensuring the removal of all unsavory materials.

Although these approaches led to a number of sites being forcibly shut down, the appropriateness of the methods used is still questionable. Certainly child pornography is not an issue that any right-minded person would support, but it does not necessarily follow that this makes the use of hacking an acceptable recourse. At the bottom line, hacking is also illegal in most developed countries, so what makes "hackers against child porn" any more noble than "murderers against child porn"? Of course, it can be argued that from a moral perspective child pornography is clearly worse, and therefore, hacking may be an acceptable response against a greater evil. However, other cases are less clear-cut – at what point does hacking become an acceptable response? In any case, hacking does not represent an ideal solution in this situation as it serves to attack the symptom rather than the cause. For example, if a web site is removed, so too is potential evidence linking it to the person that set it up. In addition, the nature of the Internet is such that if information ceases to be found in one location, it will pop up somewhere else. Given the choice, it would be preferable for the individuals involved in distributing child porn to be caught and imprisoned rather than temporarily impeded.

The anti-child porn movement ultimately realized that the use of hacking would probably complicate support for their cause and hamper their ability to co-operate with law enforcement. As such, they reverted to using more traditional Internet search techniques to locate material and then inform the authorities. The change is reflected in the "official press release" on the Condemned Network site, which now specifically refers to the use of "all legal means possible" to achieve their objectives.[286] However, this change of focus was clearly not to some members' tastes. For example, in the AntiChildPorn.Org (ACPO) group, the change to legal methods resulted in less than twelve of the 250 members remaining with the group. This suggests little dedication to the cause and that the fight against child pornography was merely a flag of convenience. It is probable that those who left were more interested in having an excuse to pursue their hacking interests and would be likely to support any cause that gave them an argument of legitimacy.

For those who remain, hacking may have been abandoned as a principal way forward, but the link has not disappeared altogether. To quote R. Loxley, a hacker and a sponsor of condemned.org:

> We do it exclusively legally in any country that has adequate laws, but where there are not we do what we have to do. We are dedicated to removing not just the porn, but the people behind it from the World Wide Web. The law enforcement agencies sometimes allow us to do certain things that they can't.[287]

So, although the underlying activity (i.e. hacking) is still illegal, it is clearly one that many can support in this context as a means to an end. Indeed, if the group were described as being responsible for forcibly removing child porn sites rather than hacking them, it is unlikely that the public at large would have any objection. As such, what many would condemn as cybercrime in other circumstances is possibly viewed as perfectly acceptable if the motive appeals to a wide enough audience. Other examples of this trend are presented in the remaining sections of this chapter.

Information warfare

Never has the saying "knowledge is power" been truer than it is today. Military strength and vast financial resources are no longer a prerequisite for a successful attack upon an enemy. The knowledge of a security vulnerability of which your target is unaware or unconcerned can be the key to entering and destroying their systems. Considering the range of potential tasks for which IT systems are now employed, the consequences of this could be fundamentally damaging. Indeed, there is now the potential to undermine and disable a society without a single shot being fired or missile being launched. To see the truth of this, it is only necessary to consider how many essential areas of modern society are now so significantly dependent upon technology that its unavailability could be catastrophic. For example healthcare, banking and finance, manufacturing, transportation, and government all have a significant reliance upon technology. Undermine the technology infrastructure and consider the impact: manufacturing would cease, access to money would be frozen, and people in need of care or support would not receive it. The emerging industries of the new millennium, such as electronic commerce, could be the first victims of this new style of problem.

All of the above effects could conceivably occur as a result of an accidental incident or a lack of foresight (e.g. in the same way as the Millennium Bug issue came about). However, this section sets out to consider the potentially more alarming scenario in which technology infrastructures or services are targeted deliberately. The term Information Warfare (IW) has been used to describe the ways in which technology could be used to attack the IT infrastructure of a country or a particular company. A formal definition is provided by Dr. Ivan Goldberg, the Director of the Institute for the Advanced Study of Information Warfare:

> Information warfare is the offensive and defensive use of information and
> information systems to deny, exploit, corrupt, or destroy, an adversary's information,
> information-based processes, information systems, and computer-based networks
> while protecting one's own. Such actions are designed to achieve advantages over
> military or business adversaries.[288]

An early example of info war is the cracking of the German Enigma code at Bletchley Park during World War II. The ability to break the encrypted communications without the enemy's knowledge gave the allies a significant advantage when it came to preparing for physical aspects of the conflict. The significance of this advantage was not forgotten when the fighting finished. After the war was over, the British gave away thousands of captured German Enigma code machines to their partners within the Commonwealth as a means of achieving secure communications– without making it clear that they already had the means to intercept and decipher the messages that the machines created. Details of Bletchley Park's wartime code breaking did not become public until the early 1970s, and in the intervening years, Britain was able to continue its intelligence gathering activities, targeting the very machines that it was happily redistributing.

In more modern times, military computer systems are already known to be favorite targets for hackers. Of any systems, one would instinctively expect these to be the best defended, so being able to penetrate them is a good means for a hacker to show off his skills. Increasingly, however, it is becoming more difficult to simply dismiss all such attacks as the work of casual joyriders, and the threat of cyberwar is now being taken very seriously by major military powers. To quote Lieutenant General Edward Anderson III, the Deputy Commander in Chief of U.S. Space Command (SPACECOM), speaking at the National Strategies and Capabilities for a Changing World conference, hosted by the U.S. Army, in November 2000:

We see three emerging threats: ballistic missiles, cyberwarfare and space control . . .
Cyberwarfare is what we might think of as attacks against digital ones and zeros.[289]

The focus of the conference was to consider the critical issues and priorities for national security strategy and the essential military capabilities that would be needed in the future. Information warfare (cyberwarfare) is clearly seen as one of the major issues for the years to come.

The weaponry for cyberwarfare includes a similar arsenal to those tools and approaches that have already been deployed by hackers and other cyber criminals. Distributed denial of service and virus-based attacks are likely favorites, due to their ability to disrupt and destroy an enemy's systems. The fact that the underlying nature of the methods used is similar to that of hackers is significant in the sense that it leads to the potential for ambiguity – what may appear to be a standard hacker assault could actually represent the first phase of a cyberwar. It is for this reason that SPACECOM is formulating its information warfare strategy in collaboration with the FBI, and a key decision in the early stages of investigating an attack will be to determine whether a military or law enforcement response is required. From 1st October 2000, SPACECOM assumed the responsibility for the Department of Defense's Computer Network Attack (CNA) mission and will detail its information warfare strategy in defense Operational Plan (OPLAN) 3600. SPACECOM already held the military lead role for Computer Network Defense – to defend DoD networks against attack from outside adversaries – and inheritance of the CNA mandate can be seen as harmonizing the overall approach. From the military public relations perspective, the ability to conduct cyberwarfare is clearly presented as being advantageous, as indicated by the following (from a SPACECOM press release):

Integrating Computer Network Attack into a broader military operation will help U.S. military forces to prevail on future battlefields. In some instances, Computer Network Attack might allow an operation to succeed with less loss of life and physical destruction.[290]

This alludes to the desirability of cyberwarfare as an alternative, less bloody means of attack. What it does not indicate is that a CNA capability is actually going to be an essential element as the military landscape changes. It is not just that the concept is being incorporated to prevent loss of life and destruction – it *has* to be addressed because the attacks that could be unleashed via computers ultimately have the potential to be more damaging than physical assaults.

The U.S. is not the only country to have identified the significance of information warfare capabilities. Indeed, Lieutenant General Anderson observed that other countries, such as Russia, Israel, and China, are actually more advanced in their efforts. The Chinese viewpoint is illustrated by the following extract taken from the People's Liberation Army's official newspaper, the *Liberation Army Daily*:

> It is essential to have an all-conquering offensive technology and to develop software and technology for Net offensives so as to be able to launch attacks and countermeasures on the Net, including information-paralyzing software, information-blocking software, and information-deception software.[291]

The attraction of cyberwar from the Chinese perspective is that they could not hope to stand up to the military strength of Western nations in a traditional war. In this sense, it is possible to view technology as an equalizing force between major countries and smaller groups. This is a battlefield where success relies upon intellectual skills and software creativity as opposed to sheer volume and physical or financial resources. In short, the individuals or small groups may, theoretically, have as much chance of succeeding as a superpower. To see the potential for damage, you only have to look at the results of actions from individuals who have acted *without* a war motive and *without* government or official backing. Consider the impact that some of the hacking and virus incidents described earlier have had upon businesses in recent years. Imagine what would be possible if a more determined effort was made to co-ordinate these attacks.

Some, however, are not convinced. Critics of the defense budget, for example, have accused the military of over-playing the threat as part of a public relations initiative aimed at ensuring their budgets do not disappear as a result of cuts in conventional spending.[292] Arguments offered in support of this view are that highly sensitive government and military systems are not even connected to the Internet, and that the statistics often quoted to illustrate the number of detected attacks are rather misleading. For example, the Pentagon has revealed figures indicating the extent of attacks against its systems. In 1998, the number of incidents totalled 5,844.[293] The following year, however, the scale of the problem had almost quadrupled, with the Defense Information Systems Agency (DISA) reporting 22,144 incidents during 1999. Without any further qualification, these figures appear extremely worrying and, if taken at face value, provide a strong justification for increasing protection against cyberwar. However, the significance of the figures is very much dependent upon what is considered to constitute an "incident." Anyone willing to do some further research would discover that, in Pentagon/DISA termino-logy, an incident does not equate to a penetration of the system (which is quite obvious when you think about it, but is not normally made clear in the context of media reports). To the Pentagon, and other U.S. defense and government sites, incidents such as a series of repeated pings, network port scanning, or opening a virus-infected message would be logged as an incident. Indeed, subsequent figures from the General Accounting Office (GAO) revealed that the U.S. Army, Navy, and

Air Force experienced a total of only 600 cyber attacks in 1999 (with attacks in this case being incidents that were identifiable as someone trying to get into a system that they were unauthorized to access). However, the GAO report did, nonetheless, establish that the scale of the problem was increasing – with 715 attacks logged during 2000.[294] As an aside, the U.S. military has rethought its attitude toward the use of the Internet and has undertaken a review of the material that is published on its web sites in order to prevent sensitive information from being made available inadvertently.[295]

Critics of the military are not the only ones who may be dismissive of cyberwar. In his book, *The Next World War*, James Adams also questions the extent to which the general public perceive the threat from this direction:

> To the public, the Internet is a playground or a productivity tool. It is not the means by which their plane might be pulled from the sky or their electric power supply switched off. In keeping with the commercial tenor of the times, the most dangerous purpose to which most see the Internet being put is the draining of their bank account or the theft of their credit card number by some malevolent hacker.[296]

This viewpoint is supported by the survey results presented in Chapter 6, which indicated that although some people do perceive threats from the Internet, these are generally considered to be of a criminal nature. So what is the real nature of the threat? The question can be answered to some extent by looking at examples that have already occurred in practice.

Cyberwar in the Balkans

The escalation of violence in the Balkans during 1999 also resulted in the emergence of a new front to the war – the cyber front. During the course of the conflict, both the NATO and Serbian sides used the Internet as a means of putting their point of view forward, and presented news stories that were distinctly colored toward their own perspectives. This, of course, is no different to what one would expect from normal media reports, the difference being that the stories were visible worldwide – actually a benefit of technology, as people on both sides could see both viewpoints and obtain a more balanced perspective. In addition to such passive cyber-propaganda, the different parties' supporters also hacked into web pages in order to leave messages detailing their support. Relevant examples are shown in Figures 7.3 and 7.4. The reason for the attacks was that, for many individuals, they represented the only way in which they could attack what they saw as the enemy.

Of course, attacks such as these web defacements can be considered to have caused only minor inconvenience. However, other attacks were focused more directly at the parties involved in the conflict. The NATO web site was the target of ping bombardment from hackers in Belgrade, while other defense alliance computer systems fell victim to other forms of attempted denial of service. To quote NATO spokesman Jamie Shea, their system had been:

> saturated by one individual who is currently sending us 2,000 e-mails a day and we are dealing with macro viruses from Yugoslavia into our e-mail system.[297]

During the same period, the Serbs were found to have hacked into the British Ministry of Defense computer systems.[298] They targeted the communications systems used to send messages between U.K. military headquarters and units in the field, again in an attempt to plant viruses. At the same time, the British were engaged in similar activities against the Serbian systems, illustrating that a cyberwar was operating in parallel to the traditional warfare approaches.

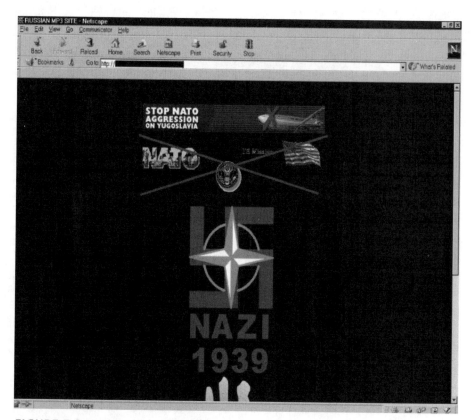

FIGURE 7.3 Anti-NATO hacking message

Cyberwar in the Middle East

September 2000 saw the breakdown of the peace settlement in the Middle East and the resumption of bloody conflicts between Palestinians and Israelis. The crisis erupted on 28th September, when the Israeli opposition leader, Ariel Sharon, attempted to assert Israeli sovereignty over holy sites shared between Arabs and Israelis in east Jerusalem. His visit to Al-Aqsa mosque (located on a site that Muslims refer to as the Noble Sanctuary and Jews call Temple Mount) ended in violent clashes that quickly spread through the occupied Palestinian territories.[299] Israeli soldiers were deployed to control the protests and the problem escalated from there. In parallel with the battles being fought on the streets, a cyberspace element to the conflict soon emerged, with both sides attacking each other's Internet sites using methods such as defacement and denial of service.

The cyber conflict began on 6th October, with pro-Israeli hackers establishing a web site to host FloodNet denial of service attacks. These work by repeatedly reloading a targeted site several times a minute, with the result that the site becomes inaccessible to legitimate traffic. A number of Hezbollah sites, including Hamas.org, fell victim to this form of attack. From this point on, the methods escalated as follows:

FIGURE 7.4 Pro-NATO hacking message

- The Israeli Internet Underground, a coalition of activists from Israeli technology companies, established a site listing details of over forty sites that had been defaced by Palestinian supporters, along with details of Israeli sites believed to be vulnerable to attack due to running services with exploitable security holes.[300]

- Two databases belonging to the American Israeli Public Affairs Committee (AIPAC) were stolen and publicly posted on the Internet by Palestinian sympathizers in Pakistan. One database contained personal details relating to AIPAC members, including around 200 credit card numbers. The other contained 3,100 email addresses of persons who had registered to be kept updated on the Israeli conflict. The perpetrator, a hacker called "Doctor Nuker," was the founder of the Pakistani Hackerz Club.[301] Such posting clearly invited the misuse of the card numbers and established the named individuals as potential targets for email harassment.

- A pro-Palestinian site was reported to be distributing hacking tools and viruses for use against Israeli targets. A range of viruses and worms (including the Melissa, Chernobyl and Love Letter varieties that were described in Chapter 5) were amongst the materials made available for download. The site encouraged visitors to utilize the tools in the intended manner, with the following oath being displayed for them to subscribe to: "I swear that I will not use these programs on anyone other than Jews and Israelis."[302]

- Unity, a Muslim extremist group, announced a four-phase plan for a so-called "cyber-jihad" against the Israelis. Phase one focused on crashing government sites, phase two encompassed financial targets such as the Bank of Israel, phase three targeted Internet and telecommunication service providers, and phase four related to the destruction of e-commerce sites.[303]

The nature of the attacks in the cyberwar could be considered somewhat trivial when compared to the 300 or so lives that had been lost in the physical conflict during the same time period. Indeed, many of the attacks merely involved defacement of web sites and racial comments against the opposing side. However, what is significant is that the perpetrators are amateurs – using the medium as a means of expressing their patriotism.

Another issue to consider is the barriers to entry in the respective forms of the conflict. To participate in the physical conflict, the first requirement is to be located in the right place. There is not much you can do to help in the fighting on the streets of Jerusalem if you actually live hundreds of miles away. Even if you are living in the conflict zone, it could be argued that becoming a really meaningful participant in the battle ideally requires you to be physically fit to fight, to possess a weapon and some sort of military skill. Many people clearly would not meet these criteria. A further barrier is, of course, the personal risk involved, as being on the frontline could obviously lead to injury or even death. As such, many people may be dissuaded from doing much more than voicing their support. In contrast, the barriers to entry into the cyber conflict are much lower. All you need is a computer and access to the Internet. The appropriate targets, and the means to attack them, can all be found on the Internet itself. This is the kind of war that many more people are willing and equipped to fight. This is well illustrated by the rallying of volunteer support by the two sides, particularly in support of the Palestinians. Interested hackers of all types, from script kiddies to professionals, found a means to join in. Nor was this participation limited to those within the Palestinian and Israeli communities. As indicated above, a major effort for the Palestinians came from hackers in Pakistan.

This situation, and that outlined in the Balkans, illustrates the use of information warfare as an adjunct to traditional conflict. Cyberwar by no means took the leading role, and mass media reports were still centered upon the physical aspects of the conflict. However, the fact that cyberwar was recognized as a means of attack by both sides is significant. It provides evidence that cyberspace is perceived as a valid battleground, and represents a potential indication that cyberwar will become an inherent part of future battles. The two sides in any conflict will now be aware that cyberwar offers a means to attack, and to be attacked by, their enemy. As such, it is an area that they ignore at their peril.

Information warfare is not the only context in which cyberspace attack could be used by an aggressor. As the next section will illustrate, another widely debated issue is the potential for technologies pioneered by cyber criminals to be adopted for use in terrorist activities.

Cyberterrorism

As we begin the twenty-first century, the concept of terrorism is closely associated with images of violence, death, and physical destruction. Terrorist methods have been used for hundreds of years as a means of bringing about change, particularly in political scenarios. Historically, terrorism has been conducted by groups of people, acting in support of a common cause or belief, with the underlying intention of coercing or intimidating a target into a desired course of action. Alternatively, terrorist action can be taken as a means of revenge or as an element of a wider conflict. The FBI definition of terrorism is as follows:

Terrorism is the unlawful use of force or violence against persons or property to intimidate or coerce a government, the civilian population, or any segment thereof, in furtherance of political or social objectives.

Conventional terrorism is by no means a trivial problem to address. However, the operation of terrorists within groups (cells), and as part of some organized overall regime, presents some level of opportunity for law enforcement to monitor and detect their activities in advance. The same cannot be said of terrorist actions carried out by a disenfranchized loner. This is effectively a random occurrence and it becomes practically impossible for anyone attempting to monitor and control terrorism to predict when and where trouble might occur. To date, however, the opportunities for an individual to make a really significant impact have been limited. Unfortunately, information technology, and society's dependence upon it, effectively changes this. The Internet is an ideal environment for what computer security expert Simson Garfinkel, author of *Database Nation: The Death of Privacy in the 21st Century*, refers to as the "irrational terrorist."[304] In contrast to those who are seeking to use their actions to further a common cause or seeking to bring about a desired change, irrational terrorists are not interested in negotiation and may be acting alone. Their objective is still to cause destruction, but it is an end in itself, rather than a means of gaining leverage. Garfinkel's discussion of the issue still focuses upon physical forms of terrorism, where the outcomes are typically loss of life and destruction of property. However, the principle of irrationality can also hold true in an IT context, and in many ways, this may be considered to provide a better environment for such actions. As previous examples have shown, the combination of a personal computer, an Internet connection, and an appropriate level of systems knowledge can put a great deal of power into the wrong hands. It is easier for an individual to attain power by this means than via conventional terrorist methods.

As Garfinkel observes, even though you cannot monitor every individual, it is potentially feasible to monitor and control the distribution of the raw materials that could be used to create terrorist weapons. The tools of conventional terrorism – such as explosives, radioactive materials, and biochemicals – are not routinely available commodities, and the organizations that have them should ideally not release them on the basis of a casual request! In addition, to be able to do anything with such dangerous materials requires specialist knowledge if they are to be handled safely and then used effectively. So, for someone to be in a position to attempt a terrorist act with explosives or chemicals, they have to be able to get hold of the stuff and know exactly what to do with it when they have it. This somewhat reduces the odds that the irrational loner would be in a position to do it. What, though, if the raw materials required are a PC and an Internet connection? These are exactly the same materials that would also be used for countless legitimate activities, so obviously attempting to restrict their distribution is a non-starter. As regards the knowledge required to utilize them, there is clearly a requirement for the perpetrator to be IT literate, but beyond that there is no fundamental limit. Previous discussion has shown that attacks can be automated via software, so even relatively unskilled individuals would be in a position to do something. Those with accompanying technical knowledge could obviously do somewhat more. Practically all of the malware incidents described in Chapter 5 were the work of individuals. Although they cannot be classed as terrorist activities, they provide a very good indication of how technology enables the activities of an individual to be amplified to massive effect. As an illustration of this, consider the following situation. In early 2000, when the security risks associated with the Internet and the World Wide Web were hardly unknown, a fifteen-year-old was able to use a software package to orchestrate a distributed denial of service attack that brought a series of major sites to their knees (see Chapter 2). If a lone teenager was able to do this, what is to stop others doing the same, and what could a more mature group achieve using similar methods?

The evidence presented in earlier chapters suggests that it is possible for hackers to breach systems that we would instinctively expect to be more secure (e.g. military sites). The fact that such attacks are successful leaves systems vulnerable to more insidious threats than straightforward hacking. Recent years have witnessed the use of information technology by terrorist-type organizations. This has led to the emergence of a new class of threat, which has been termed cyberterrorism. This can be viewed as distinct from traditional terrorism since efforts are focused upon attacking information systems and associated resources rather than physical infrastructure. When viewed from the perspective of skills and techniques, there is little to distinguish cyberterrorists from the general classification of hackers. Both groups require and utilize an arsenal of techniques in order to breach the security of target systems. From a motivational perspective, however, cyberterrorists are clearly different, operating with a specific political or ideological agenda to support their actions. This in turn may result in more focused and determined efforts to achieve their objectives, as well as more considered selection of suitable targets for attack. However, the difference does not necessarily end there and other factors should also be considered. Firstly, cyberterrorists that are part of an organized group could have funding available to support their activities. This could, in turn, facilitate access to computing equipment and resources that would be beyond the means of a casual hacker. A further aspect distinguishing cyberterrorism from conventional hacking is the impact of the attack. Dorothy Denning, Professor of Computer Science at Georgetown University, suggests the following additional caveat to the definition of cyberterrorism:

> to qualify as cyberterrorism, an attack should result in violence against persons or property, or at least cause enough harm to generate fear. Attacks that lead to death or bodily injury, explosions, plane crashes, water contamination, or severe economic loss would be examples. Serious attacks against critical infrastructures could be acts of cyberterrorism, depending on their impact. Attacks that disrupt nonessential services or that are mainly a costly nuisance would not.[305]

In her May 2000 testimony before the Special Oversight Panel on Terrorism of the U.S. House of Representatives, from which the above quotation is taken, Dr. Denning further stated that the threat to date has been largely theoretical. This view is shared by members of the hacking community who, having different motives for their actions, find it hard to relate to the concept of hacking skills being used in this context. This is illustrated by the following quotation from Emmanuel Goldstein of *2600*:

> In all of the time I've been in the scene, which is a pretty long time, I've never come across anyone I consider to be a "cyberterrorist," whatever that is. Most people who talk of such creatures either have something to sell or some bill to pass. This is not to say that such a concept is impossible. But I believe the current discussions aren't based in reality and have very suspicious ulterior motives.[306]

It is certainly fair to observe that ulterior motives might also be playing a part in government enthusiasm to address the issue. Indeed, the threat posed by cyber-terrorists and other online criminals is being used as the justification for more significant powers of monitoring and interception by governments and intelligence services. For example, in the U.K., MI5 is building a £25m email surveillance center, with the government requiring ISPs to have "hardwire" links into the system so that messages can be directly intercepted.[307] This, of course, has significant implications in relation to the millions of other messages that will also be intercepted, the majority of which will be innocent.

Although Denning and Goldstein are sceptical about the existence of cyber-terrorists, it can certainly be observed that established terrorist groups (or related organizations) are currently using the Internet for a number of purposes, as described below.

- Propaganda/Publicity
  Terrorist and resistance groups have traditionally had difficulty in relaying their political messages to the general public without being censored. However, they can now use the Internet for this purpose, as demonstrated by the Irish Republican Information Service and the Zapatista Movement (see **http://www.ezln.org/**).

- Fundraising
  Some terrorist and resistance groups linked to political parties are now using the Internet for fund raising purposes. In the future this may mean that smaller groups may be able to receive the majority of their funding through online credit card donations.

- Information dissemination

  It is also possible that groups may publish sensitive information about a particular country. For example, Sinn Fein supporters at the University of Texas made details about British Army establishments within Northern Ireland publicly available on the Internet.[308] In addition, information is available about engaging in terrorist activities. For example, the *Terrorist Handbook* instructs beginners how to make explosives and weapons, and is widely referenced and available on the Internet.[309]

- Secure communications

  Terrorist use of more advanced encryption methods will result in a command system that is difficult to break and allows for the control of groups anywhere in the world. This causes a problem for the security services, as it means that they will have to spend more time and resources on trying to decrypt electronic messages. In addition, services like anonymous remailers can be used to hide the identity of message senders. These work by accepting an email message, stripping off the actual sender's address and then forwarding the content to the intended recipient under an anonymized identity. In this way, the recipient cannot directly identify the originator of the message. Although there are numerous valid applications for such technology in order to preserve privacy, there is also the clear potential for misuse in cybercrime scenarios.

Although all of the above might give cause for concern, they merely illustrate how existing activities may be simplified via new technology. The real threat in the "cyber" context is when the Internet (or the more general technology infrastructure) becomes the medium in which a terrorist-type attack is conducted. Common scenarios that are already in evidence here include denial of service and direct attacks. Denial of service has been covered in earlier chapters and it is known that the software required to carry out such attacks is widely available on the Internet. A direct attack takes the form of hacking into a computer system and then rewriting or stealing information. At the most basic level, this can be the same as web defacement, as demonstrated by the Portuguese hacker group PHAIT (Portuguese Hackers Against Indonesian Tyranny), which rewrote Indonesian government and commercial web sites in order to protest about Indonesian occupation and repression of East Timor. An example of their handiwork is illustrated in Figure 7.5, and since 1997, the group has hacked and defaced numerous systems in this manner.

Another observation is that cyber attacks offer the capability for terrorist activities with wider-reaching impacts. With traditional terrorist activities, such as bombings, the impacts are isolated within specific physical locations and communities. In this context, the wider populace act only as observers and are not directly affected by the actions. Furthermore, acts of violence are not necessarily the most effective ways of making a political or ideological point – the public and media attention is more likely to focus upon the destruction of property and/or loss of life than whatever cause the activity was intended to promote. The ability of cyberterrorism activities to affect a wider population may give the groups involved greater leverage in terms of achieving their objectives, while also ensuring that no immediate long-term damage is caused that could cloud the issue. For example, in a denial of service scenario, if the threatened party was to accede to the terrorist demands, then the situation could (ostensibly at least) be returned to that which existed prior to the attack (i.e. with service resumed). This is not the case in a physical incident when death or destruction has occurred. Of course, cyberterrorism does not have to exist on its own and could also be used in conjunction with, or to support, more traditional attacks. For example, hacking techniques could be employed to obtain intelligence information from systems, which could then be used as the basis for a physical attack.

So, what has happened to date, and does it suggest cyberterrorism to be a real threat? Some examples of incidents that could be classed as cyberterrorism (or can, at least, be seen to be closely related to it) are presented below.

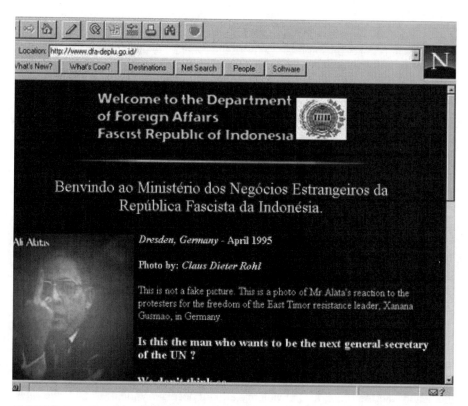

FIGURE 7.5 PHAIT hackers protest for East Timor

- In 1999 a seventeen-year-old American operating under the name Chameleon was found to be stealing satellite images from U.S. military sites.[310] Chameleon was believed to be in the employ of a follower of Osama bin Laden, the man suspected of being behind the bombing of American embassies in East Africa in 1998, and consequently at the top of the FBI's most wanted list. Chameleon was given an advance of $1,000 in exchange for the software, and promised another $10,000 and further work once it was delivered. Luckily, the FBI tracked him down before he had the opportunity to deliver the files.

- In 1998 Tamil guerrillas flooded Sri Lankan embassies with email messages, sending them 800 a day over a two-week period. The intention was to disrupt the communications capabilities, and the incident is the first known terrorist attack against a country's computer systems.[311]

- In late December 1998, a U.S. hackers group calling itself the Legion of the Underground (LoU) called for "the complete destruction of all computer systems" in China and Iraq. The group, which had previously hacked into China's human rights web site, was protesting against what it perceived as severe rights abuses by the governments in both countries and was calling upon hackers around the world to participate in attacks against their IT infrastructures. However, the declaration drew strong condemnation from other hacker groups of the day, including L0pht, the Chaos Computer Club and the Cult of the Dead Cow, who collectively referred to it as irresponsible and "nothing a hacker could be proud of."[312]

- In 1996 and 1997, an MIT graduate and self-proclaimed Internet anarchist named Jim Bell devised an online scheme that he believed could bring about the annihilation of all forms of government. In a text entitled *Assassination Politics*,[313] Bell postulated a means by which Internet technologies such as encryption, digital cash and message remailers could be used to establish an anonymous framework in which people could predict and confirm the assassinations of government officials. The idea was shared via the Cypherpunks mailing list, an online discussion area for encryption and privacy advocates. Whereas some regarded it as thought-provoking analysis of a potential consequence of the digital society, others, such as the U.S. government, took an understandably more negative view, branding Bell a techno-terrorist. Although Bell did not propose that he would break the law himself ("I'm not going to kill them off . . . other people are going to do that. I'm going to promote a system"[314]), the concern was that his ideas could incite others to do so. Indeed, the government attempted to establish a link between Bell's activities and those of another cypherpunk list participant, Carl Johnson, who was jailed in 1999 on four counts of threatening government officials in his online postings.[315]

It may be observed that some of the targets, actions, and results in these cases do not appear to be of the same level of significance or severity that one would normally associate with the concept of terrorism. This, to some degree, relates to the nature of the systems that can typically be targeted from the open Internet. In what we think of as traditional, high profile terrorist activity, the most attractive targets are those with the maximum potential for causing damage and/or attracting attention. Examples here include airports and aircraft, nuclear power plants, military installations, etc. Blowing up an aircraft with a bomb, for example, is unfortunately an established terrorist method and is guaranteed to get attention. However, achieving the same sort of result by purely cyberterrorist methods would be more difficult. Although havoc and destruction could potentially be caused by manipulating something like an air traffic control system, getting access to such systems would typically only be possible from within a private network – the systems are not visible from an Internet perspective. As such, any terrorist wishing to pick a target and cause this level of impact would currently be more likely to rely upon physical assault.

Another reason for the current lack of high-profile cyberterrorist organizations is the time and effort that it takes to establish significant attack capabilities. In August 1999, a report entitled "Cyberterror: Prospects and Implications" was produced by the Center for the Study of Terrorism and Irregular Warfare at the Naval Postgraduate School in Monterey, California. They identified three categories of cyberterrorism capability, based on escalating levels of technical skill and organizational capability:

- Simple-unstructured – capability to conduct basic hacks against individual systems using tools created by someone else. Little target analysis, command and control or learning capabilities within the terrorist organization.

- Advanced-structured – capability to conduct more sophisticated attacks against multiple systems, and possibly to modify or create basic hacking tools. Elementary target analysis, command and control, or learning capabilities.

- Complex-co-ordinated – capability to mount co-ordinated attacks and cause mass-disruption against integrated, heterogeneous defenses, and the ability to create sophisticated hacking tools. Advanced capabilities for target analysis, command and control, and learning.

It was considered that, if an organization wished to build a cyberterrorism capability, then it would take two to four years to reach the second level, and between six to ten years to reach the highest level. The study also concluded that, of the various types of terrorist organization, only those motivated by religious beliefs would be likely to pursue the highest level of cyberterror capability.

It is difficult to predict precisely how terrorist groups may use the Internet in the future. In many cases, established groups may not see the need to consider technology-based attacks if their current tried and tested methods are still producing results. However, there are several reasons why cyberterrorism may become more attractive to terrorist groups:[316]

- the risk of capture is reduced since attacks can occur remotely.
- it is possible to inflict grave financial damage without any loss of life.
- the expertise for these attacks can be hired.
- a successful attack would result in worldwide publicity, and failure would go unnoticed.
- supporters can be attracted from all over the world, with the Internet being used as a method of generating funds.
- the Internet offers an ideal propaganda tool – operating on a global basis without the option for control or censorship by individual governments.
- the capability to mount basic attacks can be developed both quickly and cheaply.

A further factor that should not be overlooked is that the terrorists of tomorrow will have grown up with the Internet and may more naturally see the target opportunities that it offers.

The seriousness with which the issue is taken can be illustrated by recent activities by national governments, such as the aforementioned formation of organizations such as the U.S. NIPC and the U.K. NISCC (discussed in the previous chapter). However, while the threats are undoubtedly serious, it is important that methods of response are not taken too far. Without appropriate control, it is possible that measures could be introduced that are harmful to society in a different way. For example, increased regulation or monitoring of our IT and communications systems could lead to the emergence (some would say extension) of a "surveillance society" in which technology is used to erode individual rights and freedoms in the name of the wider public good. Examples that could already be argued to represent a move in this direction are discussed in the section that follows.

When the boot is on the other foot

Much of the discussion in previous chapters has focused upon the activities of hackers and the threat that they pose to the security of systems such as the Internet. Although these issues must be taken seriously, individuals and businesses must also recognize that hackers are not the only threat to their privacy online. Indeed, governments and law enforcers are happy to demonize hackers for activities that are very similar to those that they themselves are not averse to engaging in. For example, evidence from recent years suggests that, with official backing, "comprehensive systems exist to access, intercept and process every important modern form of communications, with few exceptions."[317] A prime example of this is the U.S. National Security Agency's Project P-415, better known as ECHELON.

ECHELON is an electronic surveillance network with bases at locations such as Menwith Hill in Yorkshire, U.K. The system is part of an intelligence-sharing alliance between America, Canada, Britain, Australia, and New Zealand, known as the Quadrapartite, or United Kingdom-United States (UKUSA) Agreement.[318] The strongest alliance within this group is between the National Security Agency (NSA) and the U.K. Government Communications Headquarters (GCHQ), based in Cheltenham. The NSA provides funding (worth several million pounds per annum) to support the aforementioned Menwith Hill listening station, in return for which it is granted full access to the intercepted materials.

The system is capable of monitoring and scanning network traffic, with the ability to highlight any communications that contain particular keywords of interest. Such keywords might include words such as "assassination," "President," the names of known terrorist groups, world leaders, or any other terms that may be of relevance in a particular context. In spite of the obvious privacy concerns, it can be argued that such a system has a valuable role to play in various law enforcement and national/international security contexts (e.g. as an anti-terrorist defense). However, an investigation of the system that was presented in a report to the European Parliament concluded that the ECHELON system has also been at the center of commercial espionage activities. Although this may seem at odds with the concept of maintaining "national security," the interpretation of the term has been somewhat broadened to encompass economic, commercial, and corporate concerns – effectively making it fair game to spy on foreign competitors.[319, 320]

The French expressed particular concern about the commercial uses of ECHELON and conducted their own investigation to determine whether it had been used to spy on and influence international business decisions. Their resulting report claimed that it had and called for greater use of encryption in Europe in order to safeguard the privacy and confidentiality of sensitive communications.

As recognition of the sensitivity of the situation, July 2000 saw ECHELON being made the focus of a one-year investigation by thirty-six Members of the European Parliament, in order to determine the implications for European citizens and industry of global communications interception.[321] The first meeting of the resulting Temporary Committee on the ECHELON Interception System was held in November 2000, focusing upon what the system is and what it is capable of. The subsequent meeting, which commenced in March 2001, focused upon legal affairs, human rights, and privacy issues. However, when the investigation ended in July 2001, many were critical of the extent of its findings. The ultimate conclusion was that the ECHELON system almost certainly existed (a finding that was not a great surprise to many observers), but details of what it actually did were still scarce, and aspects such as its use for commercial espionage activities were played down.[322] Although the committee did not approve of ECHELON's activities, its resolution concluded that there was little that could actually be done about it, other than to step up diplomatic pressure on the parties involved. Critics felt that this was insufficient, and also observed that the committee had failed to censure other European countries, such as France, who, whilst complaining loudly about ECHELON, were actually under suspicion of using similar methods themselves.[323]

With the above in mind, it can be argued that much of the governmental rhetoric regarding the danger of hackers and their activities is somewhat hypocritical. Although the existence and operation of ECHELON was strongly suspected, it could hardly have been described as open knowledge prior to the European Parliament's investigation. Although the maintenance of such secrecy is possibly justifiable from a true national security perspective (e.g. for reasons such as defense and counter-terrorism), it is not a valid argument if it can be demonstrated that the facilities are being used for the benefit of commercial organizations.

ECHELON is by no means the only controversial example that can be cited. The aforementioned example of the U.K. Security Service's establishment of an email interception system is another illustration of how hacker-type techniques (in this case packet sniffing) are legitimized when they serve a convenient purpose. This system has a parallel in the U.S., where the FBI has a network tapping system named DCS1000 (for Digital Collection System), which is based upon a laptop computer and runs proprietary packet sniffing software.[324] Up until February 2001, the system was known as Carnivore, but the name was changed as a result of the rather predatory image that it conveyed (a fact noted by both the then U.S. Attorney General Janet Reno and the Illinois Institute of Technology, who were commissioned to produce a report about the capabilities of the system). DCS1000 systems can be deployed in locations such as ISPs, enabling communications to be intercepted from the server. The question again arises of whether the interception can be limited to traffic about which there are reasonable grounds for suspicion, or whether innocent communications will also be routinely obtained. Although the FBI argues the former (citing that monitoring can be limited to traffic to and from known Internet addresses), a counterargument is that many ISPs assign Internet addresses to their subscribers dynamically – meaning that specific addresses with which to program DCS1000 would not be known in advance, leading to the conclusion that blanket monitoring of traffic would be the only way to ensure that the desired communications could be intercepted.

News of DCS1000's capabilities caused widespread outcry, attracting criticism from a bipartisan selection of U.S. lawmakers, as well as from a range of civil liberties organizations (e.g. the American Civil Liberties Union). Their main concern was the potential for the system to snoop on the Internet communications of entirely innocent users. In order to address the concerns, the U.S. Justice Department commissioned a review to assess whether the surveillance system represented a violation of innocent users' privacy rights. The review was conducted by the Research Institute of the Illinois Institute of Technology and Chicago-Kent College of Law, who produced a report after an investigation lasting one month and costing $250,000 (£170,000). The report was generally positive, stating that the DCS1000 program (still then known as Carnivore) provides a more precise facility than off-the-shelf network monitoring software, which can be used to help ensure that agents do not get more information than that which they are entitled to obtain under court direction. The investigation did, however, highlight two potential problem areas with the tool as it then stood:

- The program allowed filter settings to be specified that "may not be appropriate or even technically feasible."[325] The filter settings determine which packets are captured, and so must be set correctly by agents in order to ensure effective use of the system and prevent the inadvertent capture of unauthorized data. It was, therefore, concluded that it needed to be made more straightforward for agents to operate.
- The use of the system lacked individual accountability, because each action within it could not be traced to a specific FBI agent. From the perspective of establishing a chain-of-custody for the collected evidence, the report stated that it would be important to be able to determine who set up a data collection and when they did so.

Overall it was concluded that when used in accordance with a court order, DCS1000 provides investigators with no more information than is permitted by a given court order. The outcome, however, did little to reassure the system's opponents, who claimed that the review was superficial, and that the team who conducted it had ties to the administration that commissioned it.[326] Concerns remained that privacy could be compromised because in order to be able to collect evidence in relation to potential criminal cases, DCS1000 would also be scanning through a huge quantity of non-criminal communications. The FBI responded to these claims by pointing out that, as DCS1000 itself sorts through the collected information in order to find evidence, the content itself is not actually seen by human eyes.

What the DCS1000 case clearly underlines is the fact that such monitoring technology has immense power and a significant potential to be exploited. The extent to which the power can be harnessed depends upon who you are – a factor that will also determine the likelihood of that power being misused. Governments and organizations like the FBI have huge resources and are, therefore, in a much better position to deploy systems for data collection, service disruption, etc. than any hackers. At the same time, one would expect more responsible utilization of the facilities. However, outside of the DCS1000 context, the FBI have attracted criticism for the methods they have used and the manner in which they have been applied. A case in point is the hacking of alleged mobster Nicodemo S. Scarfo, who was charged with masterminding loan sharking and illegal gambling operations in New Jersey. Scarfo had been using PGP (Pretty Good Privacy), a well-known encryption utility, to protect the contents of his computer from unauthorized inspection. Breaking such encryption is beyond the capabilities of even the computers at the disposal of the FBI and, as such, another approach was necessary if they were to see what Scarfo was obviously quite keen to hide.

In May 1999, the FBI applied to the courts for "authority to search for and seize encryption-key-related pass phrases," and to "install and leave behind software, firmware, and/or hardware equipment which will monitor the inputted data entered on Nicodemo S. Scarfo's computer by recording the key related information as they are entered."[327] Having obtained permission from the judge, the FBI proceeded to break into Scarfo's office and install a keystroke logging device, which was then able to record his password when he typed it in.* Using the password, the investigators could gain access to Scarfo's private encryption key, which could then be used to unlock the PGP encrypted information.

The breaking and entering, and subsequent use of keystroke logging, represented a fairly forceful approach to conducting surveillance and collecting information. Of course, by collecting all of the keystrokes entered, the FBI could not only gain access to Scarfo's password, but also to anything else that he typed while the capturing mechanism was in place. As his then attorney observed, this could have included legal correspondence, personal information or legitimate business records. The FBI's approach consequently attracted criticism from the Electronic Privacy Information Centre (EPIC), who felt that it established worrying precedents in the use of technology surveillance methods and so-called "black bag jobs" by law enforcement agencies. Of course, you may take the view that the FBI's methods were totally justified, because Scarfo was a suspected mobster and clearly had something to hide – otherwise he would not have worried about encrypting his data. However, there are numerous other reasons why someone may wish to preserve the confidentiality of their information using encryption – the PGP utility utilized by Scarfo has been an extremely popular tool for many years, and no one would presume to suggest that all those using it are doing so for nefarious reasons. The use of keystroke logging, by contrast, would be generally considered to have far fewer legitimate purposes. Certainly if such a logging device had been deployed by a hacker, few people would have difficulty identifying with the privacy infringement. At the time of writing, the exact nature of the logging mechanism used in the Scarfo case has not been disclosed, with the Justice Department insisting that

---

* Such keystroke logging could have been achieved via either a physical interception device placed within the keyboard (or between it and the computer), or using software methods, with a logging program running transparently on the target system.

secrecy is necessary in order to preserve national security, and prevent criminals from circumventing the process in the future. However, the judge hearing the case has asked the Justice Department to produce a report detailing the specifics of the method used, in order to determine whether the FBI's approach was actually lawful.[328] If it is judged not to have been, then the evidence obtained against Scarfo as a result of keystroke logging may have to be discarded, increasing the chances of him being released.

The United States is not the only country in which the interception of online communications has become a hot issue. In June 1999, the U.K. Labour Government released a consultation paper entitled "Interception of Communications in the United Kingdom." This was the first step toward what is now known as the Regulation of Investigatory Powers (RIP) Bill. On the surface, and from the perspective of the Government and the police, the Bill is presented as a means of updating legislation to allow the interception and decoding of Internet communications in the same manner as is already possible with telephone calls. Indeed, from the law enforcement perspective, this is considered to be an essential step in the fight against crime. However, as with DCS1000 in the U.S., there is an opposing group that cites significant concerns in relation to privacy (including Amnesty International and the National Union of Journalists). In addition, concern has been expressed over the impact of RIP on Internet Service Providers, who are expected to meet the costs of monitoring their own services in order to comply with the regulations. On the privacy side, concern has been expressed over provisions within the RIP Bill that enable the police to force individuals and organizations to divulge the necessary keys to facilitate the decryption of encoded information. Those failing to comply face the prospect of criminal prosecution. There is, of course, the argument that there is nothing wrong with this approach – if the parties concerned are innocent of any crime, then they should have nothing to hide. However, as some observers have noted, the issue may not always be so clear-cut. Problems could exist, for example, in cases where keys have been accidentally lost or corrupted – rendering the data inaccessible. It could then be left for the party holding the encrypted data to prove that they are not intentionally denying access. Another extreme scenario is one in which an organization or individual has been the recipient of an encrypted message (e.g. via email) for which they never had the key in the first place, but which the authorities consider suspicious. Although such problems would probably be ironed out in practice by applying common sense in the specific circumstances of a case, they raise conceptual concerns over aspects of a Bill that, in essence, is actually meant to be helping to solve problems on the Net. As with some of the examples from Chapter 6, this again illustrates the problem of introducing legislation for the information society without also raising legitimate concerns from some of the parties already involved.

SUMMARY

This chapter has shown that techniques that originally appeared in the realms of cybercrime are now being adopted to further commercial and politically oriented goals.

In the commercial sphere, ethical hackers are applying their skills for the benefit of security, taking techniques that would otherwise be regarded as illegal, and using them as the basis for business operations. Of course, the whole domain of ethical hacking is driven by cybercrime – if traditional hackers were not there to threaten systems in the first place, then the services of ethical hackers would not be required either.

The issues of hacktivism, infowar, and cyberterrorism represent more politically motivated developments. The current evidence of hacktivism seems to relate very closely to the problem of web defacement that was covered in Chapter 4. Indeed, this seems to be the main approach of hacktivists, and it can, therefore, be observed that it is the motive rather than the method that separates them from other forms of hacker.

Approaches such as information warfare and cyberterrorism are in their infancy, and at the time of writing, there are few truly significant examples that can be cited to provide evidence of how these areas may evolve in the future. Of the two, information warfare has been shown to be more developed, having already played a part in a number of real-life conflicts.

The use of interception technologies by governments and law enforcement groups has both commercial and political overtones, as well as implications for the privacy of various parties. Although in no sense are these activities considered to be cybercrimes, it is interesting to note the similarity of the underlying methods in some cases – illustrating again that it is the perpetrator and the motive that defines a cybercrime rather than the basic techniques used.

Where do we go from here?

THE PREVIOUS CHAPTERS HAVE EXAMINED THE PROBLEM OF CYBERCRIME in various guises and presented numerous examples of the incidents that can occur. In many cases it is clear that the issue is not black and white, and the associated solutions (if they exist at all) are equally complicated. In general, it is impossible to completely remove potential threats without also undermining positive aspects such as the accessibility, functionality, or convenience of the technologies concerned. There are, however, some things that can be done to add security and, hence, increase confidence in existing systems. This chapter begins by presenting an overview of such safeguards and then proceeds to offer some concluding thoughts in relation to cybercrime and its impact upon the information society.

Preventative measures

> An unfortunate side effect of these reports is that people end up thinking that securing systems and networks is hard. It's not hard, but it does take time and training, and it's an ongoing process to stay one step ahead of the bad guys.[329]

The text above quotes Dr. Charles Palmer, head of IBM's Global Security Analysis Lab, and makes the valid point that there are plenty of things that can be done in terms of introducing proper safeguards in our computer systems. This leads into the wider topic of computer security, which is now an increasingly important consideration for modern organizations, even if they have not been victims of cybercrime.

It is, of course, in an organization's interest to have adequate security, in order to protect its own systems and data. However, in years to come, this may not be the only motivation. Experience has shown that Internet systems may be made the unwitting participants in hacker activity. This can include, for example, providing an entry point from which hackers may attack other systems, or permitting software to be installed that allows them to be used in a denial of service attack upon another system. In these scenarios, the breached system itself may not suffer any loss or corruption of data, and may, to all intents and purposes, appear to be unharmed.

However, it has been predicted that organizations whose lax security enables their systems to be exploited like this may become the targets of litigation by organizations whose systems are directly harmed.[330] This is another incentive to consider appropriate protection measures.

Achieving appropriate security is often beset with problems in practice. While many organizations will happily accept the theory that security is necessary to protect systems and data, they may still harbor reservations and misconceptions that prevent it from being realized in their particular case. Examples of such misconceptions include the beliefs that:

- responsibility for security is someone else's problem.
- introduction of security will disrupt the culture of an organization and interfere with its working practices.
- implementing protection measures will represent an unnecessary financial and/or performance overhead.

However, as the numerous manifestations of cybercrime described in earlier chapters have illustrated, these excuses do not stand up. Practically any organization can fall victim to a cybercrime incident, so it cannot realistically be dismissed as someone else's problem. The "it won't happen to me" mentality is only a good defense up to the point when an incident occurs. With regard to the second misconception, security need not hinder working practices if it is properly implemented. By contrast, the occurrence of a breach may represent a significant disruption. Finally, it is true that security *can* represent an overhead in terms of cost and performance, but in view of the problems that can arise without it, it would be foolish to dismiss the issue as unnecessary.

In some cases, the dangers from abuse are already recognized, but the organizations do not consider the introduction of security to be cost-effective (i.e. the likely cost of a breach is considered to be less than the cost of installing comprehensive safeguards), and thus prefer to adopt a reactive stance. However, given the growing dependence upon information networks, a proactive attitude may become increasingly important. In addition, by introducing appropriate security measures, a system can be protected against much more than just the risks associated with cybercrime. As was illustrated back in the first chapter, there are a variety of scenarios in which a system may be threatened or compromised by accident. Appropriate attention to security will provide safeguards against many of these circumstances as well.

This section identifies a number of key areas in which security ought to be considered. The applicability of the advice is as generic as possible, but many aspects are more clearly related to organizational contexts than to domestic users.

A very good overall reference for IT security, which is gaining international recognition and acceptance, is BS 7799 – the British Standard in Information

Security.[331] This was originally released in 1995, having been derived from the best practice of thirteen major organizations, including BOC Group, British Telecom, Shell, and Marks & Spencer. Since then, the standard has been updated to account for advances in technology (particularly the increased use of the Internet and the web within modern organizations), and following the addition of a security management specification in 1998, it now comes in two parts:

- ISO/IEC 17799:2000 (Part 1) – a code of practice for information security management.
- BS7799-2:1999 (Part 2) – a standard specification for an information security management system, proving a means by which an organization can monitor and control its security.

As the reference number suggests, Part 1 has been accepted more widely than just a British Standard and has been internationally endorsed by ISO, the International Organization for Standardization. As a result, the code of practice is increasingly recognized on a worldwide basis. The recommendations that it makes are laid out in ten sections, each of which represents a top-level principle of protection:

1. Security policy.
2. Security organization.
3. Assets classification and control.
4. Personnel security.
5. Physical and environmental security.
6. Communications and operations management.
7. Access control.
8. Systems development and maintenance.
9. Business continuity management.
10. Compliance.

In most cases, the general security issues considered under these headings should be quite self-explanatory. However, a possible exception is the "Compliance" section, which explains the need for IT systems to comply with various aspects of legislation, and to be regularly audited to ensure that this is the case. The top-level headings encapsulate a total of 127 security guidelines, which then further break down into over 500 individual security controls that organizations should consider implementing in order to achieve baseline protection. The use of the term "baseline" here refers to a recommended minimum level of protection, which is generally applicable to all types of organization. However, more significant levels of protection will typically be required by organizations that have particularly sensitive systems and data, such as healthcare, banking, and government. In terms of their technological applicability, the BS 7799 guidelines encompass traditional computing scenarios, as well as more recent advances such as e-commerce, mobile computing, and teleworking.

On the surface, many of the ten headings above may not seem directly applicable to tackling the issue of cybercrime. However, this comes back to the point that cybercrime is not a problem that one should attempt to solve in isolation – it should be addressed as part of a wider security strategy. Indeed, security should not be addressed in an ad hoc manner. Protection countermeasures should be introduced in order to contribute to a defined security policy, and appropriate approaches should be selected on the basis of a formal risk assessment. Without making an assessment beforehand, it is difficult to be sure that attention is being devoted to safeguarding the correct assets or that an appropriate level of protection is being provided.

In addition to adopting such internationally recommended guidelines, organizations can demonstrate their compliance by seeking certification from national accreditation bodies. This is valuable in the sense that it provides a basis for mutual trust in business and other relationships. If your prospective partner is certified as ISO/IEC 17799 compliant, then you can have some confidence that a relationship with them will not risk compromising your organization's security or that of data shared between you.

The presentation of a full set of security guidelines and accompanying details is outside the scope of this book, and readers interested in obtaining more comprehensive information are advised to refer to the sources listed in the appendices. However, by way of an introduction to the area, this section outlines some of the principal issues that should be considered within any responsible environment. In most cases, the details provided are very brief, but in order to illustrate the further depth that is possible, a more comprehensive discussion is devoted to the topic of authentication – an issue that affects the majority of IT users to some extent. Even here, though, a much greater level of detail is still possible, and the material is restricted to some key problems and recommendations in relation to passwords.

User authentication and passwords

Given that a significant proportion of abuse has been shown to occur as a result of hackers masquerading as other users, consideration should be given to ensuring sufficient point of entry authentication. If people cannot gain access, it narrows the range of damage that they can cause. By far the most common form of authentication is the password, whereby a claimed identity is verified by the possession of secret knowledge. Other methods of authentication exist, such as the use of physical tokens or the assessment of biometric characteristics (e.g. fingerprint, face, or voice recognition), but the simplicity and low cost of passwords makes them the *de facto* choice, and they are consequently used in around 97 percent of systems.[332] Unfortunately, while they can provide relatively strong protection if used correctly, the security of passwords is often compromised by their users.

One of the most common problems is that people select their passwords badly, choosing words that they think only they would know, but which hackers could often determine if they were willing to do a bit of research first. Examples here include things such as the name of a spouse or other relative, names of pets, car registration numbers, etc. Other common examples of poor password choices are the words "secret," "password," "sex," "love," "money," "wizard," and "god" (with the last couple being particularly favored by egotistical system administrators). The words "qwerty" and "fred" are also popular choices, as a result of the close proximity of the keys making them easy to type. Finally, people are very fond of reusing their login name as the password if the system will permit it.

In addition to being vulnerable to hacker guesswork, poor choice of passwords serves to make them more vulnerable to automated cracker tools such as L0phtCrack and others that were discussed in Chapter 4. Therefore, as a guideline, passwords should be at least eight characters long and should include at least one non-alphabetic character (e.g. a number or a symbol character). This increases the number of possible character permutations that an attacker using the brute force approach would have to try, hopefully frustrating the success of such an attack.

In some cases, people are even aware that their passwords are not sensible, but rationalize their poor choice on the basis that they are not worried if anyone else accesses their account, as their information is not secret. This viewpoint overlooks two significant factors. Firstly, it only considers their information from a confidentiality perspective. If someone was to use the victim's account and then corrupt or delete the information, it is unlikely that the victim would welcome the extra work required to recreate it all. In addition, people may overlook how sensitive their own material actually is. For example, desktop PCs are often used to hold personal information such as the names and addresses of friends and business contacts – would they really want a hacker to have these? Secondly, users might not appreciate that somebody gaining unauthorized access via their account may just want to get a foothold within the system and are not specifically interested in *their* information. There are a variety of potential reasons why someone may wish to do this, as previously highlighted in the discussion at the start of Chapter 4. Reiterating some of these issues, the key points are that hackers may be able to:

- use the compromised account as a cover for nefarious activities, which would then be traced back to the hijacked system rather than their own. The legitimate account holder may then need to prove that they were not responsible.

- utilize the system as a repository for warez etc., which could again lead to problems for the legitimate account holder if discovered by a third party.

- use the compromised account as a starting point for exploiting other vulnerabilities, by which the intruder may then be able to escalate his privileges and gain access to other more sensitive resources or materials within the same system. In this sense, a poor password that makes it easy for someone to gain unauthorized access to the system not only threatens the account holder's own data, it also jeopardises the security of other users, even if they have taken care to choose their own passwords effectively.

Poor selection is by no means the only way in which users can compromise the protection. Passwords frequently remain unchanged for months (even years) at a time, unless the system forces the user to do so. The disadvantage with this is that if the password has been compromised (or is in the process of being cracked), then the masquerader has an ever-increasing window of opportunity in which to use it. Most systems offer an option to make the password automatically expire after a set period of time, and administrators should configure the system to enforce this, as users are unlikely to do it of their own volition. An appropriate lifetime for a password in normal circumstances is thirty days, although on highly sensitive systems a change every seven to fourteen days may be considered more appropriate.* A good password system will maintain a password history and thereby prevent the same word from being reused for a few months (which guards against crafty users who might otherwise be tempted to simply alternate between two passwords when prompted to change). An unfortunate side effect in cases where passwords are changed more frequently is that users often resort to writing them down so they are not forgotten. The result is that passwords can be found jotted down on post-it notes on monitors, underneath keyboards, and in desk drawers, all of which can be easily found by other people if they are motivated to look.

If passwords are to be used as the only method of authentication, users must be educated in the correct way to use them. Table 8.1 presents a set of example guidelines that could be presented to users in relation to some dos and don'ts for using passwords.

---

* The author has worked on systems, belonging to a defense contractor, where a new password of at least 14 characters was required every week.

TABLE 8.1 Password protection guidelines for users

Do not assume that you are safe just because you have some kind of password on your account. Although passwords are normally stored and transmitted in encrypted form, they are still vulnerable to attack or compromise. Someone will not normally try to crack your password by sitting there and typing different combinations. Automated password cracking programs are freely available on the Internet and can do all the hard work on the impostor's behalf.

Do not choose words that can be found in a dictionary – password cracking tools have in-built dictionaries and can match these within seconds.

Do not choose passwords that someone who knows you (or cares to do a bit of research about you) might be able to guess. Examples here include names of partners, children, pets, car registration numbers, elements of your address, etc.

Do not share your password(s) with anyone, including colleagues. Anyone who knows your password can immediately assume all of your access rights and privileges on the system. If you need to share your data or resources with other people, there are always more secure ways of doing so.

Do not write your password(s) down. It may be a good memory jogger for you, but someone else could probably find the information as well.

Do not choose the same password for all of the systems that you use. This is effectively putting all of your eggs into one basket as, once someone breaks or discovers one password, all of your systems are vulnerable.

Do not assume that, just because you feel that your system contains no information that you regard as confidential or sensitive, it does not matter if someone gains unauthorized access to it. Confidentiality is only one aspect of the problem. People gaining access could change or destroy your files, impersonate you on your email system, or use your account as a starting point for a more serious breach of security.

Do change your password on a regular basis (e.g. once a month). It is always possible that your current password may have been illicitly obtained without your knowledge. Changing the password regularly will force the impostor to obtain or break your new choice – which may not be feasible if you have followed other aspects of this advice. Once you have changed your password, **do not** revert to using the previous one again at a later time.

Do choose passwords of at least nine characters in length, including a combination of both numbers and letters. Using numbers as well as letters increases the number of possible character permutations that an automated password cracking program must try in order to crack a password by brute force.

continued

TABLE 8.1 Password protection guidelines for users (*continued*)

Do consider using a scheme that will help you to remember your passwords more easily (i.e. so that you do not have to write them down or choose obvious ones). You could, for example, choose the first letters of a phrase that you find easy to remember. For example, using this technique, the phrase "the quick brown fox jumped over the lazy dog" yields a password of "tqbfjotld." Add a number to it (e.g. your day or month of birth) and you have a totally meaningless looking password such as "tqbfjotld3," which you *should* still be able to remember and type quite easily.

Auditing and monitoring

A good way to identify if anything is amiss is to watch what is actually going on in the system. Auditing offers a means to achieve this, and can record a log of security-relevant events for later inspection. Audit mechanisms can be employed at the operating system level and by certain applications, and can reveal signs of external penetration attempts as well as internal misuse. Given that it is a passive measure, however, such signs will only be revealed through examination of the data. As such, it is important to look at what is logged, as otherwise the auditing process is just placing an additional overhead on the system in terms of processing and storage. Luckily, a variety of tools can be used to simplify this analysis and create suitable reports for system administrators.

The collection of audit data can also be valuable as evidence in the event of a security breach. Having said this, however, careful attackers will try to cover evidence of their activities by modifying or deleting any log entries that might have recorded such details. As a result, auditing alone may not always be sufficient. A more proactive measure, which is actually increasingly essential with Internet accessible systems, is the use of Intrusion Detection Systems (IDS), which can actively watch for signs of hacker activity by monitoring network traffic and host-based activity. If potential problems are identified, the IDS will be able to alert the system administrator and, in some cases, invoke automatic responses to contain the situation.

Keeping backups

If a hacker or a virus comes along and trashes your data, a very good safeguard is to have a backup copy of it from which things can be restored. In fact, backups are vital as more than just a safeguard against cybercrime – there are many other security threats that may result in loss of data, such as equipment failure and physical hazards like fire and flood.

In order to be of real use, backups should be made on a regular basis, and frequently enough to ensure that, if the occasion arises to use them, they will enable the majority of data to be recovered. The sensible frequency will depend upon the type of organization and the extent to which the data content of the system changes over time. If the data is fairly static, then a weekly backup may suffice. If, however, there are thousands of transactions per week, then daily backups may be more appropriate.

In order to properly safeguard vital data, backups themselves should be protected. The disks or tapes should be stored safely, well away from the machines on which the master copies of data are held (to guard against incidents like fire). Organizational users should also consider testing their ability to *recover* from backups, in order to ensure that the process is known and effective if a genuine requirement should ever arise.

Of course, having backups does not mean that any security breach can then simply be dismissed as a trivial inconvenience – there will still be a significant amount of effort involved in restoring from backups and recreating any data that was entered since the last backup was made. In addition, normal operations will be disrupted while this is being done. As such, backups should be regarded as one of the vital last lines of defense, which you would always hope not to need.

Anti-virus measures

As Chapter 5 has illustrated, protection against viruses (and other forms of malware) is, unfortunately, essential in the modern IT environment. Luckily, however, the means to provide effective safeguards is readily available in the form of anti-virus (AV) software, which can scan memory, files, and incoming email messages for signs of infection.

Systems should be configured to automatically run a virus scanner at start-up, without offering the user the option to bypass the process. The AV package can then run transparently in the background throughout the time that the system is in use. Users should be explicitly instructed not to disable the scanner, and if they do so, their system should be excluded from the network.

New virus definitions can become available on a daily basis and it is, therefore, important to ensure that scanning software is kept up to date. Without this, the safeguard will diminish over time as it ceases to provide protection against new strains. Many AV packages now offer the facility to take care of this automatically and can download vendor-issued updates over the Internet.

Even with AV software installed, it is important to take care not to compromise the protection by reckless use of the system. Programs and documents that are obtained or received from unknown or untrusted sources should be handled with appropriate care. And, as incidents such as Melissa and the Love Bug have shown, even things that appear to come from friends may not be exactly what they seem.

In view of the risks, special care should be taken with:

- programs and other materials downloaded from untrusted Internet sites.
- unexpected email attachments.
- floppy disks of unknown origin.

From an organizational perspective, staff should be educated about the risks, and appropriate controls introduced to prevent them from downloading materials from the Internet or bringing them in from home in an unrestricted manner.

Education and awareness

Security will only be implemented and maintained effectively if people understand what they have to do about it. This applies throughout an organization, and affects people at all levels, from end users to system administrators.

For end users, the principal requirement is to instil awareness of security policy and compliance with good practice in relation to things such as passwords and viruses. From an organizational perspective, this may dictate a requirement for initiatives such as staff education and awareness programmes.

Users should be made aware of the tactics that hackers may employ in order to steal passwords and gain unauthorized access. This will hopefully ensure that they are less susceptible to methods such as social engineering. It is also essential for users to know the acceptable bounds of their own access and activities, and to be made aware of relevant cybercrime laws, so that they do not inadvertently put themselves in the position of breaking the rules.

At the other end of the scale are system administrators, and here too there are requirements to acquire security skills and keep up to date. At the baseline level, it demands that administrators are familiar with the security facilities available within the operating systems and applications for which they are responsible, as well as how to properly configure them. Professional training courses are offered that address these specific issues, albeit at a price in many cases. However, the known cost of undertaking training is probably preferable to the unpredictable cost of a security breach.

It is also important for administrators to keep a watchful eye on security advisories in order to ensure awareness of the latest threats. This book has presented an overview and examples of some of the incidents that have occurred up to 2001. However, the nature of cybercrime will doubtless advance to yield new attacks, which will be documented by future authors. However, maintaining appropriate protection requires a more proactive awareness strategy than waiting for new books to provide information about new threats. Fortunately, there are a number of sources of appropriate material such as CERTs, Bugtraq, and vendor-specific lists (e.g. Microsoft security bulletins). Vigilant administrators should subscribe to these and try to ensure that they act upon any relevant advisories that are issued.

System administration and maintenance

As illustrated in earlier chapters, many security breaches result from the fact that systems have not received appropriate attention in terms of some fairly straight-forward safeguards. As such, system administrators have a number of key responsibilities. In addition to co-ordinating many of the aforementioned activities, they must ensure that:

- any operating system and application level security safeguards are enabled. Although these are frequently available, in many cases they are disabled in a default installation.

- the latest software updates and patches are installed. As Chapter 4 highlighted, hackers tend to attack systems running older versions of software in order to exploit known vulnerabilities. Many vendors will make patches freely available via their web sites, and have electronic mailing lists that are used to advise subscribers of new releases.

- anti-virus software is in use and is up to date.

- a separation is maintained, if possible, between those systems that hold sensitive data and those that are publicly accessible via the Internet and World Wide Web (remembering that earlier chapters have indicated the vulnerability of Internet systems).

- appropriate restrictions are imposed upon Internet access, to prevent unauthorized traffic from entering and leaving the organization. This can be achieved using firewall technologies, which can inspect network packets and selectively accept or block them based upon the security policy.

- the effectiveness of protection is tested and maintained. The former can be ensured by commissioning an independent assessment, as well as by penetration testing (subjecting the system to the same assault as it would be expected to face from hackers). The requirement for maintenance recognizes that, once implemented, security cannot just be forgotten about. New threats and forms of attack are guaranteed to emerge, and if protection remains static, a system will not be safe against them.

It should be noted that the recommendations presented above are indicative rather than exhaustive considerations, and organizational users in particular are advised to consider more comprehensive guidelines, such as those of BS7799. However, even following BS7799 will not give you 100 percent protection against cybercrime – indeed, there is no such thing as 100 percent security. Being secure is like trying to hit a moving target, but it is possible for all parties to significantly improve their chances by following good practice and maintaining vigilance.

Vandalizing the information society?

Is the threat of cybercrime really going to make any difference to people's attitudes toward using IT? Security experts and the media may theorize that general concern could hold back the development of the information society, but at the same time it can be argued that things are developing quite nicely regardless. For example, the web has been assimilated into the mass market and the public consciousness far quicker than various technologies that preceded it, including televisions, video recorders, and mobile phones. And this has occurred in a domain (i.e. computing) where crime was already known to exist. There was no equivalent criminal downside for the potential adopters of televisions and the other technology examples above to consider, but they still rose to prominence less rapidly. This suggests that it is really other factors, primarily cost and the potential benefits, that are the main influences over whether a technology will be adopted.

Of course, the threat of cybercrime *does* make a difference in many ways. It is because of such threats that we have to endure irritants such as multiple passwords, virus scanners, etc. Many people encounter these every time that they use IT, but they may not fully appreciate or understand the reasons. Indeed, the security software's existence may become transparent to them, or at least perceived as a seamless element of everyday operation. People place an automatic confidence in the protection they have available and then happily forget about the threat that it is there to combat.

So, what of the future? As long as the Internet contains insecure systems, the problem of cybercrime will continue. From the merely inquisitive intruders gaining unauthorized access to hunt for interesting information, to the propagators of destructive viruses, the problems are unlikely to ever go away. To date, the main impacts have largely been felt by organizational users. In the future, however, domestic users may increasingly find themselves becoming more of a target. Until now, these users have gained access to the Internet via dial-up lines, with the result that their phone line is tied up while they are online. In scenarios where there are call charges to be paid or the household has only one phone line, this largely precludes the idea of the PC being permanently connected to the Internet. With the advent of newer technologies such as ADSL (Asymmetric Digital Subscriber Line), however, this situation may change. ADSL offers an "always on" Internet connection, making machines directly and permanently accessible. Domestic machines connected in this manner could, therefore, represent a continually open target for hackers,[333] placing home users in a potentially dangerous situation that they have not previously had to face. From the opposite perspective, ADSL technology offers broadband communication capabilities, increasing the data rate from the paltry 56kbps of traditional modems to as much as 8Mbps. From the domestic cyber-criminal's perspective, this makes them a more useful tool for launching attacks such as denial of service, as they are able to pump out data much more quickly.

Many domestic systems are currently based upon security-light operating systems such as Windows 95/98/ME. If they are to become permanently visible on the Internet, a much greater level of security is appropriate, which may nullify any future distinction between business and domestic operating systems. Average home users will also find themselves having to be much more concerned about security than they are at present. A permanent Internet connection means that their computer will have an online presence long enough for it to be noticed by hackers (using either manual methods or the type of automated scanning tools discussed in previous chapters). By contrast, systems that are connected via modems are there for such short and unpredictable periods that it makes them unattractive targets. In addition, they are assigned their Internet addresses dynamically each time they connect, so the address of a particular machine will continually change – further undermining its usefulness as a target.

With the above points in mind, it is clear that security can no longer be dismissed as merely someone else's responsibility, and it may fall to the individual to take appropriate precautions. Such precautions could include the purchase and use of personal firewall software – a significant departure for the domestic user, whose only previous contact with security on their own system may have been simple passwords (and, in many cases, even that facility might not have been utilized). However, emerging operating systems, such as Microsoft's Windows XP will offer a far greater range of security functionality (including a firewall) as standard – the challenges then are to ensure that the users appreciate they ought to use them and can understand how to do so.

Of course, computer abuse is by no means the only barrier to the success of the information society – unfriendly technology, unreliable software and many other such factors will also provide genuine reasons for doubt. Having said this, cybercrime is different in the sense that it represents a deliberate attempt by one party to inflict damage upon others. In a way, however, the existence of groups such as hackers, virus writers, and cyberterrorists lends credibility to the concept of a cyberspace information society. Any true society will always include elements that many of its other members would consider to be undesirable. However, it also indicates that the information society is unlikely to be the Utopian ideal that many have predicted. Technology will not solve all of the problems from our current society – many will simply re-emerge in different forms.

The underlying message throughout this book has largely been that cybercrime is an undesirable feature of the information society, which we should seek to combat. An interesting alternative opinion, at least with regard to hackers, is provided by Dr Gerald Kovacich, a former information systems security officer and high-tech crime investigator:

We should have a global hacker appreciation day dedicated to all the hackers, phreakers, crackers, nuts, weirdos, and associated other human beings who surf, spam, use, misuse and abuse the global information infrastructure. Because of their crazy personalities, criminal conduct, and all round blatant disregard for rules, laws and government controls, they have kept millions of people employed, made all our lives more interesting, our work more challenging, and our information security market – and world economies – growing![334]

Dr. Kovacich's opinion comes from the belief that hackers have a role to play against oppressive forms of government control and restriction of freedoms. The main thrust of the paper from which the above quote is taken focuses upon how governments may seek to use hacker activities as an excuse to increase their own laws and controls in a manner that would otherwise be considered unreasonable. However, this quotation, offered as a parting thought in the paper, is perhaps too generous and too all embracing. Although it is easy to agree that the existence of hackers does serve to keep people employed, this does not make all of their actions worthy of praise. That would be like saying society needs murderers, otherwise homicide detectives would lose their jobs.

So are hackers performing a useful service in any way? Considering for a moment only those hackers who would claim that their motivation is the exploration of systems, the probable answer is "Yes." It is certainly preferable for security vulnerabilities to be established through unauthorized, but benign, exploration, as opposed to being discovered as a result of a malicious attack or commercial espionage. It can be argued that the existence of hackers prevents complacency on the part of software vendors, and motivates them to give security due consideration in product design (or at least to rectify the problem quickly when a vulnerability is exposed). The prospect of hackers constantly nipping away at their systems is also likely to have a positive effect upon the vigilance of system administrators. It can also be argued that the success of these hackers in exposing security vulnerabilities serves to "raise the bar" and put the ability to break into systems beyond the reach of the casual masses. There are, however, two caveats to this. Firstly, the ability to actually penetrate a system is not a prerequisite for causing trouble, as the victims of denial of service attacks can testify. Secondly, while some hackers content themselves with exposing vulnerabilities, others occupy their time by creating toolkits that automate the task and, thereby, allow the masses to get their feet in the door again. Another problem, of course, is that the benign explorers represent only a subset of the overall hacker community. Others may be more interested in financial gain or outright vandalism of the penetrated system. However, until their motivations become clear, there is nothing to indicate the level of danger that unauthorized users may pose, as the methods that they use to gain access will be the same regardless. Of course, by the time the motivations are apparent, it may be too late to prevent damage. As such, there is no easy way to allow access to "friendly" hackers but deny it to others.

It would be unrealistic to expect a complete removal of the criminal element from the information society – within any society there will always be elements that are unethical or disruptive. As such, we must change our attitudes and give the issue a similar level of consideration to that which we already afford to other types of crime, such as theft from our properties. In addition, an increase in the instances of computer crime must be seen as inevitable. As the technology itself becomes more pervasive, cyberspace will become a natural environment for criminal opportunities. The widespread acceptance of this fact will be the first step in ensuring that the information society is a safe place to be.

Having said this, many of the common problems that enable cybercrime *can* already be solved with existing IT security measures. Other forms of security technology, such as intrusion detection systems, are continually improving, with more advanced capabilities that will limit the future opportunities for hackers and their ilk. So, with the technologies available or in place, the main ongoing problem is again linked to the attitudes and awareness of the people involved. Organizations must find a way to configure and maintain their systems securely. Everyone else must take their share of responsibility too, following good security practice where possible and ensuring that their actions do not compromise protection. In this sense, the information society is as safe as we wish to make it – and having such a choice is a cause for optimism.

Glossary of terms

ARPANET Advanced Research Projects Agency Network. A networking project initiated by the U.S. Advanced Research Projects Agency in the late 1960s, which later evolved into the Internet.

BIOS Basic Input/Output System. Provides the basic instructions for controlling the system hardware of a PC (e.g. for accepting keyboard input and displaying screen output).

Black Hat A term applied to malicious and destructive hackers whose activities are seen to be for the detriment of security.

Blue Box A multi-frequency tone-generating device created and used by early phone phreakers to bypass normal call charging procedures in the network.

Boot Sector The first sector on a disk, from which information is read in order to start-up the computer.

CERT Computer Emergency Response Team. The official emergency team for the Internet, formed as a result of the Internet Worm incident of 1988, which issues advisories in relation to various security issues, incidents and vulnerabilities.

Cracker A term used to specifically denote a malicious form of *hacker*. The distinction between the two terms is frequently blurred.

Daemon On Unix-based systems, a program that runs transparently at the operating system level and remains dormant until invoked by the occurrence of specific condition(s).

DoS Denial of Service. A form of attack in which legitimate access is prevented or impeded as a direct result of activities originating from unauthorized parties. A typical example would be to overload a networked system, such that it cannot respond to legitimate connection requests.

Exploit A script, program, mechanism or other technique that is used by a hacker in order to take advantage of a system vulnerability.

Firewall A system that enforces a boundary between two or more networks, with the ability to permit or deny the passage of data according to predefined security policy. The policy may specify (for example) valid source and destination systems, and permitted network services.

FTP File Transfer Protocol. A common protocol and utility for transferring files between systems over the Internet.

Hacker Someone attempting or gaining unauthorized access to a computer system.

Honeypot A program that makes it appear as if a computer is offering particular network services on its Internet ports. If an attacker targets the system and attempts to exploit potential vulnerabilities in the perceived services, the honeypot can log their access attempts.

HTTP Hypertext Transfer Protocol. The protocol (rules) used for transferring files on the *World Wide Web*.

IP Internet Protocol. The protocol used to send data from one computer to another on the Internet.

IP address A unique numeric address that is used to identify a specific machine on the Internet (e.g. 192.168.14.20).

ISP Internet Service Provider. An organization that a customer can connect to in order to obtain Internet access. Examples include companies such as AOL, T-Online and Freeserve.

Macro Virus A *virus* coded using the macro language of a desktop application such as Microsoft Word and Excel. The virus can then be concealed in any files produced by the associated application and will infect any systems on which such files are subsequently opened.

Malware A collective term for a variety of malicious software programs, including *viruses*, *worms* and *Trojan Horses*.

Multipartite A *virus* that uses two or more methods to infect a computer (e.g. boot sector and file infection).

Packet Sniffer A program that records the data sent by a computer when communicating over a network. Can be used for network diagnostic purposes, but can also be useful to hackers (e.g. for capturing information such as passwords).

Password Secret data, usually a string of characters, used to authenticate a user as being the legitimate holder of a claimed *user ID*.

Payload The action(s) that a *virus* carries out (other than replication) on an infected system.

PING Packet INternet Groper. An Internet-based utility that determines whether a specific *IP address* is accessible by sending packets to the address and waiting for a reply. Misuse of PING was a method used by early examples of *Denial of Service* attack.

Polymorphic Virus A class of *virus* that is able to change its internal structure or encryption method in order to avoid detection by anti-virus software.

Registry A feature of Microsoft Windows (version 95 and later) that is essentially a database containing details of operating system and application program configurations.

Root The highest level of access on Unix-based systems. The administrator account.

Rootkit A *hacker* tool that provides a backdoor into a system and hides the fact that it has been compromised.

Scanner A program that attempts to determine vulnerabilities of a target system by probing it for details of services it runs.

Sniffer A tool that monitors and records network activity.

Tiger Team A team of computer security experts who attempt to uncover security holes in system protection by targeting the existing defenses.

Trojan Horse A program that pretends to be something else in order to enter a system and encourage people to use it, typically resulting in unexpected and unwanted effects.

URL Uniform Resource Locator. An address that enables the location of a resource on the *World Wide Web*.

User ID/User name A unique name assigned to a legitimate user on a system to which he or she is permitted access. This name is used to log into a system and is typically accompanied by a *password* in order to reduce the possibility of impersonation.

Virus A replicating program that enters a system concealed in infected materials such as disks, files or documents. The virus carries a *payload*, which will activate at some point after infection, causing unwanted and often damaging side-effects.

War Dialler A program that automatically dials a range of telephone numbers, looking for connectables and logging details for later inspection.

Warez Hacker slang for illegally copied software.

White Hat A term applied to ethical hackers whose activities are seen to be for the benefit of security.

WWW World Wide Web. The collective name for a global network of information, accessible via the Internet.

Worm A replicating program that can spread between systems autonomously, without the need to infect a carrier in the manner that a *virus* does.

Online resources for cybercrime and security

Appropriate references for many of the specific points raised in the main chapters can be found in the numbered "Notes on sources" section. For readers interested in more general reference sources, this section presents a series of web addresses for sites that contain news and other information relevant to the topics discussed. The entries listed under each heading are by no means exhaustive, but many of the sources indicated here will also provide hyperlinks to further sites of relevance.

Online news sites

The following sites provide daily technology news stories and regularly feature reports relating to cybercrime.

TechTV	http://www.techtv.com/news/hackingandsecurity/
	http://www.techtv.com/news/virus/
The Register	http://www.theregister.co.uk
Wired News	http://www.wirednews.com
ZDNet News	http://www.zdnet.com/zdnn/

Security sites

CERT	http://www.cert.org	Computer Emergency Response Team.
CIAC	http://www.ciac.org	Computer Incident Advisory Capability.
Computer Security Institute (CSI)	http://www.gocsi.com	The Computer Security Institute. Includes surveys of computer crime and security breaches.

Crypt Newsletter	http://sun.soci.niu.edu/~crypt/	Case studies, analyses and satire of Internet culture, computer crime, and information warfare.
Freebyte	http://freebyte.com/antivirus/	A selection of freely downloadable anti-virus software.
Infowar.com	http://www.infowar.com	Information warfare resources.
Internet Fraud Watch	http://www.fraud.org/internet/intset.htm	Tips, bulletins and other information to help Internet-based consumers avoid fraud and protect their privacy.
Packet Storm	http://packetstormsecurity.org/	Non-profit organization providing Internet security information and resources.
RSA Data Security	http://www.rsasecurity.com	Security solution provider.
SANS Institute	http://www.sans.org	System Administration, Networking, and Security Institute.
SecurityFocus.com	http://www.securityfocus.com	Comprehensive security site with news and vulnerability information for different platforms.
Symantec	http://www.symantec.com	Security solution provider, including Anti-Virus Research Center.

Hacker-related sites

2600	**http://www.2600.com**	*2600: The Hacker Quarterly.*
alldas.de defacement archives	**http://defaced.alldas.de**	Mirrors of web defacements from 1998 to present day.
Attrition	**http://www.attrition.org/mirror**	Mirrors of web defacements from 1995 until May 2001.
Cult of the Dead Cow	**http://www.cultdeadcow.com**	Cult of the Dead Cow. Info and downloads (including Back Orifice).
FreeKevin	**http://www.kevinmitnick.com**	Web site established in support of Kevin Mitnick.
KevinPoulsen.com	**http://catalog.com/kevin/**	The web site of Kevin Poulsen.
Takedown	**http://www.takedown.com**	A web site dedicated to Tsutomu Shimomura's hunt for Kevin Mitnick.
The Happy Hacker	**http://www.happyhacker.org**	Various hacker-related information and links.
webcrunchers	**http://www.webcrunchers.com/crunch**	The web site of John Draper (Cap'n Crunch).

Notes on sources

1. Adams, J. 1998. *The Next World War*. Random House U.K., London, 285.

2. Toffler, A. 1981. *The Third Wave*. Pan Books, London.

3. Martin, W.J. 1988. *The Information Society*. Aslib, London.

4. Gates, B. 1995. *The Road Ahead*. Viking Press, New York.

5. Standage, T. 1998. *The Victorian Internet*. Weidenfeld & Nicolson, London.

6. Braden, R. 1989. "Requirements for Internet Hosts – Communication Layers," RFC 1122, October.

7. Network Wizards – Internet Domain Survey, http://www.nw.com/zone/WWW/.

8. Caceres, R., Danzig, P.B., Jamin, S. and Mitzel, D.J. 1991. "Characteristics of Wide-Area TCP/IP Conversations," Proceedings of ACM SIGCOMM '91.

9. Thompson, K., Miller, G.J. and Wilder, R. 1997. "Wide-Area Internet Traffic Patterns and Characteristics," IEEE Network, Nov.–Dec.

10. "Global Internet Statistics (by Language)," *Global Reach*, September 2000, http://www.glreach.com/globstats/index.php3.

11. Based on figures from International Telecommunications Union (ITU). 10 July 2000. See http://www.itu.int/ti/industryoverview/at_glance/internet99.pdf.

12. Berners-Lee, T. 1999. *Weaving the Web – The Past, Present and Future of the World Wide Web by its Inventor*. Orion Business Books, London.

13. Rheingold, H. 1994. *The Virtual Community – Finding Connection in a Computerized World*. Secker & Warburg, London.

14. "Current Total Statistics," SETI@home, 5 March 2001, http://setiathome.ssl.berkeley.edu/totals.html.

15. Electrolux Screenfridge prototype. http://www.electrolux.co.uk/screenfridge/.

16. "Washing online," The *Guardian*, "Online" supplement, 26 October 2000, 5.

17. "Tomorrow never comes," The *Guardian*, "Online" supplement, 4 January 2001, 17–20.

18. Goodwin, S. 1999. "Embedded problem," *The Computer Bulletin*, British Computer Society, July.

19. "The Y2K Date Rollover Problem on PC Systems," Micro Firmware, Inc., 1998. http://www.firmware.com/support/bios/year2000.htm.

20. "'Pocket' Virus Targets Kids," *Wired News Report*, 24 August 2000.

21. "Powergen in security scandal – thousands of debit card details open to abuse," Silicon.com News Report, 18 July 2000.

22. "Is it too late to plug the PowerGen leak?," *Computing*, 27 July 2000, 1, 15.

23. "Data Protection Commissioner washes hands of PowerGen," *Silicon.com News* Report, 13 October 2000.

24. "Security fear shuts online bank," The *Guardian*, 1 August 2000, 1.

25. "Expect more red faces over blue chip security," The *Sunday Telegraph*, 6 August 2000, 8B.

26. "Crashes turn Cahoot launch into a disaster," The *Guardian*, 13 June 2000. See http://www.guardianunlimited.co.uk/Archive/Article/ 0,4273,4028680,00.html.

27. U.K. Audit Commission. 1994. *Opportunity Makes a Thief*, Audit Commission Publications, U.K.

28. "Hacker hunt after smear campaign," *Computer Weekly*, 20 October 1994, 108.

29. Parker, D.B. 1998. *Fighting Computer Crime: A New Framework for Protecting Information*. John Wiley & Sons Inc., New York.

30. U.K. Audit Commission. 1998. *Ghost in the Machine – An Analysis of IT Fraud and Abuse*. Audit Commission Publications, U.K.

31. "2001 CSI/FBI Computer Crime and Security Survey," *Computer Security Issues & Trends*, vol. VII, no. 1. Computer Security Institute, Spring 2001.

32. "External hacker threat increases," *Computing*, 16 November 2000, 23.

33. "2001 CSI/FBI Computer Crime and Security Survey," *Computer Security Issues & Trends*, vol. VII, no. 1. Computer Security Institute, Spring 2001.

34. Anderson, J.P., 1980. "Computer Security Threat Monitoring and Surveillance," James P. Anderson Co., Fort Washington, PA (Apr.).

35. "Partner in crime," *The Computer Bulletin*. British Computer Society, May 2000, 23–5.

36. U.K. Audit Commission. 1998. *Ghost in the Machine – An Analysis of IT Fraud and Abuse.* Audit Commission Publications, U.K.

37. Nycum, S.H. and Parker, D.B. 1990. "Prosecutorial experience with state computer crime laws in the United States," in *Security and Protection in*

Information Systems. A. Grissonnanche (ed.), Elsevier Science Publishers B.V., North-Holland, 307–19.

38. "Financial losses due to Internet intrusions, trade secret theft and other cyber crimes soar," Press Release, Computer Security Institute, 12 March 2001. http://www.gocsi.com/prelea_000321.htm.

39. National Computing Centre. 1994. *IT Security Breaches Survey Summary*. National Computing Centre Limited, Manchester.

40. Survey results from Scholastic Inc. See http://www.cybercitizenpartners.org/.

41. Keynote. 2000. "Denial of service attacks this week degraded Internet performance overall according to keynote," Keynote Press Release, 12 February 2000.

42. "A frenzy of hacking attacks," *Wired News* Report, 9 February 2000.

43. "Reno: 'We must punish Mafiaboy'," *Wired News* Report, 19 April 2000.

44. "64 more charges for 'Mafiaboy' hacker," *Channel2000.com News* Report, 3 August 2000.

45. Hancock, B. "Mafiaboy prison time recommended," *Computers & Security*, vol. 20, no. 5, 348–9.

46. "Teen charged in DOS hack attack," *TechTV News* Report, 19 April 2000.

47. Whitworth, D. "Internet pest puts words in Clinton's mouth," *The Times*, 16 February 2000, 15.

48. "Prankster admits Clinton online porn joke," BBC News Online, 16 February 2000.

49. "Hotmail fallout: a mere trickle," *Wired News* Report, 31 August 1999.

50. "Hotmail hackers: 'We did it'," *Wired News* Report, 30 August 1999.

51. "Scary hole found at ZKey," *Wired News* Report, 18 August 2000.

52. "MS fingers Hotmail hackers," *Wired News* Report, 5 October 1999.

53. "'Curador' pleads guilty," *SecurityFocus News*, 29 March 2001.

54. "Curador taunts police over site break-ins," *InternetNews* report, 9 March 2000.

55. "Curador worked as e-commerce consultant," *InternetNews* report, 27 March 2000.

56. "Teen hacker escapes jail sentence," BBC News Online, 6 July 2001.

57. "Hacker praised by judge for Bill Gates prank," *The Times*, 7 July 2001, 15.

58. "Safeway shoppers hit by hacker," The *Sunday Times*, 13 August 2000, 28.

59. Levy, S. 1984. *Hackers: Heroes of the Computer Revolution*. Anchor Press/Doubleday.

60. *The Jargon File*, version 4.2.0, 31 January 2000.
http://www.eps.mcgill.ca/jargon/html/index.html.

61. Clough, B. and Mungo, P. 1992. "Phreaking for fun," Chapter 1 in *Approaching Zero: Data Crime and the Computer Underworld*. Faber and Faber, London.

62. Hancock, B. "DefCon recruiting JamFest," *Computers & Security*, vol. 19, no. 6, 493–4.

63. "Hack-umentary, the E-Film," *Wired News* Report, 14 February 2000.

64. "Q&A with Emmanuel Goldstein of *2600: The Hacker's Quarterly*," CNN.com. http://www.cnn.com/TECH/specials/hackers/qandas/goldstein.html.

65. *Walk on the Wild Side*, A Big Star in a Wee Picture Production for Channel Four Television, 1993. Produced by Stuart Cosgrove and first broadcast 2 February 1994.

66. "Cyber Attack," *Panorama*, BBC Television, 3 July 2000.

67. *Data Protection Act 1998*. Her Majesty's Stationery Office (HMSO), U.K.

68. Directive 95/46/EC of the European Parliament and of the Council of 24 October 1995 on the protection of individuals with regard to the processing of personal data and on the free movement of such data. 1995. http://www.ispo.cec.be/legal/en/dataprot/directiv/directiv.html.

69. "A Portrait of J. Random Hacker," Appendix B, *The Jargon File*, version 4.2.0, 31 January 2000. http://www.eps.mcgill.ca/jargon/html/Appendix-B.html.

70. Marchand, M. 1987. *La Grande Aventure du Minitel*. Larousse, Paris.

71. Poster, M. 1990. *The Mode of Information: Poststructuralism and Social Context*. Polity Press, Cambridge.

72. Poulsen, K.L. 1995. Letter to Judge Manuel L. Real. 9 February 1995.

73. "Addicts of Net share gamblers' symptoms," *The Times*, 9 August 2000, 4.

74. Young, K., Buchanan, J., and O'Mara, J. "Cyber-disorders: The mental health concern for the millennium," *CyberPsychology and Behavior*. See also http://www.netaddiction.com/articles/cyberdisorders.htm.

75. Sterling, B. 1992. *The Hacker Crackdown*. Penguin Books Limited, London.

76. *Trusted Computer System Evaluation Criteria*. U.S. Department of Defense standard 5200.28-STD, December, 1985.

77. Homepage at http://mgmua.com/hackers/.

78. Ratnasingham, P. 1998. "The importance of trust in electronic commerce," *Internet Research*, vol. 8, no. 4, 313–21.

79. "Credit card fraud hits the Internet," *The Times*, "Interface" supplement, 26 November 1997.

80. Levy, S. 1984. *Hackers: Heroes of the Computer Revolution*. Anchor Press/Doubleday, 26–36.

81. Mizrach, S. 1997. "Is there a Hacker Ethic for 90s Hackers?" http://www.infowar.com/hacker/hackzf.html-ssi.

82. "The art of system profiling," *2600 Magazine*, Summer 2000, 6–8.

83. "A hacker's guide to being busted," *2600 Magazine*, Spring 1999, 24–9.

84. Statalla, M. and Quittner, J. 1996. *Masters of Deception: The Gang That Ruled Cyberspace*. Harperperennial Library.

85. Dr-K. 2000. *A Complete H@cker's Handbook: Everything you need to know about hacking in the age of the web*. Carlton Books, London.

86. Clough, B. and Mungo, P. 1992. "The Illuminati Conspiracy," Chapter 7 in *Approaching Zero: Data Crime and the Computer Underworld*. Faber and Faber, London.

87. "Hackers to users, Feds: Internet is 30 minutes from disaster," *Internet Week*, 22 May 1998.

88. "Hackers seek venture capital," Silicon.com, 14 April 2000.

89. "Scenes from a mall," *CNN In-Depth Specials – Hackers*. CNN.com, 29 March 1999.

90. "Hackers: Uncle Sam wants you!," *ZDNet news* report, 28 July 2000.

91. "DefCon recruiting JamFest," *Computers & Security*, vol. 19, no. 6, 493–4.

92. "Hackers in suits? Gadzooks!," *Wired News* Report, 14 July 2001.

93. "Hackers" web site. http://www.mgmua.com/hackers/.

94. "Q&A with Emmanuel Goldstein of *2600: The Hacker's Quarterly*," CNN.com. http://www.cnn.com/TECH/specials/hackers/qandas/goldstein.html.

95. "Cap'n Crunch FAQ (Frequently Asked Questions)." http://www.webcrunchers.com/crunch/FAQ.html.

96. A transcript of the article can be found on the web at http://www.webcrunchers.com/crunch/esq-art.html.

97. Malone, M.S. 1999. *Infinite Loop – How Apple, the World's Most Insanely Great Computer Company, Went Insane*. Aurum Press, London.

98. Witness Testimony, Mr Kevin Mitnick. U.S. Senate Committee on Governmental Affairs hearing – "Cyber Attack: Is the Government Safe?," 2 March 2000. See http://www.senate.gov/~gov_affairs/030200_mitnick.htm.

99. See http://www.takedown.com.

100. Penenberg, A. "Mitnick speaks!," *Forbes Magazine* interview 5 April 1999. http://www.forbes.com/tol/html/99/apr/0405/feat.htm.

101. See http://www.discovery.com/area/technology/hackers/mitnick.html for a copy of the poster.

102. Hafner, K. and Markoff, J. 1991. *Cyberpunk: Outlaws and Hackers on the Computer Frontier*. Fourth Estate Limited.

103. Platt, C. 1995. "The mad-scientist myth figure," *Computer Underground Digest*, 7, 95.

104. *The Guinness Book of Records 1999*. 1998. Guinness World Records Ltd., 178.

105. "Guinness Book of Records" parody site. http://www.guinessrecords.com/.

106. *Guinness World Records 2000 – Millennium Edition*. 2000. Guinness World Records Ltd.

107. "Mitnick gets out of Lompoc," *Wired News* Report, 21 January 2000.

108. Zuckerman, M.J. "The latest version of Kevin Mitnick," *USA Today Tech Report*, 20 November 2000.

109. "A Chat with Kevin Mitnick," ABCNEWS.com. 8 May 2000.

110. Poulsen, K.L. 1995. Letter to Judge Manuel L. Real. 9 February 1995.

111. Poulsen, K.L. 1990. Letter to Timothy J. Rogan. 5 September 1990.

112. See "The Littman Game." http://catalog.com/kevin/links.html.

113. "Patch available for 'malformed help file' vulnerability," Microsoft Security Bulletin (MS99-015), 17 May 1999.

114. Denning, D.E. 1999. *Information Warfare and Security*. Addison-Wesley.

115. "How to eliminate the ten most critical Internet security threats: The experts' consensus," Version 1.32, The SANS Institute, 18 January, 2001. http://www.sans.org/topten.htm.

116. "Patchwork security – Software 'fixes' routinely available but often ignored," CNET News.com report. 24 January 2001.

117. "Crackers attuned to schools," *Wired News* Radio Report, 28 February 2001.

118. "2001 CSI/FBI Computer Crime and Security Survey," *Computer Security Issues & Trends*, vol. VII, no. 1. Computer Security Institute, Spring 2001.

119. "Party poopers," The *Daily Telegraph*, "Connected" supplement, 24 December 1996, 7.

120. See http://www.2600.com/conserv_hacked/ mm028978/index.html for the hacked version of the page.

121. "Security firm's site defaced," *Wired News* Report, 30 November 2000.

122. "ATTRITION: Evolution," 21 May 2001.
http://www.attrition.org/news/content/01-05-21.001.html.

123. "Hacker taps into 24,000 credit cards," The *Sunday Times*, 25 June 2000,
Main section, 14.

124. "TCP SYN flooding and IP spoofing attacks," CERT Advisory A-96.21, 19
September 1996.

125. Akass, C. "On the straight and narrow – not," *Personal Computer World*,
February 2000, 57.

126. Evans, M.P. and Furnell, S.M. "Internet-based security incidents and the
potential for false alarms," *Internet Research*, vol. 10, no. 3, 238–45.

127. "Let the web server beware," *Wired News* Report, 23 December 1998.

128. Security Administrator's Tool for Analyzing Networks – SATAN. General
Information. http://www.fish.com/~zen/satan/satan.html.

129. "Influence of Satan divides IT industry," *Computer Weekly*, 13 April 1995, 4.

130. "Cap'n Crunch FAQ (Frequently Asked Questions)."
http://www.webcrunchers.com/crunch/FAQ.html.

131. See http://www.bo2k.com/about.html.

132. "Count Zero – Member of the Cult of the Dead Cow," ABCNEWS.com.
http://archive.abcnews.go.com/sections/tech/DailyNews/chat_countzero.html.

133. "A Note on Product Legitimacy and Security," Back Orifice 2000 Release
Information, Cult of the Dead Cow, 10 July 1999.
http://www.bo2k.com/legitimacy.html.

134. Prigg, M. "Hacker software hijacks Windows," The *Sunday Times*, 9 August
1998, Section 3, 14.

135. L0phtCrack 2.5 readme file, L0pht Heavy Industries, Inc.

136. "Boston hackers post on web site easy-to-use program they claim can steal
Windows NT passwords," *CMP Media Inc.*, 16 April 1997.

137. "IMPORTANT note to all NT/W2K IIS admins/users," Daniel Docekal, Posting
to Windows NTBugtraq Mailing List, 14 August 2000.

138. "MS server attack tool unleashed," *Wired News* Report, 16 August 2000.

139. Chiliarchaki, P. 2000. "Security Analysers – Admin Assistants or Hacker
Helpers?," M.Sc. thesis. Department of Communication and Electronic
Engineering, University of Plymouth, Plymouth.

140. Noack, D. "The back door into cyber-terrorism," APBnews.com Report, 2 June
2000.

141. "IE 5.5 hole lets hackers into personal records," CNET News.com Report. 26 September 2000.

142. Statistics obtained from http://www.microsoft.com/technet/security/current.asp.

143. Hurt, E. "The New Security War," *Business2.0*, 31 October 2000. http://www.business2.com/.

144. "Patchwork security – Software 'fixes' routinely available but often ignored," CNET News.com report, 24 January 2001.

145. Noack, D. "The back door into cyber-terrorism," APBnews.com Report, 2 June 2000.

146. *Draft Convention on Cyber-Crime (Draft No. 19)*, Council of Europe, PC-CY (2000) Draft No. 19. Strasbourg 25 April 2000.

147. "EU cybercrime treaty puts users at risk, warn experts," *Computer Weekly*, 24 August 2000, 3.

148. Schneier, B. 2000. *Secrets and Lies: Digital Security in a Networked World*. Wiley, New York.

149. "Oh, how the CCC has evolved," *Wired News* Report, 30 December 1999.

150. Brunnstein, K., Fischer-Hübner, S., and Swimmer, M. "Classification of computer anomalies," Proceedings of the 13th National Computer Security Conference, Washington, D.C., 1–4 October 1990, 374–84.

151. National Computing Centre. 2000. *Business Information Security Survey 2000 (BISS 2000)*. National Computing Centre, Manchester, 6.

152. Brunnstein, K., Fischer-Hübner, S. and Swimmer, M. "Classification of computer anomalies," Proceedings of the 13th National Computer Security Conference, Washington, D.C., 1–4 October 1990, 374–84.

153. Landler, M. "'Love Bug' creator proclaims his fame," *SiliconValley.Com News* Report, 22 October 2000.

154. Cohen, F. "Computer viruses – theory and experiments," originally appearing in IFIP-SEC 84 and also appearing as an invited paper in *Computers and Security*, vol. 6, no. 1, 22–35. See also http://www.all.net/books/virus/index.html.

155. "Three minutes with Fred Cohen, virus trends tracker," PCWorld.com, 14 November 2000.

156. "I love you, free virus scanning software," *IEEE The Institute*, vol. 24, no. 8, August 2000, 4.

157. "Top ten viruses reported to Sophos in July 2001," Press Release, Sophos, 3 August 2001. http://www.sophos.com/pressoffice/pressrel/uk.

158. "Sophos six-month summary of virus activity," Press Release, Sophos, 18 July 2001. http://www.sophos.com/pressoffice/pressrel/uk.

159. Details taken from W97.Melissa.A virus overview. Symantec AntiVirus Research Center. http://service1.symantec.com/sarc/sarc.nsf/html/W97.Melissa.A.html.

160. "Creator of 'Melissa' Computer Virus Pleads Guilty to State and Federal Charges," Press release, U.S. Department of Justice, 9 December 1999. http://www.usdoj.gov/criminal/cybercrime/melissa.htm.

161. "Mac users hit by Melissa macro virus," *The Register*, 19 January 2001.

162. Hafner, K. and Markoff, J. 1991. *Cyberpunk: Outlaws and Hackers on the Computer Frontier*. Fourth Estate Limited.

163. "How the slimy worm works," *Wired News* Report, 4 May 2000.

164. "Worm suspect list grows to 40," *Wired News* Report, 16 May 2000.

165. "Love Bug case dead in Manila," *Wired News* Report, 21 August 2000.

166. "Cyber Attack," *Panorama*, BBC Television, 3 July 2000.

167. "Virus suspect is *really* wanted," *Wired News* Report, 23 August 2000.

168. "New love: a whole lot of nothing?," *Wired News* Report, 19 May 2000.

169. "MS finally addresses email hole," *Wired News* Report, 15 May 2000.

170. F-Secure virus descriptions. F-Secure Corporation. http://www.f-secure.com/v-descs/qaz.htm.

171. "Hackers crack into MS system," *Wired News* Report, 27 October 2000.

172. "The patch MS forgot to apply," *Wired News* Report, 6 November 2000.

173. "Hackers steal Microsoft secret codes," *The Times*, 28 October 2000, 1.

174. "Bill's nightmare," Editorial, The *Mirror*, 28 October 2000, 6.

175. "MS hacker's shorter stay," *Wired News* Report, 30 October 2000.

176. "How MS played cat and mouse," *Wired News* Report, 30 October 2000.

177. "Mitnick doubts Microsoft story on intruder," *TechWeb Technology News*, 1 November 2000.

178. *Cyber Threats and Information Security: Meeting the 21st Century Challenge*, Center for Strategic and International Studies, Washington, D.C., December 2000, 7. http://www.csis.org/homeland/reports/cyberthreatsandinfosec.pdf.

179. "Report: Microsoft hack a U.S. security risk," *CNN.com News* Report, 29 December 2000.

180. Details taken from CIH virus overview. Symantec AntiVirus Research Center. http://www.symantec.com/avcenter/venc/data/cih.html.

181. "'Pocket' virus targets kids," *Wired News* Report, 24 August 2000.

182. "Worm turns on wireless," *Wired News* Report, 6 June 2000.

183. Details taken from VBS.Timofonica worm overview. Symantec AntiVirus Research Center.
http://www.symantec.com/avcenter/venc/data/vbs.timofonica.html.

184. "Prank leads to fears about mobile security," *ZDNet UK News* Report, 9 August 2000.

185. "Worm Turns on Wireless," *Wired News* Report, 6 June 2000.

186. "The sad tale of Chris Pile's 15 seconds of fame," *Crypt Newsletter*, 1996.
http://www.soci.niu.edu/~crypt/other/pyle.htm.

187. "Italy jails zoologist in Aids scam," *Computing*, 13 May 1993, 1.

188. Kabay, M.E. "Identification, authentication and authorization on the World Wide Web," ICSA White Paper.

189. Fisher, M.J. "moldovascam.com," *The Atlantic Online*, September 1997.

190. "2000 CSI/FBI Computer Crime and Security Survey," *Computer Security Issues & Trends*, vol. VI, no. 1. Computer Security Institute, Spring 2000.

191. "Why worm writer surrendered," *Wired News* Report, 14 February 2001.

192. "Virus threat gains momentum," *Datamation*, 1 April 1995, 22.

193. "Feds crack hacker gang," *Datamation*, 1 April 1995, 15.

194. "Oh, no!," *Datamation*, 1 April 1995, 15.

195. "Surf is no longer up," *Datamation*, 1 April 1995, 18.

196. "World at large," *Datamation*, 1 April 1995, 16.

197. "FBI Newsletter gulled by 'Net joke,'" *Crypt Newsletter*.
http://www.soci.niu.edu/~crypt/other/quant.htm.

198. "No fool like an April Fool," The Editor's Page, *Datamation*, 1 April 1995, 8.

199. Rushe, D. "Digital television steals march on home shopping rivals," The *Sunday Times*, "Business" supplement, 5 September 1999, 4.

200. "Watch out – the invisible virus is on its way," *Silicon.com News* Report, 21 February 2001.

201. Leyden, J. "Risks from hybrid Linux/Windows virus low," *The Register*, 28 March 2001.

202. "Symantec Protects Users Against VBS.LoveLetter.A," Symantec Press Center news release, 4 May 2000. http://www.symantec.com/press/2000/n000504b.html.

203. Rheingold, H. 1994. *The Virtual Community – Finding Connection in a Computerized World*. Secker & Warburg, London.

204. Seminar presentation by Detective Sergeant Clive Blake (Metropolitan Police Fraud Squad). British Computer Society Information Security Specialist Group seminar, "Casting the Runes," London, February 2000.

205. Bequai, A. 1999. "Cyber-crime the US experience," *Computers & Security*, vol. 18, no. 1, 16–18.

206. Parker, D.B. 1989. "Consequential loss from computer crime," in Grissinnanche, A. (ed.), *Security and Protection in Information Systems*. Elsevier Science Publishers B.V., North-Holland, 375–9.

207. "ICM Poll – The Internet – January 1999," ICM Research. http://www.icmresearch.co.uk/reviews/1999/internet-99-jan.htm.

208. "Anti-Piracy – Crackdown 99." Business Software Alliance. http://www.bsa.org/uk/antipiracy/crackdown99/.

209. "Computers turned my boy into a robot," The *Daily Mirror*, 18 March 1993.

210. "Building Confidence in Electronic Commerce – A Consultation Document." Department of Trade & Industry. 1999. Document reference URN 99/642.

211. "Electronic Commerce & Public Policy," Supplement to *Information Technology & Public Policy*, Journal of the Parliamentary Information Technology Committee, Spring 1999, 1.

212. Hancock, B. "Security Views," *Computers & Security*, vol. 18, no. 3, 1999, 184–98.

213. "2000 Internet fraud statistics," *Internet Fraud Watch*. http://www.fraud.org/internet/lt00totstats.htm.

214. "Online auction survey summary," National Consumers League, 31 January 2001. http://www.nclnet.org/onlineauctions/auctionsurvey2001.htm.

215. *Your Choice. How eCommerce Could Impact Europe's Future*. Anderson Consulting. 1998. http://www.ac.com/services/ecommerce/ecomrept.pdf.

216. Information Security Survey 1998, KPMG Information Risk Management, London. 1998. http://www.kpmg.co.uk.

217. "Online fraud is increasing," *MSNBC News* Report, 3 November 2000.

218. "Casting the runes," British Computer Society – Information Security Specialist Group, Newsletter, Spring 2000.

219. "Partner in crime," *The Computer Bulletin*, British Computer Society, May 2000, 23–5.

220. "New Hi-Tech Crime Investigators in £25Million Boost to Combat Cybercrime," U.K. Home Office News Release, 13 November 2000. http://wood.ccta.gov.uk/homeoffice.

221. e-commerce@its.best.uk, Performance and Innovation Unit Report, September 1999. http://www.cabinet-office.gov.uk/innovation/1999/ecommerce/index.htm.

222. "Protecting the critical national infrastructure," National Infrastructure Security Co-ordination Centre, http://www.niscc.gov.uk/cni/cniinfo.htm.

223. Mission Statement, National Infrastructure Protection Centre (NIPC), 1998. http://www.fbi.gov/nipc/nipc.htm.

224. "Tackling computer crime," BBC News Online, 19 April 2001.

225. "Gartner Says Most Internet Crime Goes Unpunished," Press Release, Gartner Group Inc, 7 December 2000. http://gartner3.gartnerweb.com/public/static/aboutgg/pressrel/pr20001207a.html.

226. Schifreen, R. "A hacker's story – How to understand the hacker's methods, and how to use that knowledge to protect your own systems," *Proceedings of CompSec International 1992*, Elsevier Technology, 1992.

227. Sterling, B. 1992. *The Hacker Crackdown*. Penguin Books Limited, London, 274–81.

228. Sterling, B. 1992. *The Hacker Crackdown*. Penguin Books Limited, London, 142–8.

229. Littman, J. 1996. *The Fugitive Game – online with Kevin Mitnick*. Little, Brown & Company Limited, 16–20.

230. "A chat with Kevin Mitnick," ABCNEWS.com. 8 May 2000.

231. Campbell, D. "More *Naked Gun* than *Top Gun*," The *Guardian*, "Online" supplement, 27 November 1997, 2, 3.

232. "Federal Sentencing Statistics by State," 1997 Fiscal Year. United States Sentencing Commission. http://www.ussc.gov/judpack/jp1997.htm.

233. Bequai, A. 1999. "Cyber-crime the US experience". *Computers & Security*, vol. 18, no. 1, 16–18.

234. "China executes hacker over £122,000 theft," *Computing*, 6 May 1993, 1.

235. "2 Chinese hackers get hacked!," *U.Geek*, 28 December 1998.

236. "New Interpol chiefs to tackle cybercrime," *CNN.com* report, 3 November 2000.

237. "Highway to hell?," *Computer Weekly*, 2 March 1996, 30, 31.

238. "Q&A with Emmanuel Goldstein of *2600: The Hacker's Quarterly*," CNN In-Depth Special – Insurgency on the Internet. http://www.cnn.com/TECH/specials/hackers/qandas/goldstein.html.

239. Shimomura, T. and Markoff, J. 1995. *Takedown – the Pursuit and Capture of Kevin Mitnick the World's Most Notorious Cybercriminal – by the Man Who Did It*. Secker & Warburg, London.

240. Collier, P.A. and Spaul, B.J. 1992. "The Woolwich Centre for Computer Crime Research: Addressing the need for UK information," *Computer Fraud and Security Bulletin*, August 1992, 8–11.

241. "BCS highlights court failings," *The Computer Bulletin*, British Computer Society, September 2000, 12.

242. Sinrod, E.J. and Reilly, W.P. 2000. "Cyber-crimes: A practical approach to the application of Federal computer crime laws," *Santa Clara Computer and High Technology Law Journal*, vol. 16, no. 2. Santa Clara University, 1–50.

243. Penenberg, A. "The demonizing of a hacker," *Forbes Magazine*, 19 April 1999.

244. Sinrod, E.J. and Reilly, W.P. 2000. "Cyber-crimes: A practical approach to the application of Federal computer crime laws," Santa Clara Computer and High Technology Law Journal, vol. 16, no. 2. Santa Clara University, 1–50.

245. "Legal age of consent." http://www.ageofconsent.com/ageofconsent.htm.

246. "External hacker threat increases," *Computing*, 16 November 2000, 23.

247. "Rhetoric reigns at Net crime meet," *Wired News* Report, 24 October 2000.

248. "Three Kazak men arrested in London for hacking into Bloomberg L.P.'s computer system," News Release, U.S. Department of Justice, 14 August 2000. http://www.usdoj.gov/criminal/cybercrime/bloomberg.htm.

249. *Draft Convention on Cyber-Crime (Draft No. 19)*, Council of Europe, PC-CY (2000) Draft No. 19. Strasbourg 25 April 2000.

250. "EU cybercrime treaty puts users at risk, warn experts," *Computer Weekly*, 24 August 2000, 3.

251. Global Internet Liberty Campaign Member Letter on Council of Europe Convention on Cyber-Crime, 18 October 2000. http://www.gilc.org/privacy/coe-letter-1000.html.

252. Banisar, D. "Love letter's last victim," Commentary – SecurityFocus.Com, 22 May 2000.

253. Gruenwald, J. "U.S., EU move toward cybercrime treaty," *USA Today Tech Report*, 25 September 2000.

254. Poulsen, K.L. 1995. Letter to U.S. Probation Officer Marc J. Stein. 12 June 1996.

255. Poulsen, K. "exile.com," *Wired Magazine*, January 1999.

256. See, for example, "The Condor Brief" (Kevin Poulsen, 13 May 1996) and "Mitnick Muzzled" (*Security Focus News*, 25 April 2000. http://www.securityfocus.com/templates/article.html?id=23).

257. Witness Testimony, Mr. Kevin Mitnick. U.S. Senate Committee on Governmental Affairs hearing – "Cyber Attack: Is the Government Safe?," 2 March 2000. See http://www.senate.gov/~gov_affairs/030200_mitnick.htm.

258. Penenberg, A. "Mitnick speaks!," *Forbes Magazine* interview, 5 April 1999.

259. "No word from Mitnick," The *Daily Telegraph*, "Connected" supplement, 27 April 2000, 3.

260. "Direction," *2600 Magazine*, Winter 2000-2001, 4, 5.

261. "Mitnick to challenge order barring him from writing about technology," *San Jose Mercury News*, 23 June 2000.

262. "Second sight, K. Mitnick," The *Guardian*, "Online" supplement, 30 November 2000, 14–15.

263. "Speaking Requests" page, Free Kevin web site, http://www.kevinmitnick.com/speaking_request.html.

264. "Training for cyber war," *Computer Weekly*, 27 April 2000, 28–31.

265. "eWEEK's OpenHack III Challenge Survives 5.25 Million Attack Attempts," *PR Newswire*, 1 February 2001.

266. "US Justice hires hackers," *SECURE Computing*, September 1998, 16.

267. See http://www.2600.com/hackedphiles/doj/ for "before and after" illustrations of the Department of Justice web site at the time.

268. See PricewaterhouseCoopers Technology Risk Services at http://www.pwcglobal.com/extweb/ncovrvw.nsf/docidserv/0B3C88BD49F49E87852566650052BD92.

269. See http://www.research.ibm.com/compsci/security/gsal/gsal.html.

270. O'Neill, B. "Computing and the Net: Hackers for hire," The *Guardian*, "Online" supplement, 26 February 1998, 5.

271. "Penetration Teams," subsection of "Charlatans" page on Attrition.org. http://www.attrition.org/errata/charlatan.html.

272. "Hackers unmasked," interview with Matthew Bevan on *SiliconReport Security* CD, published by Network Multimedia Television Ltd, London, 1999.

273. "Hacker startup joins e-security biz," *Reuters Limited*, 6 January 2000.

274. "PricewaterhouseCoopers warns against hackers-as-security-consultants trend," PricewaterhouseCoopers Press Release, 13 June 2000. http://www.pwcglobal.com/extweb/ncpressrelease.nsf/DocID/344F9763ADCBAC4A852568FE00464510.

275. "2001 CSI/FBI Computer Crime and Security Survey," *Computer Security Issues & Trends*, vol. VII, no. 1, Computer Security Institute, Spring 2001.

276. "Hack university: Learning from the pros," *ZDNet News* Report, 12 July 2000.

277. "'Hacktivist' vows to strike again over fuel costs," The *Daily Telegraph*, 21 September 2000, E3.

278. "Welcome to Herbland," hacked version of UK Legoland web site. See Attrition.org mirror at http://www.attrition.org/mirror/attrition/2000/09/10/www.legoland.co.uk/.

279. "Ok, so don't read the security bulletins," hacked version of Commonwealth Telecommunications Organisation web site. See Attrition.org mirror at http://www.attrition.org/mirror/attrition/2000/08/19/www.cto.int/.

280. "Anti-smoking hacker stubs out UK sites," *Newsbytes*, 16 August 2000.

281. "'Hacktivist' vows to strike again over fuel costs," The *Daily Telegraph*, 21 September 2000, E3.

282. "Protestor hits Opec website," Business Section, BBC News Online, 13 September 2000.

283. Young, K., Buchanan, J., and O'Mara, J. "Cyber-disorders: The mental health concern for the millennium," *CyberPsychology and Behavior*. See also http://www.netaddiction.com/articles/cyberdisorders.htm.

284. "The mainstreaming of kiddie porn," *Wired News* Report, 24 August 2000.

285. "Hackers' new tack on kid porn," *Wired News* Report, 4 February 2000.

286. "Official Press Release," The Condemned Network. See www.condemned.org/press.php.

287. "Hacker who wages war on child porn," *The Times*, "Interface" supplement, 15 May 2000, 5.

288. Goldberg, I. Institute for the Advanced Study of Information Warfare (IASIW). http://www.psycom.net/iwar.1.html.

289. "U.S. Army kick-starts cyberwar machine," *CNN.com News* Report, 22 November 2000.

290. "U.S. Space Command takes charge of Computer Network Attack," News Release, United States Space Command, 29 September 2000. http://www.spacecom.af.mil/usspace/rel15-00.htm.

291. Ridgeway, J. "Chinese Army pushes cyberwar barbarians at the gate," *Village Voice*, 24–30 November 1999.

292. Wayner, P. "Hacker 'attacks' on military networks may be closer to espionage," *New York Times*, 8 March 1999.

293. "Pentagon under cyber-siege," The *Daily Telegraph*, "Connected" supplement, 11 November 1999, 2.

294. "Information Security — Challenges to Improving DOD's Incident Response Capabilities," United States General Accounting Office (GAO), March 2001. http://www.gao.gov/new.items/d01341.pdf.

295. "Pentagon gets tough in war of the Web," *The Times*, "Interface" supplement, 7 October 1998, 2.

296. Adams, J. 1999. *The Next World War*. Random House UK, London, 348.

297. "Kosovo info warfare spreads," Science/Technology News, BBC web news, Thursday 1 April, 1999.

298. "Serbs hacked into MoD's computers," *Sunday Express*, 27 February 2000, 2.

299. "Q&A: crisis in the Middle East," BBC News Online, 18 December 2000.

300. "Israeli hackers vow to defend," *Wired News* Report, 15 November 2000.

301. "'Hacktivism': Mideast cyberwar heats up," *ZDNet News* Report, 6 November 2000.

302. "Palestinian crackers share bugs," *Wired News* Report, 2 December 2000.

303. "Hacker war rages in Holy Land," *Wired News* Report, 8 November 2000.

304. Garfinkel, S. 2000. *Database Nation: The Death of Privacy in the 21st Century*. O'Reilly & Associates, Inc., 211.

305. Denning, D.E. "Cyberterrorism," Testimony before the Special Oversight Panel on Terrorism, U.S. House of Representatives, 23 May 2000. See http://www.terrorism.com/documents/denning-testimony.shtml.

306. "Q&A with Emmanuel Goldstein of *2600: The Hacker's Quarterly*," CNN.com. http://www.cnn.com/TECH/specials/hackers/qandas/goldstein.html.

307. "MI5 builds new centre to read e-mails on the net," The *Sunday Times*, 30 April 2000, 1.

308. "Ulster security details posed on the Internet," *The Times*, 25 March 1996.

309. Anonymous. 1994. *The Terrorist's Handbook*. Available on Internet/WWW.

310. "Cyber Attack," *Panorama*, BBC Television, 3 July 2000.

311. Denning, D.E. "Cyberterrorism," Testimony before the Special Oversight Panel on Terrorism, U.S. House of Representatives, 23 May 2000. See http://www.terrorism.com/documents/denning-testimony.shtml.

312. "LoU strike out with international coalition of hackers," Joint statement by 2600, The Chaos Computer Club, The Cult of the Dead Cow, !Hispahack, L0pht Heavy Industries, Phrack and Pulhas. 7 January 1999. http://www.cultdeadcow.com/news/statement19990107.html.

313. Bell, J. *Assassination Politics*. http://www.zolatimes.com/v2.26/jimbell.htm.

314. "Crypto-convict won't recant," *Wired News* Report, 14 April 2000.

315. "Guilty verdict for cypherpunk," *Wired News* Report, 20 April 1999.

316. Warren, M. 1998. "Cyber terrorism," Proceedings of SEC-98 – IFIP World Congress, Budapest, Hungary, August 1998.

317. Campbell, D. 1999. *Interception Capabilities 2000*. IPTV Ltd, Edinburgh, Scotland. http://www.iptvreports.mcmail.com/ interception_capabilities_2000.htm.

318. Gauntlett, A. 1999. *Net Spies – Who's Watching You on the Web?* VISION Paperbacks, London.

319. Campbell, D. 1999. *Interception Capabilities 2000*. IPTV Ltd, Edinburgh, Scotland. http://www.iptvreports.mcmail.com/ interception_capabilities_2000.htm.

320. Poole, P.S. 1999/2000. "ECHELON: America's Secret Global Surveillance Network," http://fly.hiwaay.net/~pspoole/echelon.html.

321. "The spy in your server," The *Guardian*, "Online" supplement, 10 August 2000, 2–3.

322. "Echelon Furor Ends in a Whimper," *Wired News* Report, 3 July 2001.

323. "Europe should tackle home-grown Echelons, says MEP," *The Register*, 6 July 2001.

324. "The spy in your server," The *Guardian*, "Online" supplement, 10 August 2000, 11.

325. From Section 5.8, *Independent Technical Review of the Carnivore System – Final Report*, 8 December 2000, IIT Research Institute, Maryland. http://www.usdoj.gov/jmd/publications/carniv_final.pdf.

326. "Positive 'Carnivore' review draws immediate fire," *Newsbytes Report*, 14 December 2000.

327. "FBI hacks alleged mobster," *Wired News* Report, 6 December 2000.

328. "Judge wants keyboard logger info," *Wired News* Report, 9 August 2001.

329. "Q&A with IBM's Charles Palmer," CNN In-Depth Special – Insurgency on the Internet. http://www.cnn.com/TECH/specials/hackers/qandas/palmer.html.

330. "Security expert warns of litigation," *Computer Weekly*, 20 April 2000, 1.

331. British Standards Institution. 2000. *Information Technology. Code of Practice for Information Security Management*. BS ISO/IEC 17799:2000. 15 February 2001.

332. KPMG. 1998. *Information Security Survey 1998*, KPMG Information Risk Management, UK. http://www.kpmg.co.uk.

333. "Hacker fears over fast Net links," The *Daily Telegraph*, "Connected" supplement, 25 November 1999, 2.

334. Kovacich, G.L. "Hackers: freedom fighters of the 21st century," *Computers & Security*, vol. 18, no. 7, 573–6.

Index

Abbey National 16
Abene, Mark 71
Active Server Page (ASP) technology 127
Active-X 72
Adams, James 2, 249
addiction *see* Internet Addiction Disorder
Adleman, Professor Leonard 151, 152
ADSL (Asymmetric Digital Subscriber Line) technology 280
agrarian society 1
Agricultural Bank of China 215
aliases 48–9
Allen, Paul 47
Amazon.com 30
Ambulance virus 145
America Online 158
American Israeli Public Affairs Committee (AIPAC) 252
analyzer tools 117–20, 128–31, 134
Anderson, General Edward III 246–7
Anderson, James 25–6
anti-virus software 134, 155, 277–8
Apple Computer 84
Approaching Zero (Clough and Mungo) 45
Argus Systems Group 232
ARPANET 4–5, 85, 89
Ashcroft, Dr. Keith 53–4
ASP (Active Server Page) technology 127
Assassination Politics 259
Asymmetric Digital Subscriber Line (ADSL) technology 280
AT&T 71, 83
Atlanta 2600 hackers 75
ATM machines 11
Attrition 103, 106, 108, 133
auctions online 204–5
Audit Commission 21–6, 28
auditing 276
availability 19–20

Back Orifice (BO) 74, 120–4, 135
    Professional Plug-in 127
backdoor programs 102, 148
backing-up data 276–7
Badtimes hoax virus 182–3
Balkans 249–50
Ballmer, Steve 164
Banisar, David 225
Bank of America 71
banking 12, 15–16
Baran, Paul 4
Barclays Bank 15–16
Bedworth, Paul 201, 213, 217
Bell, Jim 259
Bell Telephone 46–7
BellSouth 70, 212–13
Berners-Lee, Tim 7
Bevan, Matthew ("Kuji") 92, 214, 238
BIND vulnerability 98
biometric user authentication 273
BIOS chip 169
"Black Hat" hackers 42, 45, 65
Blake, Clive 26
Bloomberg Business News 222
"Blue Adept" 35
Blue Box 46–7, 82–3, 84
bombs 148–9
boot-sector viruses 146
BoW Newsletter 66
British Standard in Information Security (BS7799) 270–2, 279
BskyB 186
buffer overflow attacks 96–8
Business Software Alliance (BSA) 193

Cahoot 16
Cap'n Crunch (John Draper) 46, 82–4, 120
"Capture the Flag" contest 77
Carnivore system 263

CCU (Computer Crime Unit) 207
CERN 7
CERT 118, 133
CGI (Common Gateway Interface) scripts 98
Chamberlain, John 14
"Chameleon" 259
Chaos Computer Club 71–2, 140, 198
Charlie Board 84
chat rooms 32
Chernobyl (CIH) virus 168–70
Chien, Eric 13
child pornography 243–5
China 215, 248, 259
CIAC 118
CIH (Chernobyl) virus 168–70
Circle of Deception 104
clandestine users 25
classification of abusers 25–6
classification of offences 21–4
Clinton, Bill 32
Clinton virus 184
Clipper 184
Clough, B. 45
CNI (Critical National Infrastructure) 208–9
CNN 30, 31, 32
Cohen, Fred 151–2
command modification 102
Common Gateway Interface (CGI) scripts 98
competitions for hackers 76–7, 232
computer crime
    costs 28
    definition 21
Computer Crime Unit (CCC) 207
Computer Misuse Act (1990) 69, 196, 201,
    210–12
Computer Security Institute (CSI) 24, 25, 28
computer-assisted crimes 22, 24
computer-focused crimes 22, 23
ComSec 71
Condemned Network 243–5
confidentiality 17–18
The Conscience of a Hacker 58–64
Conservative Party web site 104
conventions 74–7
Corley, Eric (Emmanuel Goldstein) 49, 80, 81,
    92, 216, 256
COSMOS phone center 85
costs of computer crime 28
costs of security 270
Council of Europe Draft Convention on
    Cyber-crime 134, 223–5
Count Zero 121–2
Courtney 135

Crackdown 99 campaign 193
crackers 42, 65
credit card crime 36–7, 204, 206
criminals, types of 24–6
Critical National Infrastructure (CNI) 208–9
CSI (Computer Security Institute) 24, 25, 28
Cult of the Dead Cow 73–4, 121, 123, 126–7
"Curador" (Raphael Gray) 35–8
customer relations 38–9
cyber warriors 44, 55
cybercrime, definition 21
"Cyberpunk" 213
Cyberpunk (Markoff) 86
cyberterrorists 44, 253–61
cyberwarfare see information warfare

"Dark Dante" see Poulsen, Kevin
Data Protection Act (1998) 51, 196
Datamation 183–4
"Datastream Cowboy" 214
date information 12–13
DCS1000 systems 263–4
DEF CON 74, 75–7, 120
defacing web sites 32, 100, 102–9, 257–8
Dell 76
denial of service attacks 29–31, 109–11
Denning, Dorothy 255–6
DERA (Defence Evaluation and Research
    Agency) 25
Digital Equipment 85, 213
distributed denial of service attacks 110
distributed processing 8–9
Docekal, Daniel 127
"Doctor Nuker" 252
Draper, John (Cap'n Crunch) 46, 82–4, 120
dumpster diving 139–40

eBay 30
ECHELON 262–3
education and awareness programs 278
Electronic Attack Response Group (EARG) 209
electronic commerce 35–8, 202–7
electronic mail 4, 33–5
    hoax messages 38–9
    and social engineering 138
enforcement agencies 207–10
Enigma code 246
espionage 72
Esquire 83–4
ethical codes 64–5
ethical hacking 231–2, 235–9
eWEEK 232
Excite 30

exotic viruses 154
exploit programs 117–20
external penetrators 25

false alarms 111–16
Farmer, Dan 117
FBI (Federal Bureau of Investigation) 263–6
file sharing 99
file viruses 146
films 78–82
    Hackers 48, 61, 79–80, 81
    Swordfish 82
    Takedown 87–8
    WarGames 48, 78–9, 198
firewalls 112, 115
Fischer, Joschka 222
fk 66
"fluxnyne" 243
Forgery and Counterfeiting Act (1981) 210–11
40Hex 66, 68
fraud 23, 206
    costs of 28
    and online auctions 204–5
    reported incidents 27
Friday 13th virus 151, 198
fuel crisis 239–43
The Fugitive (Littman) 87

Gabriel 135
gagging 136
Games, Steve Jackson 213
"Gandalf" 217
Garfinkel, Simson 254
Gartner Group 209–10
Gates, Bill 2, 36–7, 47
gatherings and conventions 74–7
GCHQ (Government Communications
    Headquarters) 262
Germany 222
Gibson Research Corporation 128
global file sharing 99
Global Internet Liberty Campaign (GILC) 224
Global Security Analysis Lab (GSAL) 236
Gold, Steve 210
Goldberg, Dr. Ivan 246
Goldstein, Emmanuel (Eric Corley) 49, 80, 81,
    92, 216, 256
Government Communications Headquarters
    (GCHQ) 262
Gray, Raphael ("Curador") 35–8
"Grey Hat" hackers 42, 238
GSAL (Global Security Analysis Lab) 236
Gullotto, Vincent 173
Guzman, Onel de 92, 149–50, 161–2

The Hacker Crackdown 71
The Hacker Ethic 64–6
Hacker Manifesto 58–64
Hackers 48, 61, 79–80, 81
Hackers: Heroes of the Computer Revolution
    (Levy) 41
hackers
    "Black Hat" 42, 45, 65
    as celebrities 77–92
    characteristics 47, 62
    choice of handle 48–9
    classification of types 43–5, 54
    competitions for 76–7, 232
    definition of 41–3
    ethical hacking 231–2, 235–9
    gatherings and conventions 74–7
    "Grey Hat" 42, 238
    harmless hackers 50–1
    hiring 231–9
    justification of activities 50–2
    motivation 52–8, 62, 281
    objectives 100–1
    origins of 45–7
    owning a system 100–1
    public perception of 28–9, 194–6,
        197–8
    self-image 47–52
    stereotypes 47–52
    "White Hat" 42, 45, 235
Hackers Unite 33–5
HackerWhacker 128
Hackerz Club 252
hacking attacks 22, 23, 24
    costs of 28
    denial of service attacks 29–31, 109–11
    on email accounts 33–5
    growth of 26–7
    web site defacement 32, 102–9, 257–8
Hacking for Girlies (HFG) 105–6
hacking groups 70*f*4
    Chaos Computer Club 71–2, 140, 198
    Circle of Deception 104
    Cult of the Dead Cow 73–4, 121, 123,
        126–7
    Hackers Unite 33–5
    Hackerz Club 252
    Hacking for Girlies (HFG) 105–6
    L0pht Heavy Industries 72–3, 124, 126–7,
        238
    Legion of Doom 70–1
    Legion of the Underground 259
    Masters of Deception 71
    PHAIT (Portuguese Hackers Against
       Indonesian Tyranny) 257–8

hacking methods
    analyzer tools 117–20, 128–31, 134
    BIND vulnerability 98
    buffer overflow 96–8
    CGI (Common Gateway Interface) scripts
      98
    dumpster diving 139–40
    exploit programs 117–20
    global file sharing 99
    HackTek 111
    IMAP vulnerabilities 99–100
    lock-picking 140–1
    mountd 99
    password mismanagement 99
    POP vulnerabilities 99–100
    port scans 96, 116, 119
    Remote Data Services (RDS) 99, 100
    Remote Procedure Calls (RPC) 98
    rootkits 101–2
    Sandmind 99
    Sendmail vulnerabilities 99
    SNMP vulnerabilities 100
    social engineering 136–9
    SYN Flooding 109–10
    system vulnerabilities 95–100
    vulnerability scanners 118, 119, 127–8,
      134
hacking publications 58–69, 70
    The Hacker Ethic 64–6
    Hacker Manifesto 58–64
    magazines and newsletters 66–9
    2600-The Hacker Quarterly 67–9, 88
HackTek 111
Hacktivists 44, 239–45
    Condemned Network 243–5
    online fuel protester 239–43
Hafner, Katie 86
harmless hackers 50–1
"Herbless" 240–3
HFG (Hacking for Girlies) 105–6
HIR 66
hiring hackers 231–9
hoax email messages 38–9
hoax viruses 181–5
Honeynet Project 133
Hotmail 33–4, 155
HSBC Holdings 242
human engineering 136

i-mode mobile phones 172
IBM 236
IDS (Intrusion Detection Systems) 276
IIS (Internet Information Server) 99, 100, 127
illicit software 22, 23, 192–3

IMAP vulnerabilities 99ƒ100
imprisonment of criminals 214–15
"in the wild" viruses 154
Indiana University 101
Industrial and Commercial Bank of China 215
information society 1–13
Information Society (Martin) 2
information superhighway 2
information warfare 245–53
    in the Balkans 249–50
    Enigma code 246
    in the Middle East 251–3
Infoseek 60
integrity 18–19
internal penetrators 25
Internet 189–90
    access options 9
    application devices 8, 9
    electronic commerce 35–8, 202–7
    interception of communications 262–6
    and kitchen appliances 9
    number of hosts 5
    number of users 6
    origins 3–6
    regulation and policing of 218–25
    and terrorism 256–7
    see also electronic mail
Internet Addiction Disorder 53–4, 217
Internet Explorer 131
Internet Information Server (IIS) 99, 100,
    127
Internet Relay Chat (IRC) 53
Internet Underground 252
Intrusion Detection Systems (IDS) 276
ISO/IEC 17799 compliance 271, 272
Israel 251–3

JANET 4
The Jargon File 42, 52
Jobs, Steve 84
Johnson, Carl 259
Jones, Andy 221
judiciary 216–20

[K]Alamar 179, 181
Kazakhstan 222
Keynote 30
KGB 72
kitchen appliances 9
"Knight Lightning" 212–13
Koch, Karl 72
Kournikova virus 181
Kovacich, Dr. Gerald 281–2
"Kuji" (Matthew Bevan) 92, 214, 238

L0pht Heavy Industries 72–3, 124, 126–7, 238
L0phtCrack 124–6
Labour Party web site 74–5, 104
lamers 45
Lecture 184
Legion of Doom 70–1
Legion of the Underground 259
legislation 210–12
    Computer Misuse Act (1990) 69, 196, 201,
        210–12
    Council of Europe Draft Convention on
        Cyber-crime 134, 223–5
    Data Protection Act (1998) 51, 196
    enforcement agencies 207–10
    enforcement and sentencing 212–16
    Forgery and Counterfeiting Act (1981)
        210–11
    global inconsistencies 220–5
    and the judiciary 216–20
    public awareness of 196
    Regulation of Investigatory Powers (RIP) Bill
        266
Levy, Elias 131
Levy, Steven 41, 64
Liberty Crack 173
Linux operating system 187
Littman, Jonathan 87, 91
lock-picking 140–1
logfile cleaners 102
logic bombs 148
Love Bug worm 147, 150, 159–63
Loxley, R. 245
lusers 45
Luthor, Lex 70
Lycos 60

macro viruses 146, 153
"Mafiaboy" 30–1, 48
magazines see hacking publications
malware 26, 143–88
    backdoor programs 148
    creation tools 178–85
    definition 143–4
    future direction of 186–7
    motivations of writers 149–51
    Personal Digital Assistant (PDA) malware
        172–3
    software bombs 148–9
    see also Trojan Horses; viruses; worms
malware writers 44, 55, 149–51
Marchand, Marie 53
Markoff, John 86, 87, 106
Martin, W.J. 2
masqueraders 25

Masters of Deception 71
MC Hammer web site 106
media reporting 197–201
Melissa virus 155–9
"The Mentor" 58–60, 70
message services 53
MI5 256
Michelangelo virus 151, 198
Microsoft 33, 34, 35, 97, 121, 163–8
    Active-X 72
    Hotmail 33–4, 155
    Internet Explorer 131
    Internet Information Server (IIS) 99, 100,
        127
    Outlook 155, 156–7, 158, 162–3
    Rapid Exposure Detection (RED) team
        231–2
    security bulletins 132, 165
    Windows NT 97, 124
    Windows XP 281
    Word 153, 157
Middle East 251–3
military systems 61–2, 246–50
Millennium Bug 12–13
MILNET 4
Minitel 53
misfeasors 26
Mitnick, Kevin 84–9, 92, 167, 198, 213,
        214–15, 219, 226–9
mobile phones 72, 171–3
Moldovan porn scam 176–7
Money, Arthur 76
Morris, Robert 158
Mosaic 6
Motorola 85, 106
mountd 99
movies see films
Movistar service 172
MP3 music files 101
multi-platform viruses 187
multipartite viruses 146
Mungo, P. 45

NASA 50, 106
National Computing Centre 28
National Hi-Tech Crime Unit (NHTCU) 208
National Infrastructure Protection Center (NIPC)
        209, 261
National Infrastructure Security Coordination
        Centre (NISCC) 208–9, 261
National Security Agency (NSA) 262
NATO 249–50
Neidorf, Craig 70
NetBIOS support 113

Network Associates 108
network sniffers 102
New York Times web site 105–6
The Next World War (Adams) 2, 249
Noble, Ronald 215–16
Nokia 85, 86
NORAD 86
NORMAL.DOT 153, 157
Notepad 164
NSFNET 5

online auctions 204–5
online fuel protester 239–43
OnTheFly worm 181
OPEC (Organisation of Petroleum Exporting
    Countries) 242–3
OpenHack III 232–3
operating systems 281
Operation Sundevil 71
Orange Book 60–1
Outlook 155, 156–7, 158, 162–3
owning a system 100–1

Pacific Bell 85, 90
packet sniffers 135
Packet Storm 66
packet switching 3–4
Pakistan 252
Palestinians 251–3
Paller, Alan 133
Palmer, Dr. Charles 269
PalmOS 173
Parker, Donn 21
password crackers 56–8, 117, 119, 135
    L0phtCrack 124–6
password management 99, 193, 272–6
patches 131, 132, 133
payload element of viruses 145
Penthouse 106
perpetrators, types of 24–6
personal data misuse 23
Personal Digital Assistant (PDA) malware
    172–3
PGP (Pretty Good Privacy) 265
Phage 173
PHAIT (Portuguese Hackers Against Indonesian
    Tyranny) 257–8
"Phiber Optik" 80, 216
Philip, Prince, Duke of Edinburgh 210
Phrack Magazine 66, 68, 212–13
phreakers 44, 45–7, 55, 83
physical tokens 272–3
Ping messages 112–13, 115
piracy 22, 23, 192–3

PitBull system 232–3
"Pod" 217
Pokey worm 170–1
policing 207–10
polymorphic viruses 146
POP vulnerabilities 99–100
Popp, Dr. Joseph 174–6, 213
pornography 23, 32
    child pornography 243–5
    Moldovan porn scam 176–7
port scans 96, 116, 119
Poulsen, Kevin (Dark Dante) 53, 89–91, 92,
    214, 225–6
PowerGen 14–15
Prestel 210
Pretty Good Privacy (PGP) 265
preventative measures 269–83
    anti-virus software 134, 155, 277–8
    auditing 276
    backing-up data 276–7
    education and awareness 278
    Intrusion Detection Systems (IDS) 276
    password protection 272–6
    user authentication 272–3
prison sentences 214–15
private work 23
Professional Plug-in 127
program viruses 146
"Prophet" 212–13
Pryce, Richard 92
public attitudes and awareness 28-9, 191–201
    and media influence 197–201
    to current legislation 196
    to electronic commerce 202–7
    to hackers 28–9, 194-6, 197–8
    to seriousness of computer crime and abuse
        193–4
    to software piracy 192–3
    to viruses 197
publications *see* hacking publications

Qaz worm 163–8
Quittner, Joshua 71

Rapid Exposure Detection (RED) team 231–2
Redhotant 108–9
Regulation of Investigatory Powers (RIP) Bill
    266
Reilly, W.P. 220, 221–2
remote administration programs 119
Remote Data Services (RDS) 99, 100
Remote Procedure Calls (RPC) 98
Reno, Janet 207
replication strategy for viruses 144

Rheingold, Howard 8, 190
Rica, Fred 238
Rome Labs 214, 238
rootkits 101–2
Roy, Jean-Pierre 31
RSA Security Inc. 106–7

sabotage 23
Safeway 38–9
"The Saint" 35–8
SAM file 124
samurai 44, 55
Sandmind 99
SANS Institute 98, 131
Santa Cruz Operation 85
SATAN 117ƒ18, 135
Scarfo, Nicodemo S. 265–6
Schifreen, Robert 210
Schily, Otto 222
Schneier, Bruce 138
script kiddies 44, 45
security bulletins 132, 165
security issues 13–20
    British Standard in Information Security
        (BS7799) 270–2, 279
    costs of security 270
    ISO/IEC 17799 compliance 271, 272
    see also preventative measures
Sendmail vulnerabilities 99
sentences imposed on criminals 214–15
Serbs 249–50
SERENDIP 9
SETI@home 9
Sharon, Ariel 251
Shea, Jamie 250
Shi Biao 215
Shields Up! 128
Shimomura, Tsutomu 85, 87, 106, 216
ShopIP 84
Short Message Service (SMS) gateway 171–2
SIM (Subscriber Identity Module) cards 72
Sinrod, E.J. 220, 221–2
"Sir Dystic" 49, 74, 92, 121, 123
Slatalla, Michele 71
Smith, David 92, 158
sniffers 119
    network sniffers 102
    packet sniffers 135
SNMP vulnerabilities 100
social engineering 136–9
software bombs 148–9
software piracy 22, 23, 192–3
Solaris operating system 99
Sophos 153

SPA** 184
SPACECOM 247
"Spot the Fed" competition 76–7
SRI International 89
Stacheldraht 30
stealth viruses 146
Sterling, Bruce 72
Stoll, Clifford 72
Subscriber Identity Module (SIM) cards 72
Sun Microsystems 85, 99, 213
Sundevil 71
support programs 102
surveillance networks 262–6
surveys 26–9, 192
Svet Namodro 127
Swordfish 82
Symantec 76, 182
SYN Flooding 109–10
system administrators 51, 128–31, 132–3,
        278–9
    courses for 238–9
system vulnerabilities 95–100

Takedown 87–8
Takedown (Markoff) 87, 106
talk and finger service 97
Tamil guerrillas 259
technology dependence 1–13
Telefonica 171
telegraph 3
telephone networks 3, 45–7
    mobile phones 72
    and viruses 171–3
television 7
Tenebaum, Ehud 92
terrorism see cyberterrorists
theft 23, 100
    costs of 28
    reported incidents 27
Third Wave (Toffler) 2
tiger team 237
time bombs 148, 151
Timofonica virus 171–2
Toffler, A. 2
trashing systems 101
Tribal Flood Net 30
Trinoo 30
Tripwire 102
Trojan Horses 57, 102, 147–8, 149, 174–6
    Liberty Crack 173
    Moldovan porn scam 176–7
    Phage 173
TRW 71, 85
"Tweety Fish" 49

2600-The Hacker Quarterly 67–9, 88

Unified Incident Reporting and Alert Scheme
    (UNIRAS) 209
Unix 55–6, 102
    talk and finger service 97
unlicensed software 22, 23, 192–3
Unsolved Mysteries 90–1
URL address modification 14–15
user authentication 272–3
    see also password management
user names 33

Vbs Worms Generator 178–81
Venema, Wietse 117
victims of cybercrime 189–91
virtual communities 8
The Virtual Community (Rheingold) 190
viruses 22, 23, 24, 144–7, 149
    Ambulance 145
    anti-virus software 134, 155, 277–8
    Badtimes 182–3
    CIH (Chernobyl) 168–70
    costs of 28
    evolution of 151–5
    exotic 154
    Friday 13th 151, 198
    growth of 153
    hoax viruses 181–5
    "in the wild" 154
    Kournikova 181
    Melissa 155–9
    Michelangelo 151, 198
    multi-platform 187
    payload element 145
    public attitudes and awareness 197
    replication strategy 144
    reported incidents 27
    and telephone networks 171–3
    Timofonica 171–2

    types of 146
    W32.Winux 187
    see also Trojan Horses; worms
Vlad 66
VMS operating system 85
vulnerability scanners 118, 119, 127–8,
    134

W32.Winux virus 187
wannabees 45
war dialers 117, 119
warez d00dz 44–5, 55
WarGames 48, 78–9, 198
The Watchman (Littman) 91
web site defacement 32, 102–9, 257–8
The Well 8
Wells, Joe 154
Werney, Steffen 140
"White Hat" hackers 42, 45, 235
Whitney, Craig 209
WildList 154
Windows NT 97, 124
Windows XP 281
Wired News 34, 35
Word 153, 157
World Wide Web *see* Internet
worms 147, 158
    Love Bug 147, 150, 159–63
    OnTheFly 181
    Pokey 170–1
    Qaz 163–8
    Vbs Worms Generator 178–81
    see also viruses
Wozniak, Steve 47, 84

Y2K problem 12–13
Yahoo! 30

ZDNet 30
ZKey 35